Of Merchants and Missions

American Society of Missiology
Monograph Series

Series Editor, James R. Krabill

The ASM Monograph Series provides a forum for publishing quality dissertations and studies in the field of missiology. Collaborating with Pickwick Publications—a division of Wipf and Stock Publishers of Eugene, Oregon—the American Society of Missiology selects high-quality dissertations and other monographic studies that offer research materials in mission studies for scholars, mission and church leaders, and the academic community at large. The ASM seeks scholarly work for publication in the series that throws light on issues confronting Christian world mission in its cultural, social, historical, biblical, and theological dimensions.

Missiology is an academic field that brings together scholars whose professional training ranges from doctoral-level preparation in areas such as Scripture, history and sociology of religions, anthropology, theology, international relations, interreligious interchange, mission history, inculturation, and church law. The American Society of Missiology, which sponsors this series, is an ecumenical body drawing members from Independent and Ecumenical Protestant, Catholic, Orthodox, and other traditions. Members of the ASM are united by their commitment to reflect on and do scholarly work relating to both mission history and the present-day mission of the church. The ASM Monograph Series aims to publish works of exceptional merit on specialized topics, with particular attention given to work by younger scholars, the dissemination and publication of which is difficult under the economic pressures of standard publishing models.

Persons seeking information about the ASM or the guidelines for having their dissertations considered for publication in the ASM Monograph Series should consult the Society's website—www.asmweb.org.

Members of the ASM Monograph Committe who approved this book are:
>   Roger Schroeder, SVD, Catholic Theological Union
>   Michael A. Rynkiewich, Retired from Asbury Theological Seminary

Recently Published in the ASM Monograph Series

Elliott, Curtis W. *Theologizing Place in Displacement: Reconciling, Remaking, and Reimagining Place in the Republic of Georgia*

Balisky, Lila W. *Songs of Ethiopia's Tesfaye Gabbiso: Singing with Understanding in Babylon, the Meantime, and Zion.*

Hovey, Kevin George. *Guiding Light: Contributions of Alan R. Tippett Toward the Development and Dissemination of Twentieth-Century Missiology.*

Of Merchants and Missions
A Historical Study of the Impact of British Colonialism on
American Methodism In Singapore from 1885 to 1910

ANDREW PEH

FOREWORD BY ROBERT SOLOMON

American Society of Missiology
Monograph Series

VOL. 40

☙PICKWICK Publications · Eugene, Oregon

OF MERCHANTS AND MISSIONS
A Historical Study of the Impact of British Colonialism on American Methodism in Singapore from 1885 to 1910

American Society of Missiology Monograph Series 40

Copyright © 2019 Andrew Peh. All rights reserved. Except for brief quotations in critical publications or reviews, no part of this book may be reproduced in any manner without prior written permission from the publisher. Write: Permissions, Wipf and Stock Publishers, 199 W. 8th Ave., Suite 3, Eugene, OR 97401.

Pickwick Publications
An Imprint of Wipf and Stock Publishers
199 W. 8th Ave., Suite 3
Eugene, OR 97401

www.wipfandstock.com

PAPERBACK ISBN: 978-1-5326-3436-9
HARDCOVER ISBN: 978-1-5326-3438-3
EBOOK ISBN: 978-1-5326-3437-6

Cataloging-in-Publication data:

Names: Peh, Andrew, author. | Solomon, Robert, foreword.
Title: Of merchants and missions : a historical study of the impact of British colonialism on American Methodism in Singapore from 1885 to 1910 / by Andrew Peh; foreword by Robert Solomon.
Description: Eugene, OR: Pickwick Publications, 2019 | Series: American Society of Missiology Monograph Series 40 | Includes bibliographical references and index.
Identifiers: ISBN 978-1-5326-3436-9 (paperback) | ISBN 978-1-5326-3438-3 (hardcover) | ISBN 978-1-5326-3437-6 (ebook)
Subjects: LCSH: Great Britain—Colonies—Southeast Asia—History—19th century. | Methodist Church—Singapore—History. | Missionaries—Singapore—History. | Singapore—Church history.

Classification: BX8316.S55 P35 2019 (print) | BX8316.S55 (ebook)

Manufactured in the U.S.A.

to ma and pa

thanking the Lord for the both of you, always

Contents

Tables ix
Foreword by Robert Solomon xi
Preface xv
Introduction xvii

Chapter One
Strange Bedfellows: Merchants and Missionaries 1
    Introduction 1
    Statement of the Problem 9
    Theoretical Framework 10
    Research Questions 15
    Delimitations 16

Chapter Two
The Colonial Contact 18
    The East India Company 18
    Sir Stamford Raffles and the Founding of Singapore 23
    The Straits Settlements 32
    Mutiny in India 37
    The Crown Colony 41
    British Policies in the Crown Colony 42
    Conclusion 50

Chapter Three
The March of Methodism 52
    Christianity in the Colonial Era, before 1886 52
    British Methodism: A Missed Opportunity 64

American Methodism: New Beginnings 66
Pioneers of Methodism in Singapore 94
Conclusion 101

Chapter Four
Methodist Maneuvers 103
    Circumventing Colonial Policies 103
    Methodists and Evangelism 114
    Methodists and Education 121
    Methodists and Ethics 148
    Conclusion 180

Chapter Five
Action, Reaction, and Transformation 183
    Conclusion 183

Appendices 209
Bibliography 305

Tables

Table 1   The Trade of Singapore 1824–1913 ($ million)
Table 2   The Growth of Trade of Singapore
Table 3   ACS Enrolment from 1886 to 1911
Table 4   A Comparison of Singapore's Ethnic Population Ratio
Table 5   Government Education Expenditure and Allocation of Funding
Table 6   Income, Expenditure, and Cost of Instruction for ACS, RI, and SJI, 1888–1902
Table 7   Comparison of Percentage Passes in Three Schools in Singapore
Table 8   Comparison of the Total Number of Chinese Immigrants by Gender
Table 9   Occupation and Ethnicity of Interviewees of the Opium Commission
Table 10 Comparison of Percentage of Trade Revenue Derived from Opium Traffic and Percentage Expenditure on Education

Foreword

Recently, on my way to visit a friend in Orchard Road, I was driving along Stamford Road, named after Sir Stamford Raffles who "found" Singapore in the early nineteenth century. The road is part of a historical section of old Singapore and I took time to notice the architectural intricacies of some of the old buildings that have been wisely preserved and spruced up, and continue to be used. One of the buildings was known for much of the twentieth century as the MPH Building, a three-story Edwardian style building.

    I told my friend of the buildings I noticed on my way, mentioning in particular the old MPH Building, which is now used by the Singapore Management University. Having studied in a school nearby a long time ago, he remembered the building fondly. I told him that MPH originally stood for Methodist Publishing House; he was surprised to hear that as he had always known MPH as standing for Malaya Publishing House. The Methodist Mission in Singapore began in 1885, when a church (Wesley Methodist) was established after Bishop James Thoburn and Dr. William Oldham led a preaching mission. Soon after a school, Anglo-Chinese School (ACS), was started in 1886. A printing press was set up in 1890 under the leadership of William Shellabear. This press became the famous Methodist Publishing House in 1906 and moved to its new premises in Stamford Road in 1908. Its scope of operations was expanded rapidly and it took on a new name, the Malaya Publishing House, in 1927.

    A stone's throw away, on Coleman Street, stood the Methodist Chapel (Wesley Methodist Church), which moved to nearby Fort Canning Road in 1908, and still has a commanding presence there. ACS, which started existence in Chinatown, moved to occupy premises in Canning Rise adjacent to the Methodist Chapel in 1887, and was located there until 1994. The school saw various phases of construction and expanded to other areas in the city. The former school building is currently used as the National Archives. Also in Coleman Street was the Methodist Book Room set up in 1893, which now houses the Singapore Philatelic Museum.

What is noteworthy is that within a small area in the historical district of Singapore is a living reminder of the dynamism of the Methodist Mission in Singapore: a church, a school, and a publishing house. It is a historical and architectural testimony to the "pluriform mission" that Rev. Dr. Andrew Peh explains and demonstrates in this book. Today, people use the terms "wholistic mission" or "integrated mission," but pluriform mission as done by the Methodists focused on a multiplicity of fronts, including evangelism and church planting, education, publishing, and social outreach. This was not new to the Methodists, for John and Charles Wesley and the early leaders of Methodism in the eighteenth century were known for their all-encompassing view of their mission of "spreading scriptural holiness across the land." They planted Methodist societies (churches) that spread and grew rapidly, set up schools, ministered to the poor and marginalised, and were active publishing and challenging social ills and finding solutions.

Dr. Peh has done excellent work in describing the energetic and creative way in which the early Methodists in Singapore went about carrying out their multi-pronged mission, each aspect strengthening the others. He offers inspiring portraits of some of the early pioneers: William Oldham (church planting and education), Sophia Blackmore (education, social ministries), and William Shellabear (publishing, church planting).

These mission narratives are set in the context of British colonial rule in Singapore, which took various forms—first in treating the island as a territory under the rule of the British East India Company in Calcutta, then as a crown colony ruled directly from London. Amid these changes were issues connected with the goals and concerns of the colonial government. Dr. Peh shows that their primary aim was commercial trade and profitability. The need to maintain social order was subsumed under this central purpose. This explains how educational opportunities for the local population were inadequate and were generally directed at producing clerical staff for the colonial administration. Also vices such as prostitution and opium addiction were tolerated and made use of to generate income. Such an attitude created a *laissez faire* social environment into which the early Methodist missionaries arrived. That the colonial government had restrictions on evangelistic work could be seen in the 1874 Pangkor Treaty as well as the government's insistence that the mission schools that the Methodists set up in quick succession focus on providing a secular education. Dr. Peh shows how the Methodists got around such restrictions through their creativity, perseverance and commitment to their mission.

By so doing, the author musters evidence to argue that the relationship between the American Methodist Mission and the British colonial government was not a hand-in-glove one or even a partnership because of their somewhat different goals and concerns, which at times led to cooperation but in other instances led to policies and actions that were in opposition. More often than not, it was an indifferent posture on the part of the colonial authorities. Dr. Peh puts to rest the notion that the missionary movement, at least in the case of the early Methodist mission in Singapore, was a willing and subservient partner of colonial interests. The evidence suggests otherwise, in that the missionaries were not often on the same page with the colonial merchants and magistrates, for example in the way they saw education as a way of producing indigenous leadership and developing the local communities, and in the way they opposed policies related to opium consumption and trade and gambling on moral grounds.

This book is not only an added resource for those interested in the relationship between missionaries and colonial rulers (for which Dr. Peh must be congratulated and thanked), but also provides an interesting and inspiring narrative of early Methodist missionary work in Singapore that showcases the industry, passion and nimble creativity of the missionaries, a narrative that challenges us today on many fronts, both in our own devotion to Jesus and how we do God's mission in our complex world.

Bishop Emeritus Robert Solomon
The Methodist Church in Singapore

Preface

This marks the completion of an important chapter in my life for which I am deeply thankful to our Lord, Jesus Christ, who has orchestrated every detail of this work. I thank all who made possible the completion of this work, by their persevering prayers, their prodigal presents, and their persistent presence.

I dedicate this work to my parents, whose lives are a continual instruction and inspiration to me. I am grateful for my family, both immediate and church, for the love and support all these years. I am indebted to the various churches (Bukit Panjang Methodist Church, Charis Methodist Church, and Grace Methodist Church), the Chinese Annual Conference of the Methodist Church in Singapore), Trinity Theological College as well as the many individuals (Barry and Serene Leong, Boon Hock and Emily, Casey and Cynthia Lin, Ricky and Valerie Ho, Rev. and Mrs. Khoo Cheng Hoot) who supported my studies at Asbury Theological Seminary.

I thank the faculty at Asbury Theological Seminary who had played a significant part in developing my interest in mission history and especially my mentor, Dr. Terry Muck, for his patience and his constant encouragement at times when completing this work seemed impossible. I thank also those friends, who have assisted me especially in the transcription of the archival materials, making an important task so very much less tedious. I thank especially my extended family—Jay Watts, Court and Lori Fender, Dennis and Sylvia Chan, Edmund Koh, Bernard Yee, Tan Teck Haur, Teo Kim Kiat, Nathanael Goh, and Adalric Mesina Chang—for standing alongside me

The list of people to thank seems to grow longer as I recount the blessings that the Lord has provided through them, as lives intersect with life and where iron sharpens iron. Be it for a brief moment in time or for a significant part of the journey, each of you whom the Lord has graciously allowed our paths to cross have had a significant influence and impact in my life and for which I am indebted.

Soli Deo Gloria!
Andrew Peh

Introduction

The relationship between colonialism and mission has been one that is often accused of collusion and complicity. While there have been a fair amount of research pertaining to colonialism, most of these are derived from the African, Indian or South Pacific contexts. This research deals with the specific case of interaction of American Methodism with British colonialism in Singapore at the close of the nineteenth century. It seeks to investigate if Christianity (American Methodism, in this case) came to Singapore on the coattails of the British colonial administration.

It is evident that British colonialism provided the necessary precondition for Methodist mission in Singapore. It may also be said that Methodism and British colonialism had a symbiotic relationship which enabled the colony to be administered with minimal cost and yet with maximum efficiency, especially in regard to education. With a preoccupation on commerce and trade, the colony was administered in an atypical *laissez faire* context which worked to the advantage of the Methodist mission, as it very quickly embarked on a *pluriform* mission, reaching different ethnic groups with the different means of presenting the Gospel.

The research yielded archival documentation that in regards to efforts at evangelism and church planting, education mission as well as matters involving ethics and Christian witness, the Methodist missionaries were constantly appealing against colonial administrative policies and praxes. Despite the implications of the Pangkor Treaty, the Methodists continued to minister to the local indigenous people and migrant population, through mission and evangelism. Despite the paltry grant they received from the colonial administration and prohibition against proselytism, the Methodists went ahead and established an effective Christian academic institution that until today, continues to be at the forefront of education in Singapore. Despite the nonchalance of a colonial administration against such social malaise as opium addiction, prostitution and poverty, the Methodists penetrated different levels of society to work for the benefit of those affected. Despite the colonial emphasis on economic profitability for a free port such as Singapore, the Methodists laboured instead to free the people with the Gospel of Jesus Christ.

The conclusion arrived through research of historical documents and various archival records, both secular and ecclesiastical, is that the charge of complicity of mission and colonialism is a generalization that is tenuous in the case of Methodism's advent and growth in Singapore.

1

Strange Bedfellows: Merchants and Missionaries

INTRODUCTION

THE RELATIONSHIP BETWEEN COLONIALISM and Christian missionary expansion in the nineteenth and twentieth centuries continues to be a contentious issue in recent scholarship on the colonial-missionary enterprise. On one side of the spectrum, there are some evangelicals who assume that the Protestant missionary movement, as a civilizing mission, was pure both in its intention to spread the gospel as well as in its adoption of the means to do so. On the other hand, there are also those who perceive the missionaries as no more than cultural and theological imperialists who rode on the coattails of the colonizers. A good number of authors who emerged from the post-colonial period hold on tenaciously to their belief that the missionary expansion since the sixteenth century is but one arm of Western aggressive imperialism. Various key scholars and authors (Lal Dena[1] and Kwame Nkrumah[2]) from the post-colonial societies also find it difficult to shake off the oft-held notion that first comes the missionary, then comes the resident, and finally, the regiment. In more recent developments, however, there has been literature from a growing number of historians (Jacob S. Dharmaraj[3] and Dom Felice

---

1. Dena, *Christian Missions and Colonialism*.
2. Nkrumah, *Neo-Colonialism*.
3. Dharmaraj, *Colonialism and Christian Mission*.

Vaggioli[4]) as well as anthropologists (Jean and John Comaroff[5]) who offer a somewhat "balanced" perspective, while hinting at their suspicion that these two forces have been "strange bedfellows."

Be that as it may, the general tenor of most colonial studies accuses the Christian missionary movement as being a co-conspirator, in constant connivance with the exploitative activities of colonial rule, through conquest, commerce, code of law, and "civilizing mission." The church is still seen as a part of the colonial enterprise and not surprisingly, there are many who are skeptical of the church's missionary efforts. There is a need to determine the part played by the missionaries in a colonial context; were they in collusion with the colonial administration or where they guileless in their goal of proclaiming the Gospel? This becomes the context that this research deals with, in the specific case of British colonialism in Singapore at the close of the nineteenth century.

While there may be an increasing number of writers from previously colonized countries who are emerging from the shadows and giving voice to their thoughts on the various aspects of colonial administration, there seems however, to be paucity in literature that deals directly with the issue of colonialism and missions. One of the earliest and to date, one of the more important books to deal with the twain (colonialism and missions) is Stephen Neill's *Colonialism and Christian Missions*. Writing in the 1960s, Bishop Stephen Neill's work remains as a significant pioneering endeavor to address the paucity of a subject that continues to have implications for the mission of the church today.

Neill's presentation of interrelationship between colonialism and missions comes across as equitable. It shows the missionary as being a true child of his/her time, culture and mind, where the blunders of the colonial administration are also found in the principles, practices and behavior patterns of the missionary. Neill is not prepared to excuse or rationalize colonialism, and the injustices and evils that accompanied it, and neither does he condone the paternalistic and colonial mindset and attitude of the missionary. Though the missionary's pattern and praxis often coincided with the colonial powers and more often is found to be in cooperation with the colonial rulers, especially if it benefited the ministry, Neill maintains that the missionary's motive, purpose and principles are qualitatively different from those of the colonialists. More often than not,

---

4. Vaggioli, *History of New Zealand*.
5. Comaroff, *Of Revelation and Revolution*.

the missionary was a voice for the native population under colonial rule, though Neill does not discount the fact that there have been occasions when the missionaries compromised their solidarity with those among whom they ministered. Nonetheless, Neill held that the missionary was first and foremost a Christian and a messenger of the Gospel, who sought the welfare of the people whom he/she had come to serve.

In his conclusion, Neill is conscious that he writes at a time when colonialism was coming to a close and at a time where

> one age has died and another is striving to be born. We stand in the time of birth pangs, in which the future still remains obscure. The time has not yet come, at which it will be possible to pass a fully objective judgment on the epoch which has now decisively come to an end.[6]

Neill notes the extreme positions that many have held, either in condemnation or in commendation of the cooperation between missionaries and the colonial powers. For Neill, when all the detractions made by the opponents of missions have been fairly faced, and some of them admitted, however, one cannot deny the fact that "as a result of the Christian mission in the colonial period, the Christian Church exists in every corner of the earth."[7] Neither can one discredit the fact there still remains a vast accumulated treasure of unselfish service rendered to the colonized/colonies because of the missionary's primary motivation of love for his/her Lord, for the people and the land. Ultimately, Neill is optimistic about the mission of God, regardless of the methods humans employ; for Neill,

> mission will continue till the end of time. The successful accomplishment of mission depends, humanly speaking on the open-eyed and whole-hearted acceptance of the two conditions, of total engagement with men in their needs and total detachment from them in desires.[8]

In more recent studies that investigate the relationship between Protestant missions and colonialism (British imperialism, to be more specific), Brian Stanley's contribution is significant. In *The Bible and the Flag: Protestant Missions and British Imperialism in the Nineteenth and Twentieth Centuries*, Stanley identifies both popular and non-professional

---

6. Neill, *Colonialism and Christian Mission*, 422.
7. Neill, *Colonialism and Christian Mission*, 424–25.
8. Neill, *Colonialism and Christian Mission*, 425.

theses that have been propounded on the alleged complicity of Protestant missions with British imperialism. Stanley defines the essence of imperialism as

> control by an alien national or racial group; such control may be primarily political or primarily economic, and need not imply formal territorial rule; it may also be contrary to the original intentions of the imperial power, or only indirectly related to those intentions.[9]

Stanley identifies three forms of imperialism; firstly imperialism in the form of colonization (as with the "growth" of the British Empire in North America and the colonization of Australasia); secondly in the form of colonialism, where "legal sovereignty has been ceded to or usurped by the imperial power"[10] without the large scale human settlement; and thirdly, the "informal imperial control, in which the imperial power wields predominant influence in a territory without resort to either human settlement or formal political rule."[11] Interestingly, in looking at the forms of colonial rule in the context of Singapore, this third form of imperialism perhaps best defines the kind of colonial administration experienced in Singapore. Stanley surveys the various definitions of imperialism and provides also an important history for the interpretation of imperialism[12] as a platform from which he challenges the traditional arguments against British Imperialism. He noted that distinct from our present day understanding of colonialism, "for the duration of the nineteenth century, 'colonialism' was the term applied to describe the network

---

9. Stanley, *Bible and the Flag*, 35.
10. Stanley, *Bible and the Flag*, 34.
11. Stanley, *Bible and the Flag*, 35.
12. Stanley submits that "the word 'imperialism' has undergone twelve distinct changes since its origins in the 1840s, according to a major study by R. Koebner and H. D. Schmidt." Interestingly, the term, originated in the 1840s in France, where it denoted the desire to restore to France the glories of national greatness, which were hers under the Emperor Napoleon Bonaparte. It was Napoleon's nephew, Louis Napoleon, who revived this notion of romantic nationalism. Hence, in its early usage, from between 1850s to 1870, for the Englishman, the term signified not so much his country's overseas possessions but rather a style of domestic politics in France, which is characterized by militarism, bombast, and scant respect for constitutional liberties. Imperialism remained a term of heavily negative connotations at least until the 1880 general elections in Britain. See Stanley, *Bible and the Flag*, 35–39.

of increasingly informal ties binding Britain to the white settler colonies and was not normally employed in relation to India or Africa."[13]

Stanley draws upon various case studies, highlighting the missionary-imperial relationship in the British West Indies, South Africa, India, China (1792–1860), Fiji, Bechuanaland, Nyasaland, Uganda and Kenya, all of which were once under or had encountered British colonialism. In each of these cases, Stanley sought to demonstrate that often, the Bible was not an accomplice to the British flag.

With regards to the charge of complicity, Stanley points out that almost all cultures exist in a state of perpetual flux and are subject to diverse and often contradictory influences. Hence, in coming to the defense of British Protestant missionaries, Stanley forwards the view that "the choice confronting indigenous cultures has not been between change and no change but between a number of possible directions of change, some evidently more beneficial than others"[14] and that they were very rarely the sole agents of cultural change to impact the various societies.

Instead of simply reacting negatively to the critique of the Protestant missionary movement, Stanley acknowledges the movement's faults and ambiguities but at the same time he raises some serious questions for all who have come to accept the prevalent assumption that the missionaries were, wittingly or not, simply colonists in religious dress. Stanley argues instead that the missionaries were primarily evangelists, whatever else they might have been. He reasons that there is a sense in which Christianity is an "imperial" religion insofar as Christ makes "absolute demands upon all people and all cultures."[15] The missionaries, Stanley noted, had a clear and compelling grasp of the "imperial" demands of the Gospel but,

> their vision was frequently clouded by national and racial pride and in certain essential respects was distorted by the mechanistic worldview, which they had inherited from Enlightenment thought. As a result, they sometimes failed to apply the ethical demands of the kingdom of God as rigorously to their own nation as they did to the non-Western societies to which they were sent. Their relationship to the diverse forces of British imperialism was complex and ambiguous. If it was fundamentally misguided, their error was not that they were indifferent to the cause of justice for the oppressed, but that their perceptions of

---

13. Stanley, *Bible and the Flag*, 35.
14. Stanley, *Bible and the Flag*, 170–71.
15. Stanley, *Bible and the Flag*, 184.

the demands of justice were too easily molded to fit the contours of prevailing Western ideologies. In this respect, our predecessors reflect our own fallibility more closely than we care to admit.[16]

This study rests upon the foundations that have been previously laid by such esteemed mission historians as Stephen Neill and Brian Stanley. In the initial review of the history of Methodism in Singapore, there seems to be many points of correspondence with Neill and Stanley's more positive evaluation of the missionary enterprise in light of criticism against western colonialism. This study serves to continue the account of the growth of Protestant missions in this part of the world that is often overshadowed by those nations that have longer histories and feature more significantly in the colonial era of yesteryears.

In any survey of colonialism or of Christian missions, Southeast Asia is often eclipsed by both India and/or Africa. Yet the story of Christianity as it came to Southeast Asia and more specifically, Singapore in the nineteenth century, must be told. Was the British colonial experience in India or Africa "exported" to this part of Asia as well? Did Christianity come to Singapore on the coattails of the British colonial administration?

Not unlike the experience in the New World, in Africa and in India, the Christian missionary movement in this part of Asia, stands accused of complicity with British colonialism and regarded as a means by which the colonial rulers usurped what rightly belonged to the native people. It has been said of missionaries that when they first came to Africa they had the Bible and the Africans had the land. The missionaries said, "Let us pray." The Africans closed their eyes and when they opened them, they had the Bible and the missionaries had their land.[17] The church is seen as the remaining vestige of colonial rule. In a post-colonial and postmodern world, many are increasingly critical in their assessment of these Protestant missionaries. The issue at stake, however, is whether or not the missionaries contributed, intentionally and purposefully or otherwise, as colonial agents to the processes of subjugation, exploitation and the devastation of the land and the people.

The establishment of the British Empire (from about 1780 onward) accompanied the advent and subsequent rise of Protestant missions.

---

16. Stanley, *Bible and the Flag*, 184.

17. The anecdote is popularly attributed to Bishop Desmond Tutu but may also have originated from Jomo Kenyatta, the first prime minister of Kenya.

Under the auspices of trade and commercial enterprises such as the English East India Company, the gospel of Jesus Christ was simultaneously proclaimed to those colonies in South Asia and subsequently to various countries in Southeast Asia.

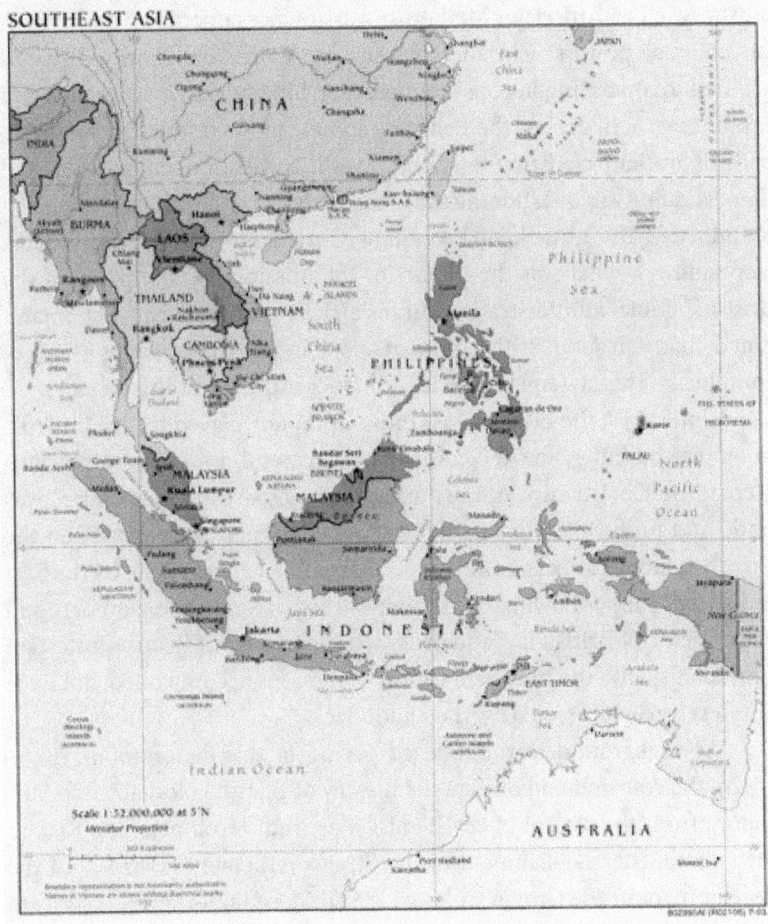

Figure 1 Map of Southeast Asia (2003)

Invariably, the missionary enterprise became increasingly entangled with British economic expansionary ideals—"commerce and Christianity" (a phrase used by David Livingstone in 1857). The diversity of races and religions (Chinese, Indians, Malays, British, Americans, Dutch, et cetera) that converged in Singapore and established themselves in this trading port, became an important factor in the British policy of religious freedom in the governing of the colony. Yet to date, not much material is available in exploring and understanding the complex relationship of Protestant (and in particular, Methodist) missions to the colonial rule in the history of the church in Singapore.

The case of Singapore is interesting in that it involves British Methodist as well as American Methodist missionaries operating under British colonial powers. Christian missionary endeavors have long been accused "of operating in consistent partnership with the instruments and exploitative activities of the British colonial rule—commerce, conquest, code of law and 'civilizing mission,'"[18] yet it is still an open question and there is validity in questioning the extent to which colonial rule advanced or impeded the growth of Protestant Christianity in Singapore. Correspondingly, what was the impact of the missionary enterprise on the British colonial administration? In his article on colonialism, Schumann noted that, "in fact, British missionary-colonial relationships were ... complex."[19] This statement provided further impetus for this research.

Until 1857, the English East India Company played the leading role in empire building, and the company was careful not to combine commerce with Christianity. At the outset, the company's "main concern was trade and profit. Its religious interest was only peripheral."[20] When the Crown assumed direct control of the commercial empire built by the East India Company following the Indian Mutiny (1857), "the gunboats and instruments of British law and order led the banner of British Protestant Christianity into the twentieth century. Missions accompanied, but were not necessarily protected by, the Union Jack."[21]

As background to the focused period of this dissertation (1885–1910), the research will outline the history of British colonialism in Singapore from the arrival of the English East India Company in 1819, to the subsequent establishment of the Straits Settlements (1826) and the development of the Crown Colony (1867). More importantly, it seeks to articulate the attendant policies of the Crown administration toward the

---

18. Schumann et al., "Colonialism," in Sunquist et al., *Dictionary of Asian Christianity*, 194.

19. Schumann et al., "Colonialism," in Sunquist et al., *Dictionary of Asian Christianity*, 194.

20. David, *Western Colonialism*, 194.

21. Chew and Chew, "Imperialism," in Sunquist et al., *Dictionary of Asian Christianity*, 362.

Anglican missionary enterprise in Singapore, as the context for the later arrival of Methodist missions.

This dissertation will then study and analyze the arrival and establishment of American Methodism in Singapore from 1885, with a main focus on the relationship between the Methodist missionaries and the British colonial administration. The research will involve the study of records that document the explicit and implicit relationships between the missionaries and the colonial administration of Singapore. In addition the research design includes an examination of the work of the Methodist mission and the corresponding influence of Methodism on the administration of colonial Singapore. This may shed some light on the dialectical relationship between British colonialism and Methodist missions.

STATEMENT OF THE PROBLEM

It is a common claim heard today in Singapore and throughout former colonies that Christian missions operated from a position of privilege by their association with colonial regimes and that that privilege implicates missionaries in the colonial project. Christian mission is perceived as complicit with colonialism. Even in modern Singapore, the Christian faith is often regarded as a legacy of the Western colonial enterprise. There seems to be a suspicion of western import and colonial legacies, which are perceived as impediments to the building of a Singaporean national identity. Not surprisingly, Christianity is often regarded as a "western religion," a vestige of the former colonial regime. This causes the faith to be misunderstood and creates an obstacle to authentic Christian mission.

This research will explore the relationship between the British colonial administration and the American Methodist mission agency in Singapore from 1885 (arrival of Methodism) to 1910 (the first 25 years). The project involves historical research in a number of archives (see Appendix A—Information on Archives) with the goal of discovering how the British colonial regime dealt with the Methodist mission and how the Methodist mission responded to the British colonial administration, thereby documenting the complex interaction between British colonialism and American Methodism.

Employing a theoretical analogy of heterogeneous catalysis[22] and a theoretical framework adapted from the work of Jean and John Comaroff,

---

22. Heterogeneous catalysis refers to chemical reaction that occurs between reactions that are catalysed by another reactant, all of which are in different physical

this research will investigate the dialectical relationship between British colonialism and the Methodist missions. The research will document the various means by which early Methodist missions in Singapore permeated the cultures and societies, albeit under the secular policies of the colonial administration. It will also include a missiological reflection on the Methodist missionary methods (programs and practices) to and with the immigrants in Singapore as well as their responses to the colonial administration, in order to glean insights relevant for a mission model for today, especially in countries in Southeast Asia, which share the similar context of colonial history.

THEORETICAL FRAMEWORK

The advent of Methodist missionaries in the wake of British colonial rule helped spark a movement as with many other stories of Methodism in Asia. Bishop Robert Solomon, the former Bishop of the Methodist Church in Singapore, called it "the story of sparks of grace that lit up spiritual fires of personal and social holiness"[23] in Singapore and spreading outwards in Southeast Asia. It is a story of change, brought about by action, reaction, interaction and transformation, among the immigrant population, the missionaries and the colonial administration. This dynamic interaction reminded me of my previous studies in the field of chemistry, specifically of heterogeneous catalysis.

Chemistry, by its very nature, is a science that is concerned with change and much of the study of chemical reactions is concerned with the formation of new substances from a given set of reactants. An example of a simple metal/acid reaction, such as that of zinc with hydrochloric acid, which may be expressed as such:

$$\text{Zn} + 2\text{HCl} \longrightarrow \text{H}_2 + \text{ZnCl}_2 \quad \text{slow reaction with no visible effect}$$

zinc   hydrochloric acid   hydrogen   zinc chloride

---

states. The catalyst is introduced to alter the kinetics of the reaction, which in other words is to speed up the rate of reaction. See Carberry, *Chemical and Catalytic Reaction Engineering*. Chapter 9 of the book deals with the topic of heterogeneous catalysis. Carberry noted, "Heterogeneous catalysis has to deal not only with the catalyzed reaction itself but, in addition, with the complexities of surface properties (different crystal surfaces, different catalytic sites, possible segregation of adsorbates (so-called island formation), contamination or deterioration of catalytic sites, and adsorption and desorption equilibria and rates" (273).

23. Goh, *Sparks of Grace*, iv.

The above reaction occurs at room temperature, somewhat slowly with no visible signs of reaction. Interestingly, the rate of the chemical reaction may be increased with the addition of a substance known as a catalyst. The addition of a small amount of copper sulphate solution increases the rate of reaction, causing greater effervescence and faster formation of the hydrogen gas. Chemically the reaction is written as:

$$\text{Zn} + 2\text{HCl} \xrightarrow{\text{CuSO}_4 \text{ catalyst}} \text{H}_2 + \text{ZnCl}_2 \quad \text{fast reaction accompanied with effervescence}$$

zinc + hydrochloric acid → hydrogen + zinc chloride

A catalyst is defined as the substance that changes the speed of a chemical reaction without undergoing a permanent chemical change itself in the process. The catalyst may react with the reactants in the process of the chemical reaction but the end result is such that the catalyst is reformed at the end of the process. Hence there is an exchange that goes on between the catalyst and the reactants. A general catalytic equation may be rendered as such:

$$\text{Reactant A} + \text{Reactant B} \xrightarrow{\text{Chemical X catalyst}} \text{Product(s) of Reaction}$$

Catalysis may be further classified as homogeneous catalysis (where the catalyst is present in the same phase as the reacting molecules) or heterogeneous catalysis (where the catalyst is in a different phase from the reactant molecules, usually as a solid in contact with either gaseous or liquid reactants). For the purposes of this proposal, it is heterogeneous catalysis that warrants our attention. An important example of heterogeneous catalysis is the use of vanadium pentoxide in the Contact Process[24] for the production of sulphur trioxide and sulphuric acid. Sulphuric acid production, which is fundamental to the production of car batteries, soap, fertilizers and various other commodities, is hence regarded as a benchmark of industrialization.

---

24. Emerson Process Management, "Sulphuric Acid Manufacturing," https://www.emerson.com/documents/automation/application-note-sulfuric-acid-manufacturing-rosemount-en-68374.pdf.

Without using the complicated chemical terminologies,[25] we may say that a catalyst may act through any of the following three paths in changing the speed of a chemical reaction (called chemical kinetics):

a. by increasing the proximity of two or more of the reactants.

b. by increasing the opportunity of reaction.

c. by decreasing the energy requirement for reaction, or in layman's terms, decreasing the difficulty of reaction.

Although in heterogeneous catalysis the catalyst itself does not undergo any chemical change, yet there is often some degree of change, albeit physical. The example of vanadium pentoxide, employed as a catalyst in the Contact Process, highlights this physical change. While chemically it is still vanadium pentoxide as it facilitates the formation of sulphur trioxide, the catalyst is physically amalgamated into a mass, quite unlike the original but yet retaining its chemical qualities as catalyst.

The chemical effect of heterogeneous catalysis serves as a useful analogy to the issue of the Methodist missionary enterprise under British colonialism in Singapore. The colonial administration provided the necessary factors that facilitated the advent of Methodism in this part of Southeast Asia. Thus, British colonialism was catalytic to the advent of Methodism in Singapore, where "Pax Britannica was a precondition of missionary activities."[26] In the process of catalysis, the interchanges brought about various degrees of change primarily to the missionaries and to the people of Singapore and secondarily to the colonial administration in Singapore, however minute or subtle those secondary effects may be. Chemically, the reaction formula may be expressed in the following manner:

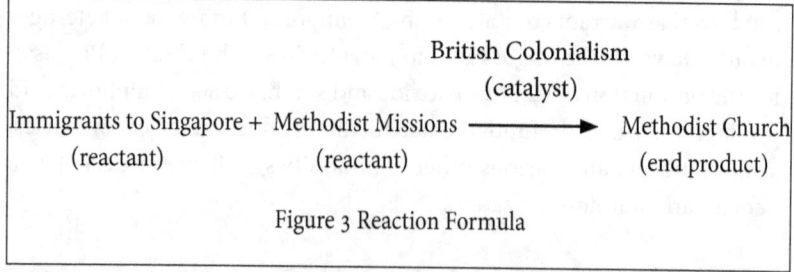

Figure 3 Reaction Formula

25. See Brown, LeMay, and Bursten, *Chemistry the Central Science*, 523–25, for a more detailed description of the steps involved in heterogeneous catalysis.

26. Olaf Schumann et al., "Colonialism," in Sunquist et al., *Dictionary of Asian Christianity*, 195.

The chemical model of catalysis provides a working analogy in understanding the mechanism between colonialism and Methodist missions, though it should be cautioned that as with most analogies, there is a limit when the analogy is taken to extremes.

This study of the relationship between British colonialism and Methodist missions in Singapore is further informed by Jean and John Comaroffs' view of colonialism as a dialectical process. The Comaroffs deal with the concepts of ideology and hegemony, where ideology may be understood as the external form of some social order while hegemony is the enforced worldview that is manifestly powerful. The Comaroffs understand colonialism as not merely taking over the land, but also taking over the consciousness of the people. They also perceived that the impact of colonialism had a counter-effect on the colonialists as evidenced by the responses of the colonized. The Comaroffs suggest that, as the "ways of the whites" were increasingly thrust on the Tswana of South Africa, it was both suppressing (colonization of consciousness) as well as enabling (consciousness of colonization),

> The Tswana may have learned the political language of colonialism. And they may have conducted themselves according to its practical terms. But the more they were forced to comply with European forms of discourse, the more they came to rely upon, and invoke, the distinction between *sekgoa*, the ways of the whites, and *setswana*, Tswana ways. . . . Present in embryo from the start of the long conversation, it (this contrast) was to emerge as a critical trope in Tswana historical consciousness.[27]

The Comaroffs' dialectical model highlights the inevitable changes that occur in the interaction of two or more cultures. For the colonized, the changes are strikingly obvious but for the colonizers, change is also present, though often subtle. In the dialectical relationship between colonial rulers, missionaries and colonized, the period of British colonial rule in Singapore helped to precipitate both the industrial growth as well as a national movement in shaping the identity of Singaporeans, most evidently in the period following the Japanese Occupation. It may well be that Singapore's industrial growth is grounded upon the pillar of meritocracy, while the Singapore identity is founded upon multiculturalism. These twin pillars of multiculturalism and meritocracy have become the very foundation on which modern Singapore is established. In the

---

27. Comaroff and Comaroff, *Of Revelation and Revolution*, 308.

manner that British colonial policies have influenced the course of multiculturalism in present-day Singapore, it may also be surmised that the missionaries have firmed the other pillar of meritocracy through their emphasis on education in colonial Singapore. But interestingly, "arguably, the most significant and lasting effects of British Imperialism have been felt in Britain itself. Imperialism has been instrumental in shaping the British sense of national identity."[28] This study seeks to investigate the impact that British colonialism has had on Methodist missions in this part of Asia, which had a direct bearing on the methods and ministries of the Methodist missions, as well as the corresponding (perhaps subtle) influence, Methodists missionaries have had on colonial rule.

In this project, I have chosen to adopt this model with respect to the interchanges and interactions between the British colonial administration and the Methodist missionaries. Adapting the model from the Comaroffs,' the dialectical and catalytic model of British colonialism upon Methodist missionaries and the immigrants in Singapore, may be thus illustrated:

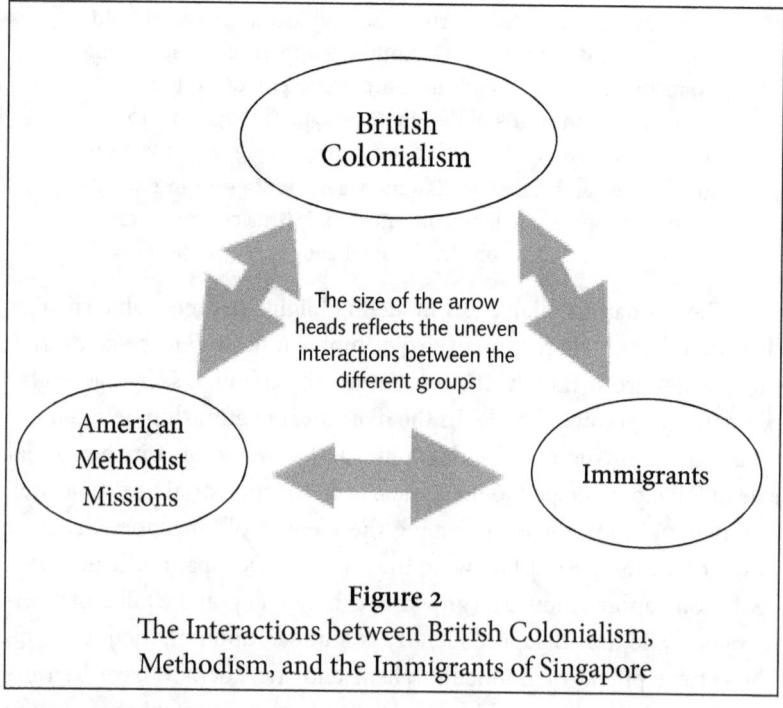

Figure 2
The Interactions between British Colonialism, Methodism, and the Immigrants of Singapore

---

28. Webster, *Gentlemen Capitalists*, 262.

The above diagram illustrates the influence that each of the groups has on the others. The British administration and the missionaries exert a more than proportionate impact on the immigrants and in the same manner, there is also a disparate effect between the colonial administration and the Methodist missionaries, which is the main focus of this research.

The framework for this research is perhaps best articulated in the following quote by Karl Jung, "The meeting of two personalities is like the contact of two chemical substances: if there is any reaction, both are transformed."[29]

RESEARCH QUESTIONS

In order to adequately and chronologically research this topic, four questions are raised and these questions guide the corresponding research methodologies:

Question #1: What were the initial policies of the colonial administration (English East India Company and the Straits Settlement) with regard to early Christian missions in Singapore?

Question #2: What policy changes toward missions were made during the period of the Crown rule (1867 onward)? To what extent did the colonial administration enforce those policies in practice? How did it affect mission praxis?

Question #3: How did the American Methodist mission respond to the policies and practices of the administration, in view of colonial positions on the propagation of religious beliefs?

Question #4: What influence(s) did the Methodist missionaries have on the colonial administration?

In addition to the four research questions, the principal area of application for this research can also be stated in the form of a question:

Application Question: What can we learn from nineteenth century Methodist missions and what applications can we make as Methodist missions grow outward to other parts of Southeast Asia today?

---

29. Jung, *CW 18*, 71.

DELIMITATIONS

The complexity of the interchanges between missions and colonialism fuels the need to better understand the uncharted waters in the history of missions and colonialism in Singapore and serves as an impetus to better understand, to articulate and to retell the story of the Methodism in colonial Singapore. In view of the vast amount of archival materials available and the expansive nature of the issue, the study will be delimited as follows:

1. This study will not examine in detail the formation of the English East India Company nor will it provide a detailed nineteenth century colonial history of Singapore. Though the previous administration under the English East India Company and the subsequent governance under the Straits Settlements, which was administered from British India, does provide the context, this study will focus primarily on the period of British colonial rule from 1860s to the early twentieth century, when Singapore was a part of the Crown Colony under the direct rule of Britain.

2. This study will not attempt to provide an exhaustive history of the advent of Christianity in Singapore. Undoubtedly the Anglicans, Presbyterians and Roman Catholics have all made an impact on Christianity in Singapore, but this study seeks to take a closer look at the advent of Methodism in Singapore and the issues and interchanges those pioneer Methodist missionaries took on with the colonial administration, specifically of the period between 1885 and 1910.

3. This study will not attempt to account for and chronicle all the evangelistic and missional efforts of all the pioneer Methodist missionaries but seeks to highlight the significant examples from among these early missionaries who have impacted the growth of the church in Singapore.

4. This study's focus is not on the colonial impact on the immigrants in Singapore but primarily on the colonial impact on the missionaries. It is noted, however, that some colonial administrative policies did have ramifications for the strategies and methods that the missionaries employed in bringing the gospel to the people.

5. As this project is primarily a historical research focusing on the period of Crown rule in Malaya, it will not engage the post-World War II history of decolonization, independence and post-colonial history in any significant detail.

2

The Colonial Contact

WRITTEN ACCOUNTS OF THE early history of Singapore are sketchy, though it is generally accepted that Singapore served as a port of the Malacca Sultanate in the sixteenth century. Gradually, Singapore was eclipsed by the increasing importance of Malacca as a trading port, first established by the Portuguese in support of their spice trade in the Far East and later taken over by the Dutch East India Company.[1]

By the late eighteenth century, Singapore had waned in significance, becoming an almost desolate island and had perhaps faded from the maps of the European colonial powers that had ventured into this part of Asia in competition for the lucrative spice trade. The island became home to only a handful of Malay fishermen and was the occasional "stopover" island of the pirates who plied the Straits of Malacca. It was the English East India Company who "rediscovered" Singapore and was able to take advantage of its important geography, located at the crossroads of the sea route between India in West and China in the East.

THE EAST INDIA COMPANY

Considering the latitude of its historical and global impact, few commercial enterprises can parallel that of the English East India Company. The Company was founded as *The Governor and Company of Merchants of London Trading into the East Indies* by a coterie of enterprising and

---

1. More popularly known by the initials VOC, *Vereenigde Oostindische Compagnie*, which was also founded in the same year as the English East India Company in 1600.

influential businessmen, and was granted a Royal Charter by Queen Elizabeth I on 31 December 1600, with the intent to favour trade privileges in the East, beginning with India. Initially, the Company had 125 shareholders, and a capital of £72,000. Due to Dutch control of the spice trade, the Company found it hard to make any impact and encountered much opposition in establishing an outpost in the East Indies. Eventually, ships belonging to the company arrived in India, docking at Surat, which was established as a trade transit point in 1608. In the next two years, it managed to build its first factory (as the trading posts were known) in the town of Machilipatnam on the Coromandel Coast in the Bay of Bengal. As it built up its influence, the Company was able to wrestle India from the Dutch in the ensuing years.

In his account of the Company's mercantile dealings with the Indians, however, Keay[2] reminds us that India was not the original object of the East India Company's operations and neither was India the final object. Much of the trade was centered initially on the Spice Islands. The spice trade, though lucrative for the handful of merchants who purchased stock in the Company's voyages, proved unpopular with the Crown, since woolen cloth, the chief mercantile item of the English trade, was not of any significant demand in Southeast Asia. Furthermore, the ferocity of the Dutch in defense of the "islands of spicerie," effectively repulsed English competition by 1650. The subsequent voyages to Siam, Japan and the Arabian dependencies also yielded little benefit. It was not until the tentative approach to India, for India's prized calicoes, that the Company began its halting transformation from business enterprise to temporarily become overlord of the subcontinent. Yet, India was perhaps an extended distraction, for throughout its history, the Company was as much about the East as about India and its most successful commercial venture was in China.

In the early part of the nineteenth century, when the company was at its zenith, the Company controlled almost half the world's trade and a tenth of the British Exchequer's revenues consisted of customs receipts on the Company's imports of tea. The geographical span of the Company's

---

2. Keay, *Honourable Company*. Keay's account of the company is significant in that he sought to differentiate the commercial enterprises of the East India Company from the colonial administration of the Raj (formal British colonial rule), which followed it, and to release the company from the Victorian notion that it was the necessary and logical precursor of British rule in India.

business empire stretched from London through India, to most of Southeast Asia and on to China.

Within much of that territory, Company officials governed with a sense of Anglo-Saxon superiority; building their own military forts, raising its own navy, dispensing justice, minting its own currency and waging war as they saw fit, when the Company's trade was affected. Without them there would have been no British Empire, and presumably, the history of quite a number of countries in Asia might have followed an entirely different course.

The English East India Company in extending their dominion in India, and whose trade with China[3] in the second half of the eighteenth century was steadily expanding, saw the need for a port of call in this region to refit, revitalize and protect their merchant fleet, as well as to forestall any advance by the Dutch in Southeast Asia.

The arrival of the British in Southeast Asia, in particular, Malaya, is almost inseparably linked together with Britain's desire to trade with China. The latter almost invariably playing some part in the activities of the former. According to Tregonning, the movements of the British eastward—from India to the Malay Peninsular, the impulse that led to the foundation of Penang in 1786, to Singapore in 1819 and the onward movement to Hong Kong in 1842—were all representative of British desire to strengthen trade with China. For the British, "the trade in tea, then, was the basic impulse that led to the expansion of British power in the Far East, and as a corollary, in Southeast Asia as well."[4] But the English traders faced a problem, for prior to the nineteenth century, before there was any trade in opium, it became increasingly obvious that the British had nothing that the Chinese did not already possess or was not quite prepared to do without. Britain could trade silver bullion but was hesitant that any silver should leave the country,

> but if Britain itself produced nothing of value to China and if Indian cotton was insufficient, fortunately, there were a few other commodities Britain could secure in exchange for which the *towkays* of Canton would exchange their tea. Chief of these were tin and pepper. And it was largely for the acquisition of these

---

3. Tregonning, *British in Malaya*. Tregonning interprets the movements of the British, eastward from India to the Malay Peninsular, as a stepping stone to Britain's mercantile scheme of trade with China.

4. Tregonning, *British in Malaya*, 5.

two commodities that Britain doggedly continued its search for a Southeast Asian base.⁵

The East India Company embarked on various mercantile missions into areas as Acheh, Bencoolen, Kedah, Perlis and eastward toward the island of Balambangan. The attempts of the British to establish trading posts in order to acquire tin and pepper, the two primary products, were to help facilitate an increasing volume of trade with China. The later acquisition of Malacca from the Portuguese helped to further establish British presence in the Malayan peninsular. The British, however, had to be cautious in these endeavors because of Dutch presence and competition.

The urgency of having to establish more trading posts to facilitate trade with China resulted in the establishment of a post in Penang, Malaya in 1786. Contrary to some historians who advanced the claim that Penang was founded for reasons of maritime strategy to serve colonial interests, historian Tregonning regards it as a misinterpretation and ignoring of the facts. He maintained that "Nearly all of the Company expeditions were commercial in intent and designed to assist the trade with China. They were undertaken not by the Navy, not sponsored by Bombay, the naval center, but by Madras and Calcutta."⁶ In view of the Dutch presence and competition in this part of Southeast Asia, Penang was hence targeted as a commercial trading post, which was to break that monopoly, ensuring the safe passage of British trade with China. Penang's significance, however, was eclipsed with the founding of Singapore, which afforded a better harbor and a more strategic position for British interests in the spice trade.

Sir Stamford Raffles of the English East India Company intended to establish a British trading base at the southern tip of the Straits of Malacca to check the resurgent power of the Dutch government⁷ and to re-establish some British prominence abandoned by the withdrawal from Java. Circumventing the explicit directives of his immediate superiors, who were more concerned for Penang's survival than for the Company's long term interests, Raffles went ahead to acquire a legal title to the island

---

5. Tregonning, *British in Malaya*, 5.
6. Tregonning, *British in Malaya*, 33.
7. For a more detailed account of Anglo-Dutch rivalries, please refer to, "The Relationship between British Policies and the Extent of Dutch Power in the Malay Archipelago, 1784–1871," in Tarling, *Imperial Britain in Southeast Asia*, 7–27.

which later established British presence at a strategic location. Singapore, as a port, was attractive because,

> whereas all the ports of the remainder of Southeast Asia exacted customs, dues and levies, Singapore, despite numerous attempts by the Company in India to change it, began and remained a free port. Raffles should be given full credit for introducing it; that it remained so, however, unlike Penang, was due to the much more favorable locale of Singapore for trade, and to its very rapid growth.[8]

Yet in a similar manner, not unlike the situation in India, British presence in Southeast Asia was but part of the larger perspective of establishing British trade, finally and ultimately with China, the Middle Kingdom. In tandem with Keay, Tregonning traced the development of the ports of Malacca, Penang (for the most part in his book) and Singapore, and saw them as part of a scheme that was in the ultimate service of British trade with China. Tregonning concluded with the observation that summed up the primary thesis:

> Of most importance was the acquisition of the British of a place to trade—a barren island off the mouth of the Canton River. Here in Hong Kong, the British were to establish what they had been seeking for over a hundred years. Not in Penang or in Singapore had they succeeded, nor in the many other attempts in Southeast Asia. Aware though they had been of the problem, their attempts to answer it have never been satisfactory. But in Hong Kong, at last, the British had secured a mart for trade with China. With the establishment of Hong Kong, the long move east from India has ended.[9]

The inclusion of the history of Malaya (that of, Penang, Malacca and Singapore) is perhaps a piece in the grand "puzzle" of British mercantile expansion. Yet it is nonetheless a significant piece in the scheme of things for without the spice and tin trade in Southeast Asia, Britain would not have been able to penetrate the Chinese market. It is hence indicative that the history of this region cannot be taken in isolation. Furthermore, in many ways the history of Malaysia and Singapore are so intertwined that it continues to be played out in the present (as in the issue of water talks

---

8. Tregonning, *British in Malaya*, 153.
9. Tregonning, *British in Malaya*, 172.

between the two countries) even long after the British has withdrawn from Southeast Asia.

SIR STAMFORD RAFFLES AND THE FOUNDING OF SINGAPORE

Raffles was an astute officer of the Company and sought to combat Dutch designs on the monopoly of the spice trade. He perceived that the Dutch were

> actuated by a spirit of ambition, by views of boundless aggrandizement and rapacity, and by a desire to obtain the power of monopolizing the commerce of the Eastern Archipelago, and of excluding the English from those advantages which they had long enjoyed.[10]

His persistent efforts to safeguard the interests of British trade in the Malayan Archipelago would eventuate in the plan to concede to the Dutch the British trading centers in Sumatra and the exclusive control of the Straits of Sunda, while concurrently mounting British efforts to obtain a port or trading center at the southern entrance of the Straits of Malacca. With British control of a port to the northern and southern entrance of the Straits of Malacca, this would have given the British "the entire command of the only channels for the direct trade between China and Europe."[11]

Since his assumption of duties as the East India Company's Governor of Java and as Lieutenant-Governor of Bencoolen, Raffles had envisioned the establishment of an English settlement at the southern entrance of the Straits of Malacca in order to secure British commercial interests in Southeast Asia. He had plans to establish a port where ships trading with China could obtain provisions and make repairs. Raffles saw that a port further south of the Straits of Malacca was of far greater significance than British controlled Penang, primarily of its closer proximity to the Spice Islands and to China. He believed that Penang "was too far from the center of things to be an effective station," and was "so distant from the principal native ports of the Archipelago, that under

---

10. Raffles, *Memoir of the Life*, Minute to Lord Hastings, 304.
11. Egerton, *Sir Stamford Raffles*, 172.

the uncertainty of the passage up the Straits, but few native vessels are induced to go there."[12]

Raffles clearly expressed his thoughts in a paper entitled "*Our Interests in the Eastern Archipelago*" which he addressed to the President of the Board of Control of the East India Company in 1817. In the paper, Raffles forwarded his arguments that Britain should take

> immediate possession of a port in the Eastern Archipelago, the best adapted for communication with the native princes ... for the resort of the independent trade, and the trade with our allies; for the protection of our commerce and all our interests, and more especially for an entrepot for our merchandise.[13]

Raffles saw the establishment of a port and settlement in Singapore as a springboard for the expansion of British trade in the East. Giving consideration to the Dutch inevitable repossession of their colonies and the subsequent attempt to then revive their monopoly of the trade in the east, Raffles saw in the setting of a free port in Singapore, a means of upsetting their monopoly in the East. Accordingly, Raffles had no intention that these ports were to become colonial establishments. They were rather "to be looked upon as so many outposts or stations erected for the convenience and security of our general commercial interests, and not as governments intended for the rule and detailed management of a dominion."[14] In his emphases on commercial interests rather than colonial conquests, Raffles reflected Shelburne's dictum of 1782, that "We prefer trade to dominion."

In November 1818, Lord Hastings, Governor-General of India, gave tacit approval to Sir Stamford Raffles to establish trading stations at both the northern and southern tip of the Malay Peninsula. Raffles was to go first to Achin (known also as Acheh) to establish British interests there and then to go on to establish a British post at Rhio (Riau) at the southern tip of the Straits. Hastings had authorized Raffles "to secure an agreement with Acheh at the northern end and establish a post at Riau, Johor or some other southern point, provided he did not bring the Company into

---

12. Raffles, *Memoir of the Life*, 306–8. See also Egerton, *Sir Stamford Raffles*, 162–63, 166; and Boulger, *Life of Sir Stamford Raffles*, 260–71.

13. The paper is printed fairly completely in Boulger, *Life of Sir Stamford Raffles*, 268–73. The original manuscript may be found in the British Museum, Add. MSS., 31,327, f.241.

14. Boulger, *Life of Sir Stamford Raffles*, 270.

conflict with the Dutch."[15] As soon as Raffles had set sail on his mission, however, Hastings sent another somewhat contradicting dispatch that directed Raffles to "desist from every attempt to form a British establishment in the Eastern Archipelago."[16] The conflicting dispatch is somewhat demonstrative of the fact that Hastings and indeed, the superiors in the East India Company, had not decided on anything concrete except that something had to be done in the Straits of Malacca.

Aware of their vacilation, Raffles arrived in Penang, to the scene of more intrigue and Company politicking. Colonel Bannerman, the Governor of Penang, was anything but cooperative and sought to prevent Raffles from achieving his goal. Raffles' orders were to first establish the post in Achin (Acheh) to the north but Bannerman "was insistent that the Achin mission should be postponed pending certain representations he wished to make to the Supreme Government."[17] Upon which, Raffles decided to set sail for the south, embarking on the second part of his mission, undaunted by the calculated preclusions imposed by Bannerman. Unintentionally, Bannerman's hostility in preventing the Achinese mission, ensured that Hastings' second dispatch that forbade the establishment of new posts in the eastern Archipelago, did not catch up with Raffles, who was by then enroute to the south, in search of a new trading station in the Rhio (Riau) islands.

Abandoned in the seventeenth and eighteenth century in favor of other islands and ports in the southern tip of Peninsular Malaysia, Singapore had become more of a pirates' liar. Accordingly, Abdullah Munshi made this note in his account of Singapore:

> At that time, no mortal dared to pass through the Straits of Singapore, *jins* and *satans* even were afraid, for that was the booty. There also, they put to death their captives and themselves fought and killed each other in the quarrels on the division of the spoils. . . . All along the beach there were hundreds of human skulls, some of them old, some fresh with hair still remaining, some with teeth still sharp, and some without teeth: in fine,

---

15. Turnbull, *History of Singapore*, 7–9. Turnbull records that Raffles, enroute to the southern islands, received news of the Dutch's claim over Riau Islands, thereby jeopardizing the English hopes of establishing a southern base along the Straits of Malacca. The bureaucracies and internal political rivalries within the East India Company all but served to propel Raffles forward in ensuring the establishment of a southern base.

16. Egerton, *Sir Stamford Raffles*, 183–84.

17. Mills, *British Malaya*, 55.

they were in various stages of decay. Mr. Farquhar ordered them to be collected and thrown into the sea.[18]

In spite of its notoriety as a pirates' cove, Raffles surveyed the nearby islands and on 29 January 1819, Raffles landed on the island of Singapore. The next day, he concluded a preliminary treaty with *Temenggong Abdulrahman* to set up a trading post here. Despite the treaty, Raffles did not think that his legal claim on Singapore was secure since it came from the *de facto* and not the *de jure* ruler of the country. In order to squash all claims that the rival Dutch may have on Singapore, Raffles thought it expedient that he should also secure a similar treaty with the Sultan.

Singapore was a part of the Empire of Johor and that this island should have two rulers is the result of decay of this ancient empire during the seventeenth and eighteenth century. The power of the Sultan became increasing checked by the rise of the Raja Mudas, which was the hereditary office of the Princes of the Bugis merchant-pirates who had settled on the coasts of continental Johor. In 1810, with the passing of the ruling Sultan Mahmud II, the Empire was left to his two sons. Hussien, the elder was away in nearby state of Pahang and in his absence, the Raja Muda of Rhio. Raja Jaafar, convinced the younger son, Abdulrahman, to seize the throne. Hence while Hussein is the rightful heir, the *de jure* ruler, Singapore was administered by the *de facto* ruler of Johor, Abdulrahman, the *Temengong*. The Dutch treaty of 1818 which gave them control of the southern islands of Rhio was similarly concluded with Abdulrahman.

In a letter to his friend and superior, Marsden, on 31 January 1819, Raffles penned his thoughts with regards to what he expected from the British occupation of the island. He wrote:

> My Dear Sir, here I am at Singapore, true to my word, and in the enjoyment of all the pleasure which a footing on such classic ground must inspire. The lines of the old city, and of its defences, are still to be traced, and within its ramparts the British Union waves unmolested. . . . It is only now left for me to solicit your support in behalf of my more recent attempt to extend the British influence. Most certainly the Dutch had never a factory in the island of Singapore; and it does not appear to me that their recent arrangements with a subordinate authority at Rhio can or ought to interfere with our permanent establishment here. I have, however, a violent opposition to surmount on the part of the Government of Penang. . . .

18. Abdullah Abdul Kadir, *Hikayat Abdullah*, 32.

> This place possesses an excellent harbour, and everything that can be desired for a British port in the island of St. John's, which forms the south-western point of the harbour. We here command an intercourse with all the ships passing through the Straits of Singapore. We are within a week's sail to China, close of Siam, and in the very seat of the Malayan Empire. This, therefore, will probably be my last attempt. If I am deserted now, I must fain return to Bencoolen, and become philosopher. . . . I expect to conclude all my arrangements at this place in the course of a few days and then return to Penang, where I left Lady Raffles, and my anxiety to get there, on her account, is very great. From Penang my course will probably bend toward Acheen, where I have to establish the British influence on a permanent footing; from thence I shall proceed to Bencoolen. . . .
>
> If I keep Singapore I shall be quite satisfied; and in a few years our influence over the Archipelago, as far as concerns our commerce, will be fully established.[19]

As noted in the above correspondence, the acquisition of Singapore is a thoroughly commercial decision rather than one of colonial conquest. Carefully ascertaining the provisions of the treaty was confined to just the Rhio Islands and that the Dutch could lay no claims over Singapore, Raffles wanted to ensure an indisputable claim in the ensuing diplomatic contest over the sovereignty of Singapore and hence he sought to formalize the treaty with Hussien, the rightful heir. Raffles well understood that the *Temenggong* was the *de facto* ruler of Singapore, while Hussein, whose power was checked, was nonetheless the undisputable *de jure* ruler of Singapore. Raffles perceived that:

> if the Company's title to Singapore was based merely on the Temenggong's grant, the Dutch might be able to overthrow it on the ground that theoretically he had no right to make the cession. But with a grant signed by both the "de facto" and the "de jure" sovereigns, the Company's title was legally unassailable.[20]

Raffles entered into negotiations with Hussien and persuaded him to come to Singapore and be installed as the rightful Sultan of Johor. On 6 February 1819, a formal treaty was concluded with Sultan Hussein of Johor and the *Temenggong*, the *de jure* and *de facto* rulers of Singapore respectively. The treaty agreements were that the Company was given

19. Boulger, *Life of Sir Stamford Raffles*, 311.
20. Mills, *British Malaya*, 51.

the rights to build a factory on the island and that both the *Sultan* and *Temenggong* will not enter into any other treaty negotiations with any European or American powers. In return, the Sultan Hussein was to receive a comfortable pension from the East India Company as long as he lived and in return he was only to give the rights for the Company to build a factory on the island.

Though London was still doubtful of Raffles' somewhat hasty and perhaps seemingly insubordinate tactics in acquiring Singapore, for fear of a direct conflict with the Dutch, Singapore however, proved to be a prized settlement. Within a year, 1820, Singapore was earning revenue, and three years later, its trade surpassed that of Penang. In letter to his cousin, Dr. Raffles, Raffles wrote:

> My settlement of Singapore continues to thrive most wonderfully. It is all and everything I could wish, and if no untimely fate awaits it, promises to become the emporium and the pride of the East. I learn with much regret the prejudice and malignity by which I am attacked at home for the desperate struggle I have maintained against the Dutch. Instead of being supported by my own Government, I find them deserting me and giving way in every instance to the unscrupulous and enormous pretensions of the Dutch....
>
> Were the value of Singapore properly appreciated, I am confident that all England would be in its favour. It positively takes nothing from the Dutch and is to us everything. It gives us command of China and Japan, with Siam and Cambodia, Cochin China, etc—to say nothing of the Islands themselves. What you observe regarding the introduction of British cottons through this port to China is a most important question. The affair is perfectly practicable, and nothing more easy. I had framed a plan, and am still bent upon the object; but until I know from England how I am to be supported in what I have so far done, it would be premature to suggest any speculation. Confirm Singapore and establish my authority in the Archipelago on the principle I have suggested, and it will not be long before there is abundant demand for this description of our manufactures at least. Upwards of 10,000 tons of raw cotton are annually sent to China from our territories in India. Why should we send our raw produce to encourage the industry of a foreign nation at the expense of our own manufactures? If India cannot manufacture sufficiently cheap, England can; and it is idle to talk of the cheapness of our goods unless we can bring

measure clothed from England. No people study cheapness so much; and if we can undersell them, we have only to find the way of introducing the article. The monopoly of the East India Company in England, and of the Hong merchants in China precludes the idea of anything like fair competition in our own ships, or at the Port of Canton. Not but the East India Company can, and perhaps will, assist as far as in them lies; but their ships are too expensive; the articles would also pass through the Hong merchants before they reach the general trader and consumer; and their intermediate profits would form another barrier.

At Singapore, however, every object may be obtained. Let the commercial interests for the present drop every idea of a direct trade to China, and let them concentrate their influences in supporting Singapore, and they will do ten times better. As a free port it is as much to them as the possession of Macao; and it is here that their voyages should finish,—the Chinese themselves coming to Singapore and purchasing. They have the means of importing into the different ports of Canton without the restraints and peculations of the Hong merchants. Many of the Chinese viceroys are themselves engaged clandestinely in external trade, and Singapore may, as a free port, thus become the connecting link and grand entrepot between Europe, Asia, and China. It is in fact fast becoming so. Vessels come from China to Singapore in five days.[21]

In spite of the trade growth of Singapore, it perhaps is important to note that in 1819 Raffles had in fact only acquired for the East India Company treaty rights to establish a British enclave within a Malay kingdom (of Johor). John Crawfurd, the second Resident of Singapore, noted that the treaty Raffles obtained:

> amounted to little more than a permission for the formation of a British factory.... There was really no territorial cession giving a legal right of legislation.... The native chief was considered to be the proprietor of the land, even within the bounds of the British factory.[22]

From 1819 to 1823, Singapore was technically administered by a system of "tripartite rule" of the Malay Sultan, the Temenggong, Major William Farquhar, Raffles' first appointed (British) Resident of Singapore Despite Farquhar's efficient administration, Raffles intervened and

21. Boulger, *Life of Sir Stamford Raffles*, 311–12.
22. Mills, *British Malaya*, 63.

reassigned Farquhar and initiated negotiations of a new agreement with the *Sultan* and the *Temenggong*. The Convention of 7 June 1823 extended the Company's control over the entire island, apart from the Sultan's and Temenggong's reserves and from thence, British laws would be enforced "with due consideration to the usages and habits of the people"[23] and at the same time respect was to be accorded to Malay laws and customs with reference to cases involving religion, marriage and inheritance "where they shall not be contrary to reason, justice or humanity."[24] The Convention however, stopped short of ceding sovereignty to the British.

In 1824, two new treaties formalized Singapore's status as British possession. The first was the Anglo-Dutch Treaty of March 1824, by which the Dutch withdrew all objections to the British occupation of Singapore. The second treaty was made with *Sultan Hussein* and *Temenggong Abdu'r Rahman*, with Dr. John Crawfurd, the assigned Resident, on 2 August 1824, by which the two owners ceded the island outright to the British East India Company in return for increased cash payments and pensions. With this purchase, control of the whole island and Britain's legal sovereignty over Singapore was finally acknowledged.

Notwithstanding the fact that it was Crawfurd, who finally made Singapore a British possession,[25] it is however, Raffles, who helped to definitively shape the future of Singapore. "The vision, the energy and the effrontery, which made Singapore the success that Balambangan and Penang had never been, were Raffles.'"[26] While on his journey toward Penang, Raffles did the thing that was most logical to him, which was perhaps frowned upon by his contemporaries: he used the time to learn Malay. This proved to be the key that unlocked the East to his infinite curiosity. Raffles was a natural linguist and was later to delve more deeply into the other Asian languages. He compiled dictionaries, grammars and vocabularies as well as collected and translated some ancient manuscripts. In turn, this knowledge of the local languages not only gave him deep understanding of and sympathy with the peoples of the various regions in Southeast Asia, but also opened up in his spare hours, the virtually unchartered areas of Southeast Asian history, archaeology, literature, music, art and anthropology. He is also well known for his love of

23. Buckley, *Anecdotal History*, 106–7.

24. Buckley, *Anecdotal History*, 107.

25. Please see http://www.scholars.nus.edu.sg/post/singapore/history/chew/chew10.html.

26. Keay, *Honourable Company*, 449.

botany, for which the largest bloom in the world is named after him, the *Rafflesia*. His voracious appetite made him an authority on Asian people and culture.

Raffles' knowledge of the region, his love for humanity and his hatred for oppression made him a man ahead of his time. His achievements in Singapore are unique—not only did he plan the layout of the city, he drafted Singapore's Constitution and set up a legal system, instructed the magistrates, set up everything from a Land Registry to a Post Office, from protection against fraud to licensing auctioneers, from port regulations to the minimum width of roads, he also set as the crowning piece of this his "political child," that "the port of Singapore is a free port and the trade thereof is open to all ships and vessels of every nation free of duty, equally and alike to all."[27]

Very much in tandem with the development of a free port was Raffles' project for an institution of higher education since he held firmly to the belief that "education must keep pace with commerce in order that its benefits may be ensured."[28] His pride and his joy then were the foundation of a college (first named the Singapore Institution and later renamed Raffles' Institution) and the development of a botanical garden; both of which are well established in present day Singapore! He may be regarded as a visionary not only in his founding and establishment of entrepot trade in Singapore but also for his belief that colonies did not exist for the benefit of the mother country but rather vice versa. In regard to the multicultural identity of Singapore, Raffles instructed to "let native institutions so far as regards religious observances, marriage and inheritance be respected when the same may not be inconsistent with justice and humanity, or injurious to the peace and morals of society."[29]

Raffles' hope to continue building his Singapore "dream" was prematurely terminated when he was recalled to London. In his place, he picked Dr. John Crawfurd with the cherished hope that Crawfurd would continue establishing Singapore as a premier free port and to build upon the work he had begun. Crawfurd, however, was somewhat differently motivated. He "regarded Raffles' provisions for representative government, higher education and moral upliftment as visionary, utopian, and

---

27. Boulger, *Life of Sir Stamford Raffles*, 102.
28. Turnbull, *History of Singapore*, 26.
29. Egerton, *Sir Stamford Raffles*, 233–35.

premature. He jettisoned them in order to promote what he held to be Raffles' most sensible ideas, notably his commercial policy."[30]

Crawfurd's administration of Singapore was from the period of June 1823 to August 1826 and this period saw vigorous growth in population, trade as well as revenue. The first census taken in January 1824 reflected a total population of 11,000 inhabitants that was composed of Malays (the largest community), Chinese, Bugis, Indians, Europeans, Armenians and Arabs. With the surge in population, Crawfurd was hence able to extract revenue from such vices as opium and gambling dens, a practice that went very much against the moral grain of his predecessor Raffles. It was Farquhar's approval of such vices on the newly established trading port that led to Raffles' reassignment of his Residency in Singapore. Nonetheless Crawfurd's economic policies were primarily motivated not by moralities but mercantile surpluses. Turnbull noted that "Singapore quickly achieved a commercial success beyond Raffles' hopes, but his moral and educational policies soon crumbled."[31]

THE STRAITS SETTLEMENTS

In a bid to streamline the administration among the three British possessions in the Straits of Malacca, the East India Company united Singapore with Malacca (secured from the Dutch) and Penang in 1826, forming the Presidency of the Straits Settlements. Penang was the seat of the administration of the Straits Settlement and Penang's Governor, Robert Fullerton assumed the concurrent position as the Governor of the Straits Settlement. In the same year, the royal charter of justice, that had been requested by Crawfurd in the administration of Singapore, was granted to the Straits Settlements. Based in Penang, the Recorder was to make trips to both Malacca and Singapore on a rotation basis to ensure judicial administration. The system however was not effective since the first Recorder, Sir John Claridge, refused to leave Penang due to disputes regarding travel expenses and allowances. He was subsequently recalled to London and dismissed in 1829.

Though Singapore was economically thriving, the Straits Settlements however proved to be an administrative challenge collectively. Turnbull noted,

---

30. Turnbull, *History of Singapore*, 26.
31. Turnbull, *History of Singapore*, 32.

Saddled with a big civil establishment and an elaborate judicial system, the government could not extract enough revenue to administer the scattered settlements.... the Company faced an acute financial crisis in India, and in 1830 it swept away the expensive superstructure in the Straits Settlements. The Presidency, the Governor and his Council were abolished and the Settlements were reduced to the status of a Residency dependent on the Presidency of Bengal.[32]

Hence the administration of the Straits Settlement came under the auspices of the Indian office of the East India Company in 1830. Against this background, Singapore's initial growth in 1819–24 was vigorous while the total trade growth for the period from 1824 to the 1850s was also impressive. This success came at the expense of Singapore's older sisters, Malacca and Penang. It was recorded that "by 1825 . . . its (Singapore's) trade was more than double that of Penang's, the older establishment, and six times that of Malacca's."[33]

The growing prosperity of Singapore, which attended Raffles' policy of free trade, attracted immigrants from areas around the region. Singapore increasingly became the locus of various people from all across the East as well as the West, such as the Bugis, the Chinese, the Indians, the Persians and the local Malays, converging on this little island for the purpose of trade. Singapore's population expanded rapidly. In 1827, the total population was about less than 16,000 and by 1836, it had nearly doubled to more than 30,000. Many of these traders were to make for themselves a home and by 1860, the population had grown to a little more than 80,000.

By 1827, the Chinese immigrants had overtaken the Malays as the largest single ethnic community and by 1867, they accounted for about 65 percent of the population. Most of the Chinese immigrants hailed from Southeast China, in particular the provinces of Guangtung and Fujian, which accounts for the majority representation of dialect groups being Hokkien, Teochew, Cantonese and Hakka respectively.

In 1845, the Indians comprised less than 10 percent of the population of Singapore but by 1860, the Indian population had become the second largest totaling approximately 13,000 with the majority of them hailing from South India. The growth of the Malay population was sustained but they had lost their predominance by the late 1820s and again

32. Turnbull, *History of Singapore*, 35.
33. Peterson, *Far East*, 202.

in the 1860s when they were overtaken by Indian immigrants. The other significant minority groups included the Bugis, Arabs, Jews as well as the European population, whose relatively small numbers was disproportionate to their influence, which Crawfurd candidly and perhaps paternalistically attributed as "the life and spirit of the Settlement" and without whom there would be "neither capital, enterprise, activity, confidence or order."[34]

On a micro-scale, Singapore has been a meeting point of indigenous Malays, immigrant Chinese and Indian and colonial Europeans. The British had their share of problems and issues in governing multiracial Singapore because "Singapore proved to be an extraordinary place to rule. By its compactness and complexity it was a showcase of British rule in the East. At certain crucial moments, it was a test-case without precedent."[35]

The increase trade volume attracted a corresponding increase of migrant population, which presented budgetary problems in the administration of Singapore and the Straits Settlements. In seeking to balance the budget, the officials from both Singapore and the Indian office of the East India Company made periodic proposals to tax Singapore's growing trade—a measure that would have caused Raffles to turn in his grave. This was however vehemently opposed by the merchants. Furthermore the principle of free trade had already been accepted by the East India Company's Board of Control in London in 1826 and the merchants in Singapore zealously protected any moves to overturn it. For Singapore, "free trade became a sacred cardinal principle and any threatened infringement was opposed vehemently as commercial heresy."[36] In 1836, Calcutta, the headquarters of the Bengal office had proposed port duties in order to finance anti-piracy measures in Singapore but the merchants once again succeeded in defending the free trade status as they managed to obtain a veto from the Company in London.

Of this tension between maintaining the status as a free port and balancing the budget of day-to-day operations in the Straits Settlements, particularly in Singapore, Turnbull accurately highlighted the difficulty of maintaining the balance:

> Hampered by lack of money and shortage of officials, administration was light and lax, providing a semblance of law and

---

34. Crawfurd, *Journal of an Embassy*, 383.
35. Lee, *British as Rulers*, xii.
36. Turnbull, *History of Singapore*, 50.

order but scarcely touching the lives of the inhabitants. This *laissez faire* policy and the absence of taxes and restrictions benefited trade but led to deficiencies of government, particularly in the provision of security and social services. It also meant that the different communities retained and developed their own organizations, virtually outside the pale of official administration.[37]

While the governing of Singapore presented a challenge, the figures for Singapore's trade reflected an accelerated growth rate (See Table 1—The Trade of Singapore, 1824–1913).

Table 1: The Trade of Singapore 1824–1913 ($ million)

Year	Imports	Exports	Total	Index
1824	6.6	5.0	11.6	1.9
1833	9.1	7.6	16.7	2.7
1843	13.1	11.5	24.6	4.0
1853	15.5	13.4	28.9	4.6
1863	29.8	25.4	55.5	8.9
1873	47.9	41.8	89.7	14.4
1883	79.2	68.2	147.4	23.7
1893	124.0	108.5	232.5	37.4
1903	299.3	257.7	557.0	89.5
1913	349.7	272.4	622.1	100.0

Source: Holloway, *Commerce of Singapore, Annual Trade Returns*, Singapore.

The above figures include and are demonstrative of:

- Riau-Johore, *orang laut* and other Malay and Bugis trading networks in the area.
- Traders and settlers coming from Malacca to Singapore.

---

37. Turnbull, *History of Singapore*, 50.

- A geographical position well adapted to take more trade from East Malaya than Malacca, and midway between the Indian Ocean and South China Sea.

Attendant to Raffles' free trade policy was the naval prowess of the British Empire. Trade in Singapore was backed by the primacy of the East India Company vessels. The Company also enjoyed a certain amount of protection from the Royal Navy, which was stationed in India and at times patrolled the Straits of Malacca, with Penang at the northern entrance and Singapore at the southern entrance of the Straits. This was notably so from the mid-1830s, with joint European anti-piracy efforts reducing the pirate *prahu* fleets to a marginal or near non-existent threat (for larger European and Chinese vessels anyway) by the 1850s.

As a part of the Straits Settlement, the growth of Singapore in the initial years, were phenomenal but as Wong Lin Ken[38] demonstrates, it later leveled to a more steady growth rate.

Table 2: The Growth of Trade of Singapore

Year	Total trade in millions (exports and imports)
1824	$11.9
1833	$16.7
1843	$24.6
1853	$28.9
1856	$55.5

Source: Wong Lin Ken, "Commercial Growth in Singapore"

The Straits Settlement, which was at this point of time administered by the Indian Office was to face a new chapter following 1857, as British India was swept with changes in colonial rule precipitated by what is the Indian Mutiny, also variously known as the *Sepoy Mutiny of 1857* or India's "First War of Independence" (as referred to by most Indian history books).

---

38. Wong Lin Ken, "Commercial Growth in Singapore," in Chew and Lee, *History of Singapore*, 51.

MUTINY IN INDIA

British rule in India was founded upon the strength of the Army, made up of both British and Indians and was a force to be reckoned with. The British troops formed a small yet crucial minority and were very often Irish while the majority (8 out of 10 who served in the Indian Army) were *sepoys*, who were of the traditional warrior caste, a matter for which was inseparably connected with their religious fervour, whether they were Hindus, Muslims or Sikhs.

The uprising was catalysed by a seemingly trivial point; based upon rumours that the cartridges to be issued for the new Enfield rifles were lubricated with animal fat. The ends of these cartridges had to be bitten off before use and hence for the Hindus, Muslims and Sikhs, it amounted to defilement, being in contact with animal fat, especially if it was cow fat for the Hindus or pork fat for the Muslims. To the *sepoys*, this was yet another covert attempt of the British at the colonization of not only their land but also of their minds. The rumours had precipitated a mutiny, fueling the general dissatisfaction with such areas as military pay, privileges and on a much larger scale, politics of British colonialism. "Thus it was that a shot began a conflict before it had even been loaded, much less fired."[39]

What started among the infantry men, rising in revolt against their superiors in the 19th Bengal Infantry stationed at Berhampur on 10 May 1857, quickly gained momentum and spread to other battalions such as in Meerut, near Delhi and from thence with astonishing rapidity across the northwest, to Delhi, Benares, Allahhabad and Cawnpore. Though it started as a mutiny in the military ranks, it welled into the senseless rampage and massacre of anything and every European they came across. These acts of senseless violence were often further abetted by local mobs, underscoring the tacit support of the locals. While it might have been initially a military insurrection at the start, in a wider sense, it highlighted the general dissatisfaction of the people again their colonial masters and may indeed be a reaction of the indigenous population to rapid changes in the social order engineered by the British. It was equally a reaction against the religious and even more so, cultural insensitivity of the British officers against the indigenous population. For them, the British "government was simply a euphemism for oppression under the imperial

---

39. Ferguson, *Empire*, 146.

sanction of Moghul authority."⁴⁰ In Delhi, the Muslim mutineers sought to oust the British forces with the help of the somewhat reluctant and indisposed Bahadur Shah Zafar, the last of the Mughul emperors.

The flames of insurrection were fanned and the brutality of both the mutineers as well as the British Army may be found in the history books, for which the antagonists were portrayed as perpetrators of lurid atrocity; dependent on whose pen these accounts originated. While there are not as numerous accounts of the mutiny from Indian perspectives, the diligence and evenhandedness of some of the British chroniclers⁴¹ provide a glimpse from the side of those who failed in this military coup.

Britain, however, was able to triumph with the help of various sections of the Indian Army that remained loyal, such as the Gurkhas and the Sikhs. And when all of the mutinous units finally surrendered on 20 June 1858, the British sent the last Mughal emperor Bahadur Shah Zafar into exile in Burma, thereby formally ending the Mughal Empire in India. British colonial powers in India were also transformed as a result of the Mutiny as India was henceforth not to be ruled by the East India Company but directly by the Crown. Britain was to assume direct rule over India, beginning the period of the British Raj.

In seeking to provide a reason for the uprising, which seriously threatened British rule in India, each of the parties involved sought to absolve itself of all blame; the colonial administration pointed the finger to Christian missionaries, for unbridled zeal, while some quarters among the Christians place the blame among other things, on the Hindu faith of the people. Ferguson, quoting the Baptist preacher Charles Spurgeon's address to a 25,000 strong congregation, which somewhat echoed Pope Urban's call to crusade, highlights the incredulous reason(s) Christians in London, believed was the root cause for such a tragedy:

> My friends, what crimes they have committed! . . . The Indian government never ought to have tolerated the religion of the Hindoos at all. If my religion consisted of bestiality, infanticide and murder, I should have no right to it unless I was prepared to

---

40. Keay, *Honourable Company*, 292.

41. Wild, *East India Company*. In his account of the mutiny, Wild draws on accounts that were sympathetic to both sides of the insurrection. Where history seems to record the events from the perspective of the victors, Wild is able to present voices among various sources that provide a balance in demonstrating that the British army commanders and those officers in the company were themselves no "saints" and were culpable in the mutiny of 1857. Please see 175–79.

be hanged. The religion of the Hindoos is no more than a mass of the rankest filth that imagination ever conceived. The gods they worship are not entitled to the least atom of respect. Their worship necessitates everything that is evil and morality must be out it down. The sword must be taken out of its sheath, to cut off our fellow subjects by their thousands.[42]

Such a view should not be understood as the dominant view, as other Christians, notably Dr. David Livingstone, proposed a more nuanced critique of the economic endeavours under the auspices of the East India Company. For him, the Great Mutiny was a result of insufficient missionary activity, which stood in direct contradiction of the Company's position that the zealotry of the missionaries had resulted in this bloodshed. In a lecture at Senate House, Cambridge University, Dr. Livingstone maintained:

> I consider we made a great mistake when we carried commerce into India, in being ashamed of our Christianity.... Those two pioneers of civilization—Christianity and commerce—should ever be inseparable; and Englishmen should be warned by the fruits of neglecting that principle as exemplified in the management of Indian affairs.[43]

Livingstone's recommendations, however were not heeded as Britain reacted to the Mutiny by re-organising the structure of British India. The fear of reprisals on a national basis with the attendant rise of nationalism, echoed in British historian Sir John Seeley's evaluation of the Mutiny, resulted in India coming under direct rule of the Crown:

> We could subdue the mutiny of 1857, formidable as it was, because it spread through only a part of the army, because people did not actively sympathize with it, and because it was possible to find native Indian races who would fight on our side. But the moment a mutiny is but threatened, which shall be no mere mutiny, but the expression of a universal feeling of nationality, at that moment all hope is at an end, as all desire should be at an end, of our preserving our Empire.[44]

The Mutiny resulted in the dispossession of the British East India Company of its functions in India. The Company could not survive the

---

42. Ferguson, *Empire*, 151.
43. Ferguson, *Empire*, 155.
44. Tarling, *Nations and States*, 61.

Mutiny which resulted in the abrupt termination of the British East India Company's rule in India as well as in the Far East in the ensuing years. On 2 August 1858, the India Bill was passed and power was officially transferred to the British Crown. All the Company's remaining assets in India, inclusive of armies, navies, churches, colleges, treaties, territories, vessels and vassals, warehouses and whorehouses alike, everything became vested in Her Royal Majesty Queen Victoria. The last Chairman of the Company Colonel Sykes died in 1872 and in the following year dividends on the Company stock ceased to be paid and in 1874, the Charter of the Company which had been renewed in 1854, finally expired. Wild noted that "the Company had simply ceased to be, without a bang, nor even a whimper."[45]

India was hence to be governed by the appointment of a Viceroy who was to be the chief executive and from thence, Britain embarked on a program of reform by seeking to integrate Indian higher castes and rulers into the government. According to British official Charles Raikes, the Mutiny had exposed "the fatal error of attempting to force the policy of Europe on the people of Asia."[46] In taking over governing India, British policy was henceforth to govern with, rather than against, the grain of the traditions of the local indigenous peoples. The change from Company to Crown rule was enacted with Queen Victoria's issuance of a Proclamation on 1 November 1858, which stated,

> Firmly relying Ourselves on the truth of Christianity, and acknowledging with gratitude the solace of religion, we disclaim alike the right and the desire to impose Our convictions on any of Our subjects. We declare it to be Our royal will and pleasure that none be in anywise favoured, none molested or disquieted, by reason of their religious faith or observances, but that all shall alike enjoy the equal and impartial protection of the law, and We do strictly charge and enjoin all those who may be in authority under Us that they abstain from all interference with the religious belief or worship of any of Our subjects on pain of Our highest displeasure.[47]

The effect of the Proclamation was a return to the heightened differentiation between colonial economic interests and the Christian endeavours of the missionary organizations operating in the colonies. Hence in

---

45. Wild, *East India Company*, 180.
46. Ferguson, *Empire*, 155.
47. Philips, *Evolution of India*, 33.

the period following the Mutiny, missionary organizations were increasingly perceived as expendable appendage to the Crown.

THE CROWN COLONY

The results and events following from the Indian Mutiny were to also impact British mercantile interests in the Far East as well as in Southeast Asia. With the eclipse of the Company and the India Bill of 1858, the Straits Settlements subsequently also came under the authority of the Crown. Hence, "once the East India Company had ceased to be, the Crown's eastern interests in all these areas came more closely to resemble the Indian model."[48] From the demise of the Company, the Straits Settlements was administered from the Calcutta office.

When rumours swept through Singapore that the Indian prisoners was planning a similar uprising, perhaps emboldened by the Mutiny in the same year 1857, this created some unrest among the merchants. The general feeling of unease was further exacerbated by the news that the Company office in Calcutta had planned to send the dangerous prisoners from Calcutta's jails to be interned in Singapore[49] in order to free up prison cells for mutineers. In response, the European merchants called for a meeting that passed a resolution backing European merchants in Calcutta in their demands for the abolition of the East India Company. The Singapore merchants made a further request for the separation of the Straits Settlements from the Indian office and for the Straits Settlement to come under the direct jurisdiction of London.[50]

The petitioning process took a confusing decade before any news was received. While the Straits Settlements comprised Singapore, Malacca and Penang, curiously it was a petition that was put forth by Singapore alone, perhaps because the immediate futures of the other two ports were not at all affected by the decisions from the Calcutta office. While the House of Commons had received the petition favourably, the overriding concern was the potential expense of the defence of the Straits Settlements. The Crown was unwilling to undertake any financial commitment that would prove burdensome and interestingly would not accept the

---

48. Wild, *East India Company*, 84.

49. According to Turnbull, *History of Singapore*, these dangerous prisoners began to arrive in Singapore while the petition was in process. Worried by such a turn of events, the European merchants therefore made the push for the petition to be received with greater urgency. Please refer to pp. 71–72.

50. *Singapore Free Press*, 17 September 1857; *Straits Times*, 22 September 1857.

claim that Singapore was of strategic importance to British interests in the Far East, "at once the Gibraltar and the Constantinople of the East."[51]

As history unfolded, in 1866, the War Office, however, became interested in Singapore as an alternative British military base for part of the forces stationed in Hong Kong, where the mortality rate of troops stationed there was increasingly threatening to be a scandal. Hence as the defence expenditure became a non-issue and on 1 April 1867, the Straits Settlements became a Crown Colony under the jurisdiction of the Colonial Office in London.

The transfer of administration of the Straits Settlements, and in particular for Singapore, coincided also with the advent of the steamship in the mid-1860s and the opening of the Suez Canal in 1869. These major developments in technology and politics, further catapulted Singapore's importance. Singapore became a major port of call for ships plying between Europe and East Asia. With the development of rubber planting, especially after the 1870s, it also became the main sorting and export center in the world for rubber. Before the close of the nineteenth century, Singapore was experiencing unprecedented prosperity and trade expanded eightfold between 1873 and 1913.

BRITISH POLICIES IN THE CROWN COLONY

While the British East India Company since its foundation may have espoused the Christian faith, the Company had at the same time drawn a clear distinction between the Company's economic purposes and the zeal of those who sought to enter the Company's territories as missionaries. Hence the Company had consistently resisted any missionary activities on its territories. Brian Harrison in his account of the missionary work of Robert Morrison, pioneer missionary in Malacca and Singapore noted that the English East India Company, though it had "exclusive control of British shipping to China as well as India, was not in favour of introducing Christian missionaries into the eastern world at this time."[52] It was only in 1813 when it became more lax on this ban. Yet this change of attitude to missionary activity after 1813 was apparently a decision forced upon the Company directors due to the fresh impetus of the Evangelical movement back in London. It was in a sense a limited victory for missionary interests; the missionaries had gained the official sanction to go

---

51. Turnbull, *History of Singapore*, 74.
52. Harrison, *Waiting for China*, 1.

to places where the Company was established (primarily India) while at the same time, the Company retained the right to exercise their authority in proscribing missionaries from their protection, if they are viewed as potential liability in the effective operation of the Company in those areas.

Despite the laxity in enforcing the ban, Company and colonial officers were often suspicious of the missionaries and sought to avoid unnecessary clashes. The missionaries were often more sensitive to the indigenous peoples and presented a dissonant voice to Company interests. In their reports, missionaries have written about cultural sensitivities of the Muslim soldiers serving in the Indian Army. Had the East India Company taken note of these findings, perhaps the history of the Company's dealings in India might have taken a very different trajectory.

In the final report of the Select Committee on Aborigines (British Settlements), the general tenor of the British government, as highlighted by historian Andrew Porter, was consistent with the conclusions of missionaries such as Samuel Marsden (New Zealand). The report noted that "the effect of European intercourse... has been, upon the whole, hitherto a calamity upon the native and savage nations." It went on to propose that non-intervention and the absence of regulation would serve no national interest and in the review of the previous engagements and considerations of the way forward, the committee recommended, not merely in self-interest but also bearing in mind obligations and responsibilities, the following:

> The British Empire has been signally blessed by Providence and her advantages, are so many reasons for peculiar obedience to the laws of Him who guides the destinies of the nations. These were given for some higher purpose than commercial prosperity and military renown.... He who has made Great Britain what she is, will inquire at our hands how we have employed the influence He has lent to us in our dealings with the untutored and defenceless savage; whether it has been engaged in seizing their lands, warring upon their people, and transplanting unknown disease and deeper degradation ... or whether we have, as far as we have been able, informed their ignorance, and ... afforded them the opportunity of becoming partakers of that civilization, that innocent commerce, that knowledge and that

faith with which it has pleased a gracious Providence to bless our own country.[53]

Andrew Porter in assessing the report unequivocally noted that though "paternalistic in tone, unquestioning of Britain's self-evident superiority, the Report was at the same time perceptive, in its deeply critical assessment of British neglect and expatriate activities."[54] The report highlighted the difficulties of British rule (be it formal or informal) over different ethnicities and/or cultural groups but was at the same time cognizant of the fact that without intervention the conditions would not be any better. In their recommendations, the Committee was conscious also of defining the principles of a system that might "enforce the observance of their (indigenous) rights."[55]

Though the report's primary focus was on the aboriginal peoples in the South Pacific, the influence and implications of the Committee's Report had wider consequences on other British colonies and settlements in the Asia-Pacific region. It was also to be influential particularly in the way the British handled the polity and administration of so diverse a population in the Strait Settlements (and Crown Colony).

It should be noted that "religion was but one motive out of the constellation of motives"[56] that triggered the Great Mutiny in 1857. From this bloody episode in the Company's history, the British learnt lessons that were to have implications for British rule not only in India but also in other British possessions, such as in Southeast Asia where the indigenous population groups were more prominent. The effect of the 1857 Mutiny was to highlight to the British that the minorities were a group not to be casually dismissed and that the way to rule India (and indeed also the Crown Colony) was to work at balancing the communal interests of

---

53. *Report from the Select Committee on Aborigines (British Settlements)*, PP (1837) 7 (425), 74–76, as quoted in Porter, *Religion versus Empire?*, 143.

54. Porter, *Religion versus Empire?*, 143.

55. *Report from the Select Committee on Aborigines (British Settlements)*, PP (1837) 7 (425), p 3. Porter, in his comments on the report (*Religion versus Empire?*) interestingly noted that the report recommended that all labour legislation and contracts should be regulated to preserve the freedom and that the sale of land should be closely controlled to guarantee just returns, not least in the form of "religious instruction and education" should native inhabitants want them.

56. Lee, *British as Rulers*, 255.

the various ethnic groups. In a sense, as Hardy puts it "administration is manipulation."[57]

Singapore was unique among the many British trading ports in the east, in that it was a meeting place of various distinct people groups from South Asia, North Asia and a myriad of other people groups from Southeast Asia. Multiculturalism and the inherent part played by religions is a legacy that Singapore inherited when Raffles first established Singapore as a center for entrepot trade. It was a cosmopolitan trading port, where different cultures congregated and interacted with each other. The Indian Mutiny of 1857 was hence an important lesson for the British Crown, in regard to the administration of Singapore (and Malaya), in view of a more diverse composition of the immigrant population, compared with most of the other British trading ports.

With the Crown taking over the government of India in 1858, the Straits Settlements becoming a Crown Colony in 1867 and the demise of the British East India Company in 1874, Singapore and the Malay States became the loci for some important colonial administrative decisions. As far as Malaya was concerned, the official policy toward the Malay States and Singapore complied with the tenor of the Queen's proclamation. In the period following the transfer to direct rule from London, the most important policy that was to be enacted in the Malay States was outlined later in the Pangkor Engagement of January 1874.

There are a few studies on the Pangkor Engagement and what happened in 1874 has long been considered an important watershed in the colonial history of Peninsular Malaysia, as evidenced by the works of such as Frank Swettenham, R.J. Wilkinson, R.O. Winstedt and Rupert Emerson.[58] More recently, the Pangkor Engagement is seen as symbolic of the formal taking over of the administration of the Malay states by the British. It "marked the beginning of a long-term arrangement between the British and the Malay states which allowed the British not only administrative but also political and economic control over the Malay Peninsular."[59]

---

57. Hardy, *Muslims of British India*, 64.

58. While the works of these former colonial officials may not be specifically concerned with the events and developments in 1874, the assumption, however, is that the Pangkor Engagement was a pivotal turning point in the history of Malaysia. Please see Swettenham, *British Malaya*; Wilkinson, *History of the Peninsular Malays*; Winstedt, *Malaya and its History*; and Emerson, *Malaysia*.

59. Khoo Kay Kim, *Western Malay States*, 8.

The Pangkor Engagement of 1874, also known as the Pangkor Treaty, was a treaty signed between the British and the Raja of Perak on 20 January 1874 on the island of Pangkor, off Perak in Peninsular Malaysia. This signing of the treaty is significant in the history of the Malay states as it signposted the beginning of official British involvement in the policies of the Malay states. It was also to have implications on British rule in Singapore due to proximity, both geographical and political.

Perak was a major tin producer throughout the nineteenth century, leading Britain, which had already obtained the Straits Settlements of Penang, Malacca and Singapore, to consider Perak of significant importance. However, local strife between the local Malay elites and frequent clashes between Chinese secret societies disrupted the flow of tin from the mines of Perak.

In 1871, Sultan Ali, the ruler of Perak passed away. The state of Perak had a rather complex succession system. While Raja Abdullah should have been appointed as the next Sultan of Perak, it was however, Raja Ismail who was elected. Concomitantly, two Chinese secret societies known as Ghee Hin and Hai San constantly waged battle against each other for control of the tin mines. Raja Abdullah later asked for the British help to solve these two problems. The British immediately saw this as a great opportunity to expand its influence in Southeast Asia and strengthened its monopoly on tin. As a result, the Pangkor Treaty of 1874 was signed.

Raja Ismail, who was sidelined by the British, did not attend the meeting arranged between Sir Andew Clarke and Raja Abdullah. Raja Ismail obviously did not recognize the agreement but was powerless in pitting himself against the alliance between Raja Abdullah and the British. As a result, Raja Abdullah was made Sultan and Sir J. W. W. Birch was appointed as Perak's first British Resident after the Treaty came to force.

The agreement dictated the following points:

A. Raja Abdullah was acknowledged as the legitimate Sultan, thereby replacing Sultan Ismail who would be given a title and a pension of $1000 a month.

B. The Sultan would receive a British Resident whose advice had to be sought and adhered to in all matters except those pertaining to the religion and customs of the Malays.

C. All collections and control of taxes as well as the administration of the state was to be carried out under the purview of the Sultan but arranged according to the Resident's advice.

D. The Minister of Larut would continue to be in control, but would no longer be recognized as a liberated leader. Instead, a British Officer, who would have a vast authority in administrating the district, would be appointed in Larut.

E. The Sultan and not the British government, would pay the Resident's salary.

Of the fourteen articles of the Pangkor Engagement,[60] more than half were directly concerned with British mercantile interests, while the rest were concerned with peaceful administration that indirectly affected British trading interests in the Malay Peninsular. Nonetheless, the British were astute in drafting the treaty especially when it came to matters regarding religious sentiments and sensitivities. The sixth article of the Pangkor Engagement reads:

> That the Sultan receive and provide a suitable residence for a British Officer to be called Resident, who shall be accredited to his Court, and whose advice must be asked and acted upon on all questions *other than those touching Malay Religion and Custom*. (emphasis mine)

In all above provisions, the Treaty of Pangkor made explicit the involvement of the British Resident in his advice and counsel on all matters except those pertaining to the Malay religion [that is, Islam] and customs, which came under the purview of the Malay ruler.[61] Following this agreement, the British actively became involved in three other Malay states; Negeri Sembilan, Selangor and Pahang. These states along with Perak later became the Federated Malay States. In a recent study, Carolina Lopez's evaluation of the Pangkor Engagement noted well that "the British system which separated matters of religion and state did not fit with the

---

60. For the original copy of the treaty, see Sir Andrew Clarke's letter to the Earl of Kimberley of the Colonial Office, dated 26 January 1874, in "Inclosure 7" (Engagement with the Malay Rulers) and "Inclosure 9" (Engagement with the Chinese factions). The record can be found in Colonial Office Records 273 (CO. 273) under the title *Correspondence relating to the affairs of certain native states in the Malay Peninsula in the neighbourhood of the Straits Settlements* [microfilm].

61. See Gullick, *Rulers and Residents*.

Malay understanding."[62] Be that as it may, the Pangkor Engagement more than articulates the *laissez faire* attitude of the British.

This *laissez faire* approach is also evident in the extension of British administration of the different ethnic as well as dialect groups among the immigrants. Through the Residents such as Crawfurd and those following, the practice of taxing vices such as gambling and opium houses was enacted in Singapore. Curiously, in the early administration of Singapore, the practice of taxing these vices were auctioned or sold off to individuals or groups. This principle extended to individual communities, where the administration (with little manpower with language expertise/ability to carry out policy on the ground), relied on community leaders' cooperation. As and when matter went beyond control, military force was used as a last resort.

This reliance, which later decreased as the state became stronger, reached its apogee in the "Chinese Protectorate." This was established in 1877, after the "Post Office riots" of the previous year. In 1876, Teochew merchants inspired riots against a new Post Office taking their business of handling remittances to China. To strengthen supervision and understanding of the Chinese, William Pickering was appointed the first Protector. It was only through such an appointment that the colonial administration could start to try and curb the abuses in "coolie" importation and contracts. The following highlights the chronology of administrative measures enacted by the office of the Chinese Protectorate:

> 1877: Chinese Protectorate commenced supervision of Chinese immigrants and labour
>
> 1880s: Extended supervision to brothels
>
> 1889: Chinese Advisory Board created
>
> 1890: Societies Ordinance was effected by Governor Clementi Smith, to suppress dangerous societies and register others brought into force

From such a system of administration, it is evident that if British policy provided the "iron framework" of law and security, the sinews of growth was still very much among the immigrant Asian population. As a free port, Singapore was a case where the colonial office sought to minimize operations and administration costs in order to maximize trade revenues. It should be noted that British policy was not simply about free

---

62. Lopez, *British Presence*.

trade, but also *laissez faire* ("leave alone" or minimal intervention) and rooted in indirect rule. It may have indeed been already prevalent in the manner in which the East India Company conducted their mercantile enterprises. In the case of Singapore and Malaya, these three foundation stones—*free trade, laissez faire and indirect rule*—were crucial. Through them, the British were able to maximise individual effort and reward; and they were hence able to minimize the costs of administering British rule in the archipelago. The primary motivating force in all these trade negotiations, (the Anglo-Dutch Treaty), these engagements (Pangkor Treaty), colonial acquisitions and administrations through negotiations served the one primary goal of the British colonial administration, which is economic profitability and sustainability.

In the Crown Colony (Penang, Malacca, and Singapore), the Anglican Church under the auspices of the London Missionary Society (LMS) started its work, but the colonial administration also took a *laissez faire* attitude toward Christian missions, and other religious organizations. The following perhaps best sums up British colonial policy on the administration of the colonies of the British Empire:

> Colonial administrators had to work out the details of policy whereby order and good government could be assured to immense populations of a primitive sort with a minimum expense to the British taxpayer, but with the assured preservation of an open door for British trade and the safeguarding of the civilizing enterprises that British missionaries had devoted two generations of effort to creating.[63]

The British carried this policy of non-interference, only to the extent of vigorously opposing any attempts at evangelization amongst the Malays by Christian missionaries even though there was no formal prohibition in this direction. There were no such reservations on the part of the British in as far as the other immigrant races were concerned. As a result of the British policies, Islam as a religion of the indigenous population was preserved and became further entrenched as the primary religion of the Malays, where to be Malay is synonymous with being a Muslim. The Pangkor Engagement may well be reflective of the overarching British concerns with regards to establishing their economic empire, in contradistinction to the traditional notion of colony.

---

63. Egerton, *Short History of British Colonial Policy*, 392.

CONCLUSION

In surveying the nature of British colonial rule in Southeast Asia, it perhaps is true to say that British imperialism in Southeast Asia was more about trade[64] rather than about territory. It is an account of extending British mercantile interests and more often than not, any territorial expansion (for most if not all of Southeast Asia) was indistinguishably tied with British trade. Indeed, the British presence in this region was an extended "diversion" of the East India Company's trading interests with China.

The British were involved firstly in securing ports and establishing trading factories, in order to facilitate trade with China, though China was more interested in the produce of Southeast Asia than what the Company had to offer. For these reasons, the East India Company, operating from India, acquired a series of additional ports between 1786 and 1824. In 1786, Penang was acquired from the Sultan of Kedah. Initially, Penang well served the Company's interests as it was sheltered from the monsoon winds and was a centre for collecting Southeast Asian produce for the China trade. Through the gutsy Raffles, Singapore was acquired through agreements signed between 1819 and 1824 not through use of force but through wit and negotiations. Singapore's better position, precisely midway between the Indian Ocean and the South China Seas, soon turned it into the premier Southeast Asian port in a couple of years. In the Anglo-Dutch Treaty of 1824, the British were able to wrestle Malacca from the Dutch, who were then more willing to give it up because Malacca had been eclipsed by Singapore.

The acquisitions of the ports were facilitated through the establishing of a sphere of economic influence. Prior to the Opium War, Britain had the lion's share of the trade with the East, compared with the other western powers. With the waning of Dutch influence (due to the Dutch-French rivalry in Europe), Britain was able to exert her dominance over the Straits of Malacca. In a move that mutually benefited English and Dutch interests, both countries signed the Anglo-Dutch Treaty on March 1824, for which British sovereignty over the Malayan peninsula was recognized and Malacca was handed over to the British. In return, Britain acknowledged Dutch sovereignty over all the "East Indies" (Indonesia), except Acheh and handed its Sumatran port, Bencoolen, to the Dutch.

---

64. This is what Robinson and Gallagher referred to as "the imperialism of free trade." Gallagher and Robinson, "Imperialism of Free Trade," 1–15.

In 1826, Britain inked the Anglo-Thai Agreement, where Britain recognised the historic Thai claims to sovereignty over some territories of the northern Malay States. The Agreement also secured the independence for Perak from Thai control, thereby effectively setting a limit to how far down south the peninsula the Thais could penetrate.

British naval dominance, based from the eastern ports of India, ensured no other powers threatened its trade dominance on the Malayan peninsula. The British shrewdly included the Straits Settlements (the ports of Penang, Malacca and Singapore) to control the trade. Furthermore, through the various treaties, rather than conquest, they extended their sphere of influence as they excluded neighbouring powers from the Straits Settlement hinterland in the Malay Peninsular.

With its trading interests secured and a general "sphere of influence" demarcated, Britain was happy to use informal influence in the remaining Malay States. Hence following the Indian Mutiny of 1857 and prior to the Pangkor Treaty of 1874, Britain adopted a policy of non-intervention. In 1867, the Colonial Office gave orders that Governors (of the Strait Settlements) should not interfere in the affairs of the Malay States. Though Britain became embroiled in the ensuing struggle for power among the various Malay States, which culminated in the signing of the Pangkor Treaty in 1874, yet as noted in the above account, British intervention was necessitated to protect and ensure British trading interests and economic profits.

British presence in Singapore was hence very closely related with trade. Rather similar with the East India Company's initial foray into India, Britain's interest in Singapore was scarcely territorial (expansion) and much less missional. In establishing British presence in South East Asia, the necessary platform was made ready for the introduction of Christianity and American Methodism in the late nineteenth century. Formal British rule and one which had little regard in terms of missionary fervour was the precursor to Methodist mission in Singapore. It was this *laissez faire* climate of British rule that formerly catalysed Methodism in Singapore.

3

The March of Methodism

CHRISTIANITY IN THE COLONIAL ERA, BEFORE 1886

THE ADVENT OF CHRISTIANITY in Singapore closely follows the founding of the island by Sir Stamford Raffles of the East India Company. This somewhat modeled the situation for the ports of Malacca and Penang which were established earlier. Malacca had a significant Christian presence and it was from Malacca that the Roman Catholic missionaries and Protestant missionaries began to arrive in Singapore. With the establishment of the ports along the Straits of Malacca, the London Missionary Society started pioneering missionary work first in Malacca and later in Singapore.[1] It must be noted however that in the early stages, most of these missionaries were bound for China and their stay in Singapore served more as a stopover. Among them was a Dr. William Milne who was sent by the LMS to China in 1813. But due to China's closed door policy with regard to Christian missionary work, the setting up of the Ultra-Ganges Mission by Milne in Malacca in 1815 was an expedient decision. Not only was the Ultra-Ganges Mission a ground to gather experience and establish contacts with the highly migrant Asian trading societies, it was regarded as a prelude for the new mission field in China that these missionaries hoped to see open. It was in these tangential "new" places in Southeast Asia that Protestantism began to take root.

Sent by the London Missionary Society (LMS), missionaries such as William Milne and Robert Morrison initiated Christian ministry in

---

1. Sng, *In His Good Time*, 22.

Singapore as early as the 1820s. Coming overland from Malacca, these LMS missionaries were hence able to circumvent the Company's strictly enforced rule of not mixing commerce with Christianity. Furthermore, their presence was welcomed as they were able to minister to the spiritual needs of a steadily growing number of British (and later European) merchants.

Raffles' patronage was a significant factor in the introduction of Christianity to Singapore. Initially somewhat indifferent, Raffles however had a "change of heart" which was evidenced by various efforts he implemented to bring about improvements in his administration; one of the most important of which is his intention to found a school, which came to fruition when he selected a plot of land on 12 January 1823, when he returned to Singapore, to build the "Institution." In his correspondence with his cousin Dr. Raffles dated the same day, Raffles wrote about his dream for some kind of independence for the very newly founded British colony and his desire for it to gain a momentum in its growth independent of his "intervention." In his letter, Raffles wrote,

> The progress of my new settlement is in every way most satisfactory, and it would gladden your heart to witness the activity and cheerfulness which prevails throughout. Every day brings us new settlers and Singapore has already become a great emporium. Houses and warehouses are springing up in every direction, and the inland forests are fast giving way before the industrious cultivator. I am now engaged in marking out the towns and roads, and in establishing laws and regulations for the protection of the person and property. We have no less than nine mercantile houses (European); and there is abundant employment for capital as fast as it accumulates. I cannot help thinking the soil of Singapore also opens a fine field of European speculation, and that some hundreds of our countrymen, with a very small commencement, might soon realize a handsome independence' but more of this when we meet, which I hope, will be e'er long—that is to say, within a year after you receive this, as my determination is, God willing, to quit this country, at all events by the end of the present year.[2]

With regards to the missionary work, Raffles continued,

> The death of my friend, Dr. Milne of Malacca, has, for a time thrown a damp on missionary exertions in this quarter; but I

2. Boulger, *Life of Sir Stamford Raffles*, 331–32.

expect Mr. Morrison, of China to visit this place in March, and I hope to make a satisfactory arrangement with him for future labours. The two missionaries who are here are not idle: Messrs. Milton and Thomson, the former in Chinese and Siamese, and the latter in Malay and English printing.

I have selected a spot for my intended college, and all I now require is a good headmaster or superintendent. It is my intention to endow it with lands, the rents of which will cover its ordinary expenses. I am also about to commence upon a church, the plan of which is already approved.

Raffles' dream to establish the college went beyond just a building. His vision for Singapore was in a sense ahead of his times. In a subsequent meeting, he outlined four educational objectives that were to have significant bearing on the future of Singapore. J. S. Nagle in his book, *Educational Needs of Malaya* recorded the objectives as such:

From the Minute which he read to the leading residents of Singapore on 1 April 1823, it will be noted that he gave expression to four very significant educational goals or objectives. (1) Advancement of the native peoples in social culture and a firm foundation for the Empire: "While we raise those in the scale of civilization over whom our influence or our Empire is extended, we shall lay the foundation of our Dominion on the firm basis of justice and mutual advantage." (2) National identity and international influence: "and cultivation of mind seems alone wanting to raise them (these Eastern countries) to such a rank among the nations of the world as their geographical situation and climate may admit." (3) Moral progress: "Commerce being therefore the principle on which our connection with these Eastern States is formed, it behooves us to consider the effect it is calculated to produce.... Education must keep pace with commerce in order that its benefits may be assured and its evil avoided." (4) Social and economic improvement through the development of an effective native leadership" "The progress of every plan of improvement on the basis of education must be slow and gradual, its effect silent and unobtrusive, and the present generation will probably pass away before they are felt or appreciated, but a single individual or rank raised into importance and energy by means of the proposed institution may abundantly repay our labour by the establishment of a better order of society in his neighbourhood, by the example he may set and by the resources of the country he may develop." Such were the worthy and far-reaching educational goals set up by the Founder of the Colony.[3]

Raffles also wrote to William Wilberforce, a parliamentarian and an influential philanthropist, requesting for financial support as well as missionary support to establish the college. In another letter to his cousin, Raffles surmised,

> I have set on foot for the spread of knowledge and the growth of moral principles throughout the Archipelago. Much of my time has been devoted to these objects and if I am able to carry out my plan for the establishment of a native College in Singapore, the system will be complete.[4]

He was also in correspondence with LMS missionary Robert Morrison, who had taken over the task from Milne.

Raffles managed to lay the foundation stone for the proposed college on 5 June 1823 and was wrestling for a written undertaking from the directors of the East India Company, though he was to leave Singapore three days later. His newly appointed successor, John Crawfurd was tasked to oversee the rest of the plans. The Governor-General of Bengal replied to Raffles' letter in November of 1823 (six months later!) stressing caution against haste as the permanency of Singapore as a British possession was still being sorted out. The Court of Directors of the East India Company replied in May 1825 to the Resident of Singapore, Crawfurd stating that such an educational project seemed premature given the uncertainty of Singapore in the Company's scheme of operations. Evidently, Raffles' optimism was not shared among the ruling hierarchy of the East India Company, whose sight seemed still very much focused on China as the cherished prize of British mercantile ambitions.

Crawfurd submitted a report on 7 February 1826 to the East India Office that not only halted all possibilities of fulfilling the dream but also completely overturned all that Raffles had done. Unlike Raffles, he saw the scheme of the Institution as too extensive and expensive, and refused to authorize the allocated funds of four thousand dollars promised by Raffles on behalf of the East India Company. He was willing insofar as to invest only in the elementary vernacular education rather than the English collegiate education proposed by Raffles. Furthermore,

---

3. As quoted by Doraisamy, *150 Years of Education in Singapore*, 8.
4. Doraisamy, *150 Years of Education in Singapore,*, 7.

in contradistinction to Raffles' educational objectives, Crawfurd tended toward a paternalism that saw the chief benefit of education as a means to accustom the "Asiatic to regular habits of subordination." Morrison in his account, laid blame on "Crawfurd, the infidel doctor-civilian," who "did all the mischief he could to Singapore and overturned the Institution."[5]

Crawfurd's proposal to abandon Raffles' original plan sounded the death knell and aborted the hopes and dreams that Raffles had so carefully nurtured for Singapore in regard to education. This created a gap for which missionaries arriving later in Singapore would seek to fill. In a way this episode also marked the premature end of what might have been a partnership between mission societies (such as LMS) and the East India Company. There were other overtures in seeking some kind of patronage, but the officials of the Company tenaciously upheld their beliefs that interests in Singapore and the Straits Settlements were to be strictly driven by commercial considerations.

Not unlike the situation that the LMS faced in China, the American Board of Commissioners for Foreign Missions (ABCFM), had to divert their manpower to Singapore due to difficulties faced in China, which had become increasingly hostile to Western exploitations, later precipitating the Opium War. The invitation of Robert Morrison of the LMS to join in the missionary work of Singapore was hence given some serious consideration. This resulted in the arrival of the first ABCFM missionary Rev. Ira Tracey in Singapore on 24 July 1834 and was joined later by a printer, Alfred North. The ABCFM was born within the matrix of the second Great Awakening in the United States of America and was the largest of the American Protestant mission organizations whose goal was the conversion of the whole non-Christian world. Though aware of the dismal reports of the LMS missionaries in this region, the ABCFM was more optimistic than the British missionaries and the major strategy employed in Malaya was the printing and distribution of Christian literature.

The entrance of ABCFM occurred at a time when Spain had closed the Philippines to all Protestants just as the Portuguese had done to Macau. As with regards to Indonesia, the Dutch would only grant permission to Dutch nationals where missionary work was concerned in Java. Singapore under British rule seemed to be the ideal place to begin the work of mission and to act as a centre for the ABCFM's missionary efforts

---

5. Harrison, *Waiting for China*, 75.

in this region. The news of the only LMS missionary C. H. Thomsen's plan to leave Singapore due to ill health gave further impetus for the Board to act in sending their missionaries to fill the gap. While it may not be certain if such a decision was due to this understanding that the ABCFM was to take over the work of the LMS that had planned to withdraw from Singapore, this miscommunication was to be a serious point of contention between missionaries of the two societies in Singapore.

In contrast to the LMS missionaries, the instructions given to the ABCFM's missionaries were clearly one of a church-state divide. The instructions were such:

> Your civil relations will demand very careful attention. The government of the country, whether Christian, Moslem or pagan will be your government. . . . Avoid forming connection with the government . . . as far as possible shun official intercourse with it. . . . Do not aim to attract the attention of the government.[6]

The ABCFM missionaries quickly set about their work and started printing and distributing Gospel tracts and Scriptures. Attention was also directed to organizing schools in order to raise indigenous pastors and leaders. There was also a great deal of correspondence concerning the establishment of a seminary. To the credit of the ABCFM, there was a genuine concern to reach the Malays as well as the Chinese with the hope of establishing an indigenous church, as evidenced by the requirement to learn either the Malay or the Chinese language as part of the preparation for missionaries appointed to Singapore.

In 1835, a scheme was further mooted, presumably by Ira Tracey, which called for the establishment of a Christian colony, a "reenactment" of the story of the pilgrim fathers in New England, albeit in a different context. It was envisaged that a group of Christian farmers would be transplanted in Singapore and that each family would reach several Malay or Chinese children and bring them into their homes to train them both in arable farming as well as the Gospel. The objective was to establish a farming community that was at the same time grounded upon Christian principles. There was a flurry of correspondence between the directors of the ABCFM as well as the East India Company that looked upon such a project with approval in so far as it benefited the economy. As Singapore was under the jurisdiction of the Indian Office, an official request was

---

6. Twenty-seventh Annual Meeting ABCFM, 1936 133, as quoted in Haines, "History of Protestant Missions," 169.

sent to Calcutta and subsequently referred to London. More would have transpired in seeing this plan to fruition had not a financial recession in 1836 curtailed the funds for such an ambitious project, set the Board in a debt of $40,000 and squashed the plans altogether. When London finally responded by turning down the request in 1839, the American Board's interest was beginning to wane.

At about that time in 1837, a representative from the Church Missionary Society (CMS) arrived in Singapore, with the intention of establishing a mission in this part of Southeast Asia. The CMS, which represented the evangelical wing of the Church of England, was founded in 1799 and like most of the missionary organizations, the CMS set their target for the evangelization of the Chinese as Britain and other European nations began to explore trading opportunities with the Chinese. On January 1837, Edward Squire and his wife began his work as CMS missionaries in Singapore. But since most of the Company's Anglican chaplains were from the LMS, it became obvious that the missionary efforts of any of the CMS missionaries were not welcomed. Unperturbed, the Squires began to draw closer to the missionaries from the ABCFM and learnt both Malay and Chinese from the ABCFM missionaries.

Work was started in bringing Malay and Chinese bibles into Singapore and by December 1837, Edward Squire initiated work among the much neglected Tamil and Portuguese community here in Singapore. They also directed their attention to often neglected work of education for girls in Singapore. There was also a plan to establish a boarding school and an orphanage:

> It may be remarked that orphan children would be admirably suited to become inmates of a seminary such as is here contemplated, from the fact that no one possessing any claim upon them. From such a seminary in process of time you may reasonable hope to draw readers and instructors both for Chinese and Malays.[7]

With all these plans, Squire and his wife left abruptly for Macau, seemingly in response to the possibility of establishing a mission work closer to China. There, his wife's health deteriorated and they returned to England. At their Fortieth Annual Meeting, in 1840, a small record of the CMS effort indicated that they would resume the mission only after

---

7. CMS record, December 1838, 298, as quoted in Haines, "History of Protestant Missions," 193.

greatly enlarged resources were available. Hence the quick arrival and abrupt departure of the CMS from Singapore left the ABCFM and the LMS to continue the mission work in Singapore.

Squire's departure coincided with the arrival of three missionaries from the Board of Foreign Missions of the Presbyterian Church, USA, (BFMPC) which had decided at the General Assembly of the Presbyterian Church in USA to set up a Board of Foreign Missions, thereby superseding the former interdenominational agencies, especially that of the ABCFM.[8] The BFMPC also saw that the harvest was plentiful in China and the report of the Western Foreign Missionary Society stated,

> This great people, not more remarkable for the extent of their territory, and the number of their population than for their ignorance of the true God, have of late engaged the thoughts of professing Christians in all parts of our country. . . . In every island in the Eastern Archipelago, Chinese emigrants are to be found. . . . And only men of right spirit are wanted to carry to these accessible, perishing thousands the bread of life.[9]

The three missionaries Rev. John Mitchell, Rev. and Mrs. R. W. Orr set sail from New York to Singapore in December of 1837, with the aim of surveying the Eastern Archipelago to establish a mission station that would be strategic to their goal of reaching the Chinese. Until access to China's vast interiors were possible, the advance guard were to find places without the Middle Kingdom in order to make preparations for the work of evangelization of the Chinese.

When the three missionaries arrived in April 1838, John Mitchell contracted tuberculosis. Though terribly sick and weak, he insisted on going along on a trip surveying the various mission stations on the west coast of Malaya (Malacca, Penang and Province Wellesley) and died subsequently. Orr's first report to the Board confirmed veracity of all that was said concerning the prospects of mission in China, calling it "the world's greatest mission field and the place where Christianity was destined to have its noblest triumphs,"[10] but at the same time, he cautioned against

---

8. The ABCFM had until this time (1837) been the organization through which the Presbyterian Church in the USA had channeled their manpower and resources with regard to foreign missions. The Board of Foreign Missions was formally organized on 31 October 1837.

9. Fifth Annual Report of Western Foreign Missionary Society, May 1837, 17–18. As quoted by Haines, "History of Protestant Missions," 197.

10. *Foreign Missionary Chronicle*, Dec. 1839, 377-78, as in Haines, "History of

overlooking the claims of Malaya. Tragically, before more work could be done in Singapore, the Orrs were compelled to leave Singapore within a year of their arrival (1838) due to ill health. The lack of manpower, health issues and the similar problem of a recession in the USA led to the somewhat premature cessation of the work of the BFMPC in Singapore.

Following this recall, on 25 February 1841, the ABCFM also decided to pull out of the work in Singapore in order to focus their energies and resources on China. In the eight year period from 1834 to1841, the ABCFM recorded five adult Chinese baptisms and printing of fourteen million pages of literature as the tangible fruits[11] of the mission work in Singapore. The decision was a difficult one especially for the missionaries who are directly involved but the final decision is due to a complex number of factors which include such as the personal and health issues of the missionaries as well as organizational factors such as budgets and financial constraints, inadequate staffing, difficult working relationship with the LMS and not the least the preoccupation with China as the "real" field of labour. The Board's overarching mission philosophy as indicated in the Annual Meeting was that "the comparative value of different fields cannot always be known without experiment: but when experience on this point is gained, it is the part of wisdom to give it due influence on our proceedings."[12] Hence by 1843, the Singapore "experiment" for the ABCFM (and for that matter, all the others missionary organizations) had come to a close and all the remaining work was handed over to the LMS.

About the time of the departure of the BFMPC and before that of the ABCFM, an Anglo-Indian, trained in New Brunswick, USA, Benjamin Keasberry sailed from America with the intention of heading toward Canton. When the ship made a transit in Singapore, Keasberry disembarked with little knowledge that this "transit" was to last a major part of his ministry years, with the impact spreading toward Malaya as well as Indonesia. In his work among the Malays, Hadji Abdullah recorded in his Hikayat[13] that he saw in Keasberry a person who sincerely had the welfare of the Malays at heart. Within a short time of his arrival, Keasberry established a school for the Malay children and a preaching chapel,

---

Protestant Missions," 187.

11. Thirty-second Annual Meeting Minutes, ABCFM, 1841, 144, as quoted in Haines, "History of Protestant Missions," 219.

12. Haines, "History of Protestant Missions," 219.

13. Hikayat Abdullah, 233, as quoted in Haines, "History of Protestant Missions," 222.

both of which saw initial growth that further spurred his plans for the organization of a Malay Church. This initial and important work among the Malays finally persuaded the LMS to take him on as a missionary to the Malays in Singapore. Keasberry however left his legacy in the work of establishing a Chinese church in Singapore. "The Straits Chinese Church is an ever living memorial of the selfless devotion of Mr. Keasberry."[14]

It was at about this time that the political developments in East Asia were to deal a devastating blow to a fledging missionary enterprise in South East Asia. In March 1839 the Qing Emperor appointed a new strict Confucianist commissioner, Lin Zexu, to oversee the ban of opium trade[15] at the port of Canton. In halting the trade, confiscating the large amount of opium and thereafter destroying the whole cargo of opium that amounted to about a year's supply, the British merchants who traded in opium were enraged and accused the Chinese of destroying their personal property, inciting punitive political and military retaliations. The British responded by sending a large British Indian army. The superiority of the British fleet and their firepower wreaked havoc along the coastal cities. Moving up the Yangtze, Britain flexed her military prowess and forced the Qing Court to sign the Treaty of Nanking in 1842 and subsequent "unequal treaties" that ceded various ports to Britain and her allies. Hong Kong was ceded to Britain and five other Chinese ports—Canton, Amoy, Foochow, Ningpo and Shanghai—were opened to trade with the other foreign powers. The "unequal treaties" signaled a period of humiliation for China and opened China up to trade and also western exploitation. But at the same time it presented a prized opportunity for Christianity to once again enter China, albeit on the coattails of the western imperial powers.

The Treaty of Nanking meant implicitly that the harvest field of China was hence accessible to even other mission sending organizations. Their long cherished dream of reaching the Chinese with the Gospel was becoming a reality and as a result many of the missionary societies diverted their manpower and resources in establishing the work in

---

14. Sng, *In His Good Time*, 25

15. The British East India Company pursued a monopoly on production and export of opium in India after Britain conquered Bengal in the Battle of Plassey in 1757. It was with opium from India that Britain was able to trade more profitably with China. Though banned from importation of opium, British merchants resorted to smuggling the drug into China through the ports such as Canton, which soon thrived as more Chinese became addicted. Hence exports of opium to China skyrocketed from an estimated 15 tons in 1730 to 75 tons in 1773.

China. In 1843, the LMS sent a letter to all the missionaries in Malaya, requesting them to proceed to Hong Kong for a conference to discuss the possibilities that China engenders. The conference concluded with a unanimous decision to close all the stations of the Ultra-Ganges Mission in the Eastern Archipelago, with the exception of Singapore and to move all the work to Hong Kong and the other ports of China. An article in the LMS publication, *The Missionary Magazine*, reflected the importance the LMS (and for that matter, all the other missionary organizations of that time) attached to the work in China:

> Are all the Ultra-Ganges stations to be swept away like a dream, where Christ has been honoured and preached for so many years? Yet, if a sacrifice must be made, no one can question it, when one third of the human race, known for their crimes... asks for the human interposition of England. Centuries are looking down from the Himalayas to see the first evangelists bring to these benighted millions the Gospel of Christ.[16]

Though paternalistic and condescending in tenor, it nonetheless highlights the penultimate goal of these Protestant mission organizations of the nineteenth century. In the following year, the LMS ratified the recommendation of the Hong Kong conference but was ambivalent about the situation in Singapore for the time being. But in 1846, both the remaining missionaries, Stronach and Keasberry were ordered to close the work and move on to Hong Kong. Keasberry, however, chose to remain and he wrote to the LMS, unwilling to abandon the work he had established:

> I cannot reconcile myself to the thought of this station being given up, in view of the present prospect of usefulness which it holds among the Malays both in the school and in the preaching to the adults. My earnest request is that I be allowed to remain here and labour for the poor Malays. Can it be considered too much to have one missionary to break to them the bread of life?[17]

As his request was not granted, Keasberry resigned from the LMS and stayed on. The departure of various LMS missionaries for China as well as the increasing influx of Scottish expatriates and other Europeans of the Reformed tradition necessitated the request for a Presbyterian minister as early as 1846. As an Anglican, Keasberry transcended

---

16. Haines, "History of Protestant Missions," 232.
17. Haines, "History of Protestant Missions," 233.

denominational boundaries in cooperating with the first minister of the Presbyterian congregation, Rev. McKenzie Fraser, helping them acquire a church building for the growing Presbyterian congregation, through his appeals to the LMS, which was given various parcels of land by the British government in Singapore. In that regard, the birth of the Presbyterian Church in Singapore is inseparably linked to the London Missionary Society and the Anglican Church in Singapore.

The departure of the LMS in 1846 exemplified the spirit of the time; for it in no uncertain terms demonstrated that China was the focus of not only the East India Company but also of most (if not all) of the missionary sending organizations or societies. Singapore was a colonial outpost, a stepping stone to the larger mission field of China. Singapore never figured as a missionary destination among the various missionary societies. The missionaries did come to Singapore and began some form of ministry in the early and mid-nineteenth century. Most of which, however, involved catering to the spiritual needs of the expatriate population of the Company officials who were stationed in Singapore. The Anglican Church as well as the Presbyterian Church (established at a later date) was set up to minister to the spiritual needs and well-being of the European community in Singapore. The Anglican Chaplaincy that served the migrant Anglican and Scottish expatriates became "more like an extension of an exclusive European Club and the Cathedral served as a focal point for not only the religious but also the social life of the community."[18]

With all the reappointments of missionaries to a fast opening China by brute military force and unequal treaties, only three Protestant missionaries resided in the Straits Settlements; J.C. Bausum, an independent German missionary in Penang, Miss M. Grant of the Society for the Promotion of Female Education in China, India and the East[19] (SPFE) and Benjamin Keasberry in Singapore.

Miss Grant continued the work of earlier LMS missionary Mrs. Dyer, who had established a school for Chinese girls in Singapore. Almost single-handedly, Miss Grant continued the work of this most unusual mission school in the Far East, in that the pupils were either abandoned Chinese girls or those rescued from slavery. Hence the name of the school was the Chinese Girls' School. She was later joined by Miss

---

18. Diocese of Singapore, *Visions Unfold*, 9.

19. The society was organized in London in 1834 in response to an appeal by a missionary, Rev. David Abeel of the ABCFM, to pioneer more ministries among women and girls in the East, such as India, China, and the regions surrounding.

Sophia Cooke who laboured tenaciously and gave to the school a status which it still maintains today.

Apart from the establishment of a chaplaincy to the Europeans in the Straits Settlements by the Presbyterian Church, the only other more prominent Protestant witness included the somewhat isolated efforts of these missionaries in maintaining those ministries formerly established by the LMS missionaries. It is not surprising then that in the period following the departure of the LMS missionaries, the next forty years or so is described as the "wilderness years"[20] of Protestant missionary history in Malaya (including Singapore). Keasberry wrote to no avail many pleading letters for more help in the work. He wrote similar appeals to the ABCFM to reconsider and sent appeals also to the Wesleyan Methodist Missionary Society.

BRITISH METHODISM: A MISSED OPPORTUNITY

While most records attribute the first arrival of Methodists in Singapore to the efforts of Bishop James Thoburn of the South Indian Conference of the Methodist Episcopal Church, this perhaps ignores the much earlier initiatives of the British Methodist missionaries. Though the Wesleyan Methodist Missionary Society (WMMS) might not have responded in an official capacity to the appeals of Keasberry, there was nonetheless a lone response from one of the missionaries of the Wesleyan Methodist Missionary Society (WMMS) as early as 1856. Not unlike the other missionary societies that were jumping at the opportunity to enter China via the treaties that China was coerced into signing, the WMMS had hoped to enter China through the port of Canton. Among the British Methodist missionaries who arrived, was Josiah Cox, who was born at Tipton, Devon, England in 1828 and trained for the Methodist ministry at Richmond College. He was one of the first Methodist missionaries to go out to China where he arrived in 1852. Methodist efforts at that date were located in Canton and there Cox laboured together with fellow missionaries Beach and Piercy.

During the Taiping Rebellion[21] (1850–1864) Cox became acquainted with Hong Jin, the brother of the Taiping leader, Hong Xiuquan. He

20. Haines, "History of Protestant Missions," 245.

21. The Taiping Rebellion was one of the revolutionary attempts against the Ch'ing (Qing, ethnic Manchurians) Dynasty in the nineteenth century to bring about political, social, and cultural reforms. The Qing Dynasty was seen by the Chinese majority as ineffective and corrupt foreign rule. The Chinese defeat in Opium War and

had hoped that Hong Jin's position could facilitate the opening of a mission in Nanking, the seat of the rebellion. But as the Rebellion fuelled on, it became apparent that the safety of the missionaries was not to be compromised and various missionary societies began to recall their missionaries. The WMMS recalled their missionaries and all but Cox left Canton. In a report of the work of the missionaries, it was recorded:

> All the missions party arrived in safety with the exception of Mr. Cox, who remained behind at Canton. At first he continued at the Hospital of the LMS, when that was no longer safe, he removed to the factories, and finding studies there impossible, he resolved on visiting the numerous Chinese settlers in the British Possessions in the Straits of Malacca. On 23 November, he left Hong Kong in the ship *Lancashire Witch*, and on the 8th day afterward anchored in the harbour of Singapore. Under date of December 22, 1856, he thus describes his positions and employments:
>
> "The blessing of God is, we trust, resting on our work. A few Christian friends here render us hearty assistance. We have been out among the Chinese every day. They gladly receive our books and though the Canton dialect is not spoken by one-third of the settlers, who number altogether many thousands, we find this preaching from house to house affords many opportunities of unfolding 'the unsearchable riches of Christ.' By the kindness of our friends we rented a small house near the locality of the Canton-speaking Chinese. In our front room we have held an evening meeting for conversation on God's word and prayer. The attendance has been gratifying. God has not left us without the promised help of His Holy Spirit. Surely He will enlighten

---

the surrender of the various ports to western powers further fueled the anti-Manchu sentiment, which was strongest in the south among the laboring classes. The rise of the Taiping Rebellion was closely related to the work of the Christian missionaries in Southern China as the ports were being opened for trade with the western imperial armies. The leader of the rebellion, Hong Xiuquan, had initial contact with Christianity through a tract given by a missionary. The tract, "The True Principle of the World's Salvation," was written by the first Chinese Protestant preacher, Liang KungFa (Ah Fah), who was the first convert of William Milne. Hong Xiuquan envisioned a new society built on heterodox Christian principles and named it the Heavenly Kingdom of Great Peace, 太平天国. At the height of the rebellion, Nanjing was captured in 1853 and tens of thousands of imperial army soldiers as well as civilians were massacred. The rebellion was finally quelled by the Qing army, aided by French and British forces, in July 1864. For more information on the Taiping Rebellion, please refer to Spence, *God's Chinese Son*.

some of these dark dead souls. Little can we do, oh Christ! Our hope is in Thee!"

A recent letter states, that up to Feb. 22, Mr. Cox continued at Singapore in health and safety.[22]

Cox's close working relationship with the LMS is evident in his letter in *The Wesleyan Missionary Notices, relating Principally to the Foreign Missions, 3rd Series, Vol IV for the Year 1857*, London, Wesleyan Mission House, 1857. But his hope of establishing a work in Singapore was not to be fulfilled as the head office preferred for him to continue his ministry in China. Cox then turned his attention to the opening of a mission in the densely populated cities of Hankow (Wuhan) and Wuchang on the Yangtze. In 1863 the first Methodist Mission House in Hankow was opened. With Cox's departure, the possibility of a Methodist presence faded and was to be rekindled about 29 years later with the arrival of Methodist missionaries from the Methodist Missionary Society[23] of the Methodist Episcopal Church, USA, toward the end of the century.

AMERICAN METHODISM—NEW BEGINNINGS

The Methodist Church in Singapore hence derives its formal beginnings from a missionary initiative of the South India Conference, of the Methodist Episcopal Church, USA, led by Rev. Dr. James Mills Thoburn

---

22. *Report of the Wesleyan Methodist Missionary Society*, Archival manuscripts at School of Oriental and African Studies, University of London.

23. The Methodist Missionary Society was formed in 1819, and in that year established the mission to Wyandot Indians in Ohio. Nathan Bangs (1778–1862) was the principal founder and secretary of the Methodist Missionary Society. It was recorded: "It is obvious that almost its entire business was conducted by Dr. Bangs for many years. In addition to writing the constitution, the address and circular, he was the author of every Annual Report, with but one exception, from the organization of the society down to the year 1841, a period of twenty-two years. He filled the offices of corresponding secretary and treasurer for sixteen years, without a salary or compensation of any kind, until his appointment to the first named office by the General Conference of 1836. That he has contributed more than any other man living to give character to our missionary operations, by the productions of his pen and his laborious personal efforts, is a well authenticated fact, which the history of the church fully attests." And though the initial years of the society was without a recognizable missionary, toward Bangs' sunset years, the society had a growing list of missionaries that numbered no less than four hundred, representing the Methodism in many parts of the United States, in South America, Norway, Sweden, Germany, Switzerland, Bulgaria, as well as in Asia, India, and China. The above quote is taken from Stevens, *History of the Methodist Episcopal Church*.

in 1885. The initiative to send the Methodist missionaries arose from a somewhat narrow perspective of primarily meeting the spiritual needs of the English-speaking "diaspora" in all British territories, not unlike those initial purposes of the Anglicans or Presbyterians that have arrived in Singapore earlier. A British resident in Singapore, Charles Philip, had been in correspondence with Rev. Thoburn, urging him to begin Methodist work in Singapore. There was also a request by a Scots merchant based in Singapore to Bishop John Hurst, enroute to India to administer the 1883 Conference, against the neglect of the vast territory of Southeast Asia.[24] These correspondences form the backdrop of the Methodist mission in Singapore

The sequence of events following the arrival enlarged the vision of the one sent, Reverend William Fitzjames Oldham, and have since grown to encompass ministries to the different people groups who have come to eke out a living amidst the increasing thriving trading economy in Singapore.

At the Conference in Hyderabad in December of 1884, the paramount question fielded was, "Whom shall we send?" Finally, a decision was reached to send William Fitzjames Oldham and his wife to establish the work in Singapore. Regarded as the "Founder of Singapore Methodism," Oldham, the son of a British army officer, was born in India, completed his theological education at Alleghany College and Boston University, in the United States of America and was on his way back to minister in India where he was informed of his appointment to Singapore in 1884. His appointment was a result of the response to Charles Phillips'[25] "Macedonian call" to the Methodist Church in India to "Come over ... and help us."[26] Oldham on reflection later wrote:

> I had prayed for some days that God will make me willing to go to any post in all India which I might be sent, and I at last had reached a point where I felt that I was perfectly willing for any place selected for me in all this Empire: but it never once dawned

---

24. Lau, *From Mission to Church*, 1.

25. Charles Philips was the head of the Seamen's Institute, which was based in Singapore. He was a Wesleyan, a layman, who had for some time cherished the thought of a Methodist missionary presence in Singapore. In view of the late arrival of the Methodists, Philips had also been active in supporting the work of the Anglican and Presbyterian churches in Singapore. He helped to found the first Methodist Church in Singapore together with Oldham, who regarded him as the "true father of Methodism in Singapore." Please refer to Sunquist et al., *Dictionary of Asian Christianity*, 659.

26. Sng, *In His Good Time*, 110.

upon my thoughts that they would shoot me clear through the empire and fifteen hundred miles out on the other side.[27]

Dr. Thoburn, his wife, Anne accompanied Oldham and another Ms. Julia Battie, an organist from the Calcutta Church and together they set sail for Singapore, while Mrs. Oldham was to join them later after she bade farewell to her mother in India. On 7 February 1885, the steamer *SS Khandalia*, sailed into the harbor in Singapore and they were greeted there by Charles Phillips who two years earlier had written to Thoburn in seeking his help to establish a mission there in Singapore. His meeting the arriving missionaries was an orchestration of the Lord Himself, for Phillips was not aware of their impending arrival. He went to the pier only because of a dream he had the night before. Accordingly, Philips was so convinced of his dream that even though he had no prior notice of their arrival, Philips "decided to rush down to Tanjong Pagar Dock to await the steamer. His expectation was soon confirmed. A steamer did arrive and on it was a party of Methodist missionaries."[28]

Divine orchestration was also evident in the provision for the venue where the missionaries were to conduct a series of evening meetings. Accordingly, the Assistant Municipal Secretary, John Polglase, a Wesleyan had offered to do all he could to obtain the Town Hall as the venue. When the matter came before the Municipal Council, three votes were cast for and three against and the deciding seventh vote, which set the venue, was cast by a non-Christian Chinese! That same evening, the group of newly arrived missionaries held a service at the Town Hall, attended by 150 persons who were drawn by Thoburn's reputation as an articulate preacher. Thoburn stood before the people and announced his text, "'Not by might, nor by power but by My Spirit' saith the Lord"!

Many different people were gathered at the Town Hall that evening; British men and women, some Tamils from India and Ceylon (present day Sri Lanka), a few Chinese from the coastal regions of China, and also one inquisitive English-speaking Malay, as noted by Oldham. And of that evening, he recorded:

> Dr. Thoburn took charge of the service.... With simplicity and directness, the speaker stated that the audience would reassemble from evening to evening, that their numbers would increase, that not by might of human eloquence, nor by the

---

27. As quoted of Oldham by Doraisamy, *March of Methodism*, 6.
28. Sng, *In His Good Time*, 110.

power of human persuasion but by the direct pressure upon their minds and their hearts, many of these before him would be convicted of their sins and some of them would turn to God and find newness of life. The service was so exceedingly simple and the effect was so profound that all the anticipations of the speaker were more than fulfilled on the nights that followed. Dr. Thoburn himself often referred to the ten days at Singapore as being marked by a very distinct sense of the immediate presence of God. At the close of this brief mission those had openly accepted the Gospel was called together and a church was born.[29]

Within a few days of the arrival of the missionaries in February of 1885, a series of five evening meetings were organized in the Town Hall where seventeen responded and were subsequently organized to become the nucleus of the first Methodist Church in Singapore. John Polglase was subsequently elected to all the positions that had to be filled by laymen, whilst fourteen others were accepted as probationary members.

Thoburn returned to Calcutta after an intense ten days of ministry in Singapore, the result of which was the formation of the Methodist Church on Sunday, 22 February. As the Indian Conference gave Oldham his pastoral appointment to oversee the mission work in Singapore, Thoburn further charged him as follows, "Methodism appoints you an herald to a nation and there must be continual overflow to your activities which will never end until you overtake all Malaysia."[30]

Oldham literally took hold of Thoburn's charge to have a "continual overflow to your activities" such that the story of the birth and spread of Methodism in Singapore and Malaya is so closely intertwined with church planting along ethno-linguistics lines, evangelism, education, publication and social concerns and outreach. It is in this regard that the model of Methodist mission work in Singapore has been called "a pluriform mission,"[31] where each of these strands of the mission work is so closely intertwined and interwoven in forming the tapestry that would be the hallmark of Methodism in Singapore.

---

29. Oldham, *Thoburn*, 132–33.

30. As quoted of Oldham by Doraisamy, *March of Methodism*, 8.

31. A term used as the title of chapter seven of a book on Oldham by Bishop Theodore Doraisamy. Doraisamy, *Oldham*, 50–56. Among the various chroniclers of the history of Methodism, it seems likely that the term was first applied to Oldham's mission work and strategy by Doraisamy.

It is well documented that Methodist churches were first established along linguistic considerations,[32] yet the work that the missionaries were involved in, such as the founding of schools and the mission work among those socially deprived and/or marginalized was not limited nor compromised by neither language nor ethnicity. Within just a year, the Methodist mission was making inroads to the various difficult migrant communities and employing various different means of access. Oldham perhaps understood mission as more than just building churches; that mission was more than just evangelizing the migrant population, be they the migrant workers from India and China or the colonial officers of the East India Company. Mission was all that together and more; and in that regard, the story of the arrival of the Methodists in Singapore reflects a mission that is "multidimensional in order to be credible and faithful to its origins and character."[33]

This "pluriform mission" makes the recording of the history of Methodism in Singapore challenging as there seems to be so many different movements in various different directions. In a rather short period of time, American Methodism has permeated Singapore in a manner where no other missionary efforts have done so in terms of breath and depth of their impact. A brief chronology of the first twenty-five years of Methodism will perhaps help illustrate the case:

Twenty-Five Years in Brief[34]

1885	Arrival of J.M. Thoburn and W.F. Oldham in Singapore
	Church established in February, later known as Wesley Methodist Church
	Construction began for church building in Coleman St (Dec)
1886	Founding of Anglo-Chinese School (March)
1887	Tamil work begun and Methodist Tamil Church was formed

---

32. This is best evidenced by the fact that the Methodist Church in Singapore is composed of three different annual conferences: Trinity Annual Conference (TRAC), Chinese Annual Conference, and Emmanuel Tamil Annual Conference. These annual conferences were the result of the labour of the early missionaries among the various migrant population such as the Chinese and the Indians.

33. Bosch, *Transforming Mission*, 512.

34. Adapted from Lau, *From Mission to Church*, iii.

	WFMS sends Ms. Sophia Blackmore
	Founding of Tamil Girls' School (later renamed as Methodist Girls' School)
1888	Founding of Telok Ayer Chinese Girls' School (later renamed as Fairfield Methodist Girls' School)
1889	Dr. Benjamin West began medical work and Chinese vernacular work, laying the work for the founding of Telok Ayer Chinese Methodist Church
	First Annual Meeting of Malaysia Mission (formed by General Conference 1888)
	Formation of First Epworth League
1890	Publishing House founded
1891	"Malaysia Message" first printed
	Work begun in Penang
1892	Malaysia Mission becomes a Conference
1894	Straits Chinese Church formed in Singapore
	Work begun in Ipoh
1897	Work begun in Kuala Lumpur
1898	Founding of Jean Hamilton Training School
1899	First Conference member goes to Malacca
	Work begun in Philippines
1901	Founding of Eveland Seminary in Singapore
	Foochow pilgrims arrive in Sarawak
1902	Malaysia Mission Conference becomes Annual Conference
1903	First Missionary to Sarawak
1904	Philippines Mission Conference formed
	W. F. Oldham returned to Malaysia as Bishop
1905	Work begun in Java and North Sumatra
1906	Work begun in West Borneo
1908	Work begun in South Sumatra
1909	First WFMS worker to Java.

Within the short span of five years, the Methodist work has grown to include the founding of three churches, Wesley Methodist Church (1885), Tamil Methodist Church (1887) and the Chinese church at Telok Ayer (1889), in three different languages. It had also established three schools; Anglo-Chinese School (1886), Tamil Girls' School (1887) and Telok Ayer Chinese Girls' School (1889) as well as a printing press by 1890. What began as a mission in 1885 had grown to be a Mission Conference in 1893 and later achieved autonomy as an independent Annual Conference in 1902. What began as a place to which missionaries were received became increasingly the place from which missionaries were sent. Methodist work began its northward growth toward Peninsular Malaysia, in Penang in 1891 and spread toward Ipoh, Kuala Lumpur and Malacca. It went eastward toward the Philippines before the turn of the century and toward Sarawak in 1901. Westward, work in Sumatra was started in 1905. Southward, Methodism began to establish mission work in Java that same year (in 1905) and in south Sumatra in 1908. Through a period of less than 20 years, the Methodist mission in Singapore had taken root and growing toward becoming a centre from whence the Good News was to be carried to the rest of Southeast Asia.

This is hence an attempt to retell the story of Methodism by describing primarily the growth in terms of the establishment of the various churches, followed by an account of the educational mission and publication ministry. But such an account is limited by the fluidity of the "pluriform mission" of the Methodists in Singapore. At the turn of the twentieth century, Methodism was only beginning to take root in Singapore through the pioneering ministry of Oldham. What started as a mission increasingly grew to become the Methodist Church in Singapore.[35] The division of the following account of the Methodist missions into such categories as the linguistic works, the education mission and printing mission is but an attempt to organize the historical data with a certain clarity and chronology. Yet it must be foremost in the mind of the reader that all these movements occurred in tandem and each had an impact on the growth and development of the other aspects of the mission work in Singapore. There is a dynamism that a neatly presented historical account fails to capture. This fluidity impinges on the various different ministries among the various missionaries, not the least Oldham himself, who was

---

35. This is the theme which is evident in Lau's book, *From Mission to Church*.

at once, the main actor in the various different scenes in the unfolding history of Methodism in Singapore.

Linguistic Work

Methodism in Singapore may have been first established through the use of English, but yet it is not limited only to the native English-speakers. The work was to grow in importance especially among the Chinese and Indian immigrants as well as the Malay speaking indigenous population as well as the Straits-born Chinese.

THE ENGLISH WORK

With Thoburn's return to India, Oldham remained in Singapore and became the first resident Methodist missionary pastor. Together with Polglase, the Methodist work in Singapore was planted. This new church that had a predominantly English congregation continued to meet in Town Hall on Sunday evenings. By December of that same year, sufficient funds were also collected to build the first Methodist church in Singapore at Coleman Street, later named as Wesley Methodist Church.[36]

THE TAMIL WORK

Besides the establishment of a predominantly English speaking congregation, missionary efforts were realized along other linguistics communities, among the Tamils, Chinese and Malays. In a rapidly growing cosmopolitan society where different cultures congregate, the Methodists were able to capitalize on creating ministries to cater to the needs of the different nationalities represented.

In establishing the church along Coleman Street, Oldham also demonstrated particular concern for the large number of Indians in Singapore. Growing up in India, the Oldhams knew Tamil and using that knowledge, Oldham visited the jails in order to preach to Tamil prisoners. He appointed as a "missionary to the Tamils" a person named Benjamin Pillai and by September 1885, they "had entered the open door of the jail and had regular service with the Tamil prisoners."[37] Oldham also minis-

---

36. Wesley Methodist Church was later re-sited to Fort Canning in 1909 and has since become the symbol of Singapore Methodism. Please refer to the website for more information on the history as well as the various ministries in the church: http://www.wesleymc.org/.

37. As quoted by Doraisamy, *March of Methodism*, 9

tered among the Tamil laborers, who had come to Singapore, in search of job opportunities and better wages. In September 1885, he received the first Tamil catechist, Mr. M. Gnanamuthu, sent from Rangoon by the Rev. J. E. Robinson. Gnanamuthu who worked as a missionary to the Tamils, who started a Tamil School for the children in the Serangoon area with an initial registration of about 45 students. By the end of 1885, Sunday and weekday services in Tamil were held by the Methodists.

In early 1887, Oldham secured the appointment of a Tamil preacher, G. W. Underwood, from the Jaffna Mission to work among the Tamil-speaking laborers. Underwood worked tirelessly at gathering Tamil Christians together as a congregation and soon assumed the responsibilities as the pastor of the first Methodist Tamil Church.[38] Underwood was also the person who later helped Ms. Blackmore in founding the Tamil Girls' School in August of 1887. When he died of pneumonia in 1890, the Rev. H. L. Hoisington came and continued his work in the Tamil church, school and prison ministry, with the assistance of Mr. Gnanamuthu. Other Tamil churches were soon organized all over the island as the Tamil work grew.

THE CHINESE DIALECTS WORK

Similarly, Singapore was the locus of the influx of numerous Chinese immigrants in search of a better life. Perceiving the growth of the Chinese immigrant population, Oldham wrote in request of a missionary to work among the Chinese and hence the Methodist mission to the Chinese began with the arrival of an American doctor, the Rev. Dr. Benjamin Franklin West, and his wife in 1888. Dr. West had come as a medical missionary but his arrival coincided with a period where there was an increasing demand for teachers in the education ministry that Oldham had founded in 1886. Rev. and Mrs. West hence found themselves more involved in teaching than in medical missions, for which he had left Cincinnati to come to Singapore.

At the first Annual Meeting of the Malaysia Mission in April 1889, Rev. Dr. West was determined that his medical training be better appreciated. His earnest plea was:

---

38. Means, *Malaysia Mosaic*, 37. Means wrote also about the exploratory trip Underwood took up the Malay Peninsular to Perak where there was a growing number of Tamils. Underwood was eager to expand the Tamil ministry northward to Malaya except for his unfortunate succumbing to pneumonia.

> Gentlemen! I did not come half way round the world to teach third standard boys! I am a doctor and there are thousands here who need my services. I gladly gave up my practice to become a missionary—but a medical missionary, my friends, and I insist that you give me a chance.[39]

As the mission in Singapore was a relatively new field, very little financial support was given and candidly, Bishop Thoburn recommended that until the Board apportioned more finances to Singapore, the missionaries where to support themselves through teaching. This was seemingly the missionary model that was appropriated for the missionaries from the Methodist Episcopal Church in Singapore. They were for most part self-supporting.

Hence for Rev. Dr. West and his wife, it was decided that they would continue to teach and also be involved in medical mission. In August 1889, West and his wife moved into the Telok Ayer district, which was an enclave for the Chinese immigrants, with its opium dens, gambling houses and brothels. They adopted the mission model common in China, of renting a house on the main street and establishing it as a center for medical, evangelistic and educational work. Dr. West apportioned his time to educational and medical missions—in the morning, he taught at the school and in the afternoons he saw patients in his home and on Sundays, his house became a gathering place for services. When the medical consultation work expanded, they were able to establish a dispensary along Nanking Street.

In his church work, Rev. Dr. West had the help of two local preachers, as well as a native Chinese "bible-woman," and in August 1889, the Chinese Methodist Church was formed. Placing himself right at the heart of the Chinese quarters, Rev. Dr. West was able to incarnate the love of Jesus to the Chinese in a very practical way. He also had a very effective ministry to the opium addicts. Consequently, it was of no surprise that many of the converts and worshippers in the church were his patients. Realizing his inadequacy in the dialects of the Chinese, he requested for a brief leave of absence to go to China to learn Hokkien, the dialect used by the majority of the Chinese and upon his return his work expanded. It is recorded that "between February and April 1892 alone, over 3500

---

39. As quoted by Means, *Malaysia Mosaic*, 39.

patients were treated at the dispensary and a congregation of 46 was meeting regularly on Sundays."[40]

With the growth in the Chinese church, other workers arrived later such as Rev. Ling Ching Mi,[41] an ordained Methodist deacon and Thong Sin San, both from China. Dr. H L E Luering, a linguist from Germany who eventually learnt to preach in Malay, Hokkien and Foochow further expanded the scope of ministry to the Chinese and by 1895, the Chinese mission was conducting meetings in almost all the major dialects.

The Peranakan Work

The early missionary efforts were undertaken by both Oldham and Blackmore, visiting homes and preaching in Malay *kampongs* (villages). Among one of the members at the English Church in Coleman Street was the Commanding Officer of the Royal Engineers at Pulau Brani, Captain William Girdlestone Shellabear, who had come to be greatly influenced by Oldham. As he was responsible for the Malay soldiers under his charge, Shellabear took upon himself the challenge of learning the Malay language from a private tutor, Encik Ismail and "quickly proved himself quite fluent and effective."[42]

Challenged by Oldham, Shellabear resigned from the army and prepared himself to be a missionary, accepting Oldham's suggestion to equip himself with the necessary knowledge and skills in the area of printing. This was to be part of Oldham's plans to set up a mission press in Singapore, for the ministry of publications for the benefit of the locals. This was to be one of Shellabear's lasting legacies in this part of the world.

In tandem with the work in establishing the printing press, Shellabear also worked tirelessly at street evangelism in the vicinity of the Press. Shellabear pioneered the Methodist work in Malay and in 1892 he started Malay services in a rented shophouse in Arab Street. Like Oldham and Blackmore, he visited the Malay families regularly and this resulted in some conversions. This was however, not lasting as most of the Malay contacts later returned to the Muslim faith. But this was not to dampen

---

40. Sng, *In His Good Time*, 122.

41. Lau, *From Mission to Church*, 36. Rev. Ling was recruited by Dr. Luering and arrived in 1897. He was the founding pastor of Foochow Methodist Church in 1897 and was later sent as a missionary to Sibu and Sitiawan, Malaysia, where the Chinese emigrants from FooChow were being settled.

42. Lau, *From Mission to Church*, 26.

his efforts, as he then concentrated his efforts on the Straits Chinese, who also used the Malay language.

Best known for his literary translation work into the Malay language, Shellabear had the opportunity to combined efforts with Blackmore in organising the Malay-speaking Straits-born Chinese (Baba)[43] church in January 1894. The Middle Road Church, or the Baba Church[44] as it came to be known, was the fourth Methodist Church to be organized and all within the span of no more than a decade. It is also important to note that it was out of this congregation that nurtured the first Baba minister, Rev. Goh Hood Keng.[45]

Education Mission

In tandem with the building of a church, Oldham was presented with an opportunity to establish an important ministry for the Methodist witness in Singapore—educational mission. In seeking to address the needs of the poor and uneducated, Oldham saw educational ministries as a concrete option and was an ardent proponent for such. The symbiotic relationship between the schools and missions forged in the early years of Methodism in Singapore remains as one of Methodism lasting legacy in the development of Singapore. Secular historian W. Makepeace wrote of Oldham:

---

43. The Peranakans, or Babas as they were known, were Straits-born Chinese who spoke a distinctive Malay instead of their mother tongue. They were descended from Chinese traders who had settled along the major trading ports of Malacca, Penang, and Singapore, along the Straits of Malacca, evolving their own distinct culture and language. The men were known as Babas and the women were known as Bibiks.

44. The Baba Church was later relocated to the current site at Kampong Kapor as there was insufficient space to cope with the various different congregations that had gathered for worship. These included not only the Babas, but also Hinghwas, Hakkas, Foochows (Chinese dialects groups), as well as the English congregation. Upon completion of the new building at Kampong Kapor in 1930, it became known as the Straits Chinese Methodist Church (Bickley Memorial). It was renamed Kampong Kapor Methodist Church in 1957. Kampong Kapor Methodist Church, "Our History."

45. Goh Hood Keng was educated in the Methodist schools and took the step of faith through the guidance of one of his teachers. Despite parental objection, being raised in a staunch Buddhist family, he remained filial to his parents and through his life testimony helped them make their decision to follow Jesus too. Goh Hood Keng became the first locally ordained pastor of the Straits Chinese Methodist Church (now Kampong Kapor Methodist Church). His one passion was "to preach Christ and Him crucified." Please refer to http://trac-mcs.org.sg/Download.cfm?DObjID=245&Mode=1&FN=/Goh%20Hood%20Keng.pdf.

> The name of the Rev. W.F. Oldham, D.D., will ever be associated with the history of the Colony.... Arriving here, he speedily won influence with all the sections of the community by his public spirit, broad-mindedness, unceasing activity and his fluency in thought and speech. The Chinese were eager to have him as tutor for themselves and their children, and freely supported him with money for his educational and even religious enterprises. Among these Mr. Tan Keong Saik and Mr. Tan Jiak Kim were conspicuous.[46]

Methodism literally stumbled upon education mission. It was not a mission model as if it had been carefully deliberated and planned for in any of the discussions between Oldham and Thoburn prior to Oldham's arrival in Singapore. And Oldham's founding of Anglo-Chinese School is as much extraordinary as Charles Philip's meeting with the missionaries who first arrived on 7 February 1885. Oldham was walking about in the Chinese enclave at Telok Ayer District, where he chanced on "*The Celestial Reasoning Association*," a group of Chinese merchants who gathered together and arranged talks and debates to encourage the learning of English. When his request to join the association was politely turned down, Oldham was instead offered an opportunity to deliver a talk on astronomy, where he met the President of the Society, Tan Keong Saik. Impressed by his presentation, Tan Keong Saik, who was also a member of the Legislative Council in Singapore, urged Oldham to help him in a presentation (in English) that he was to make before the leaders of the Chinese business community. Oldham recorded the encounter as such:

> The next morning I received a letter from one of the last evening's company asking whether I would become his tutor in the English, he wished instruction three times a week, he would pay $40.00 a month. I accepted the offer immediately; it gave me an instant entry into much of the Chinese life in the city. My pupil was a member of the legislative council in Singapore and as such was much in the eye of the local press. Presently it began to be perceived that he was making finer English speeches than he had been thought capable of and the word began to go around that in these speeches he was helped by the young man who had spoken to them on Astronomy. The result was several offers from middle aged or older men to have me become their tutors.[47]

---

46. Makepeace, Braddell, and Brooke, *One Hundred Years of Singapore*, 269.

47. Oldham, *Malaysia*, Manuscripts, as quoted by Doraisamy, *Oldham*, 35. It seems that Doraisamy was in possession of the manuscripts as he wrote the book but

Oldham, though flattered by their request, knew that his calling was "not to come to Singapore to be an English tutor for wealthy Chinese merchants,"[48] but instead offered to teach their sons, which was met with much approval. With the support of these influential Chinese merchants, who indicated their willingness to undertake all the expenses in regard to operations of the school, this became the Methodist Church's first venture into education in Singapore and birthed the Anglo-Chinese School.

Handbills were circulated in the Chinatown vicinity announcing the opening of the school:

> The Anglo-Chinese School is to be opened in Amoy Street, No. 70, on 1 March 1886. Chinese will be taught from 8a.m. to 12a.m. and English from 1.30pm to 4pm. Apply to the superintendent, W.F. Oldham, care of Lim Kong Wan and Son, 21 Malacca Street.[49]

The school started on 1 March 1886 with an initial enrolment of 13 boys, sons of the Chinese businessmen who were present when Oldham delivered his lecture at the Celestial Reasoning Association. A Chinese teacher was initially engaged to teach the class in the morning but as the demand for English far exceeded that for Chinese, Oldham later reverted to teaching the English classes in the morning and thus freed himself for other ministry in the afternoons. Those in the Chinatown vicinity came to refer to the school instead as "Oldham Mission School." The popularity of the school among the Chinese merchants spread and soon there were requests from Chinese outside Singapore who wished to send their sons to learn under the Oldhams. Nathalie Means noted in her account that Mrs. Oldham gave up a part of their home in order to house the young boarders.[50] Even so, by the end of the year (1886), class enrolment had passed the one hundred mark and the shop house space was soon too small to house all the students. Writing a report to the Board of Missions on 5 June 1889, prior to his reappointment back to the USA, Oldham noted,

---

efforts to trace the whereabouts of the manuscripts have drawn a blank.

48. Sng, *In His Good Time*, 117.

49. As quoted in Lau and Teo, *ACS Story*, 10. It is not clear if the handbills were printed in English or Chinese. In all probability, the handbills should have been composed in English and translated (possibly by Lim Kong Wan) in order that the Chinese community would have access to the information about the school enrollment.

50. Means, *Malaysia Mosaic*, 23.

> The influence of this school is very marked. Nothing like it has ever been seen here and we find that our school work opens our way in every direction. Merchants and officials are astonished to see how influential we are in the Chinese circles. The children of nearly all the leading Chinese of this port is in our school. These lads are now receiving definite instructions. Several of them are deeply affected. Two have been definitely converted. I gain access to men I could never dream of reaching otherwise. I have no hesitation in saying this is a Divinely created agency of marked power.... Our Governor in conversation with Bishop Thoburn was please to refer to me personally as a "born educationalist."... With this start (a Mission grant of $7500 granted), with Government help and local subscriptions we can secure a $30,000 property and put our school room on such a basis as will pay hundred per cent in spiritual force, in moulding power, in social influence in all things that are desirable for the upbuilding of the Messiah's coming kingdom in our midst.[51]

The growth of the school and the boarding house necessitated the search for a separate building for the boarding school. "Bellevue," a large house next to the entrance of the Governor's grounds, was put up for sale at $12,000. Oldham brought up the matter of funding the sale of the Bellevue with a Chinese banker, Mr. Tan Jiak Kim, who had been a supporter of the school. Though Mr. Tan frankly told Oldham that "he was moving too fast for the Chinese,"[52] he nonetheless agreed to help raise half the amount locally if Oldham could raise the other half from the USA. Very quickly a sum of $6200 was raised among the Chinese and Oldham wrote a second letter to Dr. McCabe of the Board of Foreign Mission explaining the agreement with Mr. Tan. McCabe's answer was, "I have put through the Board a donation of $6000 for the Singapore School, but please tell your Chinese that we cannot keep up the pace they are setting."[53] Unbeknownst to both Mr. Tan and Dr. McCabe, it was perhaps Oldham who has set the pace in ensuring the attraction of English and Christian education among the Chinese boys in the school.

The school continued to experience remarkable growth in the subsequent years (as in the table below) and in a decade, by 1896,

---

51. *Oldham's Letter to the Board of Missions, 1889.* Archive correspondence documented at the UMC Archives, Drew University, New Jersey.

52. Means, *Malaysia Mosaic*, 24.

53. Means, *Malaysia Mosaic*, 24.

Anglo-Chinese School (ACS) had become the largest school in the Straits Settlements, with an enrolment of 641 students.

Table 3: ACS Enrolment from 1886 to 1911

Year	1886	1887	1888	1889	1890	1891	1892	1893	1894	1895	1896	1897	1898
Enrolment	13	104	248	312	372	397	388	421	485	572	641	565	575
Year	1899	1900	1901	1902	1903	1904	1905	1906	1907	1908	1909	1910	1911
Enrolment	554	625	660	697	795	701	803	877	955	1074	1083	1161	1200

Source: *Anglo-Chinese School Magazine*, 1934, 13.

The school as well as the boarding school continued to grow and in time, the "Bellevue" was inadequate to house both. It was torn down in 1896 and a new building replaced it. When Oldham returned later as Bishop of Malaysia in 1904, the boarding school was renamed "Oldham Hall" in honour of him. As the enrolment of the school continued to increase, staffing as well as housing always presented a challenge. In time, the house behind "Bellevue" was purchased. The Archdeacon of the St Andrew's Cathedral who lived in close proximity to "Bellevue" supposedly remarked, "Well, I suppose the Methodists will soon be buying my house!"[54] With later funding from the Board as well as from the Women's Foreign Missionary Society, the mission went on to secure the top of the little hill, Mount Sophia[55] and established the Methodist centre there.

As Methodist missionaries, Oldham and his wife shared an educational philosophy that was inclusive. In an article, "Sound Educational Wisdom," published in the Malaysia Message in 1907, Mrs. Oldham wrote,

> There ought not to be any discrimination between evangelistic and educational work: each can be as educational or as evangelistic as the one in charge choose to make it. This applies also to

---

54. Means, *Malaysia Mosaic*, 25.

55. The Methodist Girls' School was later relocated to Mount Sophia as was the headquarters of the Methodist mission. It was also the site for the development of Trinity Theological College, a union college conceived by the leaders of the various denominations as they were interned in Changi prison during the Japanese occupation of Singapore in 1942–45. The land on which Trinity Theological College was sited was leased by the Methodist Church for the development of local pastoral and theological leadership in the various denominations.

English and native work. They are so closely related that they must stand or fall together.⁵⁶

The Oldhams understood that education was an important means of transmitting the Good News and at the same time equipping the immigrant population with the means to engage the British colonial rulers. It might well be that as they were all missionaries of the Methodist Episcopal Church of the United States of America, they were much less concerned with issues that the colonial administration were concerned with.

Even before the Anglo-Chinese School was firmly established, Oldham continued to acutely grasp the various other opportunities presented to him in establishing ministries in education among the various communities in Singapore. Oldham was also aware of the deplorable status of women at that time. As they were denied basic education, the women stood helpless against the social forces and prejudices that shaped their destiny. Adapting the Methodist mission emphasis in various parts of India, Oldham believed that one of these ways to help these women was through education.

Oldham wrote to the Woman's Foreign Missionary Society requesting for additional help. His letter of appeal coincided with a letter from Miss Isabella Leonard to Mrs. Mary C. Nind, the corresponding secretary of the Minneapolis branch of the Woman's Foreign Missionary Society, in seeking for an opening for Miss Sophia Blackmore. An Australian by birth, Blackmore met Miss Leonard in her hometown of Goulburn, Australia and had travelled with her to India while waiting for an opening to serve as a missionary in China.⁵⁷ Reviewing Oldham's plea for worker, Mrs. Nind then matched the two requests and committed the Minneapolis Branch in supporting Sophia Blackmore's work in Singapore. To the thunderous applause of the Conference delegates, Mrs. Nind prophetically declared, "Frozen Minnesota will yet, God helping her, found a mission at the equator!"⁵⁸ Meanwhile, Oldham was attending the Conference meetings in South India in 1886, where he met and challenged Sophia

---

56. *Malaysia Message*, 1907.

57. Lau, *From Mission to Church*, 6. Blackmore's mother had previously met with missionaries such as Robert Morrison of China, Robert Moffat, and David Livingstone, and had been very supportive of Blackmore's desire to go into the mission field.

58. Means, *Malaysia Mosaic*, 28.

Blackmore to assist in the work among the women and the girls in Singapore. Oldham perceived that:

> Female education, when the missionaries first came here, was very backward. It is not that there were no schools; there were, but they were struggling and not coordinating. As I emphasize and believe in female education I could not tolerate that state of affairs. Then came on the scene a pioneer missionary lady interested in education: Miss Sophia Blackmore.[59]

Sophia Blackmore was the first woman missionary appointed by the Methodist Women's Foreign Missionary Society to work in Singapore. She had, however, used her short sojourn in India to her benefit, attaching herself to various missionaries. One such missionary couple was Bishop and Mrs. Parker who had suggested to Blackmore that in her future ministries, she should "*in your work, gather in the children and help to build up a church.*"[60] This was to have a lasting impact on her ministry in Singapore.

Her arrival thus heralded for Singapore Methodism an important thrust forward in the pioneering mission work among women. And of the urgency of the times, Sophia Blackmore later recorded in her diary:

> The mission to the women of Malaya had been, from its inception, pre-eminently a work of faith and prayer and sacrifice. Because of its location as the port of call for the commerce of the eastern world, Singapore, "meeting place of nations," was not only a strategic center for missionary work but most appallingly in need of woman's work.... Dr. Oldham, founder of Methodism there, soon keenly realized this and sent most urgent appeals to the women of America to come to the rescue.[61]

Oldham had talked about Blackmore's arrival at a gathering of Indian Christians and at that meeting a Mr. Rama Krishna Rao placed a shophouse at 33 Short Street under the disposal of the mission, rent-free for the next four years for the work of education. Another businessman, Mr. Murugusu provided for the monthly payment for the teacher, which was a donation of $60 per month. Still "others gave donations for desks,

---

59. As quoted of Bishop Oldham by Doraisamy, *Sophia Blackmore in Singapore*, 66–68.

60. Blackmore, *Record of Forty Years*, p. 1 of chapter on Methodist Girls' School.

61. Blackmore, *Record of Forty Years*, 5.

benches, desks, benches, blackboard and other furniture."[62] Hence, by 15 August 1887, in less than a month after her arrival in Singapore in 1887, Blackmore was able to very quickly start an education work among the Tamil girls at the request of Tamil businessmen, not unlike the founding of the Anglo-Chinese School. Blackmore noted in her journal, the "best of all nine little girls, with earnest brown eyes and smooth black hair, dressed in their best silken garments and adorned with much jewelry were committed to our care."[63] The initial enrolment of nine Tamils girls birthed the Tamil Girls' School that later became known as the Methodist Girls' School.

While she taught the Tamil girls at the school, Blackmore tirelessly expanded her work to include the teaching of a few Chinese girls in their homes in the Telok Ayer District. Telok Ayer was the same vicinity where Oldham had a year before, set up Anglo-Chinese School. Blackmore held that "the object of our visiting in Telok Ayer was to find pupils for a Chinese girls' school. One or two of the influential families had asked us to put a teacher in their homes."[64] With the assistance and support of that same Chinese businessman, Mr. Tan Keong Siak, and other like-minded businessmen, the school was organized along Cross Street in the Telok Ayer District, in the home of a Straits-born Chinese lady who was known as Nonya Boon.[65] Sophia recorded in her journal that "in August 1888, we made a beginning with eight little girls."[66]

Within the first year of her ministry in Singapore, Blackmore had started a second school, the Telok Ayer School in 1888. As the enrolment gradually increased the school had to be relocated to nearby Neil Road. It was relocated to another site provided by the colonial administration. Mr. James Fairfield, "a generous patron of the New England, Minneapolis Branch of WFMS"[67] made a donation of $5000 in gold in response to an appeal for funding to build the new school. The school was subsequently renamed as Fairfield Methodist Girl's School in 1913:

> in honour of kind old gentlemen who during his lifetime gave more than eighty thousand dollars to the Women's Foreign

---

62. Doraisamy, *Forever Beginning I*, 13.
63. Doraisamy, *Forever Beginning I*, 1.
64. Doraisamy, *Sophia Blackmore in Singapore*, 22.
65. Doraisamy, *Sophia Blackmore in Singapore*, 13.
66. Doraisamy, *Sophia Blackmore in Singapore*, 23.
67. As indicated in the *30th Annual Report of WFMS* (1913), 36.

Missionary Society, always withholding his name. Since his death we have learned who he was and where he lived and it has been determined to name one of his schools in each country after him.[68]

Although recruitment of women teachers posed an initial problem, Blackmore worked tirelessly with the other teachers in the successful expansion of the schools ministry to serve all the communities in Singapore. A small group of ladies who assisted her included Miss Nellia Jensen, Mrs. Leicester, Mrs. McFarlane as well as Miss Hagedorn, Miss Salome Fox and Miss E. Leicester who co-laboured with her as teachers. They went about visiting homes and encouraging the families to allow the daughters to attend the schools. Together, these ladies exemplified the interests that fueled Blackmore's ministry, namely, "sharing the Gospel and convincing women to educate their daughters."[69]

Within three years, the Methodist mission in Singapore established three schools in rapid succession; Anglo-Chinese School in 1886, the Methodist Girls' School in 1887 and Fairfield Methodist Girls' School in 1888. This model of educational mission was very quickly adopted in major towns in parts of Malaya that evidenced the rise of other Methodist schools in Penang (1891), Ipoh (1895), Kuala Lumpur (1899) as well as in Malacca.

Besides her indefatigable efforts, Blackmore, like Oldham, was also not circumscribed by ministry in schools. She also initiated the work to start a hostel for girls, who were abandoned, orphaned or disenfranchised. This was to be a significant ministry, especially in a society that was prejudicial and gender discriminate, seeing baby girls as more a bane for the family. The girls' hostel was named the Nind Home, in honor of Mrs. Mary C. Nind,[70] who had been instrumental in financing Blackmore's appointment. Until its disbandment at the onset of the Japanese Occupation of Singapore following the Japanese victory over the British,

---

68. *Quarterly Review of the Minneapolis Branch of the WFMS*, 4.

69. Lau, *From Mission to Church*, 15.

70. Means, *Malaysia Mosaic*, 28. Nathalie recorded how Mrs. Nind as corresponding secretary of the Minneapolis Branch of the Woman's Foreign Missionary Society challenged the conference to bear the heavy financial burden of supporting the Methodist women's work in Singapore. An anonymous gift of three thousand dollars was received, which was later attributed to have been a donation given by Mrs. Nind herself.

the Nind Home was home to over a hundred boarders and was a thriving and self-funding ministry.

Blackmore and other women who arrived in Singapore through the WFMS were actively involved in social work chiefly among the poor, the sick and the disenfranchised, such as the lepers. The women missionaries and the wives of the other missionaries organized hospital visits in the Serangoon area. As noted earlier, they too were involved in rescue work among abused girls. Miss Josephine M. Hebinger was one significant person in this particular ministry. She wrote describing the work in a report:

> The darkness and wickedness cannot be described, eyes must see, ears must hear, lives must come in contact with the poor fallen, in order to understand. In our home, we have six girls . . . There are over three thousand women in the dens of infamy.[71]

Many of those who were rescued were given shelter in the home and were also educated at the Methodist schools and later took their places as professionals and leaders in both the church and society in Singapore. The impact of such a ministry catalyzed the establishment of similar homes in Malaya, which were also positive influences in their respective communities.

The Nind Home further birthed a church for the Peranakans or Babas, when she evangelized the Baba Chinese women who were housebound and uneducated. Working in tandem with another missionary, William Shellabear, their efforts helped to found the Baba Church, which became the first Methodist church to use Baba Malay for both the worship services as well as the Sunday School. The extent of the ministry was evidenced by the significant numbers[72] who attended the Sunday School classes.

Together with Oldham and Blackmore, William Girdlestone Shellabear is one of the pioneers of the Methodist mission in British Malaya, yet ironically, "he is better known among Malay Muslims than among Christians."[73] With his timely arrival in 1890, Shellabear "inaugurated the Methodist efforts to evangelise the Malays."[74] Prior to his call as a mission-

---

71. Report, WFMS, (1894)

72. Lau, *Sophia Blackmore*, in Sunquist et al., *Dictionary of Asian Christianity*, 89. Earnest Lau noted that at one time the attendance was well over eight hundred.

73. Hunt, Robert A., "William Shellabear," 28.

74. Satari, "Shellabear, William Girdlestone," in Sunquist et al., *Dictionary of Asian Christianity*, 759.

ary, Shellabear was appointed as Captain of the British Royal Engineers of a company of enlisted Malay soldiers, stationed in Singapore. Hoping to get acquainted with missionaries, Shellabear who initially attended the Anglican services at St Andrew's Cathedral later attended the Methodist services where he met with Oldham. Shellabear's interest in a mission to the Malays may be attributed to his exposure of the Malay soldiers he was directly in charge of and also his observation of the church's general apathy to a Malay mission work. Convicted, Shellabear broached the idea of becoming a Methodist missionary with Oldham, who had been waiting for Shellabear's response. Together they planned for Shellabear to be a part of the mission work in Singapore as Methodist's first missionary to the Malays.

In April of 1889, when Mission Board of the Methodist Episcopal Church officially recognized the Singapore work, Shellabear had the opportunity to meet with Thoburn and further consolidated the plans for him to be a full missionary to the Malays by 1890. In his annual report, Oldham wrote:

> Work among the Malays of Singapore is particularly difficult, for they are a Mohammedan people and largely belief that the white man is godless—a reputation that many a white man has but too faithfully earned. When we are really ready to move upon the Malay citadel I feel that it must be in the villages of the peninsula and the islands of the sea, where they are more accessible and less under Arab influence. Meanwhile Brother A. Fox, a local preacher, has faithfully preached during the year in the Malay *kampungs*, assisted by the ladies, who visit the Malay women in their homes. A Sunday school, too, has been kept up in the house of a Mohammedan who invited us to use his house. Pray for the Malays. They are an attractive race, but some man must give himself wholly to them. We hope next year to have such a man to go and live in their midst and itinerate among the villages outside.[75]

This man in Oldham's mind was William Shellabear. Shellabear returned to England in order to resign from the British army and to seek his father's understanding in his decision to answer God's call as a missionary. As he waited for official confirmation to be commissioned as missionary of the Methodist Episcopal Church, he wrote to Thoburn about the possible need for theological education, the learning of Arabic

---

75. *Methodist Episcopal Church Missionary Society Book of Annual Reports*, 232.

as well as other details with regards to missionary preparation. Oldham responded on Thoburn behalf and wrote to Shellabear requesting him to learn something of the trade of printing that was to serve as a means of benefitting the Methodist mission in Singapore, not only among the Malays but also to the mission as a whole.

Mission Press

Oldham understood that the printing press has always been a useful adjunct to mission, evangelism and education and he wanted Shellabear to begin a printing operation for the Methodist mission in Singapore.[76] He wrote in the American papers an article "Wanted: A Malay Printing Press" where he surmised:

> A thousand dollars will start with a few months a stream of Christian literature from Singapore which will help to irrigate the spiritual deserts that lie all around us. "The isles are waiting for His coming." Do let us send the good tidings to these millions of islanders and so prepare His way. To many of ,them our missionaries cannot reach for years to come, but we can send them bright printed pages filled with the teachings of that book "whose leaves are for the healing of the nations.[77]

Oldham also wrote to Dr. Peck of the Mission Board of the MEC audaciously requesting for the funding of Shellabears' traveling expenses from London to Singapore and went to the extent of suggesting that if the Board was unwilling to bear the expense, he would personally repay the amount for the travel.[78] From the outset, Oldham and Shellabear were aware of the possibilities and opportunities that it presented. Shellabear believed that "the Mission Press had before it the prospect of becoming a mighty force for evangelization of Malaysia"[79] and to that effect invested himself into a great volume and variety in the publication ministry.

Shellabear arrived in Singapore with his wife in October of 1890 and got down to the work of setting up the printing press and by December

---

76. Hunt, *William Shellabear*. Hunt noted that in preparing for the mission in Singapore, Shellabear spent his days back in England learning the art of printing and his evenings and weekends with the bands of street evangelists, while waiting for replies from both Thoburn and Oldham.

77. As quoted of Oldham by Doraisamy, *Forever Beginning I*, 17.

78. Oldham to Dr. Peck, 7 August 1890, No 1261-1-2: 30.

79. Doraisamy, *March of Methodism*, 24.

1890, the press was operational. Shellabear, like the other Methodist missionaries such as Luering, held firm to the promise that God's Word will not return to Him void and that the church needs to be missionary in its existence, function and work. Shellabear invested a large part of his life in the printing press[80] and at the same time displayed a deep concern to share God's word as widely as possible to all linguistic and dialect groups and in particular, the Malays. Among the first publications that the Mission press produced were Malay and Chinese Bibles, hymnals and tracts, many of which were translated by Shellabear himself. Shellabear was also translating Christian literature into Malay, with the intention of creating a complete set of Methodist literature to serve the Malay-speaking churches he had hoped to establish in Singapore and Malaya. This was his dream and his goal.

In the context of Singapore, the local press was a vocal partner in the promotion of "innocent amusement" (namely horse racing and drinking) or such as the fundamental aspects of Singapore's culture and economy vis-à-vis opium dens, prostitution and gambling dens. As a British colony, the local press was often the tool of the colonial administration and while it perceived colonialism as an uplift of the society through certain Christian values, it often resented the missionaries who were vocal and spoke up against such activities in their contributions to the local press. The two main papers were the Straits Times and the Free Press.[81] It was hence not surprising that the missionaries desired another platform to publicise their viewpoints and to solicit Christian support.

This became a reality when J. W. Floyd assumed the appointment as Mission Superintendent and proposed a monthly mission paper, *Malaysia Message*, for missionaries in Singapore and Malaysia as a step in promoting an exchange of ideas and the educating and encouragement of fellow missionaries. With Floyd as the editor, *Malaysia Message* was first printed in October 1891. Forced to return to USA, the responsibility of

---

80. Lau, *From Mission to Church*, 27. The printing press was originally known as the Amelia Bishop Press in recognition of the lady who funded the purchase of the equipment.

81. Hunt, *William Shellabear*, 70. Hunt noted that though "the gentlemanly Straits Times was scrupulous in announcing missionary meetings, it covered temperance activities with mildly ironic disdain." It was somewhat finicky against those moral castigations of the missionaries against the abuses of opium and alcoholic addiction as well as gambling or horseracing. As with regards to The Free Press, which was under the "imperialist" (Hunt's description) editor, W. G. St Clair, it was "more venomous in its contempt for those who pressed for stricter standards of morality."

editing and printing of future publications rested on Shellabear. *Malaysia Message* was not intended to be sectarian and presumably the means whereby missionaries of the different denominations and sending societies are kept abreast of developments within Singapore and Malaysia.[82] It became the main avenue in transmitting information and articles by and about Presbyterians, Brethrens and other Protestant missionaries. Its central focus was dedicated to holiness, consonant with the emphasis of the church of that era as well as Wesley's call for "scriptural holiness in the land." Hence, the Message "came to be identified with the temperance and anti-opium campaign, and the lobbying against legal gambling, for sexual purity, and the enforcement of Sunday as a holiday from paid labour."[83] In many ways it was a tool used in voicing the missionaries' concerns in regard to social reform within the Singapore society.

Beyond just a publishing ministry, Shellabear was intentional in reaching to the Malays. In the initial years in Singapore, he would be present at various open air public entertainment gatherings where crowds gathered and he would preach at these public events, calling out in Malay for a response to the Gospel. The ground proved to be hard, yet within a year, there were some Malays who may be considered as seekers in the Malay Bible study groups that Shellabear and a few other missionaries conducted. The reward to his efforts came in the person of a Malay man, Haji Abdul Shukur[84] who confessed himself a Christian after a few meetings with Shellabear and was baptized as Andreus in the Methodist Church in 1895.[85]

Though the fruits of his labour were not immediately evident, Shellabear persisted in his outreach to the Malays. His studies into the Malay language drew him into a gathering of British and Malay scholars who were gathered as the Straits Branch of the Royal Asiatic Society, which greatly honed his language and translation efforts. Shellabear published a new edition of the *History of the Malays* (*Sejarah Melayu*) in 1895 and

---

82. The *Malaysia Message* was perhaps the first intentional effort in bringing the missionaries from different denominations and missionary organizations together. Prior to this, ecumenical opportunities for such collaboration were perhaps nonexistent. The content of the monthly publications included hearty theological debates. Most notable were the debates between Archdeacon Pelham of the Anglican Cathedral and the Presbyterians on a number of theological issues.

83. Hunt, *William Shellabear*, 71.

84. Minutes of the Malaysia Mission Annual Meeting, 1892, 24.

85. *Malaysia Message*, January 1895, 43. Andreus Shukur was later forced to leave Singapore as he was threatened by local Muslim leaders. *MM, March 1895*, 57.

subsequently a series of printed edition of Malay classical literature that he and a few others had worked upon. He further produced and published both the *Malay-English Vocabulary* and *Practical Malay Grammar*. The motivation for these scholarly pursuits was his firm belief that such were essential tools in the training of future missionaries in Malay language and culture. Relationally, his literary efforts went a long way in forging strong relationships between the printing press, the colonial officials and the local communities. Interestingly, Shellabear was not myopic in his approach, in that he also studied Hokkien (a Chinese dialect) and learned to read Chinese as well and began publication in romanized Hokkien and also in Chinese!

Within a decade, the publishing work Shellabear had embarked upon had expanded into the business of book binding and publishing for markets as far afield as Burma, Taiwan, and Indonesia, and was aptly renamed the Methodist Publishing House (MPH). Shellabear was acutely aware that his calling was primarily with the Malay people, who were the inspiration for his scholarly love for the language and provided the impetus for his various publications. Increasingly he saw the need for a new Malay translation of the Bible for the continued missionary work in Malaya. That dream became a reality for him when under a joint contract with the British and Foreign Bible Society (BFBS) and the Methodist Mission, Shellabear was tasked to revise the Malay Bible.

From 1902 to 1909, Shellabear moved to Malacca to concentrate on this literary work, while he assumed other pastoral duties. There, he formed a church and school, whilst his wife set up a girls' school. By 1904 he had moved the Methodist Pastor Training School to Malacca and took charge of it as well, while acting as District Superintendent for all the Methodists south of the Malay Peninsular including Singapore. In carrying on his work in translation he also continued to be the chief editor of the MPH. Ostensibly, he found that being out of Singapore had freed him from the conflicts in church polity and provided him more opportunities to delve deeper in his study of the Malay language. Shellabear found the opportunity to immerse himself in contemporary Malay culture through his interaction with Malay Muslim teachers[86] and through that gained a definitively positive attitude of Malay culture and of Islam.

---

86. Hunt mentioned in particular a Malay Muslim teacher named Sulaiman bin Muhammed Nur, with whom Shellabear edited two books of Malay proverbs and poetry.

Earlier in the 1890s, the prevalent missionary perception of the Malays was one of "cultural prejudices against their laziness and backwardness in the context of an economically vibrant Chinese population, which was relatively open to both mission schools and conversion to Christianity."[87] As Muslims were generally more resistant to evangelism, those of the Islamic religion tended to elicit a more hostile reception. However, through his interaction with the Malay communities and with the scholars and teachers, Shellabear's opinion of the Malays underwent transformation and he perhaps was numbered as one of those lone voices who argued strongly for the value of Malay vernacular education. In his opinion, ancient Malay cultural traditions were to be regarded as the finest part of Malay society! His assessment of Islam contradicted the popularly held notion that it was but a thin religious veneer for a primarily animistic culture. His interaction with Malay culture led him to understand more clearly how Malay spirituality was derived from a genuine commitment and submission to Allah. In 1915, in an essay written for the Methodist mission, entitled "*The Influence of Islam on the Malay Race*," Shellabear urged for positive changes in attitudes toward the Malays. He further urged that the important role Islam played in the everyday lives of the Malays not be overlooked or underestimated, such that effective evangelistic bridges may be established. Following the tenor of the 1910 Edinburgh Conference, Shellabear also urged the cessation of polemical approaches in evangelism among the Malays and the commencement of establishing points of contact between Muslim spirituality and the Christian faith.

Before he left Malacca, he succeeded in publishing a translation of *The Pilgrim's Progress* in Baba Malay, as well as several scholarly editions of classical Malay literary texts. His crowning achievement was the publication of the *Malay New Testament*, a work, which remained in print up to 1972. He was also able to translate the Old Testament into Malay. The latter work was completed in 1912, and subsequently published in the following year when Shellabear returned to be with his family in the United States.

Shellabear returned to Singapore in 1912 and in his last years in Singapore, Shellabear enjoyed much success in those endeavors, which meant most to him—the establishment of Malay medium schools for girls that soon became the largest in Malaysia. He also published a Baba

---

87. Hunt, "William Shellabear," 29.

Malay Bible to serve the growing community of local Christians and he was able, with the help of Bible Society Colleagues, to eventually establish lasting contacts among the Malay boys in villages around the town center in Singapore. In recognition for scholastic achievements, he was later elected president of the Singapore Branch of the Royal Asiatic Society, which began publishing some of his most significant scholarly works in the journal.

Amidst the great leap forward in establishing these bridges in the Malay communities, Shellabear, however, found himself increasingly estranged from the Methodist mission strategy that had become increasingly dedicated primarily to its English language schools to the neglect of vernacular education. His deteriorating health further forced him to return to the United States. Taking up a position at Kennedy School of Missions in Hartford, Shellabear continued to translate Christian works for publication in Southeast Asia and later joined the faculty full-time at Hartford, teaching the language and culture of the Malays to would-be Methodist missionaries. In this the last stage of his ministry, Shellabear sought to integrate his understanding of evangelism with the religious and cultural appreciation of the Malays, seeking to draw out new missiological approaches. In the 1920s he worked on a new set of evangelistic tracts and later, on the new translation work on the Bible, Shellabear developed a new idea of presenting the Gospel in Malay, through the use of long Malay *sha'irs* (epics in verse forms). He produced *Verses on the Kingdom of God* and *Verses on the Loving Prophet*, convinced that the *sha'ir* format,[88] which the Malays were so fond of would win their attention.

In the 1930s, after a brief setback because of a stroke, Shellabear wrote and published commentaries on the New Testament in Malay. It was only with the outbreak of World War II and the subsequent occupation of Singapore that he lost contact with the Methodist Church in Southeast Asia. By the end of the war his health deteriorated and he could not continue active work as a translator. His last work was a series of translations of the Koran from Arabic to Malay, to be used as a training tool for Christian evangelists in Indonesia.

Shellabear's deep love for the Malay Muslims propelled him, in his final years studying the Koran in greater detail, and accordingly,

---

88. Hunt noted, "The beauty of Shellabear's poetry is obvious. The use of Malay literary conventions and the measured rhythm of the *sha'ir* convey an impression of Jesus moving in a Malay world, without any change to the substance of the story." Hunt, "William Shellabear and His Bible."

the Koran and its interpreters opened his eyes to riches he had not earlier imagined.... Yet despite what his Malay teachers might have wished, these discoveries did nothing to dampen his conviction that Christianity was the one true source of salvation for mankind.[89]

He died in 1948, having lived to see the end of the war, and his own children returning to carry on the work, which he began some fifty years earlier.

PIONEERS OF METHODISM IN SINGAPORE

In short, the story of Methodism involved the establishment of churches along various linguistic lines (English, Tamil, Chinese dialects and Malay) missions to women, the setting up of mission schools and a lucrative printing press. But more than just the various physical establishments, Methodism in Singapore was about the missionaries themselves. Without their passion and perseverance, perhaps the story of Methodism in Singapore would have followed the trajectory of those other missions that have preceded it and might not have left the impact it has in Singapore today. Among the many stellar examples of American Methodism in colonial Singapore, three names are particularly outstanding: William Fitzjames Oldham, Sophia Blackmore and William Girdlestone Shellabear.

As with the founding of Singapore, where Raffles' genius was in the transforming of a pirates' rendezvous into a thriving port, the same could perhaps be said of Oldham's vision and plans for Singapore. He had envisioned the mission as one that had the possibility of stretching to India westward and to China eastward, that stood in stark contrast with the earlier missionaries who perceived Singapore as a stopover, rather than as a centre from which the Gospel would expand geographically. Oldham was unequivocal as he challenged the MEC with the vision he had of Methodism in Singapore:

> The youngest daughter of Methodism in foreign lands was born 28 April 1889.... Our territory is wide, populous, needy.... For the present we have occupied but the one point—Singapore: but this is the strategic point in the archipelago.... Intrenched here we hold out our right hand to India and our left hand to China, and, looking out over the myriads of beautiful islands that lie between us and the land of the Southern Cross, our hearts swell

---

89. Hunt, *William Shellabear*, 2.

with gratitude to Almighty God that our beloved Church will share in bringing the forty millions that inhabit these seas to the knowledge of the truth that is in Jesus.[90]

Oldham's upbringing and short time of ministry in India went a long way in helping him develop his mission model for Singapore. "It has been said of Oldham that there was probably no other person of his years who had a wider acquaintance with missionary history and conditions of that era."[91] Oldham was a practical and perceptive missiologist, for as it turned out, educational missions became for the Methodist missions an increasingly important agency through which churches came to be planted also in the other South East Asian countries of Malaysia, Indonesia and the Philippines. Oldham's vision for the Methodist mission was also not limited only to Singapore but the wider regions around. In a report, Oldham wrote:

> I would say the time has come for us to plant a mission in the Malay Peninsular. The land cries out to us, and many will joyfully receive us. In Borneo another point will be opened. In consultation with our Dutch missionary brethren, whom I had the great pleasure of meeting in Batavia (Java), many points have been tentatively selected. Brother Gaebelin from German Methodism and Brother Leuring, an accomplished linguist from Keil, Germany, are on their way to help us. Says the former, "Java for Jesus is ringing in my soul." Says the latter, "I am yours for Malaysia." To the German branch of Methodism we must look for many more missionaries in the future to work in the Dutch Indies. God grant that "Java for Jesus," and "Sumatra for Jesus," and "All these thronging islands for Jesus," may ring deep in the heart of Methodist.[92]

Oldham and the Methodist missionaries after him laboured tirelessly at educational mission that resulted in the establishment of one of the most widely respected and influential education systems in Southeast Asia. Oldham had come to believed that "the educational mission was part of God's mission and all mission is committed to presenting Jesus

---

90. Oldham, *Missionary Report*, 1889, as quoted in Doraisamy, *Forever Beginning* I, 17.

91. Ho Chee Sin, Oldham, William Fitzjames, in Sunquist et al., *Dictionary of Asian Christianity*, 616.

92. Missionary Report, 1889, 233.

Christ as Truth and Light."[93] His establishment of the schools' ministry in Singapore spread with an intensity that further consolidated the impact of Methodist mission on the migrant population in Singapore and Malaysia. Increasingly, an education in the Methodist schools became very much desired, as evidenced by the enrolment statistics of the schools in the Singapore-Malaysia context.

Concomitantly, the Methodist ministry and mission among the disenfranchised women and girls as well as medical mission, help improved the social status of women and further strengthened the church in Singapore. Oldham's pastoral leadership is evident in his acumen in organizing and establishing the church along linguistic lines. He had built upon Raffles' vision of a cosmopolitan and vibrant port and ventured into a mission that sought to value the different races and ethnicities represented in Singapore. His was a vision of different ethnic communities worshipping one Lord, where diversity in culture is united under a unity in faith.

With the various ministries in place, Oldham's stay in Singapore was temporarily disrupted in view of his failing health. He returned to the United States in 1889 to recuperate and continued to minister as a university lecturer and a pastor in Columbus, Ohio. He was to return to Singapore and to Asia in 1904 as a missionary bishop of the region. Oldham's contributions in the educational missions did not go unnoticed by the colonial office. Hence it was not surprising that upon his return to Singapore, he was requested and later appointed to a government commission to investigate and eradicate the social menace of tobacco and opium addiction in the Colony. Like Wesley, Oldham also led the Methodists in Singapore in legislative and social action against the evils of alcohol, tobacco and opium. In this manner, Oldham "therefore had great influence, directly and indirectly, on the fabric of society in developing Singapore."[94] Hence not only did Oldham establish Methodism in Singapore, he too had in more ways than one, been instrumental in "spreading scriptural holiness" across the lands. The social dimension of Oldham's contribution remains understated but his legacy continues to have impact upon both the ecclesial and social fabric of the Singapore society today.

---

93. Doraisamy, *Oldham*, 44

94. Ho Chee Sin, "Oldham, William Fitzjames," in Sunquist et al., *Dictionary of Asian Christianity*, 616.

His service as missionary bishop in the east was concluded when he undertook new responsibilities as the secretary of the Methodist Board of Foreign Missions and was appointed as General Superintendent of the work in South America in 1916. He visited Singapore for the last time in 1936, at the age of 81, to participate in the jubilee celebrations of the Methodist work in Singapore. The following account attests to the fact that even in his final years, his passion for missions and evangelism did not wane:

> An elderly Chinese man watching the historical pageant which was part of the festivities was the sole surviving member of that group of 30 whom Oldham had addressed 50 years earlier at the Celestial Reasoning Society. As the Chinese sage watched the drama unfold, his soul was deeply stirred and two days later, his old friend, the aged bishop baptized him into the fold in a moving ceremony at Wesley Church.[95]

As much as Oldham is regarded as the prime motivator of the mission work in Singapore, in that same tenor, Sophia Blackmore is to be credited as his equivalent in regards to mission work among women. Blackmore's calling, her compassion, her ministry has left a legacy for the history of Methodism in Singapore. Sensitive to the different religious backgrounds of the various different ethnic communities—the Chinese, Europeans, Indians, Malays and the Peranakans, she and her team of missionary ladies have sought to and often managed to cross of those religious borders through prophetic compassion and through their speech, action and their lives dialogued with those who need to hear the Good News of Jesus Christ. Unwilling to lend tacit support to the existing discrimination in social order, Blackmore and those missionaries after her, have also worked at challenging the evil structures within society through such as educational missions and gave voice to the sufferings of the disenfranchised, the women, the orphans, the weak, the poor, the sick and the imprisoned. Blackmore has brought to Singapore a faith that has "penetrated the life of the people in its multifarious needs. There is the work of compassion as well as of conscience, of individual salvation, rescue and uplift as well as the prophetic voice of judgment and seeking to act as the agent of social and moral change."[96] In such and many

---

95. Ho Chee Sin, "Oldham, William Fitzjames," in Sunquist et al., *Dictionary of Asian Christianity*, 616.

96. Doraisamy, *March of Methodism*, 31.

ways, through the efforts of Methodist missionaries, dignity and certain equality has been restored to the status of women both within the church as well as in the society at large. The healthy state of affairs is reflected in the WFMS Report of 1909:

> To the earnest student of missionary movements, Malaysia, (at that time the term meant the whole of the Malay Archipelago) with its wide opportunities and varied population, is rich in promise for the future. Here an island empire is outline and under the strong and steady control of the British and Dutch Governments a peculiar development is slowly taking place. The new civilization is destined, under God, one day to give these lands, radiant with natural beauty, an important place in Asia's political and commercial life. Perhaps no other agency is accomplishing so much for Malaysia as the schools for boys and girls maintained by our own church. These schools are widely patronized. Former students are now scattered far and wide over the archipelago and may be found helping to sustain the varied enterprises of the church wherever it is located. Newly established Christian homes, though widely separated, are like beacon lights upon a hill, adding their testimony to the value of a Christian education. In five stations in the Malaysia Conference, the Woman's Foreign Missionary Society has established strong educational and evangelistic centres. The work in Singapore, the oldest of these stations, is in a most prosperous condition.[97]

In a subsequent WFMS Report 1918, the following tribute was written in recognition of Sophia Blackmore's ministry. The report referred to Blackmore as the "uncrowned queen" of the mission field in Singapore and noted the impact she has had on the training of women:

> In spite of a climate that has invalided home or sent to heaven nearly two score workers, she has lived to give us thirty years of royal service and is today the uncrowned queen of that mission field. A recent letter says, "Miss Blackmore has been more than the founder of woman whom we could ask to represent us on the social and philanthropic bodies composed of the best ladies in the colony and the Mission has always been represented with dignity and ability second to none." The girls and women she has trained are now holding aloft the banner of the Cross in Java, Sumatra, Borneo and in every city in the Malay Peninsular.

---

97. The general report of the WFMS 1909, as quoted by Doraisamy, *Sophia Blackmore in Singapore*, 64.

Some are teachers, some Bible women and many, happy wives and mothers in Christian homes.[98]

The legacy that Blackmore leaves resonates with and further amplifies that left by Oldham. And like Oldham, the fruits of her labour far exceeds the influence she has had on Singapore itself; it reverberates also from the educational, evangelistic and compassionate ministry that she too brought with her to the neighbouring countries.

The third person whose contributions need to be highlighted is Rev. William Girdlestone Shellabear. Shellabear was one of the few missionaries to the ethnic Malay communities in Singapore and Malaya and was at the same time a scholar, a translator, a church planter, a publisher and in his later years, a missions professor in a seminary. If education in mission schools is tied to Oldham, then mission publications is indissolubly linked with Shellabear. Shellabear's contribution to the expansion of Methodism is in his invaluable contribution in translation and publication of various works into the Malay language. Even more fundamental however is his conviction of reaching the Malays with the Gospel of Jesus. And in this regard, he remained almost as a lone voice (though with the support of Oldham, who was reappointed to the USA). He was convinced that work among the Malays and the Baba Chinese should be central in the work of the Methodist Mission in Singapore. He forwarded his argument in an article in the Malaysia Message in June 1896. This was to be his repeated plea:

> I think that it will be the policy of our mission in the near future to concentrate the efforts of our missionaries upon the settled inhabitants of Malaysia, namely the Malays, Baba Chinese and the more or less uncivilized tribes of the larger islands of this Archipelago. Only among them can we expect to found permanent, living and growing Christian communities.[99]

Shellabear was not of the same view with those who maintained the priority of the English language as a means of social uplift and thereby enabling the communication of rational Christianity. Through his

98. The WFMS Report, 1918, as quoted by Doraisamy, *Sophia Blackmore in Singapore*, 65.

99. *Malaysia Message*, June 1896, 92. Shellabear regarded the migrant Chinese and Indians workers as a transient people, since it was common for these workers to return to the homelands in China or India upon earning a substantial amount of money. This was perhaps his oversight in not envisioning that these migrant workers would in time come also to make Singapore and Malaysia their new home.

experiences in the mission field and his interaction with the Malays, he saw that a dilettantish translation of Christian literature to Malay would do little in reaching the Malays. Similarly, he felt that a Methodist Mission whose ministries did little or nothing for the Malay community would not appeal to them. Hence, Shellabear became increasingly convinced of the significance of vernacular education in regard to the Malay communities. A debate on vernacular education was carried out in the Malaysia Message throughout 1896 where Shellabear urged for a change of mind.

When the 1897 Annual Conference met, the Education Committee opted in favour of an emphasis on education using the English medium, in a tenor that was uncharacteristically condescending. The report stated:

> Let the experiment [in vernacular education] be made by those who feel called to make it, and if the theory that there is no demand for such schools shall give place to a condition that demonstrates their right to be and their usefulness, we can all join in "God speed" to them.
>
> There should be no controversy between those who are interested in such schools and those who are devoted to the development of our Anglo-Chinese schools. The higher education of these Settlements, as in India, is destined to be through the medium of English. It was a great victory won for the cause of Christianity when Dr. Duff and Governor Bentinck defeated the orientalists in the great controversy which determined that the English language and literature, impregnated with Christian thought, was to supplant the effete oriental literatures. Government is therefore, perhaps unconsciously, doing a great missionary work. It may be said that the result is skepticism toward all religion, rather than a true faith in Christianity, but someone has said that skepticism is an impossible condition for any people. The human heart cannot rest in unbelief; so that however discouraging the situation may be at times, the ultimate result must be the triumph of intelligent faith.[100]

---

100. *Report of the Education Committee, Minutes of the Malaysia Annual Conference, 1897*, 40. With regards to the colonial policy on vernacular education, the British East India Company adopted an almost purely western educational policy in most of the places under their jurisdiction. But under Crown Rule, a *laissez faire* policy was often adopted with regard to vernacular education. The arrival of the Methodist in Malaya only served to surface an issue the colonial administration was more than happy to lay dormant. The superiority of an English (Western) rudimentary education was the belief of those in the colonial administration during the time of the Methodist mission.

It must be mentioned that the context for Shellabear's concern in regard to vernacular education for the Methodist Mission included the wider mission field of Malaysia. His concerns were not directed primarily at the schools in Singapore. In view of the success of the Mission school model, many other Methodist schools were being established in the Malay Peninsular. Shellabear's appeal to the Mission Board was not to neglect the majority Malay population in Malaysia and to that end he worked toward a Malay and Straits Chinese society that was more literate in their own vernacular and from thence to expand their role in the colonial society.

Shellabear's emphasis on the vernacular education is undergirded by his deep love for the Malays. Methodism in Malaysia and Singapore may have had greater inroads among the Malays had the Mission then heeded Shellabear's appeal. His seems almost a lone voice in the repeated pleas for the Mission to give more emphasis in regard to the Malays. Where Oldham and Blackmore represented the positive steps of the Methodist Mission, Shellabear perhaps stands as a reminder of the path that Methodist Mission in this part of the world cannot afford to ignore.

CONCLUSION

British colonial administration of Singapore produced economic success in a relatively short time. However amidst the booming success in trade and the profitability of a free port at the southern tip of the Malay Archipelago, Singapore presented a host of other difficulties; social and political for the colonial administrators. And it was precisely in this context that the introduction of Methodism enabled a speedy response as Methodist mission became very quickly grounded within a relatively short time. What the Methodist missionaries achieved in the first decade of their arrival exceed that of the longer established denominations in Singapore. The speed of the binding reaction between the Methodist mission and the local population may be attributed to principally to the missionary zeal of the Methodists and also the *laissez faire* British administration of the colony.

As we survey the early Methodist missions in Singapore, we see that missionaries have brought a faith that was to penetrate the lives of the immigrant population of Singapore in a myriad of ways; through education, through medical mission, through acts of compassion and evangelism. This was the pluriform mission with that Bishop William Oldham and the Methodist pioneers employed in seeking to establish the Methodist Church in Singapore. These were rare "men and women who could cross the boundaries of race, culture and religion with a desire to learn, which was not motivated by the hope of exploitation, and with a respect not created by fear"[101] and we do well never to forget.

---

101. Hunt, *William Shellabear*, 341.

4

Methodist Maneuvers

IN ASIA, CRITICS OF Christian missions have always made much of the complicity in the relationship between the colonial rulers and the missionaries. A moral tone was lent to the mercantilist and adventurist motivation of men like Sir Francis Light and Sir Stamford Raffles by a growing belief that the British Empire was a means of improving and civilizing the world. As a member of the House of Commons noted, "In every quarter of the globe we have planted the seeds of freedom, civilization and Christianity."[1] Understandably so, colonial administrations have often been perceived as sympathetic to Christian missions in regard to the various policies and privileges provided, while the missionaries have been assumed as agents who are in collaboration with and complicit to the colonial administrators. These have been reckoned as mutually beneficial with the presumed ultimate goal of western domination of the East, economically, politically and/or culturally.

CIRCUMVENTING COLONIAL POLICIES

In the case of colonial Singapore, the truth of the matter requires further investigation. American Methodism, one of the later missionary denominations, arrived in Singapore at a time when commerce was foremost the goal of the British colonial administration. Having gained some experience in the administration of the various English colonies in the Indian sub-continent and also in Africa, the British ventured into the East armed

---

1. Huskisson addressing the House of Commons in 1828, cited by Warren, *Missionary Movement from Britain*, 30.

with more jealous zeal in ensuring and preventing missionaries from upsetting the fragile balance of religious sensitivities. Hence, to the East India Company, Christian mission was highly suspect and was regarded more of an encumbrance, rather than an aid. While the Christian ideal was forwarded in the British Parliament, what happened on the ground was perhaps rather tangential. As has been earlier noted, the East India Company's primary concern was trade and it opposed the introduction of missionaries to India and thwarted at every turn the development of the Anglican Church as a separate entity from the EIC-funded colonial chaplaincy. This paradigm was not dissimilar to their ventures into Asia, particularly Malaya and Singapore and was to be finally crystallized in 1874, in the Treaty of Pangkor, which limited the work of the church amongst the Malays as well as denied the Malays any access to the Gospel.

The Treaty of Pangkor, also known as the Pangkor Engagement, might be regarded as one of the significant turning points in the history of Malaya. Interestingly, there seems to be a dearth of research in regard to the ramifications of the treaty on mission in the Malay Peninsula. Furthermore, in those few published research papers, much emphasis is given to the economic-political impact of the Treaty whilst almost nothing has been written in regard to the sociological implications. In an unpublished research paper, Andy Heng Kian Wai commented,

> Curiously however, one branch of history with regards to 1874—be it the factors or dimensions of change, still remains very much untouched until today. That is, its religious aspect. When it comes to Pangkor Treaty, it is extremely difficult to single out a thorough research on its religious impact on, say, Christian-Muslim relations in Malaysia since 1874.[2]

The Treaty of Pangkor is significant as it determined the path that Christian mission was to maneuver in the presence of Islam in the British colonies. Before the arrival of the British and the advent of Christianity, the Islamic faith had been present in the Malay Archipelago. Although it is not possible to offer a precise date for the arrival of Islam in the Malay Peninsula, it is well accepted that Arab traders were familiar with this part of Southeast Asia as early as the ninth century and Islam might have very well been introduced via the process of economic trade.[3] By the

---

2. Heng Kian Wai, "Pangkor Treaty 1874 Revisted," 3. This paper was made available by Scott Sunquist.

3. Hunt, *Islam in Southeast Asia*. Hunt credits four different factors that facilitated

time of the arrival of the British East India Company and the subsequent transfer to direct colonial rule, Islam had taken root and had become entrenched among the people in the Malay Peninsula.

The British East India Company established its first Southeast Asian trading centre in Bengkulu (Bencoolen), on the island of Sumatra as early as 1685. The Company maintained a trading post and a garrison to protect the pepper trade. In looking for alternative routes through the Straits of Malacca, the Company subsequently gained control of Penang[4] in 1786 and later, Singapore and Malacca. Geographically, the Company's trade was very much in tandem with the colonial exploits of the other European powers, in that prior to 1871, the British were careful in following the lead of the other European powers before them, in confining their activities to coastal or island settlements.[5] They were also circumspect with regards to local economics, religious and cultural issues and deliberate in a policy of non-interference with local politics. Historian Nicholas Tarling summarises British interests in Southeast Asia as such:

> Overseas its interests became substantially commercial and economic rather than territorial and political. It saw its dominion in India, begun in the earlier phase, as essential but exceptional. Elsewhere, a combination of strategic positions and economic and political influence should suffice to protect its interests. In Southeast Asia, Britain sought security and stability: it did not necessarily seek to rule, though its power might be felt in other ways.[6]

---

the introduction of Islam to Southeast Asia. These include Islamic politics, rise of Muslim states in India, the spread of Sufi teaching, and also indirectly the advent of European colonialism in this part of Asia. Please refer to 8–21.

4. The Sultan of Kedah had sought military protection from both the Burmese and Siamese forces northward, ceded Penang to the British East India Company in 1786. Captain Francis Light of the British East India Company took formal control of the island on 11 August 1786, renaming it as the Prince of Wales Island (reverted to "Penang" after 1867). The island of Penang was hence the first British possession in the Malay States and Southeast Asia.

5. Interestingly, this keeping to coastal cities finds further corroboration in mission history by Ralph Winter's study, "Four Men, Three Eras, Two Transitions: Modern Missions," in Winter and Hawthorne, *Perspectives on the World Christian Movement*, 253–61.

6. Tarling, "The Establishment of Colonial Regimes," in Tarling, *Cambridge History of Southeast Asia*, 2:5.

Hence by 1826, the ports of Singapore, Penang and Melaka were formed into an administrative unit called the Straits Settlements, that came under British rule, via the Calcutta office. The Indian Mutiny that is a milestone in the colonial history of India also presented a ripple effect for the colonial administration in Southeast Asia. In the successful quelling of the Indian Mutiny and the full transfer and assumption for colonial administration for the Straits Settlements by the Colonial Office in London in 1867, greater political and economic influence, not restricted to the trading ports, became much more possible and perhaps even more contingent if the British were to maintain their trade supremacy in these parts of the world.

The attractions of the interior of the Malay Peninsula were not lost on the British who were keen to expand on the West coast for the mining of tin and the establishment of plantations. The competition among the other European nations in the race toward carving out a piece of the lucrative Chinese trade and greater access to the spice trade further fuelled a greater involvement of the British with the local sultans in seeking out other possibilities. One of those was the increasingly important and lucrative tin industry. British merchants in Penang and Malacca were seeking to capitalize on the tin industry and so too were the astute Chinese merchants, who as early as 1862 were competing among the rival clans for control of the tin trade.

When the ruling Sultan of Perak died in 1871, the different Chinese clans backed up the two major rival claimants to the throne, Raja Abdullah and Raja Ismail, creating a power struggle for succession. In the ensuing political chaos, the British, who had control of the trading ports of Malacca, Penang and Singapore, found themselves with a much cherished opportunity to render their "aid" in settling this political dispute.

Reverting from their initial support of Raja Ismail, the British finally lent their weight behind Raja Abdullah and managed to wrestle control in his favour on the condition that he agreed to the establishment of a British Resident, in assisting in the administration, from whom advice "must be asked and acted upon on all questions other than those touching upon Malay religion and custom."[7]

In one sense, as the first Resident-General of the Federated Malay States, Sir Frank Swettenham had claimed, the British colonial

---

7. Records of the Colonial Office, as quoted by Heussler, *British Rule in Malaya*, 55.

administration, Her Majesty's Government was "invited, pushed, and persuaded"[8] to interfere in the affairs of the Malay States. What is equally pertinent is the view that the decision "was prompted by fear that if the disordered conditions in some of the states were not ended some other power might be invited to intervene."[9] Cognizant that the other rival European powers of Germany and France might take advantage of the political upheavals to establish their respective hegemony, the British acted surely and swiftly in support of the rightful, though weaker heir of the Perak throne, Raja Abdullah did not have the potential or the power to decline this sinecure. Through this political compromise, the British was able to use this Residential system of indirect rule to exercise British political hegemony, first in Perak in 1874, and by 1895, to the rest of the Federated Malay States. This deft political manoeuvre was by no means unchallenged by the locals as evident in the assassination of the first Resident of Perak, J. W. W. Birch, within a year of his appointment.

The establishment of the Resident was a significant milestone in making the British presence increasingly felt in the Malay Peninsular. This was ratified by the signing of the Pangkor Treaty in 1874 between the British, represented by Sir Andrew Clarke, and Sultan Abdullah of Perak. Signed on 20 January 1874 on the island of Pangkor, off Perak, the treaty installed Abdullah as Sultan of Perak and gave the British Resident strong "advisory" powers that were less consultative than they were coercive. The Treaty of Pangkor is significant in the history of Malaysia as it marks the beginning of official British involvement, though supposedly indirect, in the policies of the Malay States. While initially it dealt primarily with the state of Perak, the scope was increasingly enlarged to include the rest of the "Malay states" in Perlis, Kedah, Kelantan, Terengganu and Johor. Through the installation of a colonial advisor to each of the Sultans, the other Malay States soon also came under British influence, albeit listed as indirect rule.

While there are different perceptions of British political "interference," not the least of which is the strengthening of British colonial control in Southeast Asia, British presence is also described as precipitated by the instability of the Malay states. In this process of a widening British political hegemony, it must not be forgotten that foremost on the British agenda in developing the residential system of indirect rule was the

8. Swettenham, *British Malaya*, vi.
9. Cowan, *Nineteenth Century Malaya*, 175.

desire for stability in order to ensure ongoing trade and prosperity. The British administration would not allow the increasing numbers of Chinese rival factions to disrupt, jeopardize or usurp their control of another lucrative commodity, in this case, tin. Michael Stenson commented that "The dominant reality . . .was the development of large-scale mining and plantation agriculture, with the assistance of foreign capital and imported foreign labor."[10] British intervention was limited in geographical scope as well as in the form, albeit as mandatory advisors and it seems that the "British went only as far as they needed."[11]

Be that as it may, the impact of the Pangkor Treaty should not be underestimated. The truth of the matter is that the Treaty of Pangkor may indeed be regarded as the cornerstone of British colonial policy toward the different states in the Malay Archipelago. Despite the lack of scholarship[12] in regard to the significance of the Treaty, Moses Ponniah's succinct detailing of its impact then and now underscores the magnitude of the Pangkor Engagement:

> In 1874, the Treaty of Pangkor with the Malay rulers paved the way for the British who slowly but surely influenced the Malay states till the whole peninsula came under British rule. The Christian religion was sacrificed in favour of mere trade, for the treaty required non-interference in local religion. It became the hallmark of the British system to maintain a Christian presence solely for the colonial masters. This policy had a twofold effect on the history of Christian-Muslim relations in this nation. First, the sultans of each state have become the heads of the Muslim religion, and this right is entrenched in the Constitution of the nation. Secondly the Malays have been denied the privilege of receiving the Gospel. . . . Whatever detailed adjustments might be made to this view, the treaty of 1874 underlies the clause in the present Constitution which provides religious freedom but forbids propagation of other religions to the Malays.[13]

Among the fourteen clauses of the Treaty, perhaps Clause VI was to have the most significant impact on Christian mission in the colony. The Clause reads that the Sultan would receive a British Resident whose advice

---

10. Stenson, *Class, Race and Colonialism*, 14.

11. Tarling, *Cambridge History of Southeast Asia*, 2:29.

12. Internet and ATLA searches for "Pangkor Treaty" or "Pangkor Engagement" yield only a handful of results (if any at all) most of which are not of any significance.

13. Ponniah, "Situation in Malaysia," 31–34.

had to be sought and adhered to in all matters except those pertaining to the religion and customs of the Malays. While it is true that nothing explicit *de jure*, was established in regard to missionary efforts, yet "it was widely believed, among the European circles then, that *de facto*, missionary work was forbidden, thanks to the controversial clause, 'except those touching the Malay religion and customs.'"[14] Hence the Clause made it almost impossible for the propagation of the Gospel among the Malays. This perhaps is most evident when a cursory comparison is made of Christian missionary activity and the number of converts pre-1874 and post-1874. Both missionary activities as well as the number of converts were drastically reduced post-1874 when various Malay sultans invoked Clause VI of the Treaty to curtail church work in the Malay States.

Likewise, British sensitivities to the Malay clause in the Pangkor Treaty were to have direct ramifications on the colonial administration of Singapore. Unlike the rest of Peninsular Malaysia that had a majority Malay (Muslim) population, Singapore's free trade status was a magnet to the many ethnic groups who travelled to the port-city in search of trading and job opportunities. Yet the Treaty was to have the same effect in regard to the manner in which the British viewed mission work among the Malays in Singapore, which presented a unique case in the administration of the colony.

In the history of British colonialism, not many of the colonies presented a problem such as the case in Singapore. Singapore's increasingly multi-ethnic population presented new challenges for the British colonial administration and the policy devised was to locate the various ethnic groups into different residential and communal enclaves, in accordance with the colonial "divide and rule policy." It was part of the colonial administration's tacit policy that

> communal groups usually clustered around certain districts . . . and created a typical plural society bound by an economic nexus under British colonial administration. . . . Apart from these loose ties . . . there were few things that the inhabitants of Singapore had in common. Instead, there were many racial, religious, cultural and linguistic differences to divide them.[15]

Thus, while the different ethnic groups, such as the immigrant Chinese (the majority) and Indians, indigenous Malay and various others,

---

14. Basri, *Christian Mission*, 22.
15. Yen Ching Hwang, *Social History of the Chinese*.

contributed to the economic development of the trading port, the colonial administration did little (or perhaps nothing) to develop a sense of cohesion within or between these communities. Again, this underscored the fact that British interests in Singapore were purely economic and all other issues were incidental and peripheral. These issues warranted attention only when they had direct consequences on the trade revenue.

In regard to the different ethnic groups in Singapore, the population of local Malays was not significant. Of the Javanese who immigrated, the Resident of Singapore from 1823 to 1826, John Crawfurd had earlier described them as "very good natured, docile and accessible and by no means wanting in intelligence."[16] The Indian migrants presented considerably fewer problems in part, due to the longer history of British colonial rule in India. In the wake of an ever increasing Chinese immigrant population, it was regarded as advantageous for the British colony to encourage greater volume of Indian immigrants because "in a country like this, the preponderance of any one Eastern nationality should not be excessive and because the Indians are a peaceable and easily governed race."[17] It was the Chinese immigrants who presented a conundrum for the colonial administration.

As Singapore's entrepot trade burgeoned, it attracted an exodus of migrant workers from the areas surrounding as well as from places further afield such as India and China. By 1836, the Chinese had become the predominant ethnic group, constituting 45.9 percent of the population. They comprised half the population of Singapore by 1840 and by 1901, the Chinese immigrants made up 72.1 percent of the population; almost three out of every four persons in Singapore at the turn of the century was a Chinese!

---

16. Crawfurd, "Notes on the Population of Java," 42.

17. CO273/148 435 of 15 Oct. 1887 Weld to Holland enclosing Weld's address to the Legislative Council 13 Oct. 1887.

Table 4: A Comparision of Singapore's Ethnic Population Ratio[18]

Ethnicity	1836		1840		1901	
	No.	%	No.	%	No.	%
Chinese	13749	45.9	17704	50.0	164041	72.1
Malays, Japanese and other Malays	12538	41.7	13200	37.3	35988	15.8
Indians	2932	9.9	3375	9.5	17.47	7.8
Europeans	141	0.5	–	–	2831	1.3
Arabs	41	0.1	–	–	919	0.4
Others	583	1.9	1110	3.2	5986	2.6
Total	29984	100.0	35389	100.0	226842	100.0

Source: Edwin Lee, *The British as Rulers: Governing Multi Racial Singapore*, (Singapore: Singapore University Press, 1991) xiii–xiv.

The immigrant Chinese population was not homogenous. They were organised through their dialect associations and the five dialect groups that dominated the migrants were the Hokkiens, Teochews, Cantonese, Hakkas and the Hainanese.[19] Most of these Chinese immigrants were housed in the area now known as Chinatown. This was in the plans drawn up by Raffles as early as 1822, designating the area southwest of the Singapore River for the Chinese immigrants, which was part of his more circumspect planning to zone future developments, such as planning for the area northeast of the river (the current Padang area) for government use. In this manner, Raffles' town planning directed even different dialect groups of Chinese immigrants into different enclaves within Chinatown. He went much further in differentiating the Chinese immigrants by their class such as merchants, artisans, coolie labour, which is evidenced in the close association between a particular occupation and the enclaves around Chinatown. An example of this is the predominance of undertakers along a street in Chinatown called Sago Lane that came to be known

---

18. The figures for European and Arab population were not available for the year 1840.

19. Though all these dialect groups hailed from South China, yet apart from what is common in Chinese culture, the immigrants tended to look out for those who shared a common place of origin or spoke a common dialect. And as most of these dialect clans (termed as *hoey guan* in dialect *or huiguan* 会馆 in Chinese) rivaled each other in China, they similarly imported their rivalries, in the form of secret societies/triads, to Singapore.

as "*sei yan kai*," literally meaning "street of the dead" in Cantonese.[20] It was along these ethnic/dialect lines that the Hokkiens dominated the area around Telok Ayer and the waterfront, the Teochews along Singapore River (Clarke Quay) and around Fort Canning, the Cantonese and the Hakkas further out at Kreta Ayer.

The Chinese immigrants were often dependent on their own dialect guilds or associations, known as *huiguan* (会馆), in adjusting to life in the new environment, such as with initial accommodation, keeping in contact with their hometowns as well as helping make funeral arrangements. The leaders in the guilds often acted as middlemen between the Chinese communities and the colonial administration. As these are drawn along dialect lines, clan rivalries among the different Chinese dialect groups were not uncommon. It had been reported by the colonial secretary that, "the history of this Settlement is sufficiently known to your Grace to render it unnecessary that I should dilate on the turbulent nature of its larger Chinese population and their proneness to break into disorder."[21]

As to the cause of the Chinese rivalries and riots in Singapore, historians hold various views. Some linked the secret society riots to the lucrative underground opium trade that the various clans were involved in. Another historian, Lee Poh Ping[22] attributed the instability to the unrestricted immigration policy of the British that welcomed the barrage of Chinese who were seeking better economic prospects. Given the tumultuous history of China in the nineteenth century, the opportunism of a liberal British immigration policy only served to throw open, unchecked, a welcome to a ragtag group of refugees, rebels, ruffians and racketeers. To Lee, this British policy while it supplied the demand for labour exacted a price in the form of public riots and social instability. Edwin Lee picks up on Lee's point and traces the root cause to the tremendous social dislocation and upheavals in nineteenth century China. At a time of paroxysms in China, similar upheavals in Singapore included such unrests as the Hokkien-Teochew Riots of 1854, the Coolie and Samseng Riots from 1871–1873, Riots against the Contagious Disease Ordinance and Conservancy Act in 1872.[23] All these unrests precipitated the Governor of Singapore, Sir Harry Ord to comment:

20. Thulaja, "Sago Lane."
21. CO273/22 203 of 8 Oct. 1868 Ord to Kimberly.
22. Lee Poh Ping, *Chinese Society*, 27–30, 55–58, 64–81.
23. Please refer to Lee, *British as Rulers*, 35–43, for a summary of each of these riots and the actions taken to quell the unrest.

> Of late years, the civil wars which have been waged in the interior of the country (China) have raised up bands of men who have gone about fighting and plundering on their own account until put down by the authorities, when such have been fortunate to escape with life have been obliged to fly the country.... Many of these miscreants have during the last year or two found their way to the Straits.... We have now amongst us a larger and more dangerous element of discord than we has before.[24]

The problem of the Chinese immigrants continued to escalate to such an extent that it warranted a Commission of Enquiry, that identified these thugs as "samsengs."[25] The report noted:

> It is here to be remarked that the number of the "samsengs" or fighting men, in the Straits has during the past two years very sensibly increased And this is due to the fact that the Mandarins have of late years been clearing out hordes of rowdies and bad characters who have infested a district (Tay Chew), near Swatow. Numbers of these roughs and bad characters who have escaped with their lives, have been brought to the Straits by sailing and steam vessels and are now infesting this Colony with their presence. These men accustomed to live in their own country by plunder and violence, bring with them the lawless habits they have acquired. They are attached to the various secret societies existing in the Colony, and pay implicit obedience to the orders, whatever they may be, given them by the headmen.[26]

As the problem escalated in the face of increased number of immigrants, the British colonial administration sought a solution. Adapting from the Dutch *kapitan* system,[27] the Colonial Secretary J. Douglas Dunlop crystallised a proposal that required an administrator, who was thoroughly conversant with some Chinese dialects and one who was able to create "a strong personal government in which administrators are brought into intimate relations with the people."[28] The duty of such an

---

24. *CO273/57 29 dated 2 May 1872, Ord to Kimberley.*

25. "Samseng" is the Hokkien equivalent for fighting man, that is, a thug or hooligan, one who is out to create unrest through violence.

26. *CO273/65 24 of 20 Jan. 1873, Ord to Kimberley enclosing Report of Commission of Enquiry on the Oct. 1872 riots.*

27. In the period of the Portuguese and Dutch colonial rule in Malaysia, the Portuguese and Dutch appointed *kapitans*, chiefs or headmen to keep a check on the various ethnic communities.

28. *Report of Inspector General of Police, S.S. for the year 1875 PLCSS 1876 ccxxiii.*

administrator also included the registration of the secret societies and of the Chinese merchantile firms and the title ascribed was "the Protector of the Chinese."[29] His duties included the licensing of the coolie brokers and their recruiting agents as well as the examining the circumstances of each coolie to prevent excesses and/or abuses connected with the coolie traffic, such as fraud and kidnap.[30] Though the immediate issue at hand was the social unrests created by the clans and the associated secret societies, as they clamoured for a share of the revenue as well as the loyalties of the immigrant workers, there were also the attendant issues of female Chinese immigrants who were arriving in greater numbers to work as domestic helpers as well as the exploitation of such for prostitution, especially in view of a hugely unbalanced ratio of male immigrants.

The Governor, Sir William Jervois, accepted the recommendations and thereafter depots were established for the immigrants. The dual post of Protector for the Chinese Immigrants and Protector of the Chinese Emigrants was appointed to the Chinese Interpreter, W.A. Pickering, in 1877. Pickering became the first Protector of the Chinese in Singapore.[31] He was among the first of the British officials in Singapore who could speak fluent Mandarin and Hokkien, thereby gaining the trust of many of the Chinese merchants. He was to serve in this capacity for a decade before one of the secret societies sent out an axe-wielding thug to prevent him from meddling in the affairs of the secret societies. Pickering survived that attempt but stepped down from his post, which was assumed by Sir Cecil Clementi Smith. Sir Cecil Clementi Smith enforced a Banishment Order, and an 1889 Societies Ordinance came into effect in 1890, that almost effectively wound up most of the overt operations of the secret societies.

METHODISTS AND EVANGELISM

It is against this backdrop of colonial administration of "divide and conquer" that the Methodist missionaries arrived toward the close of the nineteenth century. The government of this increasingly thriving British colony "continued to be defined along ethnic lines: the ethnic enclaves of Chinatown, Geylang Serai and Little India illustrate how racially divided

---

29. *Report of Inspector General of Police, S.S. for the year 1876* PLCSS 1876 ccxlviii.

30. For a more detailed discussion of the Protector's job description, please refer to chapter 6 of Lee, *British As Rulers*, 75–102.

31. Turnbull, *History of Singapore*, 86–90.

Singapore was."³² But this too proved to be an important means whereby American Methodism took root in Singapore. Where the colonial policy was to "divide and rule," Oldham "perfected a design of missions within a mission,"³³ organising mission along linguistics/ethnic lines. In the establishment and growth of the Methodist Church in Singapore, this practice of "divide and rule" was never challenged by the church, be it the Anglican or Presbyterian Church and also the Methodist mission. The early Methodist pioneers worked within this colonial administration to their own advantage.³⁴ The Methodist missionaries accepted this scheme of colonial administration and developed a missionary strategy, if we can talk of one, to their advantage.

Within a short span of time from the first arrival, the English Mission was organized. John Polglase, an English Wesleyan, who worked as the Assistant Secretary of the Singapore Municipality, was appointed a Local Preacher and outreach work among British soldiers, sailors and staff of the colonial administration was carried out. It was from among these that Oldham later recruited the assistance of William Shellabear in the Malay and publications work. As with most churches established in the early history of the colony, this first Methodist Church which met at the Town Hall attracted a majority of the colonial fraternity, mainly from the other denominations and also from the Roman Catholic Church. Oldham with the assistance of Polglase, worked tirelessly and drew up plans for the construction of a church building on land granted by the colonial administration. The first Methodist church was hence built at the junction of Coleman Street and Canning Rise³⁵ and dedicated for service on December 15, 1886, within two years of the arrival of the Methodists. The location of the church is significant as it was almost equidistant between the centre of the colonial administration buildings and from

---

32. Speech by RADM(NS) Teo Chee Hean at the opening ceremony of the 1997 pre-university seminar, "Singapore as Best Home: From Scenarios to Strategies" on 3 June 1997, at NUS.

33. Doraisamy, *Oldham*, 50.

34. The author has requested permission from the Land Transport Authorities for the inclusion of a map of Singapore in 1888. The map would be a vivid illustration of how the colonial administration divided the town in their planning. The fact that the Methodist mission would plant their churches and ministries in these different enclaves is a testimony of the ingenuity of the early missionaries to circumvent the colonial administrative policies and praxes. Permission for the map is still pending.

35. A simple architecture model of the first church at Coleman Street is housed at the Methodist archives, Singapore.

Chinatown, where the Chinese immigrants were settled. The church was also located within the vicinity of the Indian immigrant enclaves.

From this "centre of operations,"[36] the Methodist mission fanned out and established a work among the Tamils, Malays and the Chinese immigrants. If the colonial policy was to "rule through division," the Methodist mission worked on that principle in establishing "pluriform missions" along linguistic lines. Besides establishing the first Methodist Church among the English-speaking, there were also simultaneous attempts to reach the non-English speaking in Singapore. This was begun amongst Tamils whose language Oldham spoke, having been raised in India. Within a short few months, the Tamil Church was established in 1887. As more Methodist missionaries arrived, work was simultaneously initiated among the dialects-speaking Chinese community as well as the local Malays and Straits-Chinese. Hence within the first three years of the arrival, the English church was established and mission work was carried out among the Tamil immigrants, the Malays, the Straits-born Chinese and the Chinese immigrants.

Within a decade of the arrival of the Methodist missionaries, that is, by 1895, the Chinese mission in Singapore was conducting meetings in all the major dialects in Singapore. This was made possible through the partnership of Chinese Christian immigrants who were themselves evangelized by the missionary endeavours of the MEC-South in Southern China. It should be noted that the Chinese mission was somewhat hindered by the rapid turnover of converted immigrants, as they returned to China after a few years in Singapore.[37]

The pluriform mission is also understood as "integrated evangelism"[38] by missiologist and former Bishop of the Malaysian Methodist Church, Rev. Dr. Hwa Yung. He attributes the strength of the Methodist mission as one that was integrative, bringing together the three strands of evangelism, rescue work and education. The pioneer missionaries did not regard the social outreach through rescue work and through education as secondary to the call of missionary endeavour in Singapore but rather as true to the Methodist call to "spread scriptural holiness" throughout the land. These were but channels through which more could be impacted with the

---

36. Doraisamy, *Forever Beginning I*, 16.

37. There are a few accounts of prominent Chinese who returned and served as leaders in their communities. These include Liang Ah Fa, one of the first Chinese converts as well as Li Deng Hui. Please see Earnest Lau, "Teaching Moral Education."

38. Hwa Yung and Hunt, *Methodist Church in Malaya*.

Gospel of Jesus in more tangible aspects. Though much has been said of the significance of Methodist efforts at education as well as rescue work, Hwa and Hunt provide another perspective in asserting that important as these efforts in education and rescue work are in any historical account of the Methodist work in Singapore, "they played a relatively minor role compared with the wide range of explicitly evangelistic ministries."[39]

This wide range of explicit evangelistic ministries included house visitations, distribution of evangelistic tracts, open-air preaching at various occasions or events, including various ethnic festivals. True to the Wesleyan spirit, the salvation proclaimed in the Methodist churches evangelistic outreach was invariably twofold; the first of which is the promise of eternal life and freedom from the fear of hell, and the second, the promise of freedom from the bondage of sin, that was manifested in such social vices common among the working classes such as drinking, opium taking and gambling. These early Methodist pioneers did not merely preach a Gospel whose spiritual benefits were reserved for the future but brought to the largely immigrant population a message of salvation even in the here and now. The Good News of Jesus was to have direct ramifications in the everyday details of their lives.

Much has been recorded of the Methodist visitations that were diligently carried out by Oldham or Blackmore and later by the local preachers and subsequent missionaries.[40] This practice of visiting the homes of the people in order to encourage them to allow their children to be educated or as a practical show of care and love for the sick and disenfranchised may seem like a normal "pastoral duty." Hwa noted that "these activities were all carried out as part of an overall strategy whose success was carefully monitored."[41] This is evident in the statistical records in the

39. Hwa Yung and Hunt, *Methodist Church in Malaya*. This highlights the numerous explicitly evangelistic efforts of the Methodist mission, which are often eclipsed by the educational mission. The quantitative and speedy growth of Methodism in Singapore is perhaps achieved more through these evangelistic ministries than through the evangelism in the schools ministry. It should be noted that the Methodist mission employed whatever resources they had in enlarging the ministries. Their emphasis on schools and rescue work as described in the following pages depict the enthusiasm with which the mission was also invested wholeheartedly.

40. The reports of these home visits and various stories of conversions may be found in the conference journals containing the conference reports of the missionaries as well as the women's work of the Women's Foreign Missionary Society, at the Methodist Archives, Singapore. These reports were submitted to the annual conference, which were held since 1888.

41. Hwa Yung and Hunt, *Methodist Church in Malaya*.

Annual Conference Journals in regard to home visitations, where the details on the distribution of tracts, the meetings held and responses to the outreaches conducted are carefully noted.

The Methodist mission spared no efforts in training the local converts to partner in the ministry of home visitation and in evangelism. Chinese women converts were trained as "Bible Women" whose main bulk of ministry included home visitation. New converts were urged to share their testimonies at the various meetings and rallies conducted and Hwa noted:

> Virtually every committed lay person was pressed into service as a lay preacher or local pastor. Before 1900 practically every male full member was listed in the Journal as either an exhorter or a local preacher. In this period evangelism was closely linked with leadership development as with education. At least as far as Asians were concerned the leadership roles most wanted were those of converts committed to public witness to what Christ had done for them.[42]

Based upon ethno-linguistic considerations, these multi-lingual and multi-pronged approaches worked as an effective strategy for the growth of Methodism in Singapore. As rightly pointed out by Doraisamy,[43] Oldham's organization of the mission along these four languages is prophetic, in that these four languages came to be recognised as the official languages of the Republic of Singapore,[44] when she gained independence from the United Kingdom in 1965.

As highlighted earlier, this pluriform mission was simultaneously carried out through the various Methodist leaders; while tending to some of the English speaking congregation members, the Methodist mission quickly moved to minister among all the different ethnic groups present in Singapore as well as the Malays. While the Methodist mission had a certain freedom to work among the different races, there was however, a particular sensitivity in regard to ministry among the Malays, especially in view of the Pangkor Treaty. The Treaty of Pangkor in 1874 marked a new phase of British colonial administration. While the tenor of the Treaty was economically and politically motivated, the main concession to the Malays, that their religion and customs would not be interfered

---

42. Hwa Yung and Hunt, *Methodist Church in Malaya*.

43. Doraisamy, *Oldham*, 50.

44. Please refer to http://www.visitsingapore.com/publish/stbportal/en/home/about_singapore/demographic_and_geograhical/people_language_.html.

with, acted as a brake to missionary work amongst the Malays. Before the arrival of the Methodists, Loh Keng Aun in chronicling the Anglican Church in the region stated that "no missionary work among the Muslim Malays was considered; and their faith has always been respected."[45]

It was against such a context that Methodist missions arrived and while it may be said the full ramifications of the Treaty is perhaps more explicitly guarded in the context of Peninsular Malaysia than in Singapore, the Methodist mission work among the Malays was perhaps cautious so as not to upset Malay sensitivities. The Malay Mission in Singapore was established under a local preacher Alexander Fox and was carried on for a couple of years under William Shellabear and various short term Chinese assistants or WSFM teachers. Evangelistic efforts among the Malays differed significantly from those among the other races and from the beginning there was minimal participation from all the missionaries. It was only those missionaries who had a reasonable command of the Malay language who were set aside for this work. In the pioneering years, street preaching in Malay was the mode of sharing the Gospel in that it was not coercive and any Malay or Straits-born Chinese, who was conversant in Malay could stop and listen to the preachers. In a report of street preaching, which appeared in an American paper (GIAL, 1889), Oldham wrote:

> The younger missionaries, however, though teaching in the school, are making the acquisition of the language their chief pursuit, and in consequence of this I rejoice to report the beginnings of street preaching in the Malay quarters of Singapore.
>
> A party of three ladies, headed by sister Blackmore (W.F.M.S.) and three men, Dr. West, brother Munson and Captain Shellabear, a godly officer of the British army proceed to "Kampong Rochore" or "Telok Blangah" and commence to sing "kita berlayer." . . .
>
> Pray for Singapore. As they get the language better these missionaries will make it hotter for their audiences and we may expect the Holy Ghost to convince these poor, darkened ones. You pray while we preach.[46]

Street preaching was perhaps one of the methods employed very early on. It became increasingly evident however, that street evangelism was not accepted or even tolerated in the Malay kampongs. Few Muslims were drawn to preaching rallies and by 1891, the Methodist missionaries

---

45. Loh Keng Aun, *Fifty Years of the Anglican Church*, 5.
46. As quoted by Doraisamy, *Forever Beginning I*, 16.

established a church that had regular preaching in Malay, but this was primarily attended by the Straits Chinese congregation.[47] For the Methodist missionaries, who were cognizant of Muslim sensitivities, reaching the Straits-born Chinese, who used the Malay language, also kept the hope of eventually penetrating the wider harvest in the Malay Peninsula.

Later, more systematic work amongst Malays was initiated by Rev. William G. Shellabear. Shellabear and his helpers focused on visitation and education as means of sharing the Gospel. But even these other means proved difficult. In most cases the local Muslim religious teacher (*imam*) would be aware of these missionary activities and give explicit warnings to the villagers to avoid the Methodist missionaries. Through the avenue of literacy training by WSCS missionaries for women and girls, significantly amicable relationships were established among the Muslims but even so, Muslim converts were few and far between. It was reported that Fanny Shellabear visited one home eighty times before she managed to persuade the parents to enroll their daughter in school. The tireless effort of the Shellabears and other like-minded missionaries helped form a small congregation of Malay and Straits-born Chinese, which regrettably did not last. This was due primarily to the resistance of the Malay community, where race was synonymous with religion. As the smaller ethnic group in an ever increasing multi-cultural trading port, the Malays cherished their slower pace of life and did not see the importance or even the need for colonial influences of economic pursuits and material comforts. Religiously, Muslims were also cautious in regard to evangelism and perhaps all the more from the westerners, since it was not easy to distinguish between a British and an American.

But the decline of the Malay work may also be attributed to the fact that there was also a lack of dedicated workers in the field. Shellabear, the main person involved in the Malay mission work, was increasingly burdened with other responsibilities, especially those of the printing press. That in particular, further exacerbated the situation. When his wife died in 1895, Shellabear returned to England to recuperate. When he came back to Singapore in 1896 to assume the appointment of the Presiding Elder of the Singapore District, the Malay congregation was already in a state of permanent decline.

---

47. This was known early on as the "Malay Church" and was the initial church plant for what is known today as Kampung Kapor Methodist Church, which until today still has a Peranakan (that is, Straits-born Chinese) congregation.

As Presiding Elder, Shellabear defended vernacular education, especially among the Malays, but from the turn of the twentieth century onward, except for some medical relief in the *kampungs* (villages), the Methodists virtually abandoned most of the missionary efforts to convert the resistant Malays. There were some plans fielded afresh in 1916 for a missionary to be assigned anew to the Singapore project abandoned a decade earlier, but these plans were halted when Shellabear was unable to continue his ministry in Malaya. This work among the Malays is another important area of ministry of the Methodists that argues against any complicity or collusion of the Methodist mission with the colonial administration. While Her Majesty's Government was eager to uphold Clause VI of the Pangkor Treaty in view of Muslim sensitivities, the Methodists were unwilling to ignore the spiritual condition of the Malays in Singapore and to that end, persisted in ministering among the Malays, despite the potential perils of upsetting colonial policies. It was later "abandoned," in view of the more rapidly growing ministries and the lack of a suitable person to spearhead the work among the Malays.

METHODISTS AND EDUCATION

Besides the Methodist emphasis on evangelism, perhaps the most lasting legacy of the Methodist mission in Singapore is their work in the area of education. It has been said that it is Methodism that "has given us the founders of our Schools, the principals and the teachers who have made and continue to make our schools what they are today."[48] As has been noted in the previous chapter, Oldham's intention to venture into education was birthed in response to the requests by the Chinese merchants and what began as a modest means of education became one of American Methodism's more significant works in Singapore.

The educational policy of the East India Company is described best as non-interference. This *laissez faire* policy is best summarized by the Report of the Calcutta University Commission in 1919:

> It was no part of the policy of the East India Company during the first two generations of its dominion in Bengal to impose a western or English system of education upon its Indian subjects. . . . India would profit most if she were left free to cultivate

---

48. Ho Seng Ong, *Methodist Schools in Malaysia*, 65.

her own ancient learning and her own system of though without interference.[49]

This *laissez faire* policy equally applied to Singapore and the Malay Peninsular in the early history of education in the Straits Settlements. Whilst the India Act of 1833 advocated western education through the medium of English, there were also advocates for vernacular education. It was a review of the education policy in 1854 that adopted a model of educational policy that was aimed at encouraging educational agencies, be they religious or otherwise, to provide basic instruction with the aid of public funds under the inspection and direction of the colonial administration. While it cannot be said that the British colonial administration was indifferent to the education of the locals, however, the administration concerned itself primarily with elementary education, where more emphasis was provided in regard to vernacular education. In brief:

> British policy toward the Malays was based on the fundamental division in traditional Malay society between the rulers and the ruled . . . (and) a system of public instruction in the vernacular for the broad mass of the Malay peasantry on one hand and the successive attempts to provide a select number of Malays, for the most part the sons of Rajas and Chiefs, with an education in English on the other.[50]

What applied to Malaya was also pertinent to Singapore as the three ports of Penang, Malacca and Singapore and the whole of the Malay Peninsular was collectively termed as Malaya. It was this *laissez faire* "climate" of the colonial administration that gave the Methodist mission space to start their educational work in Singapore. In establishing the education ministry, the Methodist mission sought the support of the British colonial administration and very often they worked within the framework circumscribed by the colonial educational policies.

Prior to the Indian Mutiny, Singapore's ethno-linguistically varied immigrant settlement was governed by the British Crown through its India Office sited at Calcutta. Much of the funding was drawn from the Indian Treasury. Hence, the colonial administration was not willing to fund various projects for which it was not the immediate beneficiary and one of these was the education of Singapore's predominantly immigrant population. The colonial administration was not interested in spending

---

49. As quoted by Chelliah *Short History of Educational Policy*, 7.
50. Stevenson, *Cultivators and Administrators*, 47.

its resources on educating a transient population in English, since they ultimately cherished the hope of returning to their homelands. The one purpose for an English education was to supply candidates for nearly the whole of the subordinate appointments in mercantile colonial administration in the Colony and Native States and for clerical and other appointments in mercantile houses.[51]

The Indian Mutiny brought about the transfer of power from the East India Company to direct Crown rule. Physically, the rule was transferred from the Indian Office at Calcutta to London's Colonial Office in 1867. From 1867, Singapore was governed directly by London through the two offices of the Legislative Council in Singapore and the Secretary of State for the Colonies.

In regard to education, the administration had by 1870 adopted the policy of providing free elementary vernacular education in Malay for the indigenous population and set up a few Malay schools in the rural areas for this purpose. At the time of the arrival of the Methodist mission, the provision of an English education was not seen as vital for the general population. In a reply to questions on education in the Straits Settlements, Edward W. Shaw, the Lieutenant-Governor of Malacca, wrote on 17 September 1870,

> I consider it not only obligatory but the real interest of the Government to provide an elementary education in reading and writing free of cost for all such of the inhabitants of the Colony as choose to avail themselves to it. To learn to read and write English presupposes some acquaintance with the language and must necessarily be confined to a few. To learn to read and write Malay in the English character should be brought within the reach of all.[52]

Shaw's comments are reflective of the educational policy at that time. The colonial administration was, on the whole, not opposed to the provision of education but it was concerned with the provision of an education that served primarily the interests of the Empire. In that regard, vernacular education was emphasized, yet it was poorly administered. At the time of the arrival of the Methodist missionaries, sometime before 1886, there were only a few vernacular schools in the various Chinese dialects[53] and Tamil. These schools were set up and maintained by their

---

51. Doraisamy, *150 Years of Education*, 173.
52. Shaw, *Replies to Questions on Education*, 101.
53. During the early and mid-nineteenth century, the Chinese vernacular schools

respective communities and the colonial administration did little to support these schools.[54] This was very largely due to the assumption on the part of the colonial administration that the Chinese and Indian populations were transient, even up to the early twentieth century. The bottom line of colonial educational policy was that it favoured the indigenous Malay population at the expense of the Indians and the Chinese. This attitude is articulated in 1898:

> I can see no reason why the Government of these States should educate children to make them suitable citizens for China or southern India apart from what services they may be able to render here as Chinese or Tamil interpreters.[55]

It is also evident through the allocation of colonial expenditure on vernacular education and grant-in-aid schools, which are schools run by the missionaries with limited government funding. The table below provides allocation of government funding in regard to education, from the period 1899 to 1908.[56]

Table 5: Geovernment Education Expenditure and Allocation of Funding

Year	Total on Education	Funding for Government schools (in %)	Funding for Grant-in-Aid schools (in %)	Funding for Vernacular schools (in %)
1899	$132,177	$28,032 (21.2%)	$46,338 (35.1%)	$57,807 (43.7%)
1902	$179,965	$34,790 (19.3%)	$78,086 (43.4%)	$67,089 (37.3%)
1905	$237,911	$79,274 (33.3%)	$67,412 (28.3%)	$91,225 (38.4%)
1908	$246,027	$63,708 (25.9%)	$95,447 (38.8%)	$86,872 (35.3%)

Source: *Straits Settlement Annual Reports*, NAtional Archives, Singapore.

in the Malay Peninsular were mostly conducted through the use of various dialects. It was only after 1919 that the Chinese language became the main medium of instruction in the Chinese vernacular schools in Singapore. This was the result of the influence of education systems and teachers from Republican China. See Song Ong Siang, *One Hundred Years' History*, 26, 46, 81, 110, 424, 483, for more information on Chinese schools in Singapore.

54. Chelliah, *History of the Educational Policy*, 58, 84.

55. Federated Malay States, *Annual Reports on Education for the Federated Malay States, 1898*, cited by Watson, *Rulers and Ruled*, 162.

56. The figures are extracted from SSARs for the period 1899 to 1908.

Despite the relatively more generous proportion of government grants and funding, the system of vernacular education, as noted earlier, provided by the colonial administration was still found to be very lacking. When tasked to conduct a study into the Straits Settlements education needs and the colonial government's provision in that regard, a committee under E.E. Isemonger submitted a report in 1869 indicating that the allocated grants were insufficient for the development of a sound education system and the lack of co-ordination result in improvidence. The findings of the E.E. Isemonger report facilitated the appointment of Colonel R. Woolley in 1870 to study further and make recommendations to better improve the existing educational structures in the colony. The findings of the Committee, contained in what is known as the Woolley Report (1870) was that "the state of education in the Colony has been and is in a backward-state, and it is not its duty to suggest what should be done to improve and promote it."[57]

The Committee made the recommendation to "take the schools as they are now and by a gradual process endeavour to place them on a more satisfactory and improved basis."[58] In that respect, the Committee made three recommendations for improvement: the appointment of an Inspector of Schools, the reforming of the existing grant-in-aid system and extending and improving vernacular education, especially Malay vernacular education. Interestingly, Francis Wong noted that "other than the appointment of the first inspector, the promises held out by the report remain largely unfulfilled."[59]

It was against this educational backdrop that Oldham and those who continued with the work of the Mission perceived the opportunities that educational mission presented for Methodism, not only in Singapore but further afield in Malaya[60] as well as the Southeast Asia region. The Methodist missionaries arrived at a time when commercially, the region was experiencing renewed economic growth when British protection was extended to Malaya (Pangkor Treaty). This further attracted more Chinese and Indians seeking employment and business opportunities in the booming economy. The colonial administration's relaxation of the policy to allow more women in the colony further added to the surge in

---

57. Woolley, *Report of the Select Committee*.
58. Woolley, *Report of the Select Committee*.
59. Wong and Hean, *Official Reports on Education*, 11.
60. Please see Ho Seng Ong, *Methodist Schools in Malaysia*, 15–52.

the immigrant population. Britain's protection of the Malayan states also signalled an increased number of Europeans interested in business in the Far East. Increasingly, English gained importance as the *lingua franca* where administration and commerce in the colony was concerned. It became contingent that the mercantile community acquired a facility in English that was regarded as an avenue of social mobility and prestige.[61] Concomitantly, for the Chinese and Indian merchants, an education in English was highly esteemed in that it provided an opportunity to tap into the currents of Western scientific knowledge,[62] ensuring progress and prosperity for their posterity.

Even though the Methodist missionaries were blatantly candid that the schools they operated were run as Christian schools, it was still very much well-received by the local merchants, especially among the Chinese and Indian merchants. While there were concerns with regards to the proselytizing of the Christian faith, a majority thought it as unlikely and except for one major incident (the Isaiah Incident, which will be mentioned again later in this chapter) most of the merchants were content to send their children to the Methodist schools, ensuring the growth of the work of the Methodist missionaries. The remarkable growth of the Methodist education mission is perhaps best captured in H. R. Cheeseman's address:

> The growth in numbers and in efficiency of the (Methodist) schools within less than the lifetime of one man is almost incredible and may well be regarded as one of the most remarkable educational developments of modern Malaya.[63]

Within a year of his arrival to Singapore, Oldham established a school in the Chinatown district in view of the overwhelming demand for English education by the Chinese merchants. Oldham was careful to ensuring that while English was offered in the mornings for the boys, Chinese was taught in the afternoon. In establishing Anglo-Chinese School, Oldham did not provide vernacular education because education in the English medium was desired by the parents. In the *Malaysia Message*, it is recorded:

---

61. Wong and Ee Tiang Hong, *Education in Malaysia*, 8–9.

62. Lee, *British as Rulers*, 291–92.

63. H. R. Cheeseman in his address at the Victoria Memorial Hall, as quoted in *Malaysia Message*, Jan.–Feb. 1935, 11.

Mission schools criticized for their emphasis on the teaching of English and Western Science. Few realize that mission schools are forced to concentrate on English by the demands of their Chinese students ... and the demand for English ... come from the fact that without it, they cannot receive a good salary in the business world.[64]

Though Oldham's intentions were never made explicit, in regard to teaching English in the morning and providing Chinese education in the afternoon, it may perhaps be explained that this was firstly in tandem with the emphasis on vernacular education in the Colony and secondly it was demonstrative of Oldham's intention to not merely promote an exclusively western pedagogy. Oldham in a speech made when he returned to visit Singapore in 1927 commented, "At that time, the school provided instruction in English in the morning and in Chinese in the afternoon and that was how it came to be called by its present name."[65] It is hence for this unlikely reason that the school was named Anglo-Chinese School.

More importantly, in providing English education for the sons of the Chinese merchants, the Methodist mission had provided an avenue for the colonized to relate to the British government on their own terms. Unlike the British mission agencies or the Anglican Church or the Scottish-linked Presbyterian Church, American Methodism did not have to be too concerned with the political ramifications or sensitivities of the Colonial Office. It did, however have to be cautious in not being regarded as partial to the rich merchants or to any particular race groups and to that effect, the Methodist missionaries spared no effort in maintaining a cordial relationship with the colonial administration. The fact that a number of the prominent lay leaders[66] were also government officials or ex-British officers perhaps further helped to facilitate the mutuality in the relationship. At the same time, the Methodist missionaries were always seeking to serve the needs of the poor and needy in their visitation programmes and church ministries.

At the start of this education work, Oldham appealed for aid from the colonial administration. His application for a building grant from the government was turned down on the grounds that the colony had sufficient schools for all children of school-going age, as far as the Government

---

64. *Malaysia Message*, May 1929, 15.

65. *Anglo-Chinese School Magazine*, 1927, 18.

66. This includes John Polglase, who was the Assistant Secretary of the Singapore Municipality, and William Shellabear.

should provide educational opportunities.[67] The frosty response from the colonial administrators went further in saying that there was no land left in the Colony to be given away. Within a year, the growth of the school had reached such a proportion that it was in dire need for new premises and the tremendous response to ACS' educational offerings suggested that the colonial administration's assessment of the demand for education in 1885 had been made rather too hastily.

Given the paltry state of the education in Singapore, the British government was delighted that there were parties interested to assist in bearing the responsibilities where education was concerned. Hence for the sake of economic considerations as well as administrative efficiency, the British colonial authorities in Singapore were partial in allowing Christian missions and other private bodies to meet the colonial educational needs.[68] While the education policy was *laissez faire*, the mission schools were never entirely free to pursue their educational and evangelistic ideals. "The British authorities supported them when it suited their own purpose and placed restrictions on them when this seemed necessary in the light of their own aims."[69]

The colonial authorities proceeded cautiously in approving various grants, such as building grants and grant-in-aid upon requests by these agencies, subject to their stipulated conditions. In 1855, the provision of government grants for education was subject to two conditions: firstly that the recipient mission school be open to government inspection and secondly, that a school fee, however small the amount, had to be levied on all the enrolled students. This is further confirmed by a report given by A.E.H. Anson, the Lieutenant-Governor of Penang, in his note, *Sketch of a Scheme for Public Education Straits Settlements*. He wrote:

> First then I propose that there should be a Superintendent of Public Instruction, whose duties should be to make visits of inspection, and to examine all schools receiving grants of money from the Government....
>
> Next I would recommend that no grants of public money should be given, except to such schools the proprietors or managers of which should be willing to permit of visit of inspection,

---

67. SSLCP, 1885, B150.
68. Holmes, *Educational Policy and Mission Schools*, 1.
69. Wong and Hean, *Official Reports on Education*, 5.

and the examination of the Masters and pupils by the Superintendent of Public Education.[70]

In the events following the signing of the Pangkor Treaty in 1874, a third condition was laid; namely that public funds received should not be used for the purpose of proselytizing, and where religious instruction should not be provided during curriculum time but should be provided without any compulsion on the students. The tenor of this is well captured by Edward Shaw's recommendation, "I advocate purely secular education. Once (you) introduced the religious element, and you will educate only the class which profess the peculiar creed introduced."[71]

Thus the Colonial administration set the parameters by which the mission schools started by various Christian missions were to operate, including the Methodists schools such as Anglo-Chinese School, Methodist Girls' School and later Fairfield Methodist School. Geographical parameters, though not explicit may be inferred in locating most of the mission schools run by the various mission agencies in the urban centres. Geographically, this curtailed or at least minimised the impact of missionary activities and the draw of the mission schools amongst the predominantly rural Malay population.

This secularity in the supply of education was further articulated in a code of regulations drafted in 1902, that "no child shall be compelled to be present when such religious instruction is given, nor may any child be refused admission to a Grant-in-aid school on grounds of religious belief."[72] This secular nature of public education in colonial Singapore was thoroughly enforced as evidenced in the report on education made much later in 1928:

> While the value of ethical training for school children was recognized, the declared policy of government was to force no child to receive religious instruction or attend religious observance against the wishes of his (or her) parent or guardian. No religious instruction shall be given and no religious observance shall be practiced during the hours fixed for secular instruction, but they may be carried out either before or after the ordinary school hours.[73]

70. Anson, *Sketch of a Scheme*, 99.

71. Shaw, *Replies to Questions on Education*, 101.

72. *Code of Regulations and Government and Grants-in-Aid English and Vernacular Schools in the Federated Malaysian States.*

73. Report of the proceedings at the Education Conference held in Singapore on

Elementary, vernacular and secular: these were the main emphases in the provision of education in the colony. Training in the "three R's" was the main emphasis of the colonial administration and it did its best to ensure the provision of secular education through the annual inspection of the schools. Yet the Methodist mission's operation of the schools became the vanguard in providing English education in the colony. While the Anglicans, Presbyterians and Roman Catholics had begun to provide English education in the schools run by their respective missionaries and workers before the establishment of ACS in 1886, their schools however did not experience the same growth rate as ACS.

The growing demand for English education, particularly among the Chinese merchants, was matched with the arrival of the Methodists, which is evidenced by the following exaggerated comment in the report in 1894, that "the English education of the colony is almost entirely in the hands of the missionary bodies or committees over which the government has no direct control."[74] The statement rightly reflected the alacrity with which the mission schools, in particular the Methodist schools, were welcomed but is perhaps ill-informed in regard to the control the government had on education. The system of regular schools inspections ensured that the mission schools kept to the policy of non-proselytizing. Furthermore, as Grant-in-aid schools, the government exercised some control specifically on the core subjects that were taught in the schools. Prior to the arrival of the Methodists, the Inspector of Schools for the Straits Settlements had in 1872, drawn up a scheme to control the missionary-run schools and "vernacular" institutions.

Under the proposed scheme, schools were organized into six standards and the subject requirements for each standard were specified. These subjects were classified as "ordinary school subjects" and "extra subjects." The list for the "ordinary school subjects" included Reading, Writing and Arithmetic while the "extra subjects" included subjects such as History, Geography, Algebra, Malay, Chinese, French and German. In making such a classification, the colonial administration ensured that the school provided the basic, secular education of training in reading, writing and arithmetic, but yet at the same time gave certain flexibility for the schools to provide other courses that corresponded to their respective principles and ideals. In the "grants-in-aid" scheme, grants were given to

---

27–30 August 1928, as quoted in Wong and Hean, *Official Reports on Education*, 6.
74. SSAR 1894, 173.

students for each subject passed in the examinations and grants given for a student who passed the list of "extra subjects" was pegged at a higher level than the "ordinary school subjects." This provision was to encourage students as well as the grant-in-aid school to widen their scope of education. In 1891, 23 extra subjects were on the approved list and more were added in the following years. It was under these "extra subjects" that ACS was able to provide such subjects as "Bible Knowledge" and other Christian curriculum.

The Methodist missionaries toed the line where this policy was concerned. Yet at the same time, they circumvented the policy by providing religious instruction before and after the stipulated confines of the policy. School chapels were held before curriculum time and Bible Knowledge classes were offered on a voluntary basis. This was a microcosm of the manner in which the Methodists manoeuvred around the colonial administration that demonstrated that more often than not, the Methodist mission was in not in any way complicit with the British colonial administration. Undoubtedly, the mission was compliant to a degree that ensured their continued presence but in no way was the Methodist mission in connivance with the economic and/or political interests of the British Empire.

The policy of the British colonial administration with regards to mission schools before the turn of the century can best be described as symbiotic, though tending toward parasitism. What was certain for the colony was that so long as the mission agencies continued to provide a service that the colonial administration was not able to do so sufficiently well, this symbiotic relationship was maintained. It benefited from the mission schools' provision of English education and up to about 1900, the government expenditure on mission schools is best considered trivial since it expected the mission schools to pay their own way in providing education. The colonial administration in Singapore regarded mission schools as a cheap means of ensuring that English education was provided for, especially in the supply of trained clerical staff. This attitude is perhaps very well articulated in the Inspector of Schools' observation in the Annual Report for the year 1894:

> The cost to Government of a pupil at an Aided school (such as ACS) averages about half the amount the Government would have to pay if the pupil were attending one of the Government schools which are, of course, entirely maintained out of the public revenue. As opportunities present themselves it is advisable

therefore to allow missionaries and the other bodies to undertake the work now being done by the Government English Schools, the Government contributing toward their expenditure in the form of results grants.[75]

In this way, the administration saved money on education by allowing the missionaries to carry on educational work in Singapore. Appended below is a table that compares the income, expenditure and costs incurred between three of the top schools in Singapore, namely Anglo-Chinese School (ACS), Raffles Institution (RI) and St Joseph's Institution (SJI), from the period of 1888 to 1902. Both Anglo-Chinese School (ACS) and St Joseph's Institution (SJI) (Roman Catholic) were mission schools while Raffles Institution (RI) was largely funded by the government. The colonial administration took over the running of Raffles Institution from its Board of Trustees and, from 1903, Raffles Institution became a government secondary school.

Table 6: Income, Expenditure, and Cost of Instruction for ACS, RI, and SJI, 1888–1902[76]

Year	Income and Expenditure	Schools		
	Income	ACS	RI	SJI
1888	Government Allowance	£842.50	£13702.00	£2975.00
	Fees	£2475.00	£4570.00	£1196.62
	Private Sources	£1915.50	£3629.00	£588.92
	Total	£5233.00	£21901.00	£4760.54
	Expenditure			
	Total	£5944.00	£19027.49	£4218.11
	Cost of each pupil (average attendance)	£27.52	£47.81	£15.62
	Cost of Government to each pupil (average attendance)	£3.90	£34.43	£11.02

75. Cited by Chelliah, *History of the Educational Policy*, 84–85.
76. Table adapted from Leong P., *Methodism and Education in Singapore 1886–1914*, B.A. Academic Exercise, (Singapore: Nanyang Technological University, 1997), 38.

Year	Income and Expenditure	Schools		
	Income	ACS	RI	SJI
	Government Allowance	£6334.00	£13922.00	£4345.00
	Fees	£5808.25	£5115.00	£1978.00
	Private Sources	–	£1691.00	£2500.00
	Total	£11642.25	£20728.00	£8823.00
1895	**Expenditure**			
	Total [A]	£8163.85	£20898.86	£7385.00
	Cost of each pupil (average attendance)	£16.10	£55.29	£22.04
	Cost of Government to each pupil (average attendance)	£12.49	£36.83	£12.97
	Income	ACS	RI	SJI
	Government Allowance	£5556.00	£14483.00	£5023.00
	Fees	£10290.71	£10842.86	£5792.75
	Private Sources	£4956.66	£11474.61	£5444.00
	Total	£20803.37	£36800.47	£16259.75
1902	**Expenditure**			
	Total	£5944.00	£29461.82	£16259.75
	Cost of each pupil (average attendance)	£35.38	£54.46	£37.73
	Cost of Government to each pupil (average attendance)	£9.45	£26.77	£11.85

A Total expenditure for schools connected with missionary bodies does not reflect the real cost of the education supplied, as the teachers in these cases receive no pay or only a nominal sum, which by no means represents the real value of the service they render.

The period from 1888 to 1902 is important in that 1902 marked the year when the new Education Code changed the system of government grants-in-aid for mission schools variable grant, from one that is based on results, to a grant which is based on average attendance.[77] The table points out the different levels of financial support provided for each school and show that even before Raffles Institution became a formal government school (in 1902), Raffles Institution had consistently

77. SSLCP, Report by the committee appointed to consider the working of the System of education Grants-in-Aid in the Straits Settlements and the Federated Malay States, 1922. In Wong and Hean, *Official Reports on Education*, 81–82.

received larger amounts in government grants when compared with ACS and SJI (both mission schools) both prior to as well as after 1903.[78] It is hence proof in demonstrating the fact that mission schools, like ACS and others, received much less money from the Government than schools operated by the colonial administration. In a report given by Rev. Dr. Benjamin West, he brought before the conference the issue if more schools should be opened in view of the government's policy in regard to grants and in view of the cost of education in Methodist-run schools:

> We ought also to determine if we will open any more Anglo-Chinese Schools for it is certain that we shall be invited to undertake such schools because we conduct them at an expense far below that possible to Government or private individuals.[79]

Despite the lower costs of providing education, the standard of education provided in the mission schools consistently matched, if not superseded, that which was provided by the government schools. The Kynnersley Report made this observation:

> It is found that in the best school of a secular character such as Raffles Institution and the Free School, the fees, the Government grant and the income derived from invested funds, are insufficient to carry on the schools in a satisfactory manner. On the other hand the Anglo-Chinese Schools managed by American missionaries, and decidedly less strongly staffed, managed to practically meet all their working expenses from the fees and the Government grant alone.[80]

Increasingly, ACS was gaining popularity among the merchants in Singapore, in particular the Chinese and Indian merchants. It should be said that this support was gained through the academic and moral emphasis on the part of the early pioneers of the school. In a response to a criticism of ACS as a school that emphasized class distinctions as it was a beneficiary of the British colonial masters, Shellabear retorted with this candid response:

> In a recent issue of the Straits Times appears the Annual Report of the Raffles Institution, in which there is a criticism upon

78. SSLCP, 1902 Report.
79. West, "Presiding Elder's Report," 39.
80. Report of the Commission of Enquiry into the system of English Education in the Colony (the Kynnersley Report), 1902, in Wong, and Hean, *Official Reports on Education*, 43.

mission schools of the colony as a class, which is neither fair in its comparisons nor just in its reflections upon the ultimate loyalty and the sympathies of such schools. The report avoids giving data, which may be found in the Blue Book, and which proves that the average cost per capita of educating boys is considerably larger than in at least one mission school in the Colony, for any given year. Furthermore the mission schools in some cases receive not a penny from home to carry them on but depend entirely upon school fees and Government grants. The Raffles Institution is in a bad way when it is necessary to question the safety of entrusting the youth of the Colony to mission schools in order to build up its own cause among the prevailing population of the Colony. The best testimony to the mission schools of the Straits Settlements is the confidence the leading Chinese gentlemen put in them. Chinamen possess as much intelligence as Europeans and may be trusted to know when their interests are being served. If there were any reason for doing so the Chinese community would withdraw their patronage. The fact that this is not done is a sufficient reply to this stricture upon both the "sectarianism" and "ultimate loyalty" of our missionary institution.[81]

On the academic front, the results of the percentage passes in the annual examinations compared very favourably with the more established schools such as Raffles Institution as follows,

Table 7: Comparison of Percentage Passes in Three Schools in Singapore[82]

Year	1887	1892	1897	1898	1911
School	Percentage Passes	Percentage Passes	Percentage Passes	Percentage Passes	Percentage Passes
ACS	90	94	78	70	95.5*
RI	91	83	87	70	85
SJI	93	92	81	62	75

Source: *Straits Settlements Annual Reports*, Singapore National Archives.

81. Shellabear, *Malaysia Message*, June 1893, 86–87. This response perhaps is illuminating in understanding the continuing rivalry between the two schools that is still perpetuated even to this day.

82. The figures are derived from the SSAR for 1887, 1892, 1902 and 1911. The 1911 results are based on the report on "The Anglo-Chinese School, Singapore", published in *The Malaysia Message*, Nov 1911, 13.

The table above shows the rapid rise of ACS against the government-run Raffles Institution as well as the Roman Catholic mission school, St Joseph's Institution. Albeit that ACS had a smaller cohort of students, the statistics show that the percentage passes were able to match the other two schools which had a longer history. Within a short period of six years, ACS' results became the school with the best academic results based on passes obtained. In the Straits Settlements Annual Report of 1892, the Inspector of Schools complimented ACS as being "particularly successful in imparting a sound knowledge of English to (its Chinese) pupils."[83] The lower percentage passes for the year 1896 may be explained by the lugubrious event of that year, that plunged the school into public controversy; the "Isaiah Incident." ACS managed to shake off the encumbrances rather quickly as evidenced by the results in the following years. Hence within a short span of the establishment of the school, ACS became rather quickly synonymous with an effective and vital English education, which was very much sought after by the Chinese merchants in Singapore.

As the popularity of English rather than vernacular education increased greatly at the turn of the century, the colonial administration also began to assume greater responsibility for education, complementing rather than supplanting the role of the Aided (mission) schools in providing English education. In ACS and similarly as in other English schools, the intake in these schools doubled between 1904 and 1911 and English education progressed steadily up to 1921.[84] The Annual Report for the year 1926, pointed to the "liberality of the grants-in-aid" for these English schools which is perhaps evidence of the government's high regard for the schools. The government support for the aided-schools continued even as they co-existed with Government schools in a spirit of friendly competition. The reason was that the grant-in-aids system was an effective policy in education, for on the one hand, the colonial administration was able to recruit English-speaking clerks, who were well-trained and on the other, they were able to keep a check on the secularity of the education provided by the mission schools.

The Methodist mission was cognizant of the success of the schools in providing education and was ill-contented with the promotion of a secular English-education, which was not to the missionaries' purposes. In an appeal to not neglect vernacular education, the editor of the *Malaysia*

---

83. SSAR (1892) 174.
84. Turnbull, *History of Singapore*, 117.

Message wrote, "The purposes of the Methodist Mission—the teaching of our native people and their children to become intelligent Christians."[85] The secularizing effect of the Government policies and grants-in-aid system was already noted much earlier when the Methodist missionaries found themselves expending their energies in educational ministries that were dictated by an inflexible colonial education code. Yet they were also conscious that their true vocation was in fulfilling their missionary call. It came as no surprise that within a decade of the arrival of the Methodist mission in Malaya, the Committee on Education reporting to the Malaysia Mission Conference of the Methodist Episcopal Church concluded their report with this admonition to hold fast to their mission:

> The committee desire in closing to suggest that with increasing attendance at our school and the spirit of competition engendered by Government inspection and the grant-in-aid system, we must steadfastly withstand the secularizing influence of the conditions under which we labour and bear in mind with studious and jealous vigilance our solemn duty to impart as far as possible, along with secular instruction, a knowledge of saving truth.[86]

The Methodist schools, in particular ACS, grew in importance as it surpassed the record of the English schools run by the government. Where colonial sensitivities were concerned, the Methodist missionaries were careful to keep to the principle of non-proselytizing within curriculum time. It was about a decade after its founding that the Methodist mission and the school board found themselves embroiled in the centre of a controversy, which has come to be known as the "Isaiah" Incident. It was one that called into question the methods and motives of the Methodist missionaries and their educational ministry. In retrospect, the incident could also be regarded as one of the major tests of the Methodist mission's resolve to stand firm on its principles in the establishment of the mission school.

On 25 July 1896, *The Singapore Free Press*, one of the more prominent newspapers in Singapore, published a letter signed by "Isaiah" who accused ACS of coercion in proselytism within the school.[87] In the letter,

85. *Malaysia Message*, February 1905, 42.

86. Luering, Ferris, and Stagg, "Report of the Committee on Education," 19.

87. All the letters that were written to the Singapore Free Press as well as the Strait Times in regards to the "Isaiah Incident" are transcribed and may be found in the attached Appendix E1–9 and F1–15 respectively.

"Isaiah" highlighted his concern "of the numerous instances in which questionable pressure was used to induce the boys to become 'deeply interested'" in the Gospel.[88] "Isaiah" went further in accusing the school of beguiling Chinese sponsors by declaring on the one hand that ACS' educational work was above board and proselytizing was not openly carried out while on the other hand, the school was actively carrying out their evangelism and publicizing their success at proselytism. The principal at that time, Rev. C.C. Kelso was accused of breaking a "compact" with the school's Chinese patrons by providing Christian instruction during school hours and of compelling the boys to become Christians. "Isaiah" wrote that the "Reverend gentlemen say one thing to the rich heathens in order to get their money, and then do and act quite differently when the money is secured." "Isaiah"'s purpose for the complaint was for both the Chinese and the Government to be aware of the alleged deceit of the Methodist missionaries. He had hoped that:

> some member of the Legislative Council ought really to ask the Government whether public money should be continued to be thrown away in aid of missionary adventurers. The Government should insist on all grant-in-aid schools becoming completely non-sectarian and non-religious, by which I mean no religion must be taught as part of the day's school work. I hope Mr. Shelford, one of the oldest residents, and the senior member of the Council, will do something to check this public scandal.[89]

The other newspaper, *The Straits Times*, published a similar letter from one known as "Anti-Humbug"[90] who accused the school of being duplicitous to their patrons through their open proselytism within school hours, where he posited that it was "the unkindest thing of all that the promoters of the Mission have done is to treat their patrons with contempt."[91] In similar vein with "Isaiah," "Anti-Humbug" ostensibly took offence at an article written by Reverend D. D. Moore, published in *The Gospel to All Lands*, where Moore wrote that evanglising the "rich

---

88. "Isaiah," *The Singapore Free Press*, 25 July 1896. The full text of the letter is found in Appendix E1.

89. "Isaiah," *The Singapore Free Press*, 25 July 1896.

90. "Humbug," *The Straits Times*, 25 July 1896. Appendix F1. In both letters, the author(s) chose to use the metaphor of a serpent disguised as a dove in the description of Anglo-Chinese School.

91. "Humbug," *The Straits Times*, 25 July 1896.

heathen Chinamen required the guile of 'a serpent in disguise.'"[92] Low Aik Lim posited that a "closer study of the text of the letter is telling and perhaps showed that the writers, "Isaiah" and "Anti-Humbug" are one and the same person."[93]

On the following Monday, 27 July 1898, the Singapore Free Press persisted with charges of deception of the school's board and accused the teachers of teaching the boys to regard their parents as "heathens." In another letter to the Straits Times, "Isaiah" asserted that the Christian (and Western) teachings of the school had poisoned the innocence of the boys against their parents as they began to "look down upon their parents with half contempt and half pity."[94]

As the school and the Methodist mission sought to clarify the position and answer to the accusations, there was a flurry of letters in the newspapers. Over the next two weeks, there were also other responses that appeared in both the Straits Times and the Singapore Free Press,[95] voicing their displeasure. These correspondences and publications in the newspapers were to add both drama and trauma in the first decade of the education mission of the Methodist missionaries, which had been marked by primarily by affability and efficiency.

There had been no public complaints of such proportion until the "Isaiah Incident," which resulted in a significant number of withdrawals from the school, the subsequent transfer of some of these to other schools such as Raffles Institution as well as the resignation of three trustees of the ACS boarding school. One of the trustees who tendered his resignation, Mr. Tan Jiak Kim, made the claim that there was an original "compact" with Oldham that "*no religious teaching whatsoever was to be carried on in the school.*"[96] He was indignant that compulsion has been exercised in inducing the boys to join the religious meetings. The rich merchant, Mr. Tan Keong Siak, who funded Oldham's establishment of Anglo-Chinese School, echoed Tan Jiak Kim's allegation that Oldham had given him the assurance that the school he (Oldham) established would be a purely secular institution.[97] In another letter to the Singapore Free Press on 30

92. *The Gospel in All Lands*, 225.
93. Low Aik Lim, "Anglo-Chinese School, 27 n. 21.
94. *Straits Times*, 27 July 1896.
95. *Singapore Free Press*, 25 July 1896; *Straits Times*, 25 and 27 July 1896; *Singapore Free Press* and *Straits Times*, 29 July 1896, 30 July 1896.
96. *Singapore Free Press* and *Straits Times*, 29 July 1896.
97. *Singapore Free Press*, 29 July 1896.

July, Tan Jiak Kim made another complaint of the unequal treatment for boys who attended the chapel services and those who did not. He noted that the teachers were prejudiced against those who did not attend the services.[98]

Through the period of exchanges, the identity of the person who masterminded the "Isaiah Incident" became evident. "Isaiah" as was later revealed, was a prominent Straits Chinese, a Queen's Scholar, by the name of Dr. Lim Boon Keng. Dr. Lim was also a legislative councilor from 1895 to 1902. While he was pursuing his studies at Edinburgh, he had been introduced to Christianity, which in his estimation demanded a renunciation of his cultural heritage. It was a difficult decision as he was torn between becoming a Christian and yet retaining his Chinese cultural roots and identity.

When he returned to Singapore, Dr. Lim Boon Keng became a vocal proponent in championing the restoration of Chinese beliefs and practices. As a Straits-born Chinese, he was opposed to what he understood as channels that brought about the erosion of the Chinese heritage. He perceived that English-educated Straits-born Chinese (Peranakans or Babas) were too Anglophilic and were hence, very much alienated from the Chinese language and culture. The Peranakans were strongly attracted to Christianity (and in particular Methodism and their education methods) because it gave them a sense of spiritual and social empowerment which they felt they lacked under British rule.

The Methodist educational mission encouraged and provided the means whereby the Straits Chinese could focus on how they could advance themselves within the colonial order of Singapore society.[99] Dr. Lim well appreciated the fact that the Straits-born Chinese community inadvertently faced the struggle of divided loyalty;[100] where culturally they identified themselves with their ancestral homeland in China while politically they were subjects of the British colonial administration. And in the wake of the not too distant Opium Wars, there was that general sentiment among the larger Chinese community that loyalty to the

---

98. *Singapore Free Press*, 30 July 1896.

99. Blackburn and Fong, "Methodist Education," 333–57. Blackburn and Fong highlight the significant contributions of the Methodist education for the Straits Chinese and the complex issue of divided loyalty the Straits Chinese were subjected to.

100. See also some of these other commentaries on the issue of political loyalty and cultural identity in the Chinese community such as Turnbull, *History of Singapore*, 102–10; Wang, *China and the Chinese Overseas*, 169–74.

British crown was tantamount to sedition against their Chinese cultural heritage.

Interestingly, Dr. Lim, though himself a product of the British education, attributed all this to the work of the missionaries in the mission schools.[101] Dr. Lim believed that the problem of confused cultural identity might be resolved in modernizing Chinese traditions, discarding what he considered to be old-fashioned superstitions and practices but reviving and strengthening Confucian morality and confidence in Chinese culture. He became increasingly convinced of the importance of Confucianism, all the more so in an immigrant Chinese community that was increasingly open to western influence. Hence from 1894 to 1919, he lectured on Confucianism in the Straits Settlements.

In seeking to revive Confucianism, Dr. Lim aimed his salvos particularly against the Methodist-run Anglo-Chinese School in his bid to turn the Chinese away from the "alien influences" of Christianity and this is probably the reason that prompted his virulent attack against ACS.[102] In his efforts to revive Confucianism, Dr. Lim reserved his most vocal criticisms for the missionaries who had sought to wean the Chinese coverts from ancestor worship practices and forwarded the premise that "some parents are not good men and therefore do not deserve to be remembered."[103] His own (mis)perceptions of the Christian faith might have fueled his zeal against the missionaries as evidenced by his accusations against the missionaries for preaching a religion based on a Jewish legend, that "cannot now be seriously maintained is admitted by nearly every reasonable man."[104] Instead, he believed that Confucian teachings ought to be the religion of the future for the Straits Chinese. He alleged that "ideal Christianity as taught by Jesus . . . exist only in visions and in books."[105] There was also the corresponding notion of perceiving the missionaries as complicit with the colonial masters. Hence for Dr. Lim and his company of Confucian reformers, the missionaries were "not only the source of danger but harbingers of European occupation."[106]

---

101. Khor Eng Hee, *Public Life of Dr. Lim Boon Keng*, 22.

102. See Low Aik Lim, "Anglo-Chinese School," 28–30, for an account into the clash of cultures in the so-called "Isaiah incident."

103. SCM, 1906, 73.

104. SCM, 1904, 85.

105. SCM, 1904, 29.

106. SCM 1907, 8.

In his response to the charges from "Isaiah," the Principal of ACS, Rev. Charles C. Kelso replied in the Straits Times and denied categorically the use of compulsion in the boys' attendance at the chapel services. Kelso pointed out that that the only "compact" made with the parents was that the school would not baptize their sons without their consent and that no pressure would be exerted to induce the boys attending the school to become Christians. He explained that contrary to compulsion, often the reason for conversion was the exemplary influence of the Methodist teachers that inevitably led some boys to become Christians. And when the boys did indicate their desires to convert, the teachers, understandably, never concealed their satisfaction.[107] Writing in *The Malaysia Message*, Principal Kelso reported Dr. Lim's intention for publishing the letter as an attempt to induce the parents to send their children to the government-run Raffles Institution, which adopted a thoroughly secular approach in education.

Despite Kelso's clarification of the charges leveled by "Isaiah" against the school, Dr. Lim was decidedly taciturn. When confronted by Kelso, regarding his role in the agitation, accordingly, Dr. Lim admitted that he was "Isaiah."[108] In order that the truth of the matter was thoroughly investigated, Principal Kelso was willing to go so far as to submit the school to a public investigation with the objective of satisfying the Chinese that no compulsion had been used.[109] It seemed likely that Dr. Lim's case against the school had not been well substantiated because Kelso's challenge was never taken up by the antagonist, Dr. Lim.

Reporting the matter before the Methodist Conference that year, Kelso offered his perspective on the "Isaiah Incident." Kelso submitted that the main cause for the controversy was monetary; he believed the immediate cause of the controversy had to do with the funding for the rebuilding of the Boarding School.[110] Kelso posited that those Chinese sponsors were finding it difficult to make good their promised donation in rebuilding the Boarding School and hence found it convenient to absolve themselves of all their prior pledges by aligning themselves with "Iasaih'"s trumped up charge of coercive proselytism and complicity with colonialism. Kelso perceived that "Isaiah" had played on the cultural

107. *Straits Times*, 27 July 1896. Please refer to Kelso's reply.
108. *Straits Times*, 31 July 1896.
109. *Straits Times*, 29 July 1896.
110. MMC, 1897, 30–31. A total amount of $9000 was required for the rebuilding of the Boarding School and had been pledged by the Chinese earlier on.

sensitivities of the Chinese in order to discredit the good work that the Methodist missionaries and teachers had been labouring thus far. Another possible reason, Kelso maintained, was that the Christian value system and the efforts at moral education provided at ACS were becoming an increasingly viable and more attractive alternative to traditional Confucian values for the Straits Chinese pupils.[111] Hence for Kelso, the sudden turn of hostilities reflected a latent disposition of the Straits-born Chinese, seeking to find their cultural identity at a time where their loyalties were challenged, not the least by the historical circumstances as well as through the accusations put forward by one such as "Isaiah," that is, Dr. Lim Boon Keng. In regard to accusations, Low believed that "one must conclude that the accuser(s) knew that the charges would not hold up under scrutiny."[112]

Perhaps what is of interest is Oldham's reticence in regard to the accusations, since he would have been the best person to respond in helping to provide an explanation. Did he, as claimed by Mr. Tan Keong Siak, have a verbal or even written agreement with regards to not evangelizing the boys? If so, had he and the teachers gone back on this compact? Is his silence in this regard to be perceived as an indication of the truth in the allegations? It is perhaps difficult to ascertain if such a compact was reached, especially since prior to the "Isaiah Incident" he had never been blamed for any proselytism. There is also the added perspective that "these intelligent and shrewd Chinese merchants really believed that this man travelled all across the globe just to teach their children English."[113] In providing an explanation, Doraisamy posited that it was entirely consistent with Oldham's diffident character[114] not to be embroiled in public disputes. Specifically, the compact that Oldham allegedly made with the Chinese merchants, included the following statement that was published in the Straits Times, clarifying that, "the ultimate aim is to help in the evangelization and elevation of the non-Christian peoples of this land."[115] In view of this important explication, perhaps Oldham's taciturnity is reasonable, which might well have been for the sake of not desiring to publicly embarass his Chinese benefactors.

111. MMC, 1897, 30–31.
112. Low Aik Lim, "Anglo-Chinese School," 45.
113. *Straits Times*, 1 Aug. 1896, 1.
114. Doraisamy, *Oldham*, 82–83.
115. *Straits Times* 28 September 1899.

The accusation that the parents were kept in the dark of their children's "coerced conversion" is also incredible in view of the fact that the Principal's report of the work and ministry of the schools was always presented at the Annual Conferences, for which the records were accessible. In the Conference Report of 1894, the Principal, Munson reported that "as long as we pursue an open and wise course, we shall have no reason to fear that any injury will be done on educational work by faithful efforts to present Jesus Christ... to the young who attend our schools."[116] In another Annual Conference Report of 1902, Munson stated that "Scripture reading has formed a part of the opening services of the day with each of the classes" and that "some have been converted."[117] Granted that if language and accessibility of the Conference Annual reports might have hindered the clear communication of what the expressed purposes of ACS was or the ministry that the teachers were involved in, yet the parents' attendance at the annual Prize Giving Day abrogates their ignorance as these were much publicized events where the achievements of the school were promulgated. In the Prize Giving Day ceremony of 1890, the Guest of Honour, the Governor of Singapore, Sir Cecil Clementi Smith's compliments of the merits of a mission school, could not have been overlooked by those critical of the subversive proselytism of these mission schools:

> It is very gratifying to see that the teachers do not stop at mere standard work but devote considerable attention to what might be called, for want of a better word, moral teaching and that the large body of influential Chinese are open to their doing so. It is pleasing to see so many Chinese boys putting themselves under religious instruction and this must be productive of much good.[118]

In a public statement, Kelso categorically declared that it has always been, and would always be, the Anglo-Chinese School's policy to provide regular religious instructions, and also maintained that no one had ever been, or would be compelled to become a Christian. Together with his willingness to subject the school to a thorough investigation, these appeared to have assuaged the undue concerns of the public. And while

---

116. MMC, 1894, 14.

117. MMC, 1892, 15.

118. Song, *One Hundred Years' History*, 292; also Ho Seng Ong, *Methodist Schools in Malaysia*, 209.

the immediate ramification of the "Isaiah Incident" was the withdrawal of some of the students, it was interesting that the total enrolment at the end of the year was at 641, which was still an increase from the previous year of 572 enrolments.[119] This increase in the school's enrolment through this tumultuous episode was perhaps evidence that a larger segment of the Chinese population were either unconvinced of the charges brought against the school or were indifferent in view of the advantage of the prospects of a better education gained, as many of the supporters were non-Christians who were more appreciative of the school's balanced education. The increased enrolment immediately following the "Isaiah Incident" may in effect be read as the public's endorsement of their trust in the good work of the Methodist Mission, especially in the area of educational mission. The issue with regards to the funding for the rebuilding of the Boarding School was also settled as the school was able to secure the financial assistance of some Christian Chinese merchants as trustees. The new building was completed and eventually opened in May 1897.[120] In regard to the sensitivities of parents who objected to their sons' attendance at the chapel services, provisions were made for them to be assembled at a separate room, but apparently very few did.[121]

The "Isaiah Incident" helped to clarify the religious mission of the educational mission of the Methodists, particularly for ACS. It strengthened the conviction that religious teaching was part and parcel of school life, where for Oldham, the story of ACS was really, "a story of educational occupation accompanied, as every true education must be, with the effort to evangelise the student boys."[122] This pointed to the fact that contrary to the accusations of Dr. Lim ("Isaiah") of deceit on the part of the educational mission, the Methodist mission was rather explicit in their evangelism. Yet they were sensitive to the social context and toed the line in regard to the requirements laid down by the colonial administration, in ensuring a certain secularity in the education offered. It is significant to note that whatever "proselytism" or Christian ministry was

---

119. The figures are taken from SSAR, 1895 and 1896, 121 and 85 respectively.

120. *Malaysia Message*, May 1897, 91. Interestingly, the trustees were headed by Song Ong Siang, co-founder of the Straits Chinese British Association with Dr. Lim Boon Keng. Song was a devout Christian and served as the president of the Chinese Christian Association formed in 1889.

121. MMC, 1897, 32.

122. Ang, *Hearts, Hopes and Aims*, 20.

administered in the school, it was always without the official curriculum hours and without compulsion.

The "Isaiah Incident" was perhaps the first but definitely not the last of the accusations against the mission work of the school. In 1899, another accuser, writing under the pseudonym of "Anti-Proselytiser" made the accusation that the school teachers in ACS continued to favour boys who "showed aptitude in memory texts of Scripture."[123] He made a further claim that a school boy was offered the prospect of an American wife if he became a Christian. The principal of ACS then, John E. Banks, in his reply to the *Straits Times*, sought to clarify the matter and affirmed the Christian principles for which ACS stood for:

> All true missionaries of Christ are directly or indirectly concerned with proselytising, which has to do with the winning of people to the Christian faith and practice. All we claim is that we endeavour to this openly and fairly.[124]

In a letter the next day to the *Straits Times*, Banks categorically denied the accusations, insisting that no attempt was ever made to coerce or to induce the boys to become Christians by the promise of marriage.[125] The immediate response seemed to have sufficiently answered the charges leveled at the school yet again and unlike the "Isaiah Incident" this episode was somewhat fugacious. By the turn of the century, most of the anti-Christian sentiments had been assuaged. In an issue of *Malaysia Message*, it was recorded that those who had opposed Christian teachings in ACS now appeared to be favourable or at least neutral.[126] In the Annual Report of the Methodist Episcopal Mission of 1900, Shellabear reported,

> The parents of the boys now have a much clearer understanding than ever before as to the position of the school in regards to religious education, and no opposition has been manifested. This is an eminently satisfactory condition of affairs.[127]

The school's harshest and perhaps most vocal critic, Dr. Lim Boon Keng accepted the invitation as the guest-of-honour at a Prize-giving Day. The Methodist mission's educational work perhaps received its most

---

123. *Straits Times*, 27 September 1899.
124. *Straits Times*, 28 September 1899.
125. *Straits Times*, 29 September 1899.
126. MM, October 1914, 33.
127. Shellabear, "Annual Report of the Methodist Episcopal Mission," 609.

profound vindication when Dr. Lim also sent not only his son, Francis Lim Kho-Beng[128] and also his grandson, Albert Lim Kok Ann,[129] to be educated at ACS, where they distinguished themselves as scholars of the school!

The "Isaiah Incident" is illustrative of the issues and conflicts between the Methodist mission and the colonial administration's policy of governing a culturally diverse colony. While it was sparked off by anti-proselytism among certain pro-Chinese factions of the Straits Chinese community, it is essentially one that perceived Christianity as complicit with British imperialism. In the minds of the Chinese, the missionaries, who came under the auspices of the Methodist Episcopal Church in the United States of America, were regarded as no different from any of the British administrators and colonial masters. In their limited perspective, the Methodist schools and also the Methodist Episcopal Mission served not the purposes of the general populace but those of the colonial masters. There was no distinction in their minds between the Americans and the British, for all were perceived as "ang mohs" (red haired).

Undoubtedly, the incident highlighted two significant truths in regard to the Methodist mission. Firstly, it is evident that the Chinese still haboured suspicions of the Methodist educational work, as a veiled form of evangelism. Secondly, that the colonial administration did nothing, absolutely nothing to come to the defence of the Methodist educationists. From a colonial administrative point of view, this was perhaps deemed unnecessary precisely because the Methodist work was never regarded as a joint effort or even a partnership in the education work of the colony. Hence, in the event of public criticisms, the silence from the colonial administration starkly underscored the indifference of the colonial masters. Insofar as it was advantageous to them, they would undoubtedly "take a slice of the pie," but when problems and issues surfaced, their silence was somewhat deafening. This underscores the fact that the

---

128. Francis Lim was the second son of Dr. Lim Boon Keng. According to the *Anglo-Chinese School Magazine*, 1930, there is a record of Francis, who graduated from ACS in 1916, returning to Singapore after many years of further education in America in the discipline of motor engineering. *Anglo-Chinese School Magazine*, June 1930, 6.

129. The records of *The Malaysia Message*, January 1939, noted, "Mr. Lim Kok Ann, son of Dr. Lim Boon Keng and an old boy of the Anglo-Chinese School, Singapore has been chosen as one of Malaya's Queen's Scholar for 1939." He was to study medicine at Cambridge. The editor seems to have misrepresented the facts, as Francis LimKok Ann is the grandson of Lim Boon Keng, whose father is Walter Lim Kho-Leng, Boon Keng's third son.

colonial administrators were in fact parasitic in regard to the positive advantages they were able to leech from the Methodist mission. Their silence is strident evidence that the American Methodists were never regarded as complicit with the British colonial administration, not even in the area of education, at least not from the perspective of the colonial administration.

METHODISTS AND ETHICS

While the Methodist contribution in planting churches and in the area of education is perhaps most noticeable, the Methodists also sought to impact the society in very much the same way as they contributed to the educational history of Singapore. Besides being active in evangelism and establishing churches among the different ethnic groups in the colony, the Methodist were also very active right at the outset of the mission in their efforts at uplifting the plight of women and children. Aware of his already significant involvement in the schools and in the church, Oldham was keen for additional support in ministering among the womenfolk in Singapore. Oldham commented:

> Female education, when the missionaries first came here, was very backward. It is not that there were no schools; there were, but they were struggling and not coordinating. As I emphasize and believe in female education I could not tolerate that state of affairs. Then came on the scene a pioneer missionary lady interested in education: Miss Sophia Blackmore.[130]

And for this reason Sophia Blackmore responded. But while Blackmore may have come to be associated with what is known today as the Methodist Girls' School, in the same tenor as Oldham is inseparably linked with Anglo-Chinese School, her work however, was not at all limited to the founding of the Tamil Girls' School (which was renamed Methodist Girls' School). Blackmore was at the forefront of the Methodist efforts at ministering to the disenfranchised, the poor and destitute, those oppressed by the rampant vice trade in Singapore and womenfolk who had no voice in a culture dominated by men, be they colonial administrators or familial relations. Of the urgency of the times, Blackmore later recorded in her diary:

---

130. As quoted of Bishop Oldham by Doraisamy, *Sophia Blackmore in Singapore*, 66–68.

> The mission to the women of Malaya had been, from its inception, pre-eminently a work of faith and prayer and sacrifice. Because of its location as the port of call for the commerce of the eastern world, Singapore, "meeting place of nations," was not only a strategic center for missionary work but most appallingly in need of woman's work.... Dr. Oldham, founder of Methodism there, soon keenly realized this and sent most urgent appeals to the women of America to come to the rescue.[131]

The process of pioneering uplift work among the womenfolk and the disenfranchised has not been an easy task. The plight of women then, was such that they "were perennially prey to the whims of better-off men, and at times of crisis, it was their daughters who were sold off as slaves and prostitutes."[132] Elson added:

> The demands and effects of the period of Western domination affected women in complex and sometimes ambiguous ways. Demeaning attitudes to women allowed Westerners, particularly in the years before their political dominance was complete, to have easy recourse to prostitutes, house servants and concubines.[133]

In particular, among the Indian and Chinese emigrants, gender inequality was the accepted norm. And somewhat interestingly, in the familial context, gender inequality seemed to be inversely proportional to poverty, where survival was the key consideration.[134] The plight of girls born into virtually all strata of the immigrant or local families was nonetheless one of gross inequality and discrimination. In that particular cultural and economic milieu, baby boys were valued as heirs of the bloodline while baby girls were often regarded more as liabilities. The education of boys was of greater significance for many families whilst education of the girls was but "an extra-curricular activity," well afforded only by the rich. The Kynnersley report of 1902 attested to the prevalence of this practice:

> A few Chinese girls are privately educated, but the great majority of Straits born Chinese girls and women are left entirely

---

131. Doraisamy, *Sophia Blackmore in Singapore*, 5.
132. Elson, "International Commerce, the State and Society," 173.
133. Elson, "International Commerce, the State and Society," 173, 174.
134. Elson, "International Commerce, the State and Society," 173, 174. Elson further noted that "sexual equality was most nearly approached in poorer families where all had to contribute substantially for the unit to survive" (173).

uneducated, a fact which constitutes one of the greatest obstacles in the way of educating, in the real sense of the word, the Chinese youth in the colony.[135]

The Chinese has a proverb, 望子成龙, which literally means, "hoping for the son to become a dragon." It refers to the hopes and aspirations that all Chinese families tag on to male offsprings. And not a few families would spare any effort to ensure that this is not merely a fantasy but a reality. It may well be that Blackmore's efforts were targeted precisely against such a mindset what she commented:

> It was most difficult, however, to persuade parents to send their girls to school, for there was but little interest in female education. Part of our work, in fact, was to create this interest. One mother would say, "We do not want our girls to *makan gaji* (earn their livelihood)." Another woman told me that if her daughter studied from the same book as her son, the girl would get all the learning out of it; there might be none for the boy and he would be "*bodoh*" (stupid). The girl might be stupid—that did not matter, but the boy must be clever.[136]

This inequality in the treatment of girls and boys was evidenced not only among the Chinese immigrants but was also prevalent among the poorer Indian immigrants. For most of the emigrants struggling to eke out a livelihood in Singapore, another mouth to feed further increased the burden. Not surprisingly, many baby girls were abandoned and most of the girls of the poor families were sold into a life of servanthood, becoming "amahs," a term used to describe the pigtailed, white-blouse and black-trousers servants of colonial rulers and rich merchant families in Singapore. Of such practices, Blackmore recorded that such activities were

> carried out in an underhand way. Little girls are taken at a very tender age and trained as servants and are entirely at the mercy of their owners and get hard usage all their lives. As they grow older they work incessantly and when their duties in the house are done, they make cakes and sell them for the master's benefit. Their only hope is a decent burial.[137]

135. "Report of the Commission of Enquiry into the system of English Education in the Colony (the Kynnersley Report), 1902," in Wong, and Hean, *Official Reports on Education*, 38.

136. Doraisamy, *Sophia Blackmore in Singapore*, 22.

137. Doraisamy, *Sophia Blackmore in Singapore*, 19, 20.

It was into such a colonial society, where the children's education was a decision left to the family, where the Methodist work among the different ethnic groups challenged that norm. The Methodist missionaries worked tirelessly to counsel, to cajole, to commend and to encourage families to send their children to the Methodist schools. This explained the tremendous growth of the schools within the first five years of the arrival of the Methodists. The June 1892 issue of *Malaysia Message* published an article that reported the meeting of the Singapore Chinese Christian Association in regard to the education of Chinese women. The report highlighted on the one hand the prevalent attitude of the Chinese with regards to education for the girls and womenfolk. Yet on the other, it is demonstrative of the growing positive influence of Methodist educational mission among some of the politically and economically important people in the colony. One of the prominent Chinese merchants, converted through the Methodist mission, Mr. Lim Koon Tye highlighted the importance of literary education for the women. He detailed the advantages that the Chinese womenfolk would gain from such an education:

> (1) It would serve to expand their minds as nothing else would. (2) It would make them take an intelligent interest in social questions which closely affect them. (3) It would enable them to understand many things of which they are at present in utter ignorance. (4) It would enable them to exert an enormous and abiding influence for good over their children, and through their children over other people's children also and (5) all these things combined would have the effect of rendering Chinese maidens every day more fit to be the partners of Chinese youths, who aspire to take an important part in the affairs of these settlements so far as they affect their own countrymen.[138]

In tandem with the growth of the schools was also the setting up of a boarding school as well as a deaconess home that was a shelter for the destitute and homeless as well as for the girls who were rescued from prostitution and abandonment. This was primarily the work of the Women's Foreign Missionary Society, for which Sophia Blackmore was one of the many indefatigable missionaries. By 1893, Blackmore was assisted by two other deaconesses, Emma E. Ferris and Josephine M. Hebinger. The ministry of these women included the work among the poor, the destitute and the lepers as well as the rescue work among the women who were either abandoned, or sold into slavery or prostitution, where a much

---

138. Shellabear, "Education of Chinese Women," 74.

darker future awaited those who were sold into the trade. In a booming port of call where the colonial administration limited the number of female immigrants, prostitution was rife. It was into such a complex multicultural context that Methodism sought to bring dignity and restore certain equality to the status of women both within the church as well as in the society at large.

While the colonial administration was a little more explicit in the prohibition of the triad societies as well as other vices such as gambling, they were less ebullient with regards to prostitution. Attendant to prostitution was a host of other vices. Prior to the relaxation of the immigration law in regard to women, Singapore was the temporary home of a good number of male immigrants from China, India and the surrounding islands, who had come in search of a better salaried job. Bringing their families along was not an option as it was neither financially unfeasible nor allowed in the immigration regulations set forth by the East India Company. The population statistics indicated that the number of men overwhelmingly exceeded that of women. The following table[139] is a comparison of the composition in terms of gender for the Chinese immigrants alone,

Table 8: Comparison of the Total Number of Chinese Immigrants by Gender

Year	Total Number of Male Chinese Immigrants	Total Number of Female Chinese Immigrants	Percentage of Female Chinese Immigrants
1871	46,104	7,468	16.2%
1881	72,571	14,195	19.6%
1891	100,446	21,462	21.4%
1901	178,778	11,822	6.6%
1911	269,854	22,738	8.4%

Source: H. Marriot, *The People of Singapore* and SSAR for 1901 and 1911.

Hard labour, coupled with the harsh conditions of a tropical climate exacerbated the abuse in alcohol and drug consumption such as opium

---

139. The figures are adapted from H. Marriot, "The People of Singapore: Inhabitants and Population," in Makepeace, Braddell, and Brooke, *One Hundred Years of Singapore*, 358–59. Additional figures for 1901 and 1911 are extracted from Jarman, *Annual Reports*, 5:91 and 6:375 respectively. The total number of male immigrants may be due also in part to immigrants, who were headed to the other parts of the Malay peninsular but were coming into Singapore as a first port of entry.

and *"ganja"* (cannabis) as well as prostitution and the accompanying social problems of contagious sexual diseases and secret societies. As evidenced in the statistics in the table above, the disparity between the population based on gender provided the excuse for the proliferation of the vice trade.

Prostitution was regarded as an "imperial problem."[140] It was part of the British policy to attract thousands of coolies to work in the commercial houses, the plantations and in the port. As immigration law prohibited women, "the coolies resorted to a sort of sexual compromise which was abhorrent to the imperial mind. As a way out, the decision was made to allow women to enter the colony for prostitution."[141] This tacit regulation also provided a "solution" for a large number of British soldiers and seamen also stationed in the colony.

Yet again, the women missionaries of the WFMC were at the forefront of this ministry among the prostitutes. They were the ones who provided the shelter for girls who were often sold into prostitution and slavery by their family members. Of this work, Mrs. Violet M. Luering wrote:

> Together with Miss Hebinger, I have visited some houses of ill-fame in Malay Street and other places, and spoken to the inmates in Malay. This work, though not an easy one, has been much upon my heart as of exceeding great importance, and it will, if faithfully continued, surely bring a rich harvest.[142]

In a separate report on "Rescue Work" submitted the following year to the Women's Conference of the Annual Conference by Miss Josephine Hebinger, she appealed:

> The darkness and wickedness of some parts of the city cannot be described. Eyes must see, ears must hear, lives must come in contact with the poor fallen, in order to understand. Is it easy to look upon all this? No, but how must the Father feel, when His blood-bought children creep along the dust of the earth and see nothing but earth, never once thinking of looking up above into the face of the One who saves them that he gave all He had for them?

---

140. Lee, *British as Rulers*, 86.
141. Lee, *British as Rulers*, 86.
142. Luering, "Report of Chinese Work," 31.

> In our home, we have six girls ... there are over three thousand in the dens of infamy.[143]

This work was to grow in importance in the years following and more were recruited to assist in this effort to address this social ill. The report of work for the following year is a further indication of the dedication with which Miss Josephine Hebinger and her team carried on this work:

> Miss Hebinger was released from the Boarding School and opened rescue work early last year. She has made nearly 150 visits to brothels and homes, held prayer meetings, organized and conducted two Sunday Schools, and distributed tracts and Scriptures portions.[144]

The difficulty and resistance faced as well as the potential extent of the rescue work is best encapsulated by this report:

> Another year of work amongst the fallen, ignorant and oppressed Chinese women and children of Singapore has passed, and it has given me a fuller knowledge of the need, the difficulties, and the encouragements of this most important work of bringing liberty to the bodies and souls of our sisters, who can be found in large numbers existing in these hovels of vice.[145]

If they were not in the thick of the rescue work, the Methodist missionaries were further explicitly vocal in highlighting the extent of the vice trade and seeking Government intervention. Again in a report submitted for the Conference of 1897, Rev. F.H. Morgan reported:

> Houses for immoral purposes have greatly increased in number and boldness of inmates on the most public streets of Singapore, often in proximity to the churches and schools. Surely an effort should be made to have clean surroundings for such institutions. Again we repeat our condemnation of the traffic in women and girls for immoral purposes carried on between China and the Straits, a species of evil particularly attended by horrors.[146]

The work of these women missionaries was not limited to any particular ethnic group but among the various different enclaves of labourers and

---

143. Hebinger, "Annual Report," 1895, 32.
144. Munson, "Presiding Elder's Report," 15.
145. Hebinger, "Annual Report," 1896, 54.
146. Morgan, "Report of Committee on Public Morals," 35.

immigrant workers. They were appalled by the proximity of vices such as brothels, gambling and opium dens to the neighbourhood where the Methodist had established churches or schools. Hence tirelessly, the mission worked against these evils and continuously appealed to the colonial administration to ensure that brothels and places of ill-repute be removed wherever they are located near schools. Where the occasion warranted, there was a close partnership with the British government in protecting young women and children. This collaboration between the government and the Methodist missionaries is noted in the Report of Public Morals of the Annual Conference in 1898:

> (2) During the year, owing to the representations made by some of our missionaries, the Government has closed many houses of ill-fame which were situated in some of the main streets of Singapore, and were necessarily passed by the attendants at our Churches and Schools. We beg to place on record, with great satisfaction, the help afforded us in this matter by the Government, but whilst thankful for the measure adopted and appreciation the interest which has been stimulated, we recognize that much yet remains to be done.
>
> (3) We also desire to express our approval of the recent decision of the law courts regarding young women brought to Singapore ostensibly as barmaids, but really for altogether different purposes, and trust that careful inquiries will be made in order that the true character of such questionable places be ascertained, as advocated by *The Straits Times*, and that the proprietors of places which are proved detrimental to the welfare of the Colony be banished, as the law provides.[147]

Another one of such successes is recorded in the appeal by the Women's Conference of the Methodist Mission in the Annual Conference of 1899. The report noted the positive steps taken and in that same report remonstrated in favour of of a deportation law:

> The efforts made during the past year to suppress vice and to rescue its victims, have deepened in our hearts the feeling of responsibility in this work, and we are determined to do all in our power to remove this evil from our midst, and to arouse the public sentiment on the subject.

---

147. Amery, Banks, and Kensett, "Report of Committee on Public Morals," 26.

> We are glad to record that brothels, established in the vicinity of our schools and churches, have been removed; but the sad fact confronts us that the work of destruction is not stopped by this means, and that while those in our charge are in a measure protected, others are endangered by the removal of such houses to their neighbourhood. We deplore the fact that no deportation law exists in the Straits Settlements, whereby those found guilty of importing girls and women for immoral purposes, may be effectually dealt with.
>
> Owing to the fact that such a law exists in India, and other colonies, the Straits become a resort for the worst offenders of other countries. The recent influx of prostitutes from Manila bears witness to this alarming state of our Colony. We recommend that direct effort be made to secure the passage of a deportation law. Numerous cases are reported where women would be glad to lead an upright life, if the way were opened to them.[148]

The Methodist mission was aware that there were times when they were unable to lift their voices very loudly against the social vices, "yet we have given no uncertain sound as to our uncompromising antagonism against them."[149] In conjunction with the vice trade, the Methodist mission, as with most of the Christian community, objected also to British administration's tacit and tolerant attitude in regard to the oppression of womenfolk, especially that of indentured servants. They were also increasingly vocal against such issues. And though it was not easy to change the mindset of the people and was probably a larger obstacle to overcome in regard to colonial administration policies, the Methodist missionaries continued to plod on. They sought to educate through various articles in the *Malaysia Message* and were constantly appealing directly to the Government and also to the Christian community as well as the economically able business community to join with them in speaking up against the tacit "acceptance" of a social problem.

To the richer members of the community as well as to the sending church, the Methodist mission would also appeal for their partnership in terms of financial giving. In an appeal for funding to expand the work in building a home for destitute women, published in April 1901 issue of the

---

148. Blackmore et al., "Annual Report," 56.
149. Pykett, Banks, and Kensett, "Report of Committee on Public Morals," 29.

Malaysia Message, there is an account of one of the success stories in this very difficult ministry:

> After a great deal of labour, and various trials, some of the girls were trained to be nurses and put out to service and have proved themselves worthy. Care has been taken to place them in Christian homes, where they are visited by Mrs. Pykett and her Bible woman, this keeping in touch with them and making them feel that they are still our girls. . . .
>
> All are taught to read, each in her own languages (for we take in every nationality). . . . Their spiritual welfare is our especial care. While religion is not forced upon them, Christian teaching is given daily, and all voluntarily attend the various services of our church. With very few exceptions, all who have come to us have found salvation and peace, and are trying to live true Christian lives. These are the same class who flocked to Jesus when He was on earth, the sinful and poor. And in caring for these, and trying to lead them to Jesus, we know His will is being done.[150]

Similar to the Methodist *modus operandi* in regard to education policies, the Methodist missionaries worked within their circles of influences to effect changes and to bring about a greater attention to the social injustices of the day. Where they had the opportunity, they often appealed for improved legislation for the benefit of those disenfranchised. They worked within the colonial system, provided the education and training necessary and in so doing gave to the local population themselves a voice to speak and effect changes within the system. This is clearly evident in that most of the girls who were rescued came to take on positions of leadership in the homes, one example of which is the Deaconess Home in Singapore. Sophia Blackmore reported, "In the Deaconess Home during the year, we have had ninety-one children. Several of our girls are now teachers, they live with us and pay their board."[151] The emphasis on building the local leadership even in the rescue work was one of their priorities.

The rescue work however was not limited to Singapore as the mission also established similar homes in various cities in the Malay Peninsula, an example of which is the Alexandra Home in Penang, established in 1903. The Report of the Committee on Rescue Work noted:

150. *Malaysia Message*, Vol X No 7 April 1901, 85.
151. Blackmore, "Report of Deaconess Home," 82.

> We are glad to say that opportunities for this work have come to all our missionaries through the year in various ways. Women have been saved from lives of sin, widows been relieved, women protected from drunken and wicked husbands, and whole families supported whilst the father was laid aside owing to sickness and other troubles, all these found a refuge in the Alexandra Home. Two Eurasian and one European women was sent from Singapore through Christians friends there; in Penang six women were rescued directly from houses of ill fame; some cases of slave-girls escaping from their mistresses through ill treatment were brought to our notice, and helped. We are thankful to God for what has been accomplished in succouring these unfortunate women in a definite way. More has been done in the past year than ever before in this line. We would be glad if this Conference would suggest a plan whereby a fund might be established for the maintenance of the inmates of this Home.[152]

It is certainly acceptable to opine that in general, Methodism (and for that matter, Christianity) was not vehemently opposed to British colonialism. There was much greater "freedom" for various missionary organizations in the Straits Settlements, where British law was upheld, compared with the other Federated Malay States in the Malay Peninsula, where Islamic sensitivities were to be left unperturbed. There were however, aspects of British administration that were particularly disconcerting for Christians and particularly, the Methodists that impinged directly upon their social principles, particularly the social vices of alcoholism, opium addiction and gambling and pursuant to all that, the inordinate reliance on revenue obtained from legalizing vice in the colony.

In the Annual Report of the Committee on Public Morals, the first of which was included in the reports to the Annual Conference of 1893, the members of the committee, which comprised Rev. W.H.B. Urch, Rev. C.C. Kelso and Rev. William G. Shellabear, wrote:

> In this the first report of the Committee on Public Morals in the Malaysia Mission Conference it is a great pleasure to call attention to the fact that the Methodist Episcopal Church has borne unvarying witness against the greatest curse of the world, and need no re-adjustment to meet the advance in thought on temperance matters. We rejoice too in that advance which makes temperance, in its best and truest sense, mean total abstinence from all that intoxicates for the individual, and legal prohibition

---

152. Pykett, "Report of Committee on Rescue Work," 11.

of all traffic in alcoholic beverages for the State. We recognize it is our duty and privilege to co-operate with all wisely-conducted movements looking to the suppression of the beverage traffic in intoxicants and the spread of total abstinence principles. We recognize it as of the utmost importance that all our people in these lands should be distinguished by their total abstinence principles and practice.

We recognize it as our duty, especially at this time, to bear testimony against the iniquitous traffic in opium, and we call upon our people to exert themselves for the total abolition of the traffic for other than medicinal purposes. We desire to assure those who are actively engaged in this great work of our sympathy and co-operation.[153]

Alcoholism presented another social problem for which the Methodists were particularly robust in their efforts toward total abstinence. The report of 1894 recorded:

> The church wields a great importance in this wicked city. Our total abstinence principles are a standing rebuke to the whiskey-drinking Europeans whose moral influences upon the native races is very hard indeed.[154]

Despite the healthy growth of the Methodist mission among the various other language groups, the work in the English Church, which was primarily composed of Europeans in civil and military service, was regarded as slow. It was reported that "one reason for our slow numerical growth is that we are a 'total abstinence' church."[155] The Methodist insistence on total abstinence is also the reason for its hearty endorsement of increased levies and taxes on alcoholic beverages in the colony.

In the same token, the Methodists were vocal in regard to gambling. Sir Stamford Raffles himself held that "the practice of gaming being highly destructive to the morals and happiness of the people"[156] and was thus explicit in his prohibition of gambling. The British governors after him however, turned gambling into a revenue generating machinery. In the English Parliament, when various legislations were enacted against gambling, the first of such legislation against gaming houses in Singapore

---

153. Urch, Kelso, and Shellabear, "Report of Committee on Public Morals," 14.
154. *Annual Report*, Methodist Episcopal Mission 1894.
155. As quoted by Doraisamy, *Forever Beginning I*, 21.
156. Raffles, *Singapore Local laws and Institutions*, 11.

appeared as part of the Police Act of 1856. Subsequently several ordinances issued by the colonial administration followed, in 1870, 1876 and 1879, and finally in 1888 which was still in force at the turn of the century. But despite the legislations and ordinances, the problem of gambling in Singapore persisted and quite often with the tacit approval and assistance of the police and has persisted down to this day.[157]

As is evident from the dates, many of the anti-gambling ordinances were in place by the time of the arrival of the Methodist mission. But there were repeated measures made by various European entities lobbying for a repeal of the anti-gambling laws. It is against these intimations that the Methodist mission stood the ground in their vocal defence. An example is found in Rev. William Shellabear's articulate rebuttal that he submitted to the press but was denied publication. Indignant with the press for circumventing the issue, Shellabear published his entire response in the July 1901 issue of the *Malaysia Message*. In his incisive and impassioned rebuttal against the request for the repeal of the anti-gambling law, Shellabear wrote:

> There are Chinese parents many of whom under the gambling laws see their sons throwing away in gambling clubs the money which their fathers have earned; ask them how they would like all restrictions to gambling tables removed. The proximity of the gambling tables at Johore is bad enough without opening the door to similar institutions being established in our midst.
>
> The laws of this Colony have fortunately not been made to suit the depraved tastes of members of the Sporting Club. Our legislators can at least be congratulated on having a higher ideal than that. And it is a pity by the way that you yourself have not a higher conception of the calling of a newspaper editor than to sink to the level of advertising a lottery and advocating a vice which fastens itself upon men and women with a grip from which many do not escape until they are brought to the verge of ruin or have been converted into drunkards, rogues and beggars.[158]

Though in policy there was a ban, yet in practice, gambling was very much rampant. The Methodist mission, however, was thoroughly cognizant of the problems associated with gambling, and in this regard, they collaborated with the colonial administration in supporting the

---

157. See Kwa Kiem Kiok, "Towards a Model of Engagement," 2004.
158. Shellabear, "Repeal of our Anti-Gambling Laws," 125.

legislations banning gambling. Methodist missionaries wrote frequently against the vice of gambling. The example of Shellabear's outspoken rebuttal is a case in point of the vigor in which the mission adhered to in regard to ensuring that legislations against gambling would not be repealed.

Undoubtedly the Methodists were active in "spreading Scriptural holiness" in the colony of Singapore as evidenced by the constant work in addressing the various social ills which were attendant to an immigrant population. They were active in encouraging laws which promulgated public morality, such as laws against gambling, alcoholism, prostitution as well as laws in regard to the observance of the Sabbath rest. The insistence of Sabbath observance was encouraged as evidenced in this report:

> We note with much gratitude that the Singapore authorities do not allow cargo to be worked upon any ship, except those carrying mails and those working coals, on the Lord's Day, and we should be glad in the Government would even stop the discharge of coal on the Sabbath. We express our hope that the Government will put a stop to the running of Sunday trains, as it is not conducive to the peace and highest welfare of the people.[159]

In another report of 1906, the committee entreated:

> Many practices continue which are not at all in keeping with the honour due to the Lord's Day, and any further infringement of the rights of this day, so dearly prized by us, must ever be met by the most emphatic protests. By occasional sermons on the subject, by the use of appropriate literature and by abstinence from any personal profanation of the day, we must aim to preserve intact this day of rest and worship.[160]

In their stand for public morality, the Methodist stance is best encapsulated in the 1894 report, which made the bold statement:

> We believe that the time has fully come to assume and maintain firmly the ground that liquor shops, opium dens, gambling resorts and brothels are not necessary evils to be tacitly tolerated, or formally regulated by law. The only recognition which Christian law should give to such resorts should be in the direction of

---

159. Rutledge, "Report of Committee on Public Morals," 60.

160. Shellabear, Horley, Amery, Pykett, and Ling Thi Kong, "Report of Committee on Public Morals," 45.

abolishing them altogether and we are thankful that as a church we have in all parts of the world assumed this advance position.[161]

Where "Methodism in general has always recognized her part of the responsibility with regard to public morality,"[162] perhaps one of the most urgent and important fight for the Methodist mission was for the abolition of opium trade, which had been the bane of many Chinese immigrants and also for mainland China. Trade in opium had been a lucrative source of trade income for the empire and for many years Britain had actively encouraged this deadly addiction all for the sake of balancing its trade deficit. It has been documented that opium use began early in the history of Singapore. Interestingly, among the gifts presented by Sir Stamford Raffles to the Temenggong Abdul Rahman in 1819 was opium. The rise in trade in Singapore involved a substantial volume of the import and export of opium and not surprisingly opium (ab)use increased among both the rich and poor immigrant Chinese population. Among the rich, opium smoking was regarded as an acceptable social activity perhaps even being indicative of a social status[163] whilst among the poor, the reasons for the (ab)use was that it was regarded as a psychosomatic panacea, as a prophylactic medication against the tropical diseases such as cholera and dysentery as well as a chemical "relief" to assuage the emotional longings for homesick souls. It is hence likely that Noorman Abdullah is correct when he wrote that "opium was not regarded or constructed as a social problem in the first half of the nineteenth century, but was in fact very much an integral part of everyday life for immigrant labour."[164] The British colonial administration, in fact regarded opium use as a prophylactic against social unrests (since the drug kept the users somewhat inebriated) and to a certain extent lauded its medical "benefits." A Colonial Engineer who served in Singapore, H.E. McCallum made justifications for the medicinal use of opium among the immigrant coolies, especially since they lived and worked in conditions that were "too often reeking with fever and malaria."[165]

Gambier production and opium trade became increasingly important parts of the revenue of Singapore's trade, for which Singapore

161. Urch, Kelso, and Shellabear, "Report of Committee on Public Morals," 20.
162. Rutledge, "Report of Committee on Public Morals," 51.
163. See oral transcripts of Dr. Low Cheng Gin.
164. Abdullah, *Exploring Constructions of the "Drug Problem,"* 5.
165. McCallum, "Memorandum on the Opium Traffic."

became one of the main distribution centres in Asia. The opium trade grew rapidly such that between 1875 and 1905, the revenue gained from opium alone, constituted between 45 to 50 percent of the Straits Settlements total trade revenue. Due to the inordinate percentage of revenue, it is hardly surprising that the colonial administration was protective of this lucrative commodity and to that end, enforced various legislations to ensure a steady supply. Demand for the "panacea" was large since the new users (addicts) were being continually created among the ever increasing number of immigrant Chinese coolie workers. As was the case in South China, the widespread dependency (or perhaps addiction) of the immigrant workers as well as the merchants on this "medical panacea" provided the British with a steady revenue. Legislations were enacted to ensure the continued profitability of the opium trade and as Andersen put it, "to protect the (opium) farmer, was to protect the revenue."[166] As with the ideological principles of the East India Company earlier on, the paramount consideration was none other than commercial profit. Besides colonial merchantilic interests, historian Carl Trocki noted that Chinese merchants also encouraged the use of opium among their workers as a form of control on the workers, who reportedly spent up to two-thirds of their wages to fund their addiction. This not only lowered the production costs but at the same time also ensured a constant demand for opium within the colony. The relationships between British merchants, Chinese middleman and the Chinese labourers were pivoted on opium. Trocki understood that "the process by which this system of indebtedness and control was constructed actually lay at the roots of most of the secret society fights, riots, or conflicts that marked the history of Chinese Singapore."[167] And Trocki further astutely noted that "the study of Chinese society in nineteenth century Singapore thus cannot be separated from that of opium."[168]

Within the context of the colony of Singapore, it may be said that opium use in much of the nineteenth century, far from being regarded as a social ill, was perhaps a very much accepted indulgence. One of the reasons why it came to be perceived increasingly as a social ill may be attributed to the holiness movement and the spiritual awakening back in England. As a result, various anti-opium movements came into existence

---

166. Lim, "British Opium Policy," 52–75.
167. Trocki, *Opium and Empire*, 5.
168. Trocki, *Opium and Empire*, 223.

in the West[169] in the latter half of the nineteenth century. These developments paralleled the initiatives in China in combating opium addiction that were often tied with the Chinese nationalism. In Singapore, the anti-opium movements gained momentum especially among the more enlightened Straits-born Chinese who felt a sense of patriotism to the country of their forebears, China, in light of the Opium Wars. The Opium Wars culminated in the unequal treaties forced upon China by the Western powers, each seeking to carve for themselves a piece of China for their possession and profit. These Straits-born Chinese merchants who had received western education, were becoming increasingly critical of western imperialism and were seeking to show their support of the revolution back in China, especially in resisting the trade in and the use of opium. Among these increasing vocal entrepreneurs was Dr. Lim Boon Keng, the person who was "Isaiah" who wrote to the newspapers against proselytism in Anglo-Chinese School. It might well have been that the "Isaiah incident" was a result of his anti-imperialist sentiments, for which he misunderstood the Methodist mission, perceiving them as complicit in the agenda of British imperialism.

These more enlightened entrepreneurs, lobbied tirelessly for the elimination of four vices, namely gambling, prostitution, drinking, and opium smoking, as they were perceived as impediments to the establishment of a physically and morally robust society. Their endeavour was very much supported by the missionaries. So intent were Dr. Lim Boon Keng and his brother that, together with some of these Straits-born Chinese, they established an Anti-Opium Society in 1906 to help the addicts and to support the cause of like-minded Chinese nationals, who were seeking to unite China against the ravages of western imperialism. Among these, opium use was regarded as a sign of moral decadence. It was discouraged all the more as the Anti-Opium Society promulgated the view that its use was synonymous with being anti-nationalistic.[170]

By the 1890s, the murmurs of protest against the vices in the Straits Settlements, echoed those in London as well as in China. The

---

169. The main anti-opium organization, the Anglo-Oriental Society for the Suppression of the Opium Trade, was founded late in 1874. Interestingly, the society owed its origin to the efforts of a group of Quaker anti-opium campaigners in Birmingham. It was a little later on that the prefix "Anglo-Oriental" was dropped.

170. Chinese nationalists as well as anti-opium society activists in Singapore have persistently condemned the use of opium, blaming opium trade as that evil which increases China's debt and decreases China's prestige.

missionaries, especially with the arrival of the Methodists began to voice their discomfort with how the vices were so readily condoned. What small dissonance the missionaries created in their critique was further amplified by the work of the Straits-born Chinese that crescendoed in the formation of the Anti-Opium Society. Among the different groups of missionaries, the Methodists were probably the most outspoken. Using their own publication, they regularly featured anti-opium articles. Beginning from the first year of the publication of the *Malaysia Message*, the official monthly journal of the Methodist mission, frequent reports and articles highlighting the harm in opium use were published.[171] The *Malaysia Message* published numerous articles castigating the problem of the opium traffic and was unequivocal in denouncing the harm that it inflicts on the users and their families. One of the authors commented:

> The opium traffic is an evil, a great evil, an evil everywhere—a curse to mankind first, last and forever. The indictments made against it can scarcely be overdrawn. Whiskey is bad enough, but opium is much worse. Where the two exist together, whiskey slays its thousands; opium its tens of thousands. Every Christian man should pray and work for its destruction. To license the opium traffic is to give it the sanction of law, make it respectable and provide for its perpetuation. The Government becomes *particeps criminus* in all of its attendant evils. To derive a revenue from the opium traffic is to feed upon iniquity. It is out of harmony with the Word of God and the Christian conscience.[172]

In a report of the mission work in Singapore, the mission was acutely aware that it could not neglect the opium question as it was spending a great deal of time as well as resources, financial and personnel especially among the Chinese in Singapore. On the importance of the opium question, it noted,

> Whether we consider this question from the individual or the national standpoint, in its moral or political aspects, or its commercial or financial bearings, it is full of profound interest. It deserves the attention of all well-disposed persons of every

---

171. The articles and reports include those found in December 1891 through to the submission of the Opium Committee report in 1909. Missionaries such as Rev. Dr. Benjamin West and Rev. J. A. B. Cook, a Presbyterian minister, periodically contributed accounts of their ministry among the opium addicts through a column "Is Opium Harmless?" in *The Malaysia Message* beginning from March 1892.

172. *The Malaysia Message*, Vol I No 4 Jan. 1892, 26.

shade of religious and political opinion. It especially demands the thoughtful consideration of those who "profess and call themselves Christians." It is not a party question, but one of vast national importance.[173]

Interestingly, the May 1892 issue of the *Malaysia Message* devoted almost the entire publication to the opium question. It included an article written by Rev. Dr. Benjamin West on "*The Physical Effects of Opium*," where he noted that "through the careful and diligent enquiries and observations made by the writer on hundreds of cases of opium smokers" that contrary to the position that opium use in small quantities may be beneficial to the body, that "the continued use of opium in any quantity, however small, is detrimental to health, both physical and moral."[174]

Other articles included "*The Historical Aspect of the Opium Question*," "*The Opium Question Viewed from the Moral Standpoint*" by H. L. E. Luering and "*Opium from the Missionary Standpoint*" by William Shellabear, who were all missionaries of the Methodist Episcopal Church. In his article, Shellabear recounts,

> I have read in the columns of this very paper of parents heartlessly bartering away their offspring to get opium, and in other Christian papers I have read of mothers driving their daughters to lives of infamy for money to purchase opium, and of boys strangling their younger brothers for the sake of some article of clothing which could be sold for opium.[175]

As evidenced in this issue and the numerous other articles published, contrary to the general view that opium was smoked in moderation and that opium addicts were specifically the men, the Methodist missionaries refuted that common misrepresentation by the proponents of opium traders. They were concerted in their appeal to curtail, if not, ban the trade in opium through demonstrating the ugly truth of the physical, financial and spiritual devastation that opium brought to both individuals and society. The *Malaysia Message* also published an interview with Bishop Thoburn on the issue of opium through the perspective of India, for which Bishop Thoburn was then appointed. In that interview, the question was asked: "What position do you hold, Bishop Thoburn, on the

---

173. Cook, "Opium Traffic," 57.
174. West, "Physical Effects of Opium," 59.
175. Shellabear, "Opium from the Missionary Standpoint," 62.

question of exporting the drug to China?" To which Thoburn's unflinching reply was,

> I hold that the Government policy of acting the part of a merchant is at least a hundred years out of date, leaving out of count all moral considerations. If the Indian Government must assume the functions of an ordinary merchant, let them select some article of commerce that has no immoral tendency. Alike on moral and economic grounds, I deem the export traffic to be wholly indefensible.[176]

In yet another article, the Methodists mission reported on the growing anti-opium movement in the Malay Peninsular, that was gaining momentum both in the Federated Malay Territories as well as in Singapore. Rev. W. E. Horley wrote that contrary to popular opinion (which he confessed that he once erroneously held) that the majority of Chinese had no desire to break off opium, there was an increasing awareness of the scourges of opium use among the Chinese and an attendant move to eradicate the use among the Chinese workers. Yet again in this article, the Methodist mission held a different perspective from that of the colonial administration. Horley included in the article the following appeal:

> Will the Governments of the Strait Settlements and the Federated Malay States do anything to help remove the terrible temptations which are in these men's way? The British Parliament has unanimously condemned the trade as being morally indefensible and has opened negotiations with China with a view to gradual suppression of the traffic, *but what is our Government here going to do*? (emphasis mine).[177]

Horley concluded his article as follows:

> The question of revenue should have no weight in the matter at all. The souls and bodies of men are more valuable than money. Well has Confucius said "In a State gain is not to be considered prosperity but its prosperity will be found in righteousness. When he who presides over a State makes revenue his chief business, he must be under the influence of some small mean man." Let our legislators and governing experts find some other

---

176. "Interview with Bishop Thoburn on the Opium Question," 48.
177. Horley, "Anti-Opium Movement," 23.

ways of raising revenue, and blessing will come to them and to the people whom they govern.[178]

To that end, the Methodist missionaries or pastors with British citizenships also lobbied like-minded colonial officials. Their unstinting reprehension of opium trade and abuse, though constantly discounted by the colonial administration as they sought to justify so lucrative a trade commodity, was perhaps beginning to reap some kind of a "positive" response. This "positive" response was in the invitation by the Governor of the Strait Settlements, John Anderson, to Bishop William F. Oldham to sit on the Straits Settlements Opium Commission in 1907.

London had issued instructions to appoint such a Commission to investigate the extent of opium smoking in the Straits Settlements and to determine "the best steps to be taken . . . for minimizing and eventually eradicating the evil (of opium smoking)" within the colony. Anderson was well aware of the extent of the opium problem, as he stated that "anyone who knows this colony knows that there is undoubtedly a great amount of evil attached to excessive consumption of opium."[179] The Commission was composed of a total of six members who were all prominent citizens of the Straits Settlement—John Anderson, Tan Jiak Kim, Dr. J. Galloway, Bishop W. F. Oldham, W.R.C. Middleton and E.F.H. Edlin. Accordingly, the majority of the Commission was pro-opium, whereas "only Tan and Oldham were known to favour suppression."[180] The commission was tasked specifically to make a full enquiry into:

(1) The extent to which excessive indulgence in the smoking of opium prevails in Our Straits Settlements;

(2) Whether the smoking of opium (a) in moderation, or (b) in excess, has increased in Our said Settlements.

(3) The steps that should in your opinion, be taken by the Government to minimize and eradicate eventually the evils arising from the smoking of opium in Our said Settlements.[181]

---

178. Horley, "Anti-Opium Movement," 23.
179. SLCP, 1907:92.
180. Trocki, *Opium and Empire*, 212.
181. Anderson, *Report of the Commission*, 1.

Methodist Maneuvers 169

The immediate reaction to the appointment of the Commission sparked a series of rather spirited counter-discourses in the newspapers. The Straits Times on 17 August 1907 carried this rather stinging critique:

> We allow evils a thousand times more deadly (than opium) in our own cities with the smug complacency of the hypocrites we are. This canting desire to deprive the native of his opium has become a mania, while unctuous prelates and self-satisfied presbyters quaff their port or drink their beer, or take their night-cap of whisky and soda.[182]

Most of the criticisms leveled at the Commission were due to the fear that any curtailing of the opium trade would have severe financial repercussions on the trade revenue of the Colony. Be that as it may, a careful reading of the wording of the enquiry indicated that there was in principle no initiative with regard to eradicating opium smoking per se (italicise).[183]

The Commission took about six months and interviewed seventy-five persons and the report of its findings are contained in three volumes totaling 1,352 pages. The table below shows the race and occupation of the witnesses.[184]

---

182. *Straits Times*, 17 August 1907.
183. CO 273/328, G.D. No 308, 24 July 1907, CO No.29672.
184. Adapted from the two tables in Anderson, *Report of the Commission*, 2, 3.

Table 9: Occupation and Ethnicity of Interviewees of the Opium Commission

Occupation	Nominated by Commission		Nominated by Anti-Opium Societies		Total
	European	Chinese	European	Chinese	
Government Officers	10	1	1	–	12
Foreign Consuls	1	–	–	–	1
Christian Missionaries	1	–	2	1	4
Medical Practitioners (Under Government)	7	–	1	–	8
Medical Practitioners (Private)	2	–	1	3	6
Journalists	1	–	–	–	1
Engineers	2	–	–	–	2
Contractors	2	–	–	–	2
Merchants	1	4	–	4	9
Planters	–	3	–	–	3
The Miners	–	2	–	5	7
Pensioned Officers	1	–	–	–	1
Ship Owners	–	1	–	1	2
Bank Cashier	–	–	–	1	1
Opium Farmers	–	4	–	1	5
Broker	–	1	–	–	1
Insurance Agent	–	1	–	–	1
Labour Contractor	–	1	–	–	1
Opium Shop Keepers	–	3	–	–	3
Labourers	–	5	–	–	5
TOTAL	28	26	5	16	75

Source: *Report of Commission on Use of Opium*, Singapore National Archives.

Of the seventy-five interviewed, there were only four missionaries—Rev. J.A.B. Cook (missionary of the China Mission of the Presbyterian Church of England), Rev. Tay Seck Kin (Pastor of the English Presbyterian Church, Chinese Mission), Rev. Father V. Gazeau (Vicar, St Peter and St Paul's Church) and Rev. H.L.E Luering (pastor in charge of

Chinese churches in connection with the Methodist Episcopal Mission), all of whom were openly anti-opium in their convictions. Rev. Cook's participation as a witness in the Commission is particularly important in that it was he who recommended fifteen out of the twenty-one witnesses nominated from the anti-opium societies.

In the consolidated report, the Commission, however, maintained that it found "no reasonable grounds" to suggest that there was a major problem at hand in regard to opium use and its conclusion was that the ills spoken thereof were "usually the subject of exaggeration."[185] In downplaying the ills, the Commission drew the analogy that "the (opium) habit in its inception (was) comparable to indulgence in alcohol in the West."[186]

In providing specific answers to the three parts of the enquiry, firstly, "the extent to which excessive indulgence in the smoking of opium prevails in Our Straits Settlements," the Commission's answer was,

> We find that the vast majority of smokers indulge to an extent that may be properly called moderate, and that excessive indulgence occurs only in isolated instances.[187]

Secondly, on "whether the smoking of opium (a) in moderation, or (b) in excess, has increased in Our said Settlements?" the Commission concluded,

> We find that there has been no increase in the prevalence of the habit, and in this we include use in moderation and use in excess, during the past decade.[188]

And finally, in regard to "the steps that should in your opinion, be taken by the Government to minimize and eradicate eventually the evils arising from the smoking of opium in Our said Settlements," the Commission's conclusion and recommendations were,

> We do not find it proved that the evils arising from the use of opium have in any way increased during the past decade. We consider, however, that the circumstances surrounding the use of opium justify the Government in maintaining a closer and stricter control over it and we therefore recommend that the present system of farming the opium revenue be abolished and

---

185. Anderson, *Report of the Commission*, 1, 3.
186. Anderson, *Report of the Commission*, 11.
187. Anderson, *Report of the Commission*, 46.
188. Anderson, *Report of the Commission*, 46.

that a Government monopoly of the preparation and distribution of *chandu* be substituted.

We further consider that steps should be taken by the Government to suppress the use of opium in brothels.

We recommend that improvements should be made in the arrangements of existing opium smoking shops, but we consider there is no necessity or justification for the abolition of such shops.

We recommend that the access of all women to licensed opium shops be prohibited and we further recommend that the sale of *chandu* to all women and to children under 18 years of age be made an offence.

We consider that the price of *chandu* at present obtaining in the Straits Settlements is sufficiently prohibitive, but we are of opinion that the price in the Federated Malay States should be gradually raised to the price obtaining in the Colony.[189]

Quite within expectations, the Commission did not make any recommendations to impose a total ban on the use of opium, but reiterated the claim that opium use did indeed provide relief for the immigrant labourers who suffered from "the lack of home comforts, the strenuousness of . . . labour, (and) the severance from family association."[190] It did however recommend the prohibition of the sale of prepared or cooked opium (known as *chandu*) to all children under 18 years of age, women, as well as the suppression of opium use in brothels.

The results of the report demonstrated the limitations of the inquiry. The testimonies of several doctors were rejected only because they held anti-opium perspectives. The recommendation for a government-operated opium refuge was rejected based on costs and similarly, the registration of smokers to regulate the abuse was similarly rejected. While such an inquiry was held, it seems evident that the Commission was primarily concerned with protecting the revenue of the colony. The recommendations that they made seem to further such a presupposition, as what was put forward was more concerned with correcting some of the existing practices in order to prevent any anyone from slipping through the system without having duly paid the taxes for opium use. Thus, it is evident that the main concern was in increasing the revenue, or at least "safeguarding of the revenue"[191] rather than addressing the evil of the

189. Anderson, *Report of the Commission*, 46.
190. Anderson, *Report of the Commission*, 46.
191. Trocki, *Opium and Empire*, 213.

drug itself. Cheng Yu Wen perceived that the purpose of the Commission was in fact bureaucratic rationalization rather than moral reform. She wrote,

> The Report was mainly concerned with justifying and safeguarding the opium revenues, and where it was convenient, a few restrictive measures were introduced, provided that these did not jeopardize the revenue. Such measures were not calculated to decrease the consumption of opium. The Opium Commission Report *appears* to be the first step in the elimination of opium in the Straits Settlements, but it would be *more correct* to look upon it as a last desperate effort to justify the Government's policy of collecting revenue from opium.[192] (emphasis mine)

It is notable that Bishop Oldham was included among the members of the Commission. The fact that a Methodist Bishop rather than any of the other prominent ministers perhaps lends credence to the role that Christianity, not least of all, Methodism, has been featured in the social fabric at the turn of the twentieth century. In most of the deliberations, however, Bishop William Oldham was but a minor voice that was seemingly drowned out in the cacophonous rants of a profit driven colonial administration. In the interviews as well as the meetings of the Commission, Bishop Oldham continually questioned the jealously guarded notion that opium was neither addictive nor a health hazard. He was cognizant of the detriment that opium had both for the individual as well as for society.

It may well have been owing to the extension of the scope of the enquiry to include the Federated Malay States, the length of time taken by the commission was extended and in the final organization of the report as well as the recommendations put forth by the commission, that two of the commissioners, namely Bishop William Oldham and Mr. Tan Jiak Kim (the two in the Commission who held anti-opium views) were perhaps not represented as they were "unavoidably absent in America and Japan respectively, and that considerable time has been required to submit this report to them for signature and return."[193] And in that regard, reading the recommendations that were worded in their absence, it is not surprising that Bishop Oldham was the only person in the Commission to disagree with the summary conclusions, for which he composed and

---

192. Cheng U Wen, "Opium in the Straits Settlements," 73.
193. Anderson, *Report of the Commission*, 2.

dispatched a memorandum of dissent as well as a personal note that were both included as to the opium commission report.[194]

Bishop Oldham's *Memorandum of Dissent*[195] was to lend voice to his disagreement with regard to the Commission's answer to the first question of the enquiry on the extent of excessive indulgence in the smoking of opium. Oldham summed up his dissent accordingly:

> Much evidence shows that the course of opium user is from "playing with the pipe" occasionally, to the steady use, in which the tendency is to an increase of the daily dose. There is, from this time, pressure upon the individual's money and time to minister to the appetite already fixed. At stated times every day the drug must be used, or the person be utterly unfit for work. Whether the dose be large or small unfitness for the daily task is the penalty of omitting it. This, with the fact that, circumstances permitting, the dose tends to increase until it reaches large proportions, leads one to conclude that "moderation" in opium smoking does not exist.[196]

In regard to the steps that should be taken by the Government, Bishop Oldham proposed the following substitution in the last paragraph of the recommendations:

> We are of the opinion that the price of *chandu* in the Federated Malay States should be gradually raised to the price obtaining in the Colony, and that as public opinion grows, and all classes demand further restriction, the Government department having the matter in charge should be empowered to increase the price of *chandu*, or adopt such other measures as may lead to the increased restriction and ultimate extinction of the opium traffic. Both in restriction and ultimate prohibition, Government action should not be permitted to lag behind Chinese public opinion.[197]

Aware of the immense suffering that opium addiction inflicts upon the users, particularly among the Chinese whom the Methodist mission

---

194. As both the memorandum of dissent and the personal note from Bishop Oldham were received after the consolidated report had been sent to the printers, Bishop Oldham had to dispatch a dozen printed copies that were attached to the printed report. These were, however, fully published in the January 1909 issue of *The Malaysia Message*, Vol XVIII No 4, which are available at the Methodist Archives, Singapore.

195. "The Memorandum of Dissent" is found in Appendix G.

196. Oldham, "Memorandum of Dissent from the Majority Report," in Anderson, *Report of the Commission*, 48.

197. Oldham, "Memorandum of Dissent from the Majority Report," in Anderson, *Report of the Commission*, 48.

had since its arrival been reaching out to, Bishop Oldham's proposed recommendation contrasted with the Commission's somewhat convenient exclusion of any mention of "restriction and ultimate extinction of the opium traffic." Bishop Oldham's recommendation is significant in that it sought to incorporate the element of public opinion, pitting moral and familial considerations against purely economic interests. His inclusion of Chinese public opinion as a factor is evidence that in the Commission the growing anti-opium sentiment among the more educated members of Chinese community had been somewhat muted and or completely ignored. His recommendation hence sought to mitigate that reticence.

Bishop Oldham further included a personal note[198] together with the Memorandum of Dissent, which is also included in the Report. His note is quoted here, in full:

> When asked to accept the appointment to the Commission on Opium, I was told the conclusions would be reached in six months. The end of this period left the Commission far from concluding this work. I was therefore unable to meet with the other Commissioners when making their findings.
>
> I am obliged now, with regret and some hesitation, to express dissent from some conclusion reached, though I agree in the main with the practical measures outline.
>
> And while wholly in sympathy with what is called the "Anti-Opium" view, I would earnestly advise against any sudden measures of repression which would outrun public opinion, disorganize the finances of the Colony, and work harm rather than good to a considerable body of users of opium who have acquired the habit and who steadfastly believe that their health would be sacrificed in any attempt to suddenly cease the use of the drug without the provision of medical help.
>
> All the parties to the traffic which is now perceived, more or less clearly, not to be conducive to the public good, must patiently and intelligently find their way to better methods of restriction until by successive steps prohibition is reached. Haste and suddenness now are to be deprecated quite as much as lethargy and inaction.

His personal note provides the explanation for absence during the time the Commissioners deliberated on the final recommendations. While his dissent may be perceived as somewhat muted, in view of the

---

198. Oldham, "Personal Note," in Anderson, *Report of the Commission*, 49. Bishop Oldham's "Personal Note" is found in Appendix H.

continuous rallying of the anti-opium community, for which the Methodist mission stood alongside. Bishop Oldham was also aware that the economy of the Settlements has been much too closely tied up with the opium traffic and trade revenue. Rev. Dr. Benjamin F. West had written in the *Malaysia Message* that, "it is something appalling to think that the opium trade of this Colony is such that 65 percent of the revenue, as stated by the Honourable Mr. Shelford in a recent speech, is derived from this traffic."[199] By the turn of the century, the revenue derived from opium trade was leveled at about fifty percent of the trade revenue. The table below shows the trade revenue derived from opium traffic from 1898 to 1906[200] and the total colonial expenditure on education.[201]

Table 10: Comparison of Percentage of Trade Revenue Derived from Opium Traffic and Percentage Expenditure on Education

Year	Total Revenue of the Colony	Total Expenditure of the Colony	Total Spending on Education	Revenue derived from Opium	Percentage of Revenue derived from Opium to total Revenue	Percentage of Education Expenditure to total Expenditure
1898	$5,071,281.54	$4,587,366.57	$134,764	$2,332,186.50	45.9%	2.94%
1899	$5,200,025.50	$5,060,523.17	$132,177	$2,333,426.00	44.8%	2.61%
1900	$5,386,556.58	$6,030,739.77	$135,130	$2,333,300.50	43.3%	2.24%
1901	$7,041,685.50	$7,315,000.53	$182,678	$3,747,269.50	53.2%	2.50%
1902	$7,754,733.23	$7,600,734.08	$179,965	$3,746,729.00	48.3%	2.37%
1903	$7,958,496.07	$8,185,952.14	$180,083	$3,746,659.00	47.1%	2.20%
1904	$10,746,517.49	$10,848,988.54	$230,729	$6,357,727.83	59.1%	2.13%
1905	$11,657,423.75	$10,976,525.37	$237,911	$5,368,939.54	46.0%	2.17%
1906	$9,618,312.97	$8,747,819.42	$265,093	$5,125,506.87	53.3%	3.03%

Source: *Straits Settlements Annual Reports*, Singapore: National Archives.

199. West, "Opium Question Again," 29.

200. Table adapted from Anderson, *Report of the Commission*, 42.

201. The figures for expenditure on education are derived from the Straits Settlements Annual Reports from 1899 to 1906, available from Jarman, *Annual Reports of the Straits Settlements*, vols. 3, 4 and 5.

Hence, Bishop Oldham's advice "against any sudden measures of repression which would outrun public opinion, disorganize the finances of the Colony, and work harm rather than good"[202] is based on sound rationale in view of the economic and financial policies on which the Straits Settlements is established. The recommendation of an immediate total ban is firstly not something that the colonial administration would even deign to entertain. Furthermore, the ramifications of an immediate total curtailing of the opium traffic would be devastating, not only to the opium traders but also to the opium addicts themselves, who did not have any other medical recourse for their addiction. The repercussions would also affect the day-to-day operations within the Colony, including the education system. Indeed, the lack of a stronger protest by Bishop Oldham on behalf of the Methodists might perhaps be explained by the fact that the immediate prohibition of the opium trade would also affect adversely the education programmes, not least of all the operation of the Methodist schools. As opium trade revenues formed a significant percentage of the trade revenue of Singapore, the grants-in-aid given to the schools, including the Methodist schools were hence inevitably tied to opium revenue of the colony. Even though the colonial expenditure on education was no larger than 3 percent of the total expenditure of the colony, any drastic shortfall in income from opium trade will almost certainly impact the colonial administration's Grant-in-aid programme which was thoroughly dependent on the opium trade. It might well be clear in the minds of those in the Commission, including Tan Jiak Kim and Bishop Oldham, that any immediate prohibitive action would have had drastic repercussions.

Seen in this light, Bishop Oldham's dissent may be perceived as one that held together the goals of the Methodist mission and at the same time recognizedre the complexities of the economic and financial considerations of the colonial administration. In the same breath that he cautioned against "haste and suddenness," he too warned against "lethargy and inaction." It must be borne in mind that his was the only dissent and his consistent recommendation was on restriction leading to the ultimate prohibition of the opium trade. The restriction and ultimate prohibition was consonant with the position of the Methodist mission as evidenced by the Report on Public Morals submitted to the Annual Conference of 1910:

202. Oldham, "Personal Note," in Anderson, *Report of the Commission*, 49.

> Your committee have noted with pleasure the official utterances of His Excellency the Governor of the Straits Settlements regarding the opium traffic, intimating that the time is not far distance when this evil shall be a thing of the past in the Straits Settlements and the Federated Malay States. Toward this end that the opium traffic is not under government regulation, and that restriction for which we have long called, such as the prohibition of opium smoking in rickshaw depots and houses of ill-fame, are being imposed, and as we believe that these restrictions cannot but help, we emphatically endorse the policy of the government to this extent.
>
> We are gratified to learnt that under the leadership of the United States of America, an international conference is about to be held at the Hague to consider ways and means for the world-wide abolition of the traffic.[203]

The Opium Commission of 1907, however, was not the end of Christian involvement in anti-opium campaigning though many, if not most, Christian groups were not at all represented. It seemed that the Methodists and the Presbyterians were the ones who presented a more vocal stance against the use of opium. Quite understandably, as the official church of the colonial administration, the Anglican Church was tacit in regard to the stand against the use of opium. Given that "opium was at the heart of the of British Malaya, and its influence went beyond the financial realm,"[204] what is perhaps perplexing is that despite the multipronged approach in the missionary endeavours of the Methodists, neither they nor the Christian fraternity at large, took up the cause of rehabilitation and care of the opium addicts, in setting up houses to care for these. Yet among the interviews conducted by the Commission, a Methodist pastor and missionary, Dr. H.L.E. Luering's testimony hints at the possible reason(s) for the difficulty in the setting up anti-opium refuges in the Colony and the Federated Malay States. In his interview with the Commissioners, Dr. Luering was asked, "Do you not think it would have been much better for those associated with the exploitation of this drug to have started a small refuge where it might have been properly tested under European medical supervision?" To which his response was:

> That was proposed at the first anti-opium meeting which was held in Ipoh about 13 months ago, I believe in November 1906.

---

203. Horley, "Report of Committee on Public Morals," 37–38.
204. Trocki, *Opium and Empire*, 237.

I was present and it was then recommended that an Anti-opium Refuge should be established in Ipoh. It did not come to pass for certain reasons. First of all the initial expense was considerable. A man to take care of it in a place like Ipoh would be a rather large expense. One gentlemen of the Anti-Opium Society was very much interested in it and presented the society with a plot of land for the purpose, I think that would have been in the end more successful. However, it would probably have exhausted the means at the disposal of the society.[205]

In other words, the setting up of anti-opium refuges required a substantial amount of finances for which government grants and lease of land were a seemingly impossibility. This financial constraint perhaps made it even more difficult for the Methodist mission to be involved in establishing these anti-opium refuges. The other reason lies perhaps in the fact that the Methodist missions were rather stretched in their commitment to establishing the church, the schools ministry as well as the home for the girls.

A significant reason for the Methodist ambivalence in regard to a closer collaboration with the local Chinese in the combat against opium may be perhaps linked with the "Isaiah Incident." Dr. Lim Boon Keng, "Isaiah" himself, the key figure in the anti-opium camp, whose open criticism of Christianity and the colonial powers a decade before the Opium Commission may have imperiled any collaboration. It might well have been that there were some reservations prior and immediately following the "Isaiah Incident" but there are evidences of greater collaboration during and after the period of the Opium Commission. In regard to the anti-opium stance, both the Methodist mission and Dr. Lim Boon Keng worked in tandem in testifying before the Commission for the abolition of the opium trade. It is also significant to note that the *Malaysia Message* carried a front page article, "*Opium versus Alcohol*" that was written by none other than Dr. Lim Boon Keng himself, where he implored that "every civilized State should endeavour to restrict the use of alcohol as much as possible and should absolutely forbid the use of opium, except as a drug to be employed only by duly qualified physicians."[206]

Perhaps the strongest reason for the Methodists' ambivalence rested not so much with Dr. Lim Boon Keng but more evidently in the

---

205. Anderson, *Report of the Commission*, 556. The interview questions and Dr. Luering's replies are found in the report from pages 562–63.

206. Lim Boon Keng, "Opium Versus Alcohol," 8.

proximity between the anti-opium groups in Malaya and Singapore and the Chinese nationalist forces in China. The links between the anti-opium groups and the nationalists forces in China raised the issue of loyalties for Christians who tended to support the status quo in China. While these two groups envisioned a society freed of the ills of opium addition, the undergirding rationale was somewhat disparate. Christianity perceived opium addiction as a personal vice that had social ramifications, whilst for the Chinese, it was much more than that, opium was both a symbol and a means of western colonialism, which was synonymous with exploitation and domination. While it may perhaps be due to the concern of being too closely associated with these groups who maintained connections with similar anti-opium and/or nationalistic forces back in China, or for whatever other reasons, it was nonetheless an opportunity lost in standing with the local Chinese in providing pastoral care and support for the opium addicts and their families. The rehabilitation of the addicts became largely a work undertaken by various anti-opium Chinese groups from 1906.

Opium use persisted as a problem for Singapore and Malaya where it was estimated that one in four Chinese in Straits Settlements was an addict.[207] It was not so much the effort of the colonial administration that catalyzed the prohibition of opium but rather external forces. The worldwide Great Depression resulted in a fall of opium revenues and it was not until 1943 that the British government finally prohibited opium smoking. By which time, the Japanese already had full control of Malaya and Singapore!

CONCLUSION

The manner in which the British governed the Straits Settlements was somewhat distinct from the other colonies in Africa and South Asia. Their one obsession was that the colony, particularly, Singapore should be economically profitable as a trading port with no natural resources and in this regard, British rule in the Straits seemed distinct from other British colonies.

In looking at the Methodist maneuvers under the colonial administration, where the colonial administration's chief concern was profitability, it may likewise be concluded that such was the case for the Methodists. But while the colonial concern was for economic profitability, the

---

207. Chen So Lan, *Opium Problem in British Malaya*.

Methodist concern was for the profit of the people among whom they established their various different ministries; for spiritual nourishment, social concern, medical care and educational mission. For the Methodists, there was a sense of cooperation whenever it was beneficial to the course of the mission. But whenever colonial policies conflicted with their goals, they often sought creative solutions. This was pre-eminently seen in the government's emphasis on the provision of a secular education whose primary concern was the training of clerical officers proficient in English. Undaunted, the Methodists continued to perservere in their educational mission by positioning themselves as eligible for the governments grants-in-aid and yet holding on true to their call to teach the Word in season and out of season by providing religious instruction without the operation hours of the schools.

At the onset of the Methodist mission, while it seemed that the Methodists might have enjoyed some privilege in the sense of colonial patronage, yet a careful examination of the intentions demonstrated that more often than not, the British administrators were far more concerned in regard to their own economic interests than those of the Methodist missionaries. Policies were revised and enforced in ensuring that proselytism was not carried out in the mission schools. And where Methodist education mission was concerned, the mission schools were not the primary beneficiaries of colonial education expenditure. It was the government schools and vernacular schools that received the bulk of colonial funding. For the British colonial administration, whilst it seemed that some of the policies were made to enhance the government of the colony (such as the location of the different ethnic groups), upon closer examination, however, it was clear that even these other reasons were peripheral to that singular obsession of making trade profitable in the Colony.

But where the ethics of the British Colony were in contradiction with the biblical mandate, the Methodist mission spared no effort in ensuring that their views were communicated and represented. In contradistinction to colonial expectations, the Methodists perceived that they did:

> have therefore the privilege of having a part in determining and promoting the moral tone and sentiment which should characterize a Christian nation. We are by no means pessimists who disregard the apparent changes for the better continually taking place around us. Nevertheless we regard it as our duty to

again draw the attention of the church, the public at large and the government to the fact that there is ample scope for future improvements.[208]

This chapter has demonstrated that in their evangelism, their educational work and their social outreaches that impinged on ethics and morality, the Methodists would not be constrained by imperial demands to subscribe to the colonial policies. In such circumstances, they were not afraid to hold their ground and explore other possibilities of engaging with the colonial administration. In short, it could be said that there was a semblance of a symbiotic relationship between Methodism and British colonialism, for which the goals of both were vastly tangential rather than convergent. As highlighted in the examples, contrary to the claims, complicity was hardly a feature of the Methodist mission in Singapore.

---

208. Rutledge, "Report of Committee on Public Morals," 51.

5

Action, Reaction, and Transformation

CONCLUSION

METHODISM ARRIVED IN SINGAPORE at an opportune time, at the turn of the nineteenth century when "Britannia ruled the waves,"[1] when Britain was the superpower of the world. It has been summarized, that,

> *Pax Britannica* was a precondition of missionary activities. For once they entered colonial societies, missionaries worked to reform or abolish local cultures and religious practices, chiefly be preaching the Gospel, by promoting Western education and medicine, and by pressing colonial regimes to act responsibly.[2]

The rise of Britain in the Industrial Revolution, the eclipse of the rest of Europe by London as the dominant centre of commerce and the growth of British naval power contributed and established British supremacy and *Pax Britannica*. British dominance was maintained out of strategically located bases along almost all the lanes of every ocean and sea routes both eastward and westward,stretching throughout the globe. This dominance was to further result in the growth in trade and

---

1. The poem "Rule, Britannia" was originally published by James Thompson in 1740 as a masque, included in Alfred (Alfred the Great) and set to music by Thomas Augustine Arne in 1740. Britannia was the name given by Rome and in tandem with the rise of British naval power, since the seventeenth century, has been anthropomorphized into a symbol that blends the concepts of military might and economic superiority and empire. The poem is found in Palgrave, *Golden Treasury*.

2. Olaf Schumann et al., "Colonialism," in Sunquist et al., *Dictionary of Asian Christianity*, 195.

commerce in the colonies that were under British rule or protection. It may be surmised that without British rule around the world, it would perhaps be difficult to talk about the global structures of capitalism that we have today, nor can we take for granted the widespread use of the English language. In his candid assessment of the Empire, Niall Ferguson concluded that:

> Of course no one would claim that the record of the British Empire was unblemished. On the contrary, I have tried to show how often it failed to live up to its own ideal of individual liberty, particularly in the early era of enslavement, transportation and the "ethnic cleansing" of indigenous peoples. Yet the nineteenth-century Empire undeniably pioneered free trade, free capital movements and, with the abolition of slavery, free labour. It invested immense sums in developing a global network of modern communications. It spread and enforced the rule of law over vast areas. Though it fought many small wars, the Empire maintained a global peace unmatched before or since.[3]

Pax Britannica hence made it possible for the growth of trade and the consequent rise of global capitalism, through the vast interconnected network of trading ports further undergirded by the use of a common language, English. British presence in Southeast Asia provided an important link in this global network through the trade in spices and later, tin and rubber which became increasingly important commodities for the global market in the early twentieth century. Consequently, it is within expectations that "Singapore's trade showed a greater rate of growth between 1869 and 1914 than in the first fifty years of its modern existence, for it became an essential link between the industrial world of the West and the developing export economies of colonial Southeast Asia."[4]

For this seaport, "the long years of peaceful growth under the aegis of *Pax Britannica* had generated sufficient economic infrastructure and global trade connections to enable Singapore to survive"[5] the events of world history and to progress into the modern city state that it is today, as Singapore gained independence from British colonial rule as late as 1965.

Peter O'Brien in writing about *Pax Britannica* comments thusly:

---

3. Ferguson, *Empire*, 358–59.
4. Wong Lin Ken, "Commercial Growth before the Second World War," in Chew and Lee, *History of Singapore*, 52.
5. Chew, *Merlion at the Edge of an Afrasian Sea*.

Britain's implicit grand strategy for securing the peace, order and stability that its national interest required can be exposed as the underlying and persistent assumptions that guided governmental negotiations and actions in the state's dealings and conflicts with other powers, including the legally subordinate but in practice "quasi autonomous" administrations in charge of Britain's own dominions, colonies and dependencies overseas. The nation's "strategic assumptions" can only be exposed by careful historical analysis of the stance British ministers pursued, case by case, country by country, decade after decade in the connected but separable spheres of political, commercial, cultural and foreign—including imperial—policies.[6]

While Livingstone's "Commerce, Civilization and Christianity" is helpful in providing a panoramic perspective of British dominance and hegemony, O'Brien's statement above is significant in that he presents the case that while Britain exerted an overarching influence, yet the manner or force wherein Britain exercised her colonial powers is largely determined by the context. In other words, one cannot speak of a uniform exertion of British imperialism on all the British colonies. Britain's exercise of dominion was largely dependent on the context. British colonialism was hence differentiated in those different contexts[7] and as Britain encountered the multi-faceted issues at different times and in different places, British colonial policies were hence applied asymmetrically. Hence, while Singapore's experience with British colonialism may have arrived from India, the Indian experience is not synonymous with Singapore's, nor for that matter is the African experience is similar to the Indian encounter. Undoubtedly, there are similarities, but suffice to say that British colonialism is perhaps more nuanced than we understand it to be. It is certainly true that *Pax Britannica* was indeed a precondition that stimulated the arrival of the missionaries, yet British colonial policies were not uniform in the extent to which missionary activities in the colonies were encouraged or promoted. Colonial policies were not uniformly enforced through the British Empire and the particular context ought to be carefully analyzed on a "case by case, country by country, decade after decade" basis.

6. O'Brien, *Pax Britannica*.
7. Britain colonized various places for differing reasons. Most were for reason of trade, the production of crops, the extraction of raw materials, and the creation of markets for finished products. Some were for purely strategic interests, as in the case of Papua, which was to check the rise of German power in the Pacific.

Yet it could be said of the British Empire in Southeast Asia that the singular motivation was commercial, above all else. Britain was eminently preoccupied with commerce, with the prized final goal of trade with China. Everything else was secondary and perhaps all the major geopolitical and socio-economic policies made were subservient to this mercantile imperative. Britain's foray into Southeast Asia was particularly focused (at least initially) on spices which it could trade with China. This is demonstrated in the explicit exclusion of missionaries from the trading ships of the East India Company. The early presence of Anglican chaplaincy was for pastoral care for the expatriate community rather than for the work of mission and evangelism. Commercial trade was the major preoccupation given Singapore's strategic location.

British presence in Southeast Asia and in particular, Singapore, therefore laid the foundational infrastructures for the later arrival of the American Methodist Mission. With the Methodists, it cannot be denied that there was a hint of imperial patronage accorded by the colonial administration. But whatever colonial support afforded is oftentimes based upon economic and political expediency rather than religious considerations. Britain was not at all interested in developing Singapore in any other direction besides using it as a stepping stone in forcing open trade with China. Their extended stay was only necessitated by the political events in both China and India. In the grand scheme of British imperialism, Singapore was but an afterthought.

As the global markets traded increasingly in tin and rubber in the mid-nineteenth century, the rich hinterland of Malaysia presented further possibilities of expanding trade with China and the rest of the world. Singapore's port thus was an important piece in Britain's strategy for continued commercial dominance. British interest in the Malay Peninsula was in many ways determined by a rabid mercantilism. In contradistinction to the other Crown Possessions, the British developed a policy of non-intervention until the surge of other European powers in Southeast Asia, led eventually to the signing of the Treaty of Pangkor in 1874.

Maria Perpetua Kana noted that:

> the most important factor that finally led to greater British involvement was the realization that if peace and order was restored the rich natural resources in the interior of the Peninsular

could be better exploited and British trade in the Malay archipelago further enhanced.⁸

In a separate study on the impact of colonialism on culture through a sport such as cricket, Habibul Khondker commented:

> The British engagement in Southeast Asia was lucrative but not socially so deep. *The plantation economy in Malaya and the transshipment of goods from Singapore did not necessitate any thing more than a small bureaucratic set-up, a legal order and police.* The job was to ensure labor control with enduring consequences. The hegemony of culture was not necessary; the brute coercion—aided by a dose of opium—was quite adequate.⁹ (emphasis mine)

It perhaps is evident that British colonial interests in Singapore and Malaysia were overwhelmingly mercantile and in that regard, other concerns, including those of the missionary organizations were peripheral, if there was indeed any at all to begin with. Besides being on the periphery, Christian mission was further compromised by British colonial policies, and all the more so, in the wake of the Pangkor engagement. The Pangkor Treaty is perceived as the blueprint for formal British rule in Malaya, wherein provisions were made to safeguard Malay rights. The British concession to exclude the Malay religion and customs from the purview of the Resident was viewed as an attempt to placate the sultans by giving them a semblance of authority, at least where Malay cultural and religious sensitivities and praxis were concerned. This was again an economically and politically expedient move on the part of the British administration. Maureen Chew held that in *toto*, the commercial interests of the British unofficially and yet effectively curtailed all missionary efforts among the Malays.¹⁰ It was to further exacerbate the cultural divide between the different ethnic communities, that would ferment and erupt in the racial conflicts in the later histories of both Malaysia and Singapore.¹¹

These developments were the context in which American Methodism first arrived in Singapore in 1885. As with Britain, most if not all of

8. Kana, *Christian Mission in Malaysia*, 19.
9. Khondker, "Cricket, Colonialism, Culture and Cosmopolitanism."
10. Chew, *Journey of the Catholic Church*, 110.
11. Numerous cases of racial tension and unrest include the Maria Hertogh riots in the 1950s and racial riots in the 1960s, between the Chinese and the Malays in Singapore and even more recently between unhappiness among the Indians against the Malays in Kuala Lumpur in March 2009.

the missionary societies were focussed on establishing a Christian presence in China. China, rather than Southeast Asia, was their goal. Joseph Haines in his dissertation, studying the history of ProtestantP missions in Malaya from 1815 to 1881, before the arrival of the Methodists, makes this stinging conclusion:

> It was easy enough to justify the abandonment of Malaya when the possibility of entering China presented itself, but there does not appear to have been much regret about leaving what seemed a difficult, if not barren field of work. In the case of the L.M.S., there was a definite irresponsible attitude about the work that was left behind in that no provision was made for the schools and congregations established in Malacca and Penang. The world of the Malayan people, Malays, Chinese and Indians, was a world that the missionary did not successfully penetrate.

In the years between 1846 and 1881, Malaya remained out of the main stream of Protestant missionary activity and was largely forgotten. At the same time there was extensive Roman Catholic activity in Singapore and the Peninsula, but the state of anarchy and civil war that prevailed prevented very much movement beyond the boundaries of the Straits Settlements.

The Church of England, with its privileged position as the established church, was unable through lack of personnel to take advantage of what opportunities were available. The planning of the Anglican Bishops was directed to maintaining as a first priority the chaplaincy to the European community. Efforts that were made to combine the work of chaplain and missionary to the Asians ended in failure. Individual chaplains did try to direct the work of native catechists, but they received little encouragement from their congregations. Similar efforts to combine missionary work with a chaplaincy on the part of the Presbyterian Church were unsuccessful.

The work of J. G. Bausum, Sophia Cooke and Benjamin Keasberry met with limited success, but the absence of any organizational backing, combined with severe financial restrictions, hampered much of their work. Benjamin Keasberry's work among the Malays, both in his literature programme and manual education, pointed to new creative approaches. Work among the Malays was more and more discouraged by the British authorities for reasons of political expediency, particularly after the signing of the Treaty of Pangkor in 1874.

The long period of inactivity ended with the new political and economic development of the country and new missionary activity of the Presbyterian Church of England and the Methodist Episcopal Church, U.S.A. directed specifically to establishing a church in Malaya.[12]

Haine's account had omitted the brief and perhaps almost easily unnoticed arrival of a British Methodist missionary some decades before the arrival of American Methodism, which was the first opportunity for British Methodism to found a church in Singapore, when Josiah Cox arrived in Singapore as early as 1853. But just as it was for the East India Company, so it was with most of the missionary societies of that era: China was the goal. The focus on China accounted for the lack of funding and perhaps also the lack of interest for British Methodism to establish a work in Singapore. Enamoured by the possibilities in China, British Methodism did not seize the opportunity of rooting Methodism in Singapore. The door was left ajar and was later opened by the American Methodist missionaries.

The hiatus of slightly more than three decades before the arrival of American Methodism saw various changes in colonial administration and policies. Singapore became a Crown Colony and was administered directly from the London office (as compared with the earlier administration through Calcutta, India). Increasingly, London began to appreciate the strategic value of Singapore as a trading port. British rule undoubtedly was the precondition for the arrival of the American Methodist mission for Britain had established the physical and political stability that made it possible for the arrival of the Methodist mission. So that when the invitation was extended for American Methodism, which was based in India to come to Singapore, it was readily accepted.

The initial colonial nonchalance toward the missionary enterprise ought to be noted. The colonial administration played no significant part in facilitating the arrival of Bishop James Thoburn and Rev. William Oldham, who came to Singapore as a response to a request by a Wesleyan, Charles Philips, worshiping in a Presbyterian church, who is hence rightly regarded as "the father of Methodism in Singapore."[13] But it may be said that the colonial administration in their *laissez faire* treatment of these missionaries was indeed the climate/context which sparked the rise of Methodism in Singapore. British colonial administration was not synonymous with patronage; colonial indifference was more likely the

12. Haines, "History of Protestant Missions," 296–98.
13. Murray, "In Memoriam: Mr. C. Philips," 95.

case. While it may be true that the Methodist requests for grants of land to establish churches and to build schools were acceded to; yet it was only often after repeated appeals and notwithstanding the fact that there were often numerous attached conditions that were stipulated by the colonial administration.

British "patronage" of American Methodism is perhaps evident only because of the demand for English education. In view of the fact that there were other schools and institutions that also provided English instruction, albeit with varying religious affiliations and different directions with regards to the development of the students, British involvement in these education agencies was also varied. Yet again the overriding criterion was eminently the economic benefit to the British government. The Straits Settlements Commission Report on Education in 1902 is worded as such,

> Commerce being by far the most important interest in the Colony, it is, we think, clear that the chief practical object of our educational system would be to turn out young men properly qualified to take part in it, and it is to be hoped that a good secondary educational system in the Colony will enable mercantile firms to draw a larger portion of their mercantile assistants from the Colony than at present.[14]

There is no doubt that within the first decade of the arrival of the Methodists, the education in the schools that the Methodists established (such as ACS and MGS) was of a better quality. It perhaps is surprising too that the cost of education (per student) for the Methodist Mission was calculated as significantly less than those schools operated by the Government, such as Raffles Institution, as well as those by the other mission agencies (such as St Joseph's Institution). The government had put in place a revised grants-in-aid educational policy that promoted a secular brand of education, thereby checking proselytism in the (Methodist) schools.

In the educational policies of the colony that were revised on numerous occasions (such as in 1833, 1854, 1870, 1893, 1899, 1902) religious neutrality, costs considerations and government inspection were always the chief criteria. Yet the Methodist schools, chiefly ACS, were able to secure the government grants-in-aid every year in helping defray the operational costs of the schools. Invariably, the colonial administration's

---

14. *Straits Settlements Education Commission Report*, 17.

tacit approval of the Methodist-run schools was based upon economic considerations.

In respect to school inspections, there was hardly any hint of colonial patronage and it is perhaps more likely that the Methodist schools that were in direct competition with the government-sponsored schools would have been subjected to even with more rigour in the inspection as they were seen as rivals. In view of the secular system of education put in place by the colonial administration, it is somewhat inordinate to note that there was hardly any charge of proselytism from the School Inspector's reports. Charges against proselytism in ACS were brought forward rather by the prominent Chinese merchants who were advocates of an education that promoted Confucian values. These accusations that were published in the newspapers may perhaps be regarded as one of the major setbacks for the Methodist mission. Yet the Methodists were able to provide a response that testified to the integrity and salubrity of the instruction offered at the Methodist schools.

In the colonial administration's insistence on the provision of a secular form of education, the Methodist mission however should not be misunderstood as having compromised their primary call. Ingeniously, they circumvented the government's insistence on secular education with the provision of religious instruction before and after the official school hours, and at no compulsion to the students. This ensured that the Methodist-run schools complied with colonial educational policies but yet in no way compromised the mission they had set out to fulfil.

Various surveys[15] of the history of education in colonial societies have demonstrated that very often colonial education was designed with the aim of keeping the colonized in their place. This has in turn fueled the critique that missionary endeavours came on the coattails of the colonialism and that the two were complicit. Undoubtedly, there are strong connections between Christian mission and the work of education and much in this more positive regard has been documented by historians such as Steven Kaplan,[16] Kenneth Scott Latourette,[17] and Brian Stanley,[18] where missionaries to Africa, China and India rather than perceived as

---

15. One example of such is Carnoy, *Education as Cultural Imperialism*.

16. Kaplan, *Indigenous Responses*.

17. See Latourette, *History of Christian Missions in China*, as well as his *History of the Expansion of Christianity*, vol. 6.

18. Stanley, *Bible and the Flag*.

colluding with the colonial administration, have often used education as a means of facilitating evangelism among the indigenous population.

There have also been numerous studies carried out, for example Comaroff and Comaroff,[19] that demonstrated that the provision of education by the missionaries precipitated a platform for the people to engage the colonial administration on their terms. Andrew Porter also noted:

> There is no doubt that the spread of literacy and knowledge of other languages both widened horizons at many different social levels and greatly enhanced the ability of ordinary people to question or subvert traditional attitudes as well as imperial and colonial assumptions.[20]

An important study undertaken by Kevin Blackburn and Pauline Fong applied the Halevy theory to account for the appeal of Methodism and the Methodist schools among the Straits Chinese in Singapore, whereby they concluded that Methodism did offer a practical set of ethics that appealed to the immigrants, particularly, the Straits Chinese. The Methodist Church, which actively encouraged indigenous leadership, further lent a voice to the colonized through the provision of the necessary "empowerment" through education. Their study drew the conclusion that, "Methodist education gave the Straits Chinese a sense of empowerment even though they remained subordinates in the colonial society of Singapore."[21]

With the view of planting a church and raising an indigenous leadership, educational mission became increasingly one of the chief strategic directions that Methodism in Singapore adopted very early since their arrival in Singapore. It is significant that in writing about the work of the Anglican Church in Malaya, Dr. Alan Cole, an Anglican priest and a former lecturer at Trinity Theological College, has this to say of the Methodists:

> But it was left to the Methodist Church, almost alone of Protestant groups, to span Malaya's rapidly growing cities with a network of mission schools. . . . Schools of other denominations

---

19. Comaroff and Comaroff, *Of Revelation and Revolution*, vols. 1 and 2.

20. Porter, *Religion versus Empire?*, 318.

21. Blackburn and Fong, "Methodist Education," 357. The word "subordinates" must be understood in that the Methodist mission did not in any way seek to subvert or undermine the colonial administration. It must not be read differently from perceiving the mission as being complicit.

were almost non-existent. So the Presbyterian contribution remained exclusively Chaplaincy work, with the Scots settlers; and the Anglicans almost so; only the Methodist churches, the less concerned from the start with the problem of shepherding their own people, in that they were an American and a missionary group, began to be filled by Asian congregations, young and English-speaking.[22]

Like many other non-Methodist observers, Cole attributed the rise of Methodism in Singapore to the educational mission as well as to the work of the women missionaries. William Oldham saw in the provision of education an open door into the lives of the immigrant population of Singapore. He noted that the Methodist mission in Singapore and Malaysia, "begins to be a story of educational occupation accompanied as every true education must be with the effort to evangelize the student boys."[23] Noting the success of educational mission in Singapore, Thoburn who had initially questioned the legitimacy of schools as a mission agency was to later write: "The mission-school in some form is inseparable from ordinary missionary work."[24]

Not only was the provision of education to the immigrant population, a service to the government in providing for the colony a steady supply of clerks, it also became an important means of enabling the locals to be trained in the service of the people as well as in the service of the Lord in the church for the furtherance of the Kingdom. The twin examples who were both among the first students of Oldham are Li Deng Hui[25] and the Rev. Goh Hood Keng.[26] Li Deng Hui later responded to Thoburn's call to teach at Anglo-Chinese School in Penang before returning to China, for which the burden upon his heart was to assist in bringing about reform in China. He dedicated his life to the cause of education first in Fudan Middle School, and later taking up the position of President of Fudan University in 1917 for the next three decades. If Li Deng Hui may be held up as a representative of the secular impact of Oldham's legacy, it is perhaps fitting to regard Rev. Goh Hood Keng as representative of

---

22. Cole, *Emerging Pattern*, 15.

23. Oldham, "Malaysia."

24. Thoburn, *India and Malaysia*, 329.

25. Lau, "Teaching Moral Education by Example." This Li Deng Hui is not the same person of the same name, who was the former president of Taiwan.

26. Sng, *In His Good Time*, 158–62. See also http://www.trac-mcs.org.sg/images/pdf/boardofministry/Goh%20Hood%20Keng.pdf for a concise biography of his life.

Oldham's spiritual legacy. Rev. Goh Hood Keng became the first Straits-born Chinese to be ordained as a Methodist deacon in 1915 and an elder in 1919, while serving also as a teacher at Anglo-Chinese School. Together, Li Deng Hui and Rev. Goh Hood Keng stand as the crowning successes of the Methodist focus in educational ministries.

In a summary of almost a decade (eight years to be precise) of Methodism in Singapore and Malaya, Oldham made the following report, in which he outlines the work that had been started. The report is quoted at length below,

> The American churches have done but little for Malaysia. India on the one side, and Japan and China on the other, have presented such populous continental areas that hitherto the efforts of American Christians have been but sparsely directed to this south-eastern Asiatic archipelago.
>
> While waiting for China to open, the American Board seems to have supported a few mission stations, but on the opening of treaty ports in China these were abandoned and the missionaries proceeded to China. Two young men, Henry Lyman and Munson were sent to the Battaks of Sumatra. These pioneers were killed and eaten by the cannibal savages, and the project was abandoned. It is cheering to know that these same Battaks, since approached from the south by German missionaries, have largely yielded to the Gospel of Jesus Christ.
>
> The comparative spiritual destitution of this section of Asia was so impressed upon one of the churches of America—the Methodist Episcopal (North)—that in 1885 Bishop Hurst, then visiting India, appointed the writer of this article missionary to Singapore. A mission on a self-supporting basis was begun among the English-speaking people of Singapore, an island of great strategic and commercial importance. The island commands the Malacca Straits and is the commercial entrepot of southeastern Asia. It is one of the commercial navels of the world and floats the British flag. Its polyglot population of Malays, Tamils, Chinese and Europeans is in close touch with all the surrounding islands, with China, with India and with Europe. In the beautiful harbour of Singapore ride the ships of sea-going nations of the world. Chinese junks and Malay dhows jostle the ocean racers of England and France and Germany. A free port, knowing nothing of custom duties, except on a very few articles, here come large cargoes of tobacco, hides, rice, tea, tin, rattan, coffee, India-rubber, and sugar. Commercial activity in foreign parts is usually accompanied by two things, moral

laxity and mental alertness. The morals of Singapore are not high. The readiness of its people to receive new ideas is far beyond that usual in the East.

The American Methodist Mission, beginning work among the English-speaking people, founded a self-supporting English-speaking church. This church has never received a penny of support from without. Beginning with seventeen members, it now numbers over one hundred, and has given over a dozen mission workers to the varied enterprises that now cluster around it.

Parallel with the work in English has grown up a mission to the "Baba" or Straits-born Chinese. These enlightened and progressive Chinamen, British subjects, seeing that the American missionary really desired to serve them, rallied around him and were at the expense of over $12,000. The English Governor, Sir Cecil Smith, of that class of enlightened rulers who have made the English name famous throughout Asia, quickly perceived the usefulness of the American educational missionary project: and a large "Anglo-Chinese" School, numbering four to five hundred scholars, entirely self-supporting, is now located in Singapore. Another similar institution is fast growing up in Penang: and through the prestige and kind feeling generated by the schools our evangelistic missionaries are finding free access to the peoples around them. A medical mission, A Malay press, an orphanage, a Tamil Church and school, and constant itinerant preaching among the Malays are all forms of activity in which the American missionaries are now engaged. It would greatly help in the extension of God's kingdom among these most interesting races if some other branch of American Christians—say the Methodist Episcopal (South) or any other—would select some part of Sumatra, or, with the consent of the Dutch missionaries, some part of Java, or the Celebes, or East Borneo as a mission centre, and from there, in consultation with the Dutch or American brethren already on the field, project a wider and more insistent evangelism among these islanders. They will otherwise year by year be more firmly entrenched in Mohammedanism, with its inordinate conceit and intolerant and fierce bigotry. If anywhere in the mission world the King's business calls for haste, it is in the fair and beautiful islands of Malaysia.[27]

For Oldham and the Methodist mission, Singapore was not an afterthought! As evident in the above report, having established the work in Singapore, the vision was cast in partnering with other missionary

---

27. Oldham, *Malaysia Message*, November 1894, 7–9.

societies and growing the work centrifugally outward to the regions surrounding; northward to the hinterland in Johor and the Malay Peninsular, the Indonesian islands to the south and the west and the eastward to the Celebes and Borneo and finally establishing the work in the Philippines.

Oldham was appointed as Missionary Bishop of Southern Asia in 1904 and in that capacity Singapore became his base in his travels to the Philippines, Indonesia and parts of Malaya. He was appointed as Coordinate Secretary to the Methodist Board of Foreign Missions in New York in 1912 and Bishop to South America in Buenos Aires in 1916. Bishop Oldham retired in 1928 but continued to be active in service of the Lord. He returned to Singapore in November 1934 for the Golden Jubilee of the founding of the Methodist Church in Singapore. The work that was begun fifty year earlier was to continue to be lived out dramatically in Oldham's homecoming. Bishop Benton Bradley recounts the event at the Golden Jubilee that was to be the culmination of a work that Oldham had begun:

> In a remarkable drama, presented by the gathered talent of Methodism of the Malay world, the story of these fifty years was set forth. I sat between Bishop and Mrs. Oldham on the one side and an elderly gentleman on the other. He was Wee Hap Lung the sole surviving member of the group who had listened to the story of the stars when the young Oldham, fifty years ago, had succeeded in making his first contact with the Chinese people by offering to address the "Celestial Reasoning Association" on astronomy. The presentation of that scene of Oldham speaking to a group of gathered in a wealthy Chinese home, deeply touched the old man. I saw he was moved, and asked him how it seemed to him after a lapse of the years. He replied, "I seem to be in a dream!" He had kept in touch with the Christians, but had not become one. And here he sat, an old man, beside the aged Oldham, returned after fifty years to celebrate the establishment of the church in Singapore. Oldham had talked with him and prayed for him. The church had followed him with loving ministries and sought to win him for Christ. He had not yielded. Was it too late? Two days hence was the Sabbath. Then the celebration would end and Oldham would be gone—gone back across the seas to the America that had commissioned him fifty years ago to proclaim the loving, saving Christ. It was not too late! He would gladden the heart of his old-time guide and teacher, he would, though late, heed the call of the Master, he would join the great and glowing company of happy people who

had found what he had not yet found in fifty years of search—peace and joy of heart.

And on the Sabbath, when Malaysia's patriarch, William F. Oldham, baptized his Chinese brother whom he had first sought fifty years ago, there was a hush in Wesley Church more eloquent than words. What a consummation of a glorious ministry! Fifty-nine years before, the young surveyor, barely twenty years of age, unknown outside of Poona and Bangalore, had been "licensed to preach." And now, having proclaimed the Good News around the world, he comes back to Singapore, to his first love as a missionary, and, in the baptism of this old Chinese friend, brings to a perfection completion his wonderful ministry of almost sixty years! Let the picture hand on the walls of Methodism's portrait gallery, undimmed and unstained forever![28]

The conversion of Wee Hap Lung was indeed a fitting consummation of Oldham's life-long ministry. Together with the other pioneers of the Methodist Mission, such as Sophia Blackmore, Benjamin West, William Shellabear, Oldham brought to Singapore a faith that has "penetrated the life of the people in its multifarious needs. There is the work of compassion as well as of conscience, of individual salvation, rescue and uplift as well as the prophetic voice of judgment and seeking to act as the agent of social and moral change."[29]

It has already been noted that the colonial administration generally adopted a *laissez faire* model of treatment of missionaries. But in seeking to come to a more definitive conclusion in regard to the question, "To what extent did British colonialism facilitate or frustrate Methodist missions in Singapore?" we find another hint of the answer in perhaps one of the more unlikely places or persons. Eugene Wijeysingha, a retired Principal of Raffles Institution for which the "rivalry" between these two schools may be traced as early as the 1890s, penned these words in his chronicling of the history of the Raffles Institution with regard to British influence, he candidly noted:

> In it is shrouded the beginnings of British history in Malaya; in it is revealed the shades of differences in imperialists who came to affect the history and landscape of Singapore; in it is contained the sad plight of education in the Straits Settlements of the Nineteenth Century; in it is contained *the story of an unsympathetic colonial government toward its obligations and an*

28. Badley, *Oldham*, 6–7.
29. Doraisamy, *March of Methodism*, 31.

> apathetic lot of European merchants, who were prepared to take away what they could find in the Settlement and return nothing for the betterment of the settlement. Yet, there were those from the very same lot, who sacrificed time and reputation to contribute their share to a settlement that had made them. They strove against overwhelming odds to put the noble concept of Raffles Institution into effect.[30] (emphasis mine)

If such may be said of the British attitude in regard to Raffles Institution, which was indeed the government school, with full support by the colonial administration, it serves hence as a very telling commentary on the tremendous apathy and perhaps prejudice that the colonial administration had against the Methodist mission in Singapore and in the Malay Peninsula, in light of the overt British emphasis on profitability and secularity. Britain's initial assessment was that it did not perceive Methodism in Singapore as primarily a threat nor was it in any significant manner beneficial to colonial interests, hence, the apathy. It gave to the American Methodists sufficient space to maneuver so long as colonial economic interests and the day-to-day administration of the colony was not jeopardized nor compromised. But where the mission's direction impinged on colonial mercantile interests, such as the opium commission, Britain expressed scant interest in the mission's stance.

It may however, be said of British colonialism that it was the catalyst that sparked off a reaction for the Methodism mission, for which the effects are still evident today. In regard to an evaluation of the Methodist mission, Porter's advice must be noted,

> It is therefore essential that today's assessments of the "imperial" role of missions should take account both of the limits to their ability to control the influence of their message and to the diverse routes by which it was diffused among the populations with whom they engaged.[31]

The American Methodist missionaries envisioned as their primary call "spreading Scriptural holiness" across the lands of Singapore and Malaysia and found the means through an emphasis on evangelistic, educational and ethical ministries. The predominantly immigrant population, particularly the Straits Chinese, perceived and cherished the possibilities

---

30. Wijeysingha, *History of Raffles Institution*, as quoted in Doraisamy, *150 Years of Education*, 10–11.

31. Porter, *Religion versus Empire?*, 318.

of acquiring the English language and attaining a Western education without necessarily assimilating a western culture and the Christian faith, while the British colonial administration operated on pragmatism and profitability, with the tacit assumption of the transience of both the immigrant population as well as that of the missionaries, whose ultimate goal was China. These broadly framed the context for which culture, colonialism and Christianity coalesced in Singapore at the turn of the twentieth century.

Can it be said that the Methodist mission was complicit with the colonial agenda? From the archival records, letters, correspondences and conference meeting reports, the evidence gives scant proof of complicity and more so of "creativity" on the part of the Methodist mission to circumvent the numerous policies and restrictions that has been enforced in order to maintain secularity, in light of the ramifications of the Pangkor Treaty and the sensitivities of different ethnic immigrant population. Peter Ho's assessment is judicious:

> The hardship of these missionaries and the fact that the school's origins were independent of the Western metropoles and were, rather from the branch plant of India, reduces the notion of a conspiratorial machine controlled the missionaries to do its bidding.[32]

It would be difficult to justify that the Methodist Mission was complicit with colonial interests. In the case of Singapore, the Methodist Mission was neither staunchly opposed nor were they agents of British Imperialism. They sought to be true to a "higher calling" and when the opportunity in education presented itself to Oldham, he grabbed at it and the missionaries thereafter held on to this particular ministry with fortitude and tenacity and in that process, brought mission education to heights unattained by previous missionary societies in the region.

It may be said of the Methodist Mission, that they were propelled by their zeal in evangelism, in their efforts to establish an education mission, to minister to the sick, the disenfranchised, the womenfolk, to establish new churches, to train up local leadership in the churches and chiefly to usher in a Kingdom whose values are inimical to the agenda of the Empire. The reach of the British Empire made it impossible for missionaries to be completely independent of all involvement with the Empire. But it cannot be postulated that hence missions were complicit

---

32. Ho Zhiwen, "'Not in Your Image,'" 49–50.

with colonialism and certainly not in regard to American Methodism in Singapore. Porter's perspicacious observation is certainly the case where the Methodist Mission in Singapore is concerned. He held that:

> The great majority of missionaries displayed a fitful interest in empire, giving it their temporary and often grudging attention chiefly when it hindered evangelisation or might bring its authority to bear in a necessary defence of missions' past achievements or basic freedom to carry on their work.[33]

Oldham's leadership of the Methodist mission, Blackmore's battle against the prejudices of the society through uplifting of the place of women in society, West's medical ministry among the poor and disenfranchised, Shellabear's extensive publications in both Malay and English and later as a teacher of missionaries are all legacies that outlive their earthly sojourn. They understood that "our mission has to be multidimensional in order to be credible and faithful to its origins and character"[34] and yet at the same time, they understood their mission as *Missio Dei*, setting their personal agendas at the foot of the cross. They constantly fought against leaving but a name on plaques and monuments and their consuming passion and dedication was to the local community of Chinese, Indian, Malays and Babas, especially in their welfare, both material and spiritual. Though, for some such as Shellabear, whose commitment to vernacular ministries found little sympathy among Christians who maintained that English was the future of Methodism in Malaysia and Singapore, yet they plodded along that somewhat lonely path. They were deeply committed to the Christian gospel, and remained steadfast in their loyalty until the end of their lives. Their loves and their lives were dictated by this:

> The emotional enthusiasm of snatching a few souls from the eternal burning is more than balanced by the imperial appeal of the constructive task of bringing whole nations into their destiny of moral life, and the whole race into the spiritual Kingdom of God.[35]

The place of the Empire as it impinges on the missionary endeavour may be understood in both positive and negative terms. But as Porter

---

33. Porter, *Religion versus Empire?*, 324.
34. Bosch, *Transforming Mission*, 512.
35. Carver, *Missions and Modern Thought*, 298–99.

noted, in agreement with Neill, missionaries often report to a "higher authority."

> By and large most missionaries did not want to be imperial propagandists and colonial rulers, any more than they intended to be consistent or uncritical supporters of capitalist enterprise. The shifting character of their relations with imperial authorities and other agencies of metropolitan expansion; their ambitious dealings with indigenous rulers or interest groups; and their weakness as empire builders or propagandists, were all substantially influenced by that fact. Both those who organised mission societies and those who volunteered for missionary service wanted to share their own religious enthusiasm, to convert non-Christians, to build up churches and to promote the kingdom of God on earth.[36]

And in this same token, for the American Methodist mission, their allegiance was ultimately to God and hence we may speak of their motivation as "Imperial," in contradistinction with imperialistic. While they operated within imperialistic governance, their impulse was of a higher "imperial" order, one that superseded that of the Empire. While they worked within the context of the Empire, they worshiped and witnessed rather to the Lord of a Kingdom that is not part of this worldly system. Where Empire and Kingdom coalesced, they were ultimately citizens of the Kingdom before Empire.

In their lives and their influence, these Methodist missionaries have sought to be sensitive to the different religious backgrounds of the various different ethnic communities—the Chinese, Europeans, Indians, Malays and the Peranakans, they have managed to cross of those religious borders with prophetic compassion, and through their speech, action and their lives dialogued with those who needed to hear the Good News of Jesus Christ. Unwilling to lend tacit support to the existing discrimination in social order, they worked at challenging the evil structures within the colonial society through such, as educational missions and gave voice to the sufferings of the disenfranchised, the women, the orphans, the weak, the poor, the sick and the imprisoned. They have incarnated *Missio Dei* in this part of Southeast Asia, girded by a biblically founded understanding of *Imago Dei*, where "grammar of incarnation is not a theory of a

---

36. Porter, *Religion versus Empire?*, 323.

doctrinal claim but a praxis, an experience. It is a living relationship or relatedness and communion without marginalization."[37]

The story of the advent of Methodism in Singapore revolves around the twin themes of merchants and missionaries, of the impact of Methodist amidst a colonial context. It raises the issues of complicity, complementary, or contradiction. As introduced in the opening chapter of this research, one way to understand the impact of colonialism on Methodism in Singapore may be described through the analogy of heterogeneous catalysis.

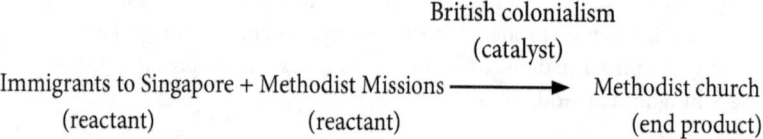

More recently, there has been much advancement achieved in catalytic research, where selectivity[38] has taken on prominence. Just as there is a certain selectivity in the chemical process, so too may be the case where British colonialism is concerned in regard to the dealings with the American Methodist Mission. British colonialism supported the mission particularly with regards to education, but only to the extent where it aided the colonial mercantile enterprise. For the colonial administration it was a partnership based upon socioeconomic and political benefits more than anything else. Colonial attitudes to the Methodist mission may be described as symbiotic,[39] and ranged between mutualism at best and parasitic at worst. There were occasions in which both the mission and the colonial administrators "benefited" from the collaborations but more

---

37. Kavunkal, "Missionary Vision for Asia in the Twenty-First Century," in Bevans and Schroeder, *Mission for the Twenty-First Century*, 165.

38. Please see Grasselli, "Selectivity Issues," 23–31. See also Cavani, Centi, Perego, and Vaccari, "Selectivity in Catalytic Oxidation," 1–3.

39. Russell, *Advances in Marine Biology*, 4–9. Symbiosis is a scientific term that was first coined by De Bary in 1879 and it is used to describe the relationship between two biological species. It is derived from the Greek words σύν (*syn*) "with"; and βίωσις (*biosis*), literally meaning living together. These interactions often result in one of the pairs benefiting entirely from that interaction. Consequently, there are three broad categories of symbiosis: mutualism (where both members benefit from the interaction), commensalism (where one member benefits while the other member is relatively unaffected), and parasitism (where one member benefits at the price of injury or death of the other member). In chapter 2, a fourth category, phoresis, which is a most akin to commensalism, is included.

often than not, the colonial office benefited disproportionately from the provision of English education in a manner that almost seem as leeching off from the Methodist advancement in educational ministries. In many cases, the Methodist mission had to innovate and creatively circumvent the various colonial policies which emphasized neutrality in regard to race and religion.

Hence perhaps in the evaluation of the relationship between British colonialism and Methodism, the term most applicable would be "catalytic symbiosis." It is undeniable that Methodism arrived at a time when the British flag was dominant and hence provided the context for which Methodism was to take root in Singapore. British colonialism provided the necessary precondition for mission in Singapore. This was the context which American Methodism was to take root and grow. But while it provided for the convenient pretext, Methodism and British colonialism took very different trajectories as the history of Singapore unfolded. Undoubtedly there were occasions of co-operation but these were often on the terms of the British colonial administration. But for American Methodism, British colonialism provided merely the context for which the Gospel took seed and bore fruit.

The fact that Methodism arrived at a time when London oversaw the administration of the Straits Settlements rather than under the auspices of the East India Company, is significant since the Company was known to have been unsympathetic to missionaries. It however should not be misconstrued that the British colonial administration was in any way sympathetic to the missionary task. *Pax Britannica* was the context and indeed the pre-condition for the arrival of the Methodists but beyond that, it was not at all in Britain's interests to be a patron for the Christian faith in Southeast Asia. Britain was content to stay neutral and with the exception of the chaplaincy work of the Anglican Church, the official church of the Empire, Britain adopted a more *laissez faire* attitude in the colonial administration, where most of the policies Britain enacted and imposed in the Straits Settlement veered toward secularity and all the more so in light of the Treaty of Pangkor signed in 1874.

The symbiotic relationship between the colonial administration and the Methodist mission through the course of history was not a linear path. It may be charted as one that at times was of mutualism, where both benefited; at times commensal, where only the colonial office benefited; and for the rest of the time, parasitic, benefiting the colonial office at the price of injury to the Methodist mission. These first three decades (from 1885 to 1912) is a story of change, brought about by action, reaction, interaction and transformation, among the immigrant population, the missionaries and the colonial administration. Karl Jung remarked that, "the meeting of two personalities is like the contact of two chemical substances: if there is any reaction, both are transformed,"[40] where the entities undergo a certain change in their encounter. The Methodist encounter with British colonialism brought about changes in the history of Singapore that continue to be played out today. Peter Ho, in his evaluation of Methodist education, the Straits Chinese and the colonial administration, makes this conclusion which is evidently the case in regard to the Methodist mission in Singapore:

> In the final analysis, the Methodists were prevented from proselytising as much as they would have liked to, the Chinese accepted more western values that their elites would have liked them to and the Government failed to have its way in English education. However, the final victor in this conflict and synthesis appears to be the Methodist Mission for ACS still bears its likeness as an evangelical institution today.[41]

Though the Methodists may have been somewhat curtailed in their Christian witness in the schools, this research affirms Ho's findings that in the final analysis, the Methodist Mission appeared to be have the predominance and the charge of complicity of mission and colonialism is a generalization, that is tenuous in the case of Methodism's advent and march in Singapore. Instead, what may be said is that the Methodists brought with them a social holiness through their pluriform mission that shook the very foundation of Britain's colonial enterprise in Singapore. Their emphasis on building indigenous leadership and empowering them through English education and positions of service in the church provided a means whereby the predominantly immigrant population was to have a voice against the inequalities that British colonialism sought to maintain, that they may speak to their colonizers on their own terms!

In Hunt's tribute to Methodist missionary, William Shellabear, he commented:

> The end of every life is not death but a legacy. For the historian, the legacy includes more than the works of life which remain after death, or even those visible influences which with

---

40. Jung, *CW 18*, 71
41. Ho Zhiwen, "'Not in Your Image,'" 49–50.

ever-diminishing force determine the shape of the unfolding world.[42]

The same may be said of each of the Methodist missionary pioneers who ministered in Singapore at the turn of the twentieth century. Regardless of their nationality, they were foremost citizens of the Kingdom rather than an Empire or a colony. Their lives help give illumination to the complexity of Christianity in the colonial society and the intricacy of contacts and conflicts between different religions in an increasingly multi-ethnic, multi-cultural and multi-religious Malaysia and Singapore. Their lives exude a rare quality in the midst of British colonialism; theirs were lives whose affection for the people was undimmed by paternalism, whose integrity was unmarred by materialism and whose faith was uncompromised by cultural and religious relativism.

Singapore has emerged from her colonial past and has become one of the more important cities in Asia. The rise has been described as meteoric and was led by Singapore's first Prime Minister, Lee Kuan Yew who in a broadcast to the people of Singapore, promised that "There will be a throbbing and humming industrial, commercial and communication center long after the British have gone."[43] In a speech given shortly after the independence of Singapore, Prime Minister Lee envisioned:

> Here we make the model multi-racial society . . . this is not a country that belongs to any single community, it belongs to all of us. We made this country from nothing, from mudflats—it is man, human skill, human effort, which made this possible. Today this our modern city—ten years from now, this will be metropolis! Never fear.[44]

Singapore has indeed grown in fulfilment of the dream that Sir Stamford Raffles had envisioned for her; as one of the largest ports, not only in Asia but of the world, and of both seaport and airport. Amidst a thriving economy that propels one forward, one must not neglect taking a backward glance at the years that witnessed the arrival of the Methodists Mission and learning from history. The advent and growth of the Methodist Mission in Singapore reminds us that economic success cannot and must not be at the expense of moral and religious life. Against

42. Hunt, *William Shellabear*, 341.
43. Lee Kuan Yew, *From Third World to First*, 53.
44. As quoted from a news clip from a video production of PM Lee's speech at the opening of the Sree Narayana Mission on 12 September 1965.

the context of British imperialism, the Methodists marched instead to a different set of orders. Their lives underscored the difference between the twin forces, one imperialistic, the other, imperial. The British Empire is no more, yet the vestiges of imperialism still remain.

There is no doubt that globalization, and the modernity that accompanies it, "provides both the single greatest opportunity the church has ever faced and its single greatest challenge."[45] The opportunity exists because "more people in more societies are more open to the Gospel in the modern world than in any previous era in history,"[46] but the challenge is that it becomes increasingly easy to lose our way amidst the different competing demands on the Christian and on the church. Singapore churches that have in recent years begun to be more actively involved in mission in various countries in Southeast Asia, must learn the lesson afresh, for in "doing church," there is a tendency to be condescending, a tendency to insisting on "doing it our way," a tendency to moulding them "in our likeness." That old imperialism may yet be reawakened in a new context that will rival again the imperial orders of the Kingdom's King.

Finally, as Methodism celebrates the 125th anniversary next year (2010), we need to be reminded of the motives and the methods with which Methodism took root and bore fruit in Singapore. In a society that emphasizes upward economic mobility—to update, upgrade, upscale, upsize and upsurge, the church must not allow materialism to eclipse her mission. Particularly, there is a concern that increasingly, the educational mission of the Methodist schools are being driven by other gains (economic or the pursuit of eminence[47]) rather than guided by the very purposes for which William Oldham and Sophia Blackmore established ACS and MGS in Singapore. In the midst of globalization and modernity, the church in Singapore has to continually look to the lessons of the past, the achievements of the present and to the challenges of the future. But amidst all these competing demands, the church in Singapore

---

45. Tulluan, "The Impact of Modernity on the Mission of the Church," in Wong Chan Kok and Lowe, *Ministry in Modern Singapore*, 152.

46. Guiness and Seel, *No God but God*, 161.

47. In an interview with ChannelNewsAsia, the former principal of ACS(I), on winning the Singapore Quality award (for efficiency), was quoted to have said the school is well placed to "meet the needs of our students, (whom) we nowadays refer to as clients or customers." It seems that such a notion where students are thus perceived runs contrary to the spirit with which the school was founded. http://www.channelnewsasia.com/stories/singaporelocalnews/view/1015981/1/.html.

(and Singapore itself) would do well not to forget that the way home is through the "lowly, the unassuming, and the imperceptible,"[48] the mustard seed faith in Jesus Christ.

---

48. Sine, *Mustard Seed Versus McWorld*, 173.

Appendices

Appendix A	Information on Archives
Appendix B	A Timeline of the History of Singapore from 1819 to 1965
Appendix C	Map of the Straits Settlements
Appendix D	A Timeline of the History of Methodism in Singapore
Appendix E1–9	Articles published in Singapore Free Press In relation to the "Isaiah Incident" (Transcribed)
Appendix F1–15	Articles published in Straits Times In relation to the "Isaiah Incident" (Transcribed)
Appendix G	Bishop Oldham's *Memorandum of Dissent*
Appendix H	Bishop Oldham's *Personal Note*

Appendix A

Information on Archives and Reports

A. Archives Collection Researched
 The National Archives (Public Records Office), London
 The British Library Archives, London
 School of Oriental and African Studies, University of London, London
 The Royal Commonwealth Society Library, Cambridge University, Cambridge
 Rhodes House Library, Oxford
 The United Methodist Archives, Madison, New Jersey
 National Archives of Singapore, Singapore
 National University of Singapore Archives, Singapore
 Methodist Archives, Singapore
 Lee Kong Chian Reference Library, National Library of Singapore
 Methodist Board of Education Archives, Kuala Lumpur

B. Colonial Government Reports
 National Archives of Singapore. *Annual Reports of the Straits Settlements, 1885–1910*
 National Archives of Singapore. *Departmental Reports of the Straits Settlements, Education, 1895–1910*
 Kuala Lumpur National Archives. *Annual Reports of the Federated Malay States, 1895–1910*
 Kuala Lumpur National Archives. *Federated Malay States Education Reports, 1905–1920*

Appendix A

C. Newspapers and Periodicals
Malaysia Message, Singapore, 1892–1935
Singapore Free Press, Singapore, 1885–1900
The Straits Times, Singapore, 1885–1920

Appendix B

A Timeline of the History of Singapore from 1819 to 1965

1819, 29 January
    Arrival of Stamford Raffles of the English East India Company.

1819, 6 February
    A treaty was signed between Sultan Hussein, the Temenggong and Raffles and the British flag was hoisted.

1822
    Raffles drew Town Plan of Singapore, established Singapore as a free port.

1824
    Signing of the Anglo-Dutch Treaty with the Dutch, withdrawing all objections of British occupation of Singapore.
    Signing of second treaty with Sultan Hussein and Tememggong Adbu'r Rahman, who ceded Singapore to the English East India Company for cash payments and pensions.

1826
    British treaty with Siam. Under terms of this agreement the sultanates of Perak and Selangor were recognized as independent, while Siamese control of Kedah was acknowledged. At the same

time, Perak ceded to Britain Pangkor Island and the Sembilan Islands for use as bases in the fight against piracy.

Singapore became part of the Straits Settlements (together with the ports of Penang and Malacca) under the rule of the English East India Company.

1830s

Opening of gambier and pepper plantations by the Chinese, which was later moved to Johor.

1852

A new deep harbour (New Harbour, later known as Keppel Harbour) was built.

1858

Singapore was still part of the Straits Settlements but was now under the rule of the Government of India.

1867, 1 April

End of rule of the English East India Company under the Straits Settlement. Singapore came under direct rule of the British Government.

1869

Opening of the Suez Canal. Singapore benefited because many ships stopped here to refuel and collect food supplies. For the next few decades, Singapore enjoyed relative peace and steady economic growth despite World War I.

1939

The Beginning of World War II.

1942, 14 February
　The Japanese captured most of Singapore. Surrender of Singapore on next day marked beginning of Japanese Occupation. Singapore renamed *Syonan-To*.

1945
　Defeat of Japanese by Allied Forces. The British returned to Singapore after the end of World War II.

1946
　Separation of Singapore from the Straits Settlements.

1950s
　Rise of Communist activities in Malaya; the British declared the state of emergency over Singapore and Malaya. This ended in 1960, when the communists were no longer a threat.

1955
　Elections gave Singapore limited self-government.

1959
　Elections gave Singapore full self-government. Lee Kuan Yew of the People's Action Party became Singapore's first Prime Minister. The National Anthem was composed.

1961
　The idea of a merger proposed by Tengku Abdul Rahman, the Prime Minister of Malaya.

1963
　The Malaysia Agreement was signed between leaders of Malaya, Singapore, Sabah, and Sarawak. Malaysia became a new nation in Southeast Asia.

1965
: Singapore was ejected from the Federation of Malaysian States, gained independence on 9 August. On 21 September, Singapore was admitted into the United Nations (UN) as the 117th member and in October, Singapore was made 22nd member of the British Commonwealth.

Appendix C

Map of Straits Settlement, 1893

Source: http://homepages.rootsweb.com/~poyntz/India/images/Straits-Settlements.JPG.

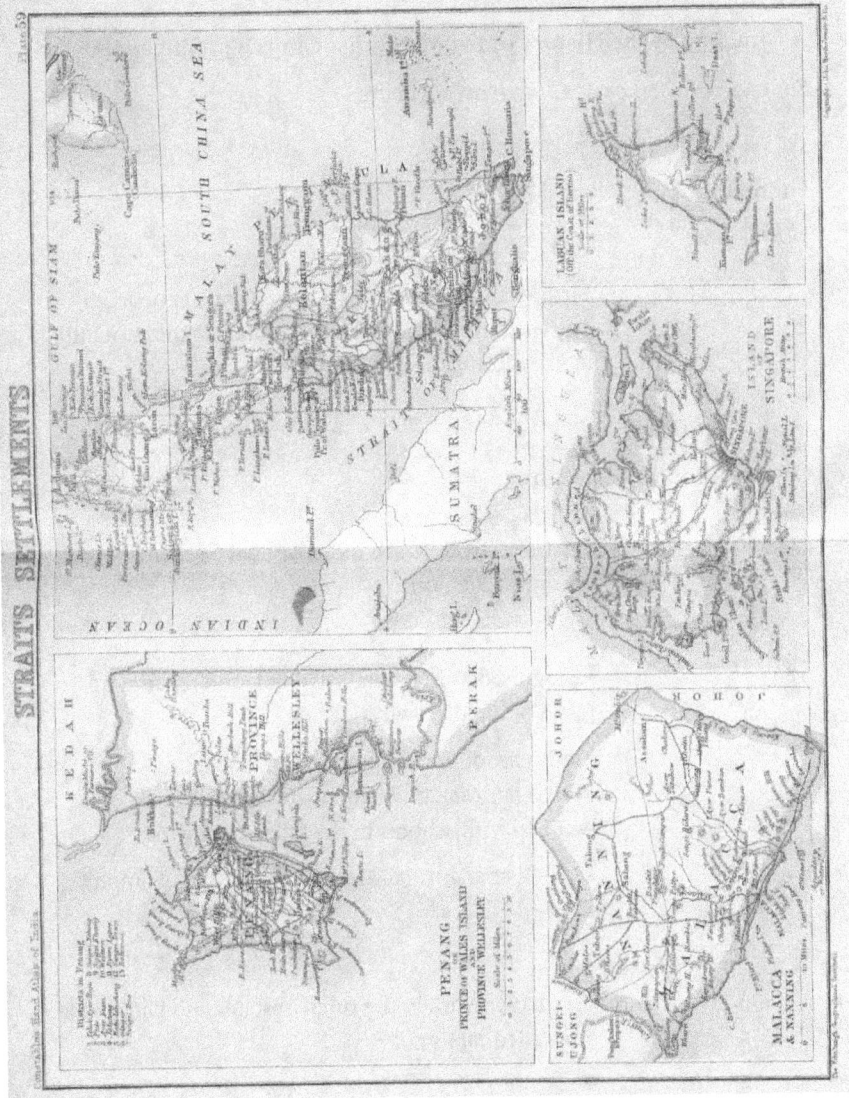

Appendix D

A Timeline of the History of the Methodist Church in Singapore
Source: The Methodist Church of Singapore

Foundations

23 Feb 1885   First Methodist "English" Church was set up as an outreach of the South India Annual Conference initiated by Rev. James M. Thoburn.

Organisation & Expansion

1888   Separated from South India Annual Conference to become a Mission.

1893   Recognised as Malaysia Mission Conference as a result of rapid growth.

Methodist outreach spread from Singapore to Peninsular Malaya where town churches were twinned with schools in the following towns:

1891—Penang; 1896—Ipoh; 1897—Kuala Lumpur; 1904—Malacca

Vernacular work in the rubber estates and villages also proceeded rapidly.

1901	Rev. James M. Thoburn established a Mission in Manila.
1902	The Malaysia Mission Conference became the Malaysia Annual Conference. Christian agricultural settlements were also established in Sitiawan (1901) and Sibu (1902).
1905	Mission in Manila became Annual Conference. Work in Java and West Borneo started.
1906	Work began in Sumatra, flourished to become the Sumatra Mission in 1922 and Sumatra Provisional Conference by 1950.
1925	The Malaysia Annual Conference was re-designated as the Malaya Annual Conference.
1928	The Netherlands Indies Mission took over the work in Java and West Borneo.
1935	Continued growth resulted in bifurcation of Malaya Annual Conference: Malaysia Chinese Annual Conference set up to reflect nature of the work of Chinese-speaking pastors.

Towards Autonomy

1940	Philippines became Central Conference separated from the rest of Southeast Asia.
1950	Southeast Asia Central Conference was constituted from remaining Conferences—Malaya Annual

Conference, Malaysia Chinese Annual Conference, Burma Annual Conference, and Sumatra Provisional Annual Conference; elected own bishop and framed its Discipline.

Subsequently, the Sumatra and Burma Conferences went their separate and autonomous ways, leaving behind the Malaysia and Singapore Annual Conferences.

1965	Singapore became an independent nation.
1968	Methodist Church in Malaysia and Singapore was officially constituted on 8 August and Dr. Yap Kim Hao was elected as the first Asian bishop.
1968	Institution of the office for the President of each Annual Conference—Singapore-Malaysia Annual Conference, Chinese Annual Conference, Sarawak Iban Provisional Annual Conference, Sarawak Annual Conference, and Tamil Provisional Annual Conference.

Becoming the Methodist Church in Singapore

1974–75	Consensus was sought to reconstitute the church on national lines.
1976	On 4 and 8 December, the Methodist Churches in Malaysia and Singapore were constituted respectively. Methodist Church in Singapore (MCS) comprised the Chinese Annual Conference, the Emmanuel Tamil Annual Conference, and the Trinity Annual Conference.
1985	MCS celebrated its centenary.

Becoming the Church in Asia

To-date | The Methodist Church and its constituent congregations continue to grow—reaching out "across the street" through its various social service projects, and "across the seas" by sending missionaries to Asian countries and beyond.

Appendix E-1

The Singapore Free Press, 25 July 1896.

The Methodist School: Self-styled "The Anglo-Chinese College"

"A serpent in disguise" according to the now-famed Rev. D.D. Moore M.A., "Member Royal Asiatic Society Malaysia" (See p.225, The Gospel in All Lands, May 1896).

Dear Sir, I take the liberty to give the above title to what I shall have to say. The subject is one of vital importance to the Chinese community, and also to the local government and the American public. The question I am about to raise is touching the American Methodist School, its methods of working, the avowed professions of its promoters as the declared to the leading Chinese on their money-collecting peregrinations, and the reports of the same reverend, Christian teachers to their home authorities or friends.

It is allowed that a tendency to exaggeration is a trait of the Yankee character, and therefore I will not say a word about the assumption of the title "College" for their school, nor for the misuse of the English word "graduate" in reference to the boys passing out of the Anglo-Chinese School, which it must be known to the world, cannot for a moment be put on the same place even with a third-rate secondary school in England. I am only sorry that my authorities, for these are the Rev. D. D. Moore* and the Rev. C. Kelso, B.A., because I feel I may do the latter injustice by linking his name with that of his reverend colleague.

The point that I wish to bring out in this communication is whether the public, chiefly, the Chinese and the Government, are aware of the methods of teaching adopted in the American "College." It is very material to the discussion to remember that the "College" is to a large extent, if not entirely, supported by funds collected from "the rich, heathen Chinaman" (Rev. D.D. Moore), and by the general public through the government grants in aid. The other aspect of the question is purely a moral one. The local promoters of the College have repeatedly declared, especially to the gullible "rich, heathen Chinamen," that their education work is honest and aboveboard, and it is notorious that they are anxious to let the heathens know that proselytising is not openly carried on. The present Principal of the College has been heard to say to Chinese that the Americans do not attempt to openly proselytise the children under their charge. It was not doubt owing largely to such representations that the reverend teachers managed so successfully to tap the unknown boards of the rich heathen, and it was in the belief that the College was a *bona fide* elementary school that the government granted to it grants in aid. Here, again, I will quote the members of the Methodist Church. Mr. Moore says, speaking of his schools in Penang: "In these schools, Christianity is openly taught. A number of our wealthy Chinese pupils are becoming Christians, and several of them are looking forward to the native ministry." Mr. Kelso also spoke in unequivocal terms: "While our success on material and academical lines is very gratifying, we feel that we have most reason to rejoice over the religious results that have been realised. (In a large lecture hall), the whole school meets every morning. The boys sing a Gospel song, the Bible is read and explained to them, and prayer is offered. These services are very inspiring and usually the boys are deeply interested. There have been a number of bright conversions in the School within the past year. . . . Thus it has come about that the leading boys in all the upper classes are professed Christians." Now these quotations prove beyond a doubt that the College is a religious seminary and I know of numerous instances in which questionable pressure has been used to induce the boys to become open "deeply interested." Some members of the Legislative Council ought really to ask the Government whether public money should be continued to be thrown away in aid of missionary adventurers. The Government should insist on all grant-in-aid schools becoming completely non-sectarian and non-religious, by which I mean no religion must be taught as part of the day's school work. I hope Mr. Shelford, one of the oldest residents, and the senior member of the Council, will do something to check this public scandal.

It may be considered by the admirers of the College that I have been unduly severe in what I have above urged. But that I am perfectly right in saying that these Reverend gentlemen say one thing to the rich heathens in order to get their money, and then do and act quite differently when the money is secured, I hope I shall prove to the ample satisfaction even of Dr. Moore, and Principal Kelso. The Rev. D.D. Moore of "the Malay Picnic" fame made a confession in the following words. "Nowhere, so much as in the East is it necessary for the Christian worker to combine the qualities of the dive and the serpent. First innocency, then subtlety, must be his motto of work." *O tempora, O mores. I really do not know whether I ought to pity the Rev. Doctor, or the pious company whom he represents.* O Dear Sir, do print the following address to the heathens in your biggest possible type. It is taken form the rare copy of "Sermons by celebrated heathens."

Hearken unto my voice, O ye rich heathens. Better bestow your plenty onto the poor which bare before you. Better far that your children and your children's children should live and die in the time-worn faith of your ancestors than that they, through your exceeding faith in the Serpent, in the guise of a dove be led into temptation and to commit the primeval sin, to wit, to receive the fruit of knowledge from the Serpent (as to venom of such serpents see Numbers 21:6.)

Now to return to the Singapore Methodist School, I believe many rich heathens sit on the Managing Board. It would be inconvenient for these gentlemen, when influence has been *subtly* obtained and had ensured the success of Mr. Oldham, were the Chinese who have been misled by them to find out that, after all, the same Reverend gentlemen who have been put before them as suitable persons to teach mankind how to avoid the Serpent have been imitating, on their unsolicited confession, the example of the accursed reptile. These amiable and rich heathens will now see for themselves that Reverend gentlemen can be very polite—can even condescend to *kowtow* to Mammon when it suits them. When the money is bagged, to use a rather vulgar expression, then the friends of these Chinese gentlemen turn round upon their patrons and call them rich heathens for their simplicity and liberality. $10,000 to build a school, $8,000 an English Church and another $10,000 a spacious bungalow. No wonder rich heathens, you are sought after. No wonder, for the sake of filthy lucre, school discipline, save the proselytising, may be so adjusted as to meet all Chinese objections. Hence the popularity of the "College." The Principal of the "College" boasts that "a year ago, one of our pupils won first place in a contest for Queen's Scholarship." Had he been a modest man, he would probably have mentioned that the said scholar received the greater part of his education at the Raffles Institution. The "College" is quite in its infancy, and it is a pity that the Principal has not sufficiently imbibed the principles of his colleague, Rev. D.D. Moore, who says in an elaborate contribution to the history of missions: "The missionary who wants to live long in the East and succeed must cultivate Patience." That is exactly what the "College" must do, and for once Mr. Moore is absolutely right.

The Chinese gentlemen on the Board of the "College" ought at once to make enquiries. They as directors must try to reform the school, or if they cannot, prevent the proselytising, then they ought to resign in a body and have nothing more to do with the school, that is to say if they agree with the principle that such a school is properly speaking not a *missions school*. The real culprits in the matter are, to speak plainly, both the heathens and the Christians. The former think they can get cheap "Colleges," without paying for teachers, whilst the latter take advantage of their delusions and ignorance to play "first innocency—then subtlety"— "to combine the qualities of the dove and the serpent."

Isaiah

PS: I beg to call the attention of the Rev. D.D. Moore to the utterance of my namesake, the Prophet, in Ch.27, 1 of the Holy Scriptures named after him.

Source:
Straits Times Archives,
Lee Kong Chian Reference Library, National Library Board

Appendix E-2

The Singapore Free Press, 27 July 1896

A Missionary Mess

There are other things besides curses that come home to roost, as some of the staff of the Methodist Episcopal Mission must now be rather painfully aware. As Artemus Ward put it once, that body may now exclaim, "There is a Krisis onto us." A moral seismic disturbance is causing the *soi-distant* "Anglo-Chinese College" to totter to its foundations. The cause thereof is simple.

According to the declarations made in a letter published on Saturday from, a correspondent who is evidently well behind the scenes it has been discovered at last that the educational work of that institution was being deliberately perverted into a system of proselytising the Chinese pupils against the desires and without the knowledge of the Chinese Board of management. It is alleged that the boys who have been entrusted to the teaching staff of the Anglo-Chinese School by their parents on the oft-repeated assurances that there would be no tampering with their religion and that the education was to be strictly a matter of the ordinary studies with a little moral everyday principle thrown in, are now being vigorously exploited as Christian 'verts without the sanction or the knowledge of their parents. There is a deliberate system of deception set up, the main object of which is to hoodwink the Board of Managers and the parents, and the teach the boys, practically, that the fathers whom they should reverence with that especial filial piety carried to so lofty a pitch against the Chinese, are mere "heathen," doomed to perdition. By specious representations of culture and glib talk of higher education the wealthy Chinese of Singapore had been systematically laid siege to, and bled to the tune of many thousands of dollars to rear a lordly College, on American lines, which was to be a pure temple of education, and not in any way open to the cloven hoof of the religious schemer.

All would have gone well—for the Mission promoters of this institution had they not been given to the usual vice of their kind—a babbling, on paper unfortunately for them, of their secret doings, as Methodist Jesuits, in the unsuspecting "Anglo-Chinese College." Just as one of their number, as a literary plagiarist, put himself in the public stocks of the New York *Independent* by going into black and white, so do the managers of the Anglo-Chinese College convict themselves of their subterranean doings when they commit themselves to printed statements in the columns of the *Gospel in all Lands*, May 1896. Whatever this print be, it has at least done the good service of hoisting the Methodist proselytisers with their own petard.

They boast therein of having practically diddled respectable Chinese gentlemen in Singapore out of large sums of money, pharisaically styling them "rich heathen Chinamen." They boast that "Christianity is openly taught" but they forget to add that they throw dust in the eyes of their "rich heathen" patrons by swearing by all that is holy that they will never, never tamper with a little China boy's beliefs. "The whole school meets daily, sings Gospel songs, hear the Bible read, and listen to prayer." Excellent, admirable in a professed proselytising agency: a contemptible, and criminal trespass upon trusting parents who have been assured that nothing of the kind goes on. "There have been a number of bright conversions," writes Mr. Kelso, the Principal. Has Mr. Kelso had the authority of the parents of those "bright Celestials" for his undermining of the religion of the pupils. Do the parents know? Do they approve? Or is the statement simply a little Mission fib, for American readers and subscribers?

The dilemma is solved by the action reported today. The Chinese trustees of the Boarding School at Bellevue have protested and have resigned in a body. Further the Chinese parents today are withdrawing their sons in large numbers, now that the Institution stands exposed for what it is, by the open declarations of its staff, made at what they doubtless imagined to be a safe distance from Singapore. To the student of human nature there is nothing to be surprised at in all this deception. The creature will always act according to its instincts and its environment.

Appendix E-2

We are authoritatively informed that in consequence of the correspondence appearing on Saturday re the Anglo-Chinese School the Chinese trustees of the Boarding School—Messrs Tan Jiak Kim, Hap Seng (Tan Kim Tian) and Tan Boo Liat (Kim Cheng and Co.)—have resigned in a body; and we also hear that a large number of the Chinese pupils of the School have been withdrawn.

Source:
Straits Times Archives,
Lee Kong Chian Reference Library, National Library Board

Appendix E-3

The Singapore Free Press, 27 July 1896

The Anglo-Chinese School

In connection with the correspondence regarding the Anglo-Chinese School, it may not be out of place at this juncture to recapitulate the history of the school as told by its promoters from time to time. The laying of the foundation stone of the present school building took place on October 5th 1892, H.E. The Governor Sir C. Smith performing the ceremony; and on that occasion it was stated that the school was founded in 1885 by the Rev. W.F. Oldham, one of the small party of Indian missionaries who visited Singapore in that year. The school was first held in a hired house in Hill Street, and afterwards in more commodious premises, and, as it was then taught, the more favourable locality, Telok Ayer. "In the month of August, 1885, on representations made by Mr. Oldham, the Government granted for mission and for educational purposes the piece of land on which now stands the neighbouring Church and School buildings. And while thanks, of course, due, first, to the Government, the trustees desire to acknowledge the hearty support afforded by the leading members of the Chinese community by stating that practically the entire course of the School-house some $5,500 was defrayed by Chinese residents. Classes met in the new building—where also the Principal, resided for some time—in February 1886, but in consequence of the increasing number of scholars and boarders the house became too small. In June, 1888, the property known as Bellevue, standing just off the government domain, and approached from Orchard Road, was purchased for a sum of $12,350 for use as a Boarding House. Here it may be again remarked that the acquisition of this property was made possible by the liberal and substantial help of a few Chinese gentlemen." The number of scholars continued to increase, and the arrangement opened "being naturally inconvenient, the position of matters was laid before government with an appeal for assistance towards enlarging the existing school premises; the appeal was favourably considered, for, on 1st December, 1889, intimation was received that a sum of $3,000 had been granted to the Anglo-Chinese School for the building purposes."

The new premises were formally opened on July 21st, 1895, and though the management of the school has never in public been avowedly sectarian, His Honour the Chief Justice, The Hon'ble Mr. Bonser, in the course of his remarks, said, "It was objected by some very worthy people that the education that was given there was not of a sufficiently distinctive religious character. Well, he was exceedingly glad it was not. He thought that if it had been attempted to carry on the School on dogmatic lines, it would have failed to enlist the sympathies of the Chinese community, and, in the second place—he was speaking perhaps, on a matter which he did not understand—but for his own part, he could not help thinking that what was commonly known as a religious education was a fraud and a deception. It was not wise, he considered, to train up boys in dogmatic truths before they could understand them... it was better to teach boys to be honest, upright and unselfish than to teach them creeds and catechisms, which they could not understand, and it was because he believed that the management of that school were endeavouring on that work that he was there that day." (applause.)

Again, on the occasion of the annual prize distribution in February, 1894, the Hon'ble W.E. Maxwell, the Colonial Secretary, said he did not wish "to touch at any length upon the subject of religious education. He knew that the founders and those principally interested in the schools were men of religion, and he honoured them for it. But they were wise, in his opinion, in not attempting in any way to interfere with the religious customs, observances and ideas of the body of boys entrusted to their charge and teaching."

No reference was made last year to the subject of religious education, but the same extracts and the actions of the Chinese trustees of the Boarding School would seem to point to the conclusion that the management of the School, to bring about such a result, have abandoned the compromise which has hitherto brought them so much in the way of assistance locally.

Source:
Straits Times Archives,
Lee Kong Chian Reference Library, National Library Board

Appendix E-4

<u>The Singapore Free Press, 28 Jul 1896 (4 Aug Ed)</u>

<u>The Methodist Mess</u>

That "honesty is the best policy" is once more exemplified in the story of what neutral observers must agree in considering as the discreditable mess that has for the time disorganised the Anglo-Chinese School. The whole trouble is due to that occasional, often chronic, spirit of crooked dealing that not unfrequently makes the average layman look askance at the practices of many professional professors of religion—no matter what the Church or creed be. In the case of the particular religious agency concerned, the difficulties are due to the fact that funds were raised from Chinese subscribers on one pretence, and applied to an object carefully disclaimed when the funds were applied for, and obnoxious to the religious feelings of the subscribers. The ordinary law of the land calls that "obtaining money under false pretences" and the criminal code provides a scale of appropriate penalties. Probably the civil law offers a process for a compulsory refund of the money originally so questionably acquired. The sordid fact is this: That the agency referred to appears to be so sharp in worldly matters as to follow with keenness the apophthegm "Mak[e] money: honestly, if ye can; but *mak[e]* money." It does not mind borrowing from certain other religious organisations the principle "Do evil, that good may come." The Chinese of Singapore have, we are convinced, the utmost confidence in the good faith and probity of the Europeans whom they meet in the course of business and in matters of social communication, local politics, and so forth. That good faith we believe to be fully justified, whether the Europeans be British or foreign. But here, on a question happily not a business affair, we find that a group of Europeans *via* America, had been convicted according to the Chinese belief, of errant bad faith and of a double dealing that in private secular life would be accounted as disgraceful and impossible amongst gentlemen. Running with the hare and hunting with the hounds, or the simultaneous cult of God and Mammon, is proverbially difficult, and if the Methodist mission people have failed to harmonise the two, it is because their conduct was sooner or later bound to be detected. There is in the case, as related publicly, a visible want of moral courage. They hoist one flag to get money, premises and pupils: then they haul it down and hoist another when they want to seduce these pupils from their parental faith. If the cause is a good one (and, conducted rightly, it is a good one) then let it be professed openly and honestly. It is perhaps demanding too much virtue that there shall be any voluntary restitution of the funds collected under false pretences from the "heathen Chinese"—they were not so-called to their faces. But let the School from now be called "Methodist Mission School," let the proselytising which is the sole justification of the School to the American mission managers, be openly declared, and the situation be honestly regularised. Are the mission people ashamed of their banner? Why then act in such a way as to make it serve to cloak the deception that has at last been discovered by the indignant Chinese parents! The Principal has given what purports to be an explanation of the case. He claims that "the School was organised as a mission and has always been known as such." To the Mission perhaps; but it was carefully impressed upon wealthy Chinese subscribers that it was not a mission they were asked to subscribe but to a secular educational establishment, where no foreign religious influences would be brought to bear on their children. Again why the exclusion of any hint at the essence of the School in its title! That is clearly left out with an object. The principal has stated in writing as follows: The only compact ever made with our Chinese friends regarding religious instruction was that no boy would be baptised without his father's consent and that no pressure would be used to induce boys to become Christians. But that Christian teachers in a mission school should exert such an influence on their pupils as to induce some of these to become Christian is inevitable, and we have never attempted to conceal our satisfaction that that should be so.

But that is a self-contradictory proposition. There is to be no "pressure" to "induce" but there is to be an "inevitable influence" to "induce."

Bearing in mind the effects and power of the adult educating mind over the impressible mind of the young pupil, can it be said that there is no pressure in such a relative position? Or that the effect of daily hearing and seeing the "inevitable" is to count for nothing? But still if the Principal had presented each Chinese parent with a printed declaration that the attendance of his child was to imply subjection to the "inevitable influences" inducing a perversion from the family faith, his position would be unassailable. Did he do so? If not, why not? The *suppresio veri* in such a case would be emphatically a *suggestio falsi*. And we again come back to our original proposition that in matters of religion, as in matters of the business and social life of a community, "honesty is the best policy." Whereas secular education is to be merely ancillary to the work of making converts, let that plainly appear on the head and front of the enterprise. Let the Principal declare in clear terms to any and every Chinese parent that it will be his object in educating the pupil, to submit him to influences whose inevitable effects may be to induce the child to separate itself from the parental creed. Only that course will exculpate him from a charge of conspiracy against the unity and harmony of the Chinese family, even under the cover of, from one particular pint of view, the worthiest of motives.

Source:
Straits Times Archives,
Lee Kong Chian Reference Library, National Library Board

Appendix E-5

The Singapore Free Press, 29 July 1896

Letter to Rev. C.C. Kelso

To the Editor,

Sir, will you be good enough to insert the accompanying letter, addressed to Mr. Kelso by myself, Mr. Tan Hap Seng, and Mr. Tan Boo Liat, in your valuable paper.

Yours truly
Mr. Tan Jiak Kim

Dear Sir,

We have read and carefully considered your explanation in the local press. In coming to our decision, we have also borne in mind what you have said to us in conversation. As you seem still to think that we are likely to compromise with you on your system of education, we wish you distinctly to understand that we have finally decided not to have any further connection with your School. In your letter to the press on the 27th, you did not give a correct account of the understanding arrived at between Mr. Oldham and the Chinese.

Our "Compact" was that no religious teaching whatsoever was to be carried on in the School. Until lately we believe this was fairly carried out. Recently, however, a change has come over the School, and although we hear the boys speak about the religious teaching, you have always denied before us that this was true, and until we saw your recent report to America we really have no substantial grounds to work upon. Now that we know your policy and recognise that, as you say, your school is "A Mission School," we feel it would be absurd for us to expect that you would abstain from religious teaching.

Further we are satisfied, after enquiry, that compulsion has been used to induce the boys to join the religious meetings during School hours.

We feel in taking this step that we are performing a public duty towards those parents who have sent their children to the Anglo-Chinese School directly or indirectly through our influence, under the impression that the School is purely secular. As this is a public matter we shall send copies of this letter to the public Press.

Yours truly
T. Jiak Kim
T. Hap Seng
T. Boo Liat

The Alleged Proselytising—The Singapore Free Press, 29 July 1896

As showing that the management of the Anglo-Chinese School have abandoned the compromise arrived at in 1885 with the Rev. W. F. Oldham, the founder of the School, the following statement by Mr. Keong Saik will be of interest in connection with the charge of proselytism which has been so freely brought against the School. No such charge could, of course, be reasonably brought against an avowedly open "mission" School, as for instance the Eastern School, bearing in mind the public declaration on the subject made by the Principal, the Rev. A. Lamont, on the eve of his departure from the Colony on leave; and that such a charge should be possible in the case of the Anglo-Chinese School shows either a lack of appreciation of the moral claims of the Chinese supporters of the School by the management, or that their assistance has been obtained through a complete misunderstanding which it has been nobody's business to clear up, in spite of the declared misgivings of the Chinese as to the intentions of those who have hitherto carried on the School.

Speaking of an interview which Mr. Oldham had with the late Mr. Kim Cheng, Tan Jiak Kim and himself in 1885, Mr. Keong Saik says that when Mr. Oldham announced his intention of starting a school here they doubted him, knowing him to be a missionary, and asked how he could establish any school without introducing religion into it. He assured them, however, that there was plenty of room both for a secular school and for religious teaching, and that the school he was about to start was a purely secular institution, apart altogether form his religious work. They believed him, and Mr. Kim Cheng was so well pleased with the idea that he immediately offered to give him a free grant of land (on long lease) for the purpose at the foot of Fort Canning. Mr. Oldham did not accept the offer, having secured a grant of land from Government, but the Chinese were invited to subscribe to the cost of the building. Mr. Keong Saik accompanied Mr. Oldham on his mission of collecting, and the surprise of the Chinese at seeing Mr. Keong Saik interesting himself on what appeared to be a mission school had to be disarmed by assurances of the secular character of the work before many of them could be induced to subscribe.

And so long as Mr. Oldham was here, Mr. Keong Saik assures us that the compact was faithfully kept. There was then no Bible reading and no hymn singing in the School, a fact which could be borne out by those of the European teaching staff who are still in the Colony. It was only after Mr. Oldham's departure that the trouble began. Ask whether the Chinese supporters of the School had not been aware of the practice of singing hymns and of reading the Bible in the School for some years past, Mr. Keong Saik admitted that he personally had suspected it for some time but was for a long time unable to prove what he heard. When he did come to know it, he ceased actively to interest himself in the affairs of the School. Others heard the same, and it was owing to these vague misgivings that some of the Chinese supporters of the School asked for a public declaration on the part of the management in 1895. That was the occasion of the remarks made by His Honour the Chief Justice, the Hon'ble Mr. Bonser, at that time one of the School Trustees, whose remarks were quoted in connection with this controversy the other day.

He had since learnt that the introduction of Bible reading and religious services dated back to the return of one gentleman connected with the management from a certain conference at Calcutta, but what he knew now he did not know for some time after the event. It was only recently, however, that the boys were compelled to listen to the reading of the Bible, and he was in a position to prove, form the statements of the boys, that on a certain day last week, the Principal gave instructions to the masters before the School, that all boys who did not attend the Bible reading were to be punished by being kept in.

Source:
Straits Times Archives,
Lee Kong Chian Reference Library, National Library Board

Appendix E-6

The Singapore Free Press, 30th July 1896

The Anglo-Chinese School

To the Editor,

Sir, in the interests of Education, since Mr. Kelso continues to deny that "pressure" had been used to induce boys to attend the religious meetings, we feel it our bounden duty to lay before the public all the facts which are within our knowledge. Will Mr. Kelso deny that up to 1890 Mr. Oldham's school was a purely secular school like the Raffles Institution and the Eastern School. In 1891 the religious exercise were introduced and we heard of them through the boys. Mr. Jiak Kim, depending on what Mr. Oldham had promised, simply told his sons and brothers not to have anything to do with them. Mr. Kelso, in reply to our letter, went completely outside facts to express his astonishment at our ignorance of what went on. We said in our letter that we had to choose between their statements of own boys and the firm denial of Mr. Kelso. We had little or no reason to suspect Mr. Kelso misleading us, and we therefore continued our enquiries without taking any step which might mean injury to the Anglo-Chinese School. When we said we were satisfied after enquiry that compulsion had been used, we referred to enquiries and investigations that had been undertaken days before Mr. Kelso published his letter asking for investigation. We have discovered a large number of the Chinese boys have already imbibed the doctrine of the Christian religion, leading them to disobedience to their parents. It is therefore untrue that religion has not been systematically taught. When "the gospel in all lands" reached our hands we saw for the first time that what we had been hearing was quite true. How could boys ask their parents for baptism unless their innocent hearts had been filled with the Christian doctrines, which must mean months of steady teaching. By having the service just when school begins, Mr. Kelso thinks he may have a subterfuge should he be attacked. Many boys who refuse to attend service are punished; a pupil teacher with cane in hand hunts up the boys who remained outside. If Mr. Kelso says that this is not compulsion, we do not know what it is. Let Mr. Kelso answer our questions. Are the boys punished by being made to stand up while those attending service sit down, and by being kept in a small room? If boys are late, they ought to be punished but not compelled to attend service. Those who are not late had no choice but to either to go to the service, or to get shut up. The public ought to know how my own boys are treated. The teachers, it seems, treat them *differently* from most other boys so that my own boys won't complain. My boys now inform me that they could do as they like and when they were threatened with punishment of any kind they asked their teachers concerned to refer to me. Other boys whose fathers have little influence had to suffer. When I found this out I made up my mind that a school capable of making such a distinction in order to enforce attendance at religious services is unworthy of support. Mr. Boo Liat when at school was treated like the other boys of "influential" families. "He was not punished but had to choose between half an hour's" idleness and attending the singing, as the service is known to boys. We have discovered that in the last week even greater efforts were made to force the boys to attend religious services.

It is absolutely incorrect that we Chinese, when we were asked for money to build the Boarding School were informed that it was to be a "Christian home," where our children were to be brought under the inevitable "Christian influences." Those who are interested in this matter may have a look at the Trust deed for this Boarding House, at present in the hands of Messrs. Rodyk and Davidson. In this deed no mention whatever is made of religion or Christian home. We gave money to build the Boarding House on the distinct understanding, as embodied in the Trust-deed, that nothing except pure education was to be given our children. It is absurd to imagine that we who are not Christians would desire to spend money in order to give our children Christian training. This is so self-evident that it is incredible that Mr. Kelso should have laboured in the public press to prove otherwise.

The matter concerned is a public one and we cannot help saying that we are sorry we cannot any longer put any trust in Mr. Kelso's promises or words, whatever may be the public opinion. I personally feel I have been misled by means not altogether worthy of Missionaries.

Yours faithfully
Tan Jiak Kim

Source:
Straits Times Archives,
Lee Kong Chian Reference Library, National Library Board

Appendix E-7

The Singapore Free Press, 3 Aug 1896

Proselytising in the Methodist School

To the Editor,

Sir, I have read the articles that have been published on the above subject, and I think occasion have arisen for me to make public a few facts which will help to correct the wrong impressions that have crept into the minds of the once liberal and generous supporters of the Methodist School—impressions that are calculated unduly to cause harm to that School.

That harm has been done to the School by "Isaiah" and his prompters is too apparent from the number of successions that have taken place among the pupils, and it becomes all the more serious and undeserving in view of the fact that the old Chinese trends have declined to submit the questions at issue to a Committee of Enquiry. They appear to be more than willing to found their judgement against the methods of that School from the one-sided statements made to them by the pupils, when formerly the statements of these very pupils had little weight with them. I for one should hardly have thought that the result of such a method of enquiry would have satisfied the mind of the ordinary common juror.

Isaiah of the Holy Scriptures was a prophet in that *he* prompted his nation to live up to a higher level of morality by pledges of blessings that would be theirs if they heard and obeyed his message. On the other hand, when I read in the papers that Mr. Jiak Kim knew perfectly well that since 1891 religious exercises have been observed daily when school began, and that Mr. Keong Saik admitted to his interviewer that after a long period of suspicion which was subsequently proved to his satisfaction to be well-founded, he had ceased "actively to interest himself in the affairs of the school," it struck me that "Isaiah" of the Singapore Free Press was really a misnomer; for was it not he who, according to Mr. Kelso had a "recently strongly defended the Bible teaching of the School at a dinner in the home of one of our prominent patrons"? *Veritas* then would rather have him styled *Vox Populi*—The mouthpiece of the populace who had prompted him to go into print. If what I have above stated is borne in mind, then the precipitous action of the three Chinese Trustees of the Boarding School at what might have appeared to be the trumpet call of "Isaiah" will reduce itself into the last step of a prearranged plan.

Mr. Kelso has replied definitely denying the charge of punishment of the pupils for not attending the service and has explained the nature of the order that was issued by him on the 24th July, but there is another point that he omitted to deal with. The letter written conjointly by the late Chinese trustees mentioned that Mr. Kelso had always denied before them that the report of the boys "about the religious teaching" was true. But having regard to the fact that when I visited the School quite recently on the repeated invitation of the Principal, and saw for myself and had explained to me what was done in the school hall the first thing every morning, and observed that no attempt was made to close the doors to any chance or inquisitive visitors, and further than there were some boys standing at the hall doors not as a punishment but from necessity through having arrived later, the hall being comfortably filled, it seems incredible that Mr. Kelso should have on any occasion given the late trustees a denial on being questioned "about the religious teaching." Had he done so, even the "subtlety" of the "accursed reptile" then would not have saved him form a terrible exposure by a surprise visit from any one of those trustees or from others on their behalf. So far as I have been able to ascertain, Mr. Kelso has ever courted visits from friends and well-wishers, not only to the educational institutional, but also to the Boarding School.

I now come to a very important part of the rupture between the parties concerned. Mr. Jiak Kim puts the question—"Will Mr. Kelso deny that up to 1890, Mr. Oldham's school was a purely secular school like the Raffles Institution and the Eastern School?" With reference to the Eastern School I fear Mr. Jiak Kim could not have remembered what he had read in an article "The Alleged Proselytising" which appeared in your last Wednesday's issue. Now as to the Raffles School does Mr. Jiak Kim, who is a trustee of that institution, not know that Sir Sanford Raffles founded his school in order to provide the natives of the settlement with religious instruction? Is he not aware that Dr. Robert Morrison, one of the pioneer missionaries to China subscribed $6000 (equivalent to about [intelligible amount] at the present rates of exchange) towards the funds on that understanding surely he must remember that until 25 years ago all the pupils of that school assembled for prayers at the opening and closing of each school day that is within [intelligible word] memory. So much as to an [intelligible word] of the schools quoted by Mr. Jiak Kim.

"Isaiah" waxed furious when referring to the Boarding School. "Every Friday afternoon, a kind of service is held. . . ." That seems to be the extent of his knowledge of what goes on there. A Correspondent in last Tuesday's issue of your contemporary publication gave further information on that subject. In that article the Correspondent only went to this extent that every Sunday "a special Sunday School meeting" was held at which "all boarders *are expected* to be present." Let me once again refer to Raffles. Till the year 1884 or 1885, there was a Boarding School connected with the Institution, and the centre block of buildings was set apart for it, until a few years before its abandonment, when the Boarding School was removed to the present site of Raffles Hotel. My information does not go further back than 1875, but between that year and 1885 there were several Chinese youths who lived in the Boarding School. There were prayers (the Order for Morning Service in the English Prayer Book) every morning at VIII at which the Chinese boys were always present, while some of the European and other boarders were not, as this went to the Chinese class of which the Chinese boys never were members. Grace was said before and after meals, and the boarders took turns in saying it. And what did the Chinese boys do on Sundays? Why, they all went or had to go to service in St Andrew's Cathedral *and that church alone* and in the afternoon to the Sunday School! These Chinese youths would gather together on a Sunday especially and spent an hour or so in singing hymns. Some of them owned Bibles and other religious books. Let the parents of those Chinese youths now come forward and say that the result of these proceedings ("proselytising" if "Isaiah" would have it) has been that their sense of filial piety has been thoroughly perverted, and that these youths have become "*put hao*" or unfilial.

"Isaiah" no doubt would be able to say how many non-Christian Chinese parents there are who ever trouble themselves for the moral education of their children and who have imparted to such children that maxim of Confucius which English (Raffles) boarders attending the now-defunct Chinese class had to imbibe that "to be a man you must cultivate filial piety." So far as his own early moral education goes, does "Isaiah" remember his beloved father more by the Confucian doctrines than by the Lord's Prayer which, as he has often said his father taught him to repeat every night at his prayers? Is it not rather this prayer "Our father in heaven" which even in his boyhood, gave him a nobler and higher conception of the meaning of filial piety, and has he not always praised his revered father for that legacy? Surely "Isaiah" will not be so uncharitable as to credit the pupils of the Methodist School with less powers of reasoning than he possessed at their age.

In conclusion, I cannot hope to succeed, where Mr. Kelso has failed to persuade the late Chinese trustees and those Chinese parents who have withdrawn their children from the Methodist School to reconsider their decision, or to appoint a Committee of Enquiry and agree to abide by the result of that enquiry, but in refusing to comply with such a request of the Principal I believe they will have cause to regret that in thus acting they have thrown overboard that salutary axiom of the best systems of law that are "A man is presumed to be innocent until he is proved to be guilty."

Dr. Lim Boon Keng

To the Editor,

Sir, Is it not somewhat surprising to find the Hon'ble Dr. Boon Keng taking such an active part in the present anti-Christian movement?

He calls himself a Christian, I believe, at least he must have done so, some years ago, and he was baptised by the Rev. J. A. B. Cook at Edinburgh, at his own request, after his professed conversion; at which time, it is said he went out of his way to renounce Buddhism, which he described as his "ancestral faith," in a speech he delivered in the church on the evening of his baptism.

Since then it appears, chameleon-like, he has changed many times, and, with a marvelous power of adaptation, seems to suit himself to the environment of the hour. But with all his change of views, (which are legion) in certain circles, he has been protesting until very recently that he is a Christian. Perhaps he does "protest too much!"

It comes with exceedingly bad grace from him to insinuate that the tortuous and poisonous characteristics of the serpent are the exclusive of those he has attacked. *Tu ipse*!

Such personal references to our Chinese medico would never have been made had he not compelled them by his action.

He appeals to *veritas*: then to *veritas* he shall go! Truth speaks calmly, not bitterly.

It may do this young gentleman good to remind him that knowledge and wisdom are not necessarily co-extensive. He has prepared a stick for his own back, and, if he receives the few blows, he must not complain.

With his many advantages, for which he has to thank his Christian friends not a little, he might have been a power for good in guiding and moderating the non-Christian Babas in their transition stage; but what has he done?

Source:
Straits Times Archives,
Lee Kong Chian Reference Library, National Library Board

Appendix E–8

The Singapore Free Press, 4 August, 1896

The Methodist Mess

From the shape being taken by the controversy over the Anglo-Chinese School, or, as it will probably hereafter be known, the American Methodist Mission School, it can be seen that it is spreading away into side issues and personal recriminations in the manner not unusual where the element of religious prejudices enters into the discussion. All that half irrelevant matter merely serves to obscure the actual cause of difference. That, we repeat, is simplicity itself. It depends primarily on the testimony of two men as to its initial stage; on the testimony of those two men plus a certain number of other persons who were interviewed by these two men, almost in every case in the presence of each other, for a certain declared purpose. Mr. Oldham is one of these men, Mr. Tan Keong Saik the other. As for the other witnesses, most of them are yet accessible, though possibly several may be dead.

To our way of thinking religion does not enter into the question at all except insofar as it refers to specific action done or not done in reference to a verbal contract which was considered to be so clearly defined that a number of people were induced to pay money for a certain purpose by virtue of that contract. The relative personal conditions were primarily of such a nature that it is absolutely incredible that any money should have been paid in the absence of such a contract, to such a person as Mr. Oldham, for such a purpose as that to which the money was devoted,—the building of the Anglo-Chinese School. Good faith was professed strenuously, continuously, apparently honestly by Mr. Oldham, and certainly honestly by Mr. Keong Saik, speaking on behalf of Mr. Oldham and in the gentleman's presence; in equal good faith, relying on the assurances, were given large sums of money bestowed for the founding of a school which as to provide non-religious general education to the sons of subscribers and the Chinese community at large.

This, and nothing else, is the root of the controversy. In examining into this, a judge or a jury would be guided by the laws of evidence that, and by the reasonable probabilities, and the inferences to be drawn therefrom. It would seem to be no more natural or reasonable that a Chinese parent would, with his eyes open, subscribe towards the perversion of the members of his family from their faith than an English or American Protestant parent or a French Roman Catholic parent, or a Turkish Mussulman parent would subscribe towards the perversion of his sons to Confucianism or Hindooism. The weight of direct evidence, and, much more, the weight of circumstantial evidence is on the side of those who claim that their money was paid only upon the assurance that no such risk was being run.

A sincere belief in Mr. Oldham's truthfulness in his declaration as to a secular education would have justified the payment of the subscriptions as far as a question of mutual trust went. But the matter, unhappily, did not end here. The money was paid over and spent, and it does not appear that Mr. Oldham, as he was morally bound to do in accepting the money, reduced the compact to writing in such a form that it would validly blind his successors to all time. But these gentlemen, having their money in the shape of structural fixtures, quite see their advantage over the unlucky subscribers. Their temptation lies in their connection with their Boards in America and in the *kudos* to be gained in mission circles by glowing accounts of "the good work" in Singapore. Because one or more of Mr. Oldham's successors fell, it must be remembered that the temptation to circumvent the "wealthy Chinese heathen" was strong, and ready to hand. Mr. Kelso has it in his power, if he chooses, to rehabilitate the shattered repute of his mission for honesty and clean dealing. Let him take the advice of any layman of good position and upright business character. He will probably find that the advice, from whatever quarter, will be of much the same description. But it is quite certain that the original subscribers have been deceived. How far wittingly, is a matter of debate.

Source:
Straits Times Archives,
Lee Kong Chian Reference Library, National Library Board

Appendix E-9

The Singapore Free Press, 11 Aug 1896

The Anglo-Chinese School

To the Editor,

Sir, Since my name has been mentioned in connection with this school, I feel it my duty to make it clear that the point of the disagreement that has arisen between the authorities of the Anglo-Chinese School and ourselves was not due to any animus on our part against the controversy in Christian religion in general. That Christianity was always tolerated when preached to adult boys and adopted by men of matured understanding is well-known to all, and as a proof of this, I need only say that the relations existing between the Christian and non-Christian Babas have always been, and are still as cordial as ever, and that a great many of the former are enjoying as much respect form the latter as any other well-conducted men do in Chinese Society. Their religious faith has not in the least lowered them in our estimation.

But what we object to is the unauthorised inculcation of foreign doctrine upon the immature minds of our children. Hence when the Rev. Mr. Oldham started the Anglo-Chinese School here the only condition exacted from him (and which, I believe, was duly observed during his stay here) was that no religious teaching should be introduced into the school during the usual school hours, that is, between 10 am and 3 pm, so that portions of the day could be devoted to religious exercises by boys of Christian parentage. In the Boarding School that Reverend gentleman also promised that no Bible teaching was to be instilled into the tender minds of our children.

On this assurance a large number of most influential men gave the full strength of their support, including the late Messrs Kim Cheng, Ong Kew Ho, Lim Eng Keng, We Boon Teck, Tan Beng Wan, and the present Mr. Jiak Kim and others. Under such auspices the School was soon largely patronised by the Chinese of all classes. The success was due, however, not to its having better or abler teachers, or to its charging a smaller fee than the Raffles, but it was caused simply by the rules regarding the age of admittance having been so relaxed, and the indulgence shewn to absentees so liberal as to meet the general views of the Chinese parents. Therefore, some years ago when I heard of the breach of this "Compact" I warned Mr. Kelso, and particularly Bishop Thoburn, that if what I had learned was true, and the Chinese community were to know of it, the parents would withdraw their children. These suspicions, however, were little thought of afterwards, consequently, when resigning the trusteeship of the Boarding-School, a few months ago, I did so on purely other grounds which I then stated in my letter of resignation, and was not in any way influenced by the above doubts.

Imagine our amazement when we accidentally came upon a copy of the *Gospel in all Lands*! In Mr. Kelso's report we found for the first time in print (for Mr. Kelso never sent his report to us) that the institutions in his charge are now in full swing as religious seminaries. We then represented to Dr. Boon Keng that Mr. Kelso's report did not agree with what the promoters of the Anglo-Chinese School had always assured us. We earnestly requested him to give expression to the feelings of the Chinese Community in this matter and in compliance with our request, the Chinese views were fully represented in the articles signed "Isaiah."

To illustrate the general tendency of the Chinese convictions regarding a question of this nature, I cannot give a better instance than that which happened only a few years ago.

When the "Poh Leong Kuk" society was at its lowest financial ebb for want of support for the Chinese Public the Roman Catholic nuns generously offered to admit all the inmates of the Refuge into the Convent free of charge, but the Chinese Committee at once declined the preferred kind offer, on account of the Convent being a religious asylum. Then, last year, when the Matron of the Society was discovered to have been tampering with the minds of the young girls in the Home with foreign religion, she was at once requested to desist from her actions, in consequence of which she resigned.

The Chinese members of the Committee of this Society are the leading men of their fellow provincials and may be taken, therefore, as the representatives of the different sections of the Chinese in this Island. If these men saw objection to the poor orphans being exposed to the influences likely to be exerted by Christian Missionaries, is it conceivable that they would knowingly permit their children to be subjected to influences which they would not allow to reach even the friendless orphans?

No doubt we made a mistake; and we are not sorry that we have been able to recognise that a mistake has been made. We certainly had at one time complete trust in the assurances made to us; and our mistake was due to our blind confidence in the Missionaries. In this connection I must emphatically repudiate the senseless insinuations that in this controversy, we are carrying on an "anti-Christian" Movement; but when some of the agents of the Mission now go amongst the Chinese at Telok Ayer and other places and publicly apply disrespectful and opprobrious terms to characterise Chinese ideas, they cannot but expect to be exposed to the indignation of the by-standers, who generally, are ignorant people on the streets.

Yours faithfully
Tan Keong Saik

To the Editor:

Sir, when the Parliament of Great Britain has been sensibly refused to admit denominational religious teaching within the walls of the English public board schools, where is the foundation for the whine of one or two interested persons over a similar policy here (infinitely more necessary) being an "Anti-Christian Movement"? Let some narrow minds "clear themselves of cant," if they can (which, however, as good old Euclid would say, is impossible).

PS: Mr. Augustine Birrel, MP, in a recent speech said:

> *Not only education, but, unhappily, the religious question was still unsettled. At the end of the 19th Christian century, we had not yet made up our minds what prayers might be safely taught to our children, or what amount of infant piety might, with safety to the State, to be enforced.*

If, therefore, in a country where one of the hundred forms of Christianity is established as a State Church it is held by the State to be inexpedient even to recognise the special tenets of that church in State Schools, much more is it impolitic, by underhand methods, to endeavour to use secular education as a decoy for the practices of proselytism. The Methodists in England, like other Non-conformists, are dead against any iota of religion being taught in public Board Schools.

Source:
Straits Times Archives,
Lee Kong Chian Reference Library, National Library Board

Appendix F-1

The Straits Times, 25 July 1896

To the Editor of "The Straits Times":

Sir, The public is under some obligation to you through your amiable, but all the more pointed, references to the Rev. D D. Moore's now celebrated pirated article on the Malays a-picknicking. The same notorious author has laid it down, as the motto of his school in "educational works," by which our Methodist friends mean proselytism in disguise, the following most astounding formula: "Nowhere so much as on the East is it necessary for the Christian worker to combine the qualities of the dove and the serpent. First, innocency, then subtlety must be the motto of his work." It has never occurred to me that it is ever necessary for a true disciple of Jesus of Nazareth either in the east or in the west—in heaven or on hell—to have anything else than *"Veritas prevalebit"* as his motto, and to say anything more than yea yea or nay nay.

This introduction will simplify what I shall have to point out. The Anglo-Chinese School of the Methodist Mission is styled in a "College" in the language of its promoters. The Principal is now out begging for money from men such as Messrs Tan Jiak Kim, Tan Hap Seng, and others. No doubt these amiable gentlemen will be told that the "College" is a purely educational institution, and that the teachers do not use their influence to proselytise. Already a large sum has been got. This is to warn others who may labour under the illusion. Mr. Kelso says in his report in the "Gospel in All Lands," May 1896, that the school work begins each morning with religious exercises, and that in the past year alone, there has been "many bright conversions." He says, also, that the leading boys in the upper classes are "professed Christians." Now, this mist be either a deliberate falsehood or mere natural tendency to exaggerate. How could the children of heathens become professed Christians if their faith had not been tampered with. But the unkindest thing of all that the promoters of the Mission had done is to treat their patrons with contempt. No thanks are expressed in their reports to America to "the rich heathens," who have been simple enough to be led by them. Mr. Jiak Kim and his Chinese colleagues on the Board of Trustees of the Singapore College may be interested to know on the indisputable authority of Rev. D. D. Moore, M.A., that they are known to the Mission which they have been misled to support—simply and truly as "rich heathens Chinamen," whose liberality is very convenient, and whose credulity is no match for the Christian "serpent." I should like to know why heathens are allowed to act as trustees to a Christian college. I challenge Mr. Kelso to say to his Chinese colleagues—rather to his "rich heathen" colleagues—what he states in his report already quoted about "the religious results" of the school being the most gratifying. I assure him that, if he only let rich heathens know the ways of the serpent, even disguised as a dove, he will find all support withdrawn. Has Mr. Kelso ever reported to his Board of Trustees the number of converts made and will he announce to them what he wrote home vis., the leading boys—"most influential Chinese"—too are "professed Christians"?

I should not have taken up so much of your space had I not been convinced that such methods of working (as a serpent in the form of a dive) does harm to other more deserving schools, which urgently need funds.

I am, &c,
ANTI-HUMBUG

Proselytising in Mission Schools

(*From a Correspondent.*)

There now exists, among the Chinese community, a decide objection to the efforts being made in missionary schools to proselytise, and the American Mission School, especially the Boarding School, is pointed out as being remarkably prominent in such efforts. It will not be out of place to refer to the early history of this school. About 11 years ago, the Rev. Mr. Oldham arrived here and commenced work in the interests of the Methodist Episcopal Church. Being an eminent educationalist, he also turned his attention to school work. He clearly saw that, to achieve success, he must make the Chinese interested. In that, he was singularly successful. Men such as the late Mr. Kim Cheng, the present Mr. Jiak Kim, and others, became quickly alive to the fact that, in Mr. Oldham, they could secure the services of a man who would give such tuition to the Chinese as they desired. A handsome sum, $4000, was raised among the Chinese for the purpose of building a school, and Mr. Oldham, practically, guaranteed that the tuition imparted should be secular This sum was doubled by the Missionary Society in New York, but, of course, was given for purposes of purely missionary work. It is quite true that, during Mr. Oldham's stay here, religious teaching was not introduced into the school, but, had he remained, it would have been impossible for him to have adhered to his compact with the Chinese. In 1891, the practice of having religious exercises in the classes was commenced, and it has gone on up to the present, when it may be said that the school is fairly a missionary one. The boys meet daily in the lecture hall, and sing a Gospel song. The Bible is then read and explained to them, and prayer is offered. Conversions have been made, and the Boarding School is considered a centre of Christian influence. A weekly prayer meeting is held, and the boys are invited to attend. An evangelical address is delivered in Malay. Several boys of the Boarding School are encouraged to go out on Sundays and hold open air meetings, while it is declared that the leading boys in the upper classes are professed Christians. A Sunday School has been organised and is carried on in opposition to the wishes of the boys' parents. It is expected to become the nucleus of an Anglo-Chinese Church. Now, if all this were done with the consent of the parents and guardians, there would be nothing to say; but the reverse is the case. This mission owes its very existence to the generosity of the Chinese. It has been most bountifully assisted by them, and, even at this moment, a large sum of money is being subscribed for rebuilding "Bellevue." In the face of this, it might be thought that the often-expressed wishes of the Chinese, that they religious views of their children should not be interfered with, would be attended to. They do not ask much. All they wish is that the boys should not be approached on the subject of religion until they have reached an age when they may reasonably be expected to understand the matter, and then decide for themselves what course they shall pursue. If the

American Mission wishes to act fairly and aboveboard with the school boys, a purely missionary school should be established, and the parents of those entering it should understand clearly that the Bible would be taught. It is quite evident, then, that the American Mission School authorities are proselytising in every possible way, on the principle that "the end justifies the means." It may concluded that this method of 'verting the children committed to their care is not known either to the parents or to such leading supporters of the school as Mr. Jiak Kim and others, and it may safely be inferred that, the moment this is fully understood, there will be no hesitation in withdrawing the boys.

Source:
Straits Times Archives,
Lee Kong Chian Reference Library, National Library Board

Appendix F–2

The Straits Times, 27 July 1896

The Charge of Proselytising

In our columns to-day the charge of proselytising levelled against the Anglo-Chinese School is repeated at great length, and with some little bitterness. In substance, the accusation made by the Chinese is that their boys are being persuaded to abandon the faith of their fathers against the wishes of those fathers. The reply of the school-master is that he forces no Chinese boys towards Christianity, that he compels no Chinese boys in the day school to join in Christian exercises, but that he is exceedingly pleased to influence boys to become Christians if that can be done by any fair and legitimate exercise of moral example and precept. We are disposed to dismiss at once the charges of bad faith in the past, because it is possible—nay it is almost certain—that those charges are based on mutual misconception. The American Christian and the Straits Chinese, who are concerned in the dispute about the Anglo-Chinese School, have both been engaged in a task on which neither of them should have entered. In the nature of things it was impossible that men who are Christian missionaries by profession can become schoolteachers among non-Christians without attempting to proselytise. These Christian teachers as the better-informed of the two parties to the contract, should have know that; but the Chinese, also, who sent their children to this school should have recognised it too. That keen, earnest, zealous, and aggressive Christians should impart to schoolboys an entirely non-sectarian teaching was in the nature of things impossible.

To-day, a very large number of boys have been withdrawn from the school, while simultaneously the Chinese merchants who assisted the school as trustees have resigned their trusteeship. To-morrow, and the next again, more Chinese boys will be withdrawn until, probably, the school will be but the skeleton of its former self. Well, it was inevitable that some day that should happen, it may as well happen today as at any other time. The teachers of the Anglo-Chinese school will now be left with a freer hand, and with a clearly explicit and definite principal to guide them. That principle is "We do not force nor urge any boys to become a Christian, but we do exercise upon him such influences as are likely to direct him to Christianity, and if these influences have that result we are pleased." It is better for these teachers that they should have a school of 200 boys on such explicitly understood terms than that they should have a school of 600 boys on terms liable to misconception, and sure to end in recrimination. On the other hand, those Chinese who do not wish to expose their sons to the possibility of being infected by Christian principles have their remedy at hand. They can send the more advanced of their boys to the Raffles School, where, although the teachers are, perhaps, professing Christians, we do not think that there is the slightest chance of any boy being influenced by Christian principles. The less advanced boys, the Chinese can at present send to Gan Eng Seng's school, which is under Chinese control and they can afterwards extend that title School till it become an advanced as well as a primary school. As touches what is to be done with those boys who are at the Anglo-Chinese School boarding house, and whose parents do not wish them to remain there, our information is that the Hon. Dr. Lim Boon Keng has been, or will be, asked to establish a scholastic boarding house of which he shall be the director, although with executive officers under him to do the main part of the work.

All this loss of scholars, all this encouragement of rival schools, may be for a time somewhat disappointing and discouraging to the teachers of the Anglo-Chinese School; but it need not in the least prevent them from persevering with their work. We take it that their chief object is to spread Christianity and English education. They will now be able to to teach Christian principles with greater energy, and without any of those difficult points of honour that may hitherto have restrained them. As touches the spread of education, on the other hand, education will lose nothing by the Raffles School being quickened into more zealous life and the Gan Eng Seng School being elevated form a primary into a secondary school. Nobody will really lose anything by the disturbance.

Source:
Straits Times Archives,
Lee Kong Chian Reference Library, National Library Board

Appendix F-3

The Straits Times, 27 July 1896

Proselytising in Mission Schools

As a protest against the attempt to proselytise in the Anglo-Chinese School, the three Chinese trustees, Messrs. Tan Jiak Kim, Tan Hup Seng, and Tan Boo Liat, have resigned their office as trustees. A number of scholars, for the same reason, were this morning withdrawn from the school, and it is very probable that more withdrawals will be made during the week. Among the Chinese, a lively feeling of indignation is manifest. It is alleged that the introduction of religious instruction is of recent date. Formally, boys were allowed on the assembling of the school to remain outside while devotions were carried on. Now, it is said, that boys neglecting to attend are detained after school hours, as a punishment. Religious instruction is now regularly given on Friday afternoons, from 2 o'clock until 3. Attendance at this is also said to be compulsory. We learn that the Chinese merchants, who have promised substantial contributions to the fund for rebuilding the boarding school, regard these innovations as relieving them from the duty of performing their promises. The money has not yet been collected; it is doubtful whether, in the circumstances, it will be.

A Correspondent Writes:

The very serious complaint that appeared in Saturday's issue of the *The Straits Times*, against the Anglo-Chinese School, on the subject of proselytising, has thoroughly awakened the leading members of the Chinese community to a sense of their duty. A deep feeling of indignation prevails at the idea that they have been so long and so cleverly hoodwinked, and steps have been taken to withdraw boys from the school, unless Mr. Kelso suppresses religious teaching therein. This he cannot consistently do; for it would be giving up work which has made Mr. Oldham and himself a reputation in America. Some effort will, no doubt, be made to patch up the matter, but, in the nature of things, such effort is not to be relied upon.

To the Editor of "The Straits Times"

Sir, I read with considerable interest in your Saturday's issue the two apparently independent attacks upon the conduct of the Anglo-Chinese Mission School. The whole case, it appears to me, can be narrowed down into a very small compass, and, consequently, I shall not need to burden you with a long letter. If, as "Anti-humbug," or that of your other correspondent, before we condemn the American Mission. And, surely, too, we shall not condemn that Mission unheard. It is the duty of the Mission, as a public institution, to justify or to endeavour to justify, its ways to the public. I do not share that unreasoning hostility to Protestant Missions that is so general in this place, and that, I feel, would tend to bias the public already in favour of their opponents. I am informed, on excellent authority, that no Chinese child is obliged, either at the day school or the boarding school, to join in or listen to the religious exercises. That is well. But the question remains as to what is the decision of the Committee in cases where the child is willing and the parent unwilling for it to be instructed in Christianity. The consent of a little child is, after all, a very meaningless thing. I do hope, Sir, that the Mission, which is doing such a splendid work among the people, will not delay an explanation.

I am, &c.,
Mustard Seed

To the Editor of the "Straits Times"

Sir, The missionary always has and always will utilise his available opportunities to propagate his faith. There is no finer opportunity in all his work than the gathering together of children in his mission schools. He has there the clay within his fingers, receptive to any impressions he cares to leave. Is it not natural, nay, inevitable, that, as a sturdy Christian, he should leave the impress of his faith upon the minds and character of his charges? It seems to me that it would be a weak-kneed sort of Christianity that he professes if he neglected to teach its truths, almost unconsciously, to the children he is instructing, even though it be ostensibly a secular instruction. And he would be but a poor enthusiast for the Master who failed to convey the truths of Christianity to the unenlightened little heathen who come to him to learn reading, writing, and arithmetic. Surely, the argument that a child should not be taught any sort of religious belief until he reaches an age of discretion is a false one. The age of discretion will enable him to decide whether the fatalistic Confucianism he learns in his Chinese home, or the Christianity he is taught in school, or the Buddhism he may study in private is to be the faith of his choice. One or two creeds more or less make little difference. Possibly, he will ultimately abandon them all, but, on the theory that there is no one so orphaned as the man without belief in a deity, presumably, he is happy who possesses many. Any way, one can scarcely expect missionaries to resist the temptation of doing a bit of proselytising under such favourable conditions as obtain in the Anglo-Chinese School. Missionaries have as much human nature as the rest of mankind.

I am, &c.,
Indifferent

To the Editor of the "Straits Times."

Sir, with your indulgence I shall examine the discussion on Proselytism in Mission Schools through the medium of your valuable columns. In my first letter I was very careful to let the promoters of the "college" speak for themselves. I wish to supplement the letter of your correspondent "Anti-humbug." To-day, I shall deal with the account of the proselytising that goes on within the "college" that has been furnished to me by the boys. It must be admitted that until quite lately—when the promoters imagined their school was firmly established on the credulity of "the rich heathens"—little or no attempt was made to coerce by school discipline, or to seduce with the subtlety of a serpent, the innocent young heathens in the "college" to adopt an unintelligible foreign religion. In justice to Mr. Oldham, it must be said that be personally never tried openly to proselytise or make converts of his pupils. His sincerity and ability, coupled with numerous personal qualities, endeared him to his Chinese friends, and, when he appealed to them for help, they met him right loyally. He certainly achieved a remarkable feat, which was possible only because of his honesty, good sense, and tact. Then he left the work to other hands, and I do not for a moment question either the piety of his successors or their desire to do good. I am not desirous of attacking persons; but, if the description of the act reflects upon the authors thereof, I can scarcely be held responsible. Public duty in the ethical world is the first law. *Patet omnibus veritas.* If Mr. Kelso chooses to say one thing to "the rich heathen Chinamen" and to do and report on another, he, surely, ought not to complain of his promises and acts being placed side by side for the information of the public, to whom the matter is even of more concern than to the Methodist Mission Society. Should such a comparison prove inconvenient to the authority who is responsible for the working of the school, it would show that, at least, a mistake had been made. The discrepancy ought to be explained to the public satisfaction, or else I fear the verdict of the *"vox dei"* must be in some such words, which are adapted from Seneca: *Turpe est aliud loqui, aliud sentire; quanto turpius aliud agere, aliud loqui.* The chines had all along been afraid that they might be dealing with "the Serpent," and the most influential among them urged for a public utterance. On the last occasion that Mr. (now Sir) W. Bonser spoke at the school, he, being one of the European trustees openly declared that in the Anglo-Chinese School religion was not taught; at least the substance of his speech went distinctly to repudiate the insinuation that the teachers directly or indirectly tried to convert the heathen children under them. At the same meeting, Dr. Lim Boon Keng thanked the then Attorney-General, and remarked on the importance of the point settled by Mr. Bonser. (See reports on the paper—Prize distribution day Anglo-Chinese School, 1893.) Mr. W. E. Maxwell, also on behalf of the principal, assured the public that no attempts at proselytising would be made. Both our former Attorney-General and Colonial Secretary must have received their information from the responsible authority of the school. Dr. Boon

Keng, who was never in any way connected with the Methodist school, must also have been led by the same authority to believe in the innocency of the school. True is the saying: *Impia subdulci melle venena latent.* These are facts which are easily capable of verification.

Now let us hear what the boys have to say. We must imagine that those concerned in the work of making converts are so injudicious as to use violent threat or force. Gentle pressure, if constantly applied, and *subtlety* can in the long run achieve more. This is the method *par excellence* of all engaged in the work of vilifying religions which they do not understand, and of recommending their own nostrums to innocent and single-minded individuals. Boys assure me that half an hour daily more or less is devoted to religious exercises. It is a mere quibble to say that the boys need not believe what they hear. It is sufficient to know that they are punished if they refused to attend the morning worship. Of course, punishment need not mean corporal punishment. A schoolmaster can punish a boy in more ways than one. One thing seems certain, and that is that boys who refuse to attend are made to "stay in." This is a formidable punishment to boys, and is enough to drive them to despair. Fancy asking a boy to choose between Christianity with the "favours" (according to school boys) of the masters and the dreary monotony of solitary confinement. I am informed that, a week ago, it was arranged that from to-day the rules about attending service are to be enforced with greater rigour. In the boarding school, too, the heathens are threatened by disfavours—if by nothing else—to join the worship of the Christian deity. Every Friday afternoon, a kind of service is held, and these wretched heathens must perforce listen against their will to the direct and indirect attacks of their revered and reverend teachers on the faith of their heathen ancestors. In time their young and innocent minds become poisoned, and, instead of loving and thinking of their parents as heathens are wont to do, they begin to look down upon their parents with half contempt and half pity, even to call them "*sesat*"—the lost ones. When rebuked for impiety by venerable old gentlemen, whom the Methodists, like other Christians, call heathens, *these pupils of Mission colleges* will say, with the approbation of their teachers: "It is the will of God." I must say that the converts of the American college are generally in my experience of them not over well read. They have simply swallowed the Methodist digest of the gospels and, *protempore* their teachers are the living oracles. It is a pity that these unfilial young heathens, before giving up the faith of their forefathers, should not read the Bible more carefully than they seem to have done.

If they had been careful students of this valuable work, they might justify their treatment of their parents in the words of the New Testament: *They shall be divided, father against son, and son against father; mother against daughter and daughter against mother; mother-in-law against her daughter-in-law and daughter-in-law against her mother-in-law.* Luke XII53. Or, again: *For I came to set a man at variance against his father, and the daughter against her mother—and a man's foes shall be they of his own household.* Matthew X35-36. These texts, which in the gospels appear as the very words of Jesus, demonstrate clearly that there could not possibly be any compromise between the Chinese ideas of *Hau Soon*, or filial devotion, and the Christian conception of the divinity of Jesus as a co-equal of the Creator. If the teachers of the American college are honest, and are sincere in their religious convictions, in plain English, if they really are Christians in profession as well as in deed, let them meet "the heathens" in open battle, and, instead of assuring "the rich heathen Chinamen" that in a professedly Christian school divine truth must be hid in a bushel for the sake of "the almighty Dollar," let them openly and sincerely avow their intention to teach the young heathens the sublime philosophy of the Jewish race, and let them say distinctly that Christianity, as commonly understood, is dead against all superstitions as *hong shui* (geomancy), *sin chu* (Tablets of Ancestral Names), and such like. In conclusion, should Mr. Kelso, hesitate to listen to my disinterested advice, and should he and his colleagues even dream of yielding to the heathens—who are bound to make a noise when they learn how they have been treated—I will commend them to consider carefully whether, as Christian teachers, they ought to come short even of the standard of a pagan or heathen teacher. Seneca is responsible for this enunciation which might well be substituted for the present motto of the method of working of the Methodist Mission. ("First innocency, then subtlety.") *quod sentiments loquacity, quod loquimur sentiamus, concordet sermo oum vita.*

I am, &c.,
Isaiah

The Rev. Mr. Kelso's answer

To the Editor of the "Straits Times"

Sir, while I think that an anonymous attack is unworthy of the attention of a respectable and honest man, I reluctantly conclude to reply in a few words to the communications regarding the Anglo-Chinese School in the Saturday's issue of the *Straits Times*, lest my silence might be misinterpreted, and an unnecessary injustice thereby inflicted on the school.

I have no apology to make for my article in *Gospel in All Lands*, to which reference is made. There is nothing in that article inconsistent with facts that were supposed to be well understood in Singapore. The article was written nearly a year ago for the purpose of describing the school and its success for the benefit of friends at home. The well-known fact that there are a few Christian Chinese boys in the school and that some of them are *influential* boys was mentioned with satisfaction. I am glad of this opportunity of making one correction. The word "college" was substituted for "school" by the Editor of the *Gospel in All Lands*. I at once wrote him on receipt of the paper in June, asking him to make the correction and protesting against the change he had made in the title.

A laboured effort is made, Sir, to create and entirely misleading impression in regard to the religious teaching of the school. The Anglo-Chinese School was organised as a Mission School has always been known as such. *The only compact ever made with our Chinese friends regarding religious instructions was that no boy would be baptised without his father's consent and that no pressure would be used to induce boys to become Christians. But that Christian teachers in a Mission School, should exert such an influence upon their pupils as to induce some of them to become Christians is inevitable, and we have never attempted to conceal our satisfaction that that should be so.*

The school has endeavoured to follow the practice of denominational schools in England in regard to religious instruction. Accordingly, no boy is obliged to attend any religious service. The Bible instruction is and always has been entirely voluntary. This is true in reference to the morning exercises and the Bible classes on Friday afternoon. These are the only occasions when any instruction in the Bible is given. No concealment whatever has ever been attempted in regard to these exercises, and the parents of the boys have been at liberty to visit the school at all times, and many of them have done so. As to the Boarding School, it was organised with the distinct understanding that the Principal and Masters were to live together in one family, eating at the same table, and that all would be expected to comply with the customs of Christian family. Accordingly the Bible has always been read and prayer offered at the table after breakfast. But no pressure has ever been brought to bear on the boys to induce them to believe in Christ either at the Boarding School or day School. The Boys have been required to do right, but always left to do as they liked about religious matters. I should be very sorry to have any one get the impression, which the contribution seems to be well calculated to convey, that I have ever written anything or said anything that could be by any possibility interpreted as disrespectful in any way to our Chinese friends or intended to deceive them. On the contrary, I have always expressed admiration and respect for the Straits-born Chinese, who have shown such a commendable industry and enterprise.

I am, &c
C.C. Kelso

Mr. Kelso's Newspaper report

The Rev. C. C. Kelso, writing to an American publication called the *Gospel in all Lands,* in May of this year, says: "While our success in material and academical lines is very gratifying, we feel that we have most reason to rejoice over the religious results that have been realised. We have a large lecture hall in which the whole school meets every morning. The boys sing a gospel song, the Bible is read and explained to them, and prayer is offered. These services are very inspiring, and usually the boys are deeply interested.

There have been a number of bright conversions in the school within the past year. The Boarding School is the centre of Christian influence."

Source:
Straits Times Archives,
Lee Kong Chian Reference Library, National Library Board

Appendix F-4

The Straits Times, 28 Jul 1896

Proselytising in Mission Schools

We learnt this morning from Mr. Kelso that sixty boys have absented themselves from the Anglo-Chinese School, owing to the circumstances that have been fully set out in these columns. The Principal does not anticipate that the secessions will increase in number, for he says that the unfortunate contretemps is due entirely to misunderstanding and misapprehension and will speedily be removed. The school routine is proceeding as usual.

A correspondent writes:-

Mr. Kelso has replied to the statements made regarding the coercive measures adopted in the Anglo-Chinese School to "vert" the Chinese boys committed to the care of the teachers in that school. Mr. Kelso steadily denies that any pressure has ever been put on the boys to compel them to be present at the religious exercises held in the school. Will Mr. Kelso try to refresh his memory as to what occurred in the school no later than Friday last? And when he has done so, he will surely withdraw that portion if his letter. Mr. Kelso alludes to the Boarding school that and says that the principal, masters and boys lived together in the same manner as would the members of a Christian family. The bible was read and prayer offered at table after breakfast. He, however, very carefully suppresses the fact that a special Sunday School meeting, at which all bounders were expected to be present, was held every Sunday in the drawing room at Bellevue; that the boys were favoured if they learned text from scripture and were able to repeat them; and that they were exhorted to speak on Christian matters. Mr. Kelso would have acted wisely had he remained silent. It is only making matters worse to put forward such a weak defence, when none was possible. The idea of baptising a Chinese boy without the consent of the parent is really rich. Does not the very thought imply that the candidate for baptism must have already been well instructed in the Christian doctrine before he could be admitted into the Church? Further comment on this is unnecessary. It is thought by some that the charge of bad faith in the past may be dismissed, and that there must have been mutual misconception. That is a very charitable way of viewing things.

MR. KELSO'S ARRANGEMENTS FOR THE FUTURE
TO THE EDITOR OF THE "STRAITS TIMES."

SIR, -

We had an interview with Mr. Lim Boon Kong, and we learned from him that the main point at issue is the question whether or not pressure has been brought to bear upon the boys in Anglo Chinese School to enforce their attendance at religious exercises in the school. That pressure has been used I have already denied in my letter of yesterday's date; but if any doubts still exist in the minds of the Chinese community on this point, we are prepared for a full investigation of the facts of the case.

We have announced to the boys this morning that these boys who do not think that it is right for them to attend religious services and those boys whose parents object to their attending will go into another room during Chapel exercises, in charged of a teacher.

We are,&c.,
KELSO,
W.G. SHELLABEAR.
Singapore, 28th July, 1896

Source:
Straits Times Archives,
Lee Kong Chian Reference Library, National Library Board

Appendix F-5

The Straits Times, 29 July 1896

Proselytising in Mission Schools

From a letter we publish today—a letter handed to us by Messrs. Tan Jiak Kim, Tan Hup Seng, and Tan Boo Liat—it will be seen that the Chinese Trustees of the Anglo-Chinese School have definitely adhered to their resignation of office. Their reason is that they are dissatisfied with the Rev. Mr. Kelso's explanation, as published in our Monday's issue. That explanation, it will be remembered that, stated that it was inevitable that Christian influence should be brought to bear on the scholars, although no pressure was, or should be, brought to bear on the boys to make them receive religious instruction against their will. The Chinese Trustees consider that even that pact has been broken. They tell us that they considered it proved that Mr. Kelso has used compulsion in imparting Christian knowledge. But the controversy really turns upon the word "influence" occurring in Mr. Kelso's explanation. The Chinese are no longer content to leave their children even under the non-compulsory influence of the Christian missionaries who conduct the school. The trustees have, accordingly, resigned, and the result of the many resignations will be that very many Chinese boys will now be withdrawn from the school.

As we said on Monday, the Chinese are not to be blamed for the step they have taken. It is altogether contrary to human nature and to the fitness of things that Christian missionaries should conduct a secular without influencing their pupils in some degree towards Christianity. The compromised that they attempted in the past was—apart from allegations of bad faith—certain to be a failure. Those Chinese, therefore, who do not wish their children to be influenced by the Christian teaching, may be right to withdraw their children. Mr. Kelso and his colleagues should face the situation. They should declare fully the policy of their school in relation to even "Christian influence." That would remove any difficulties from their path, and all doubts and confusion from the minds of the public.

Source:
Straits Times Archives,
Lee Kong Chian Reference Library, National Library Board

Appendix F-6

The Straits Times, 29 Jul 1896

Proselytising in Mission Schools:
The Chinese refuse to accept Mr. Kelso's explanations

To the Rev. C .C. Kelso, B.A.

Dear Sir,

We have read and carefully considered your explanation in the local *Press* [Straits Times]. In coming to our decision, we have also borne in mind what you have said to us in conversation. As you seem still to think that we are likely to compromise with you on your system of education, we wish you distinctly to understand that we have finally decided not to have any further connection with your school. In your letter to the Press on the 27th, you did not give a correct account of the understanding arrived between Mr. Oldham and the Chinese: our "compact" was that no religious teaching whatsoever was to be carried on in the school. Until lately we believe this was fairly carried out. Recently, however, a change has come over the school, and, although we hear the boys speak about the religious teaching, you have always denied before that this was true, and, until we saw your own report to America, we really had no substantial grounds to work upon. Now that we know your policy and recognise that, as you say, your school is a mission school, we feel it would be absurd for us to expect that you would abstain from religious teaching.

Further, we are satisfied, after enquiry, that compulsion has been used to induce boys to join the religious meetings during school hours.

We feel in taking this step that we are performing a public duty towards those parents who have sent their children to the Anglo-Chinese School directly or indirectly through our influence, under the impression that the school is purely secular.

As this is a public matter, we shall send copies of this letter to the public Press.

Yours truly
(Sd) T. Jiak Kim
(Sd) T. Hup Seng
(Sd) T. Boo Liat

Mr. Kelso's reply
To Messrs Tan Jiak Kim, Tan Hup Seng and Tan Boo Liat

Dear Sirs, in reply to your letter, which you have kindly put into my hands in anticipation of publication, I beg to say it seems to me utterly inconceivable that the friends of the school, or the Chinese community, should not know that there has been religious instruction and Bible teaching in the school, or that, the school is a Mission School. The Bible has been read in the school regularly since the first of the year 1891. Since July 1891, when for the first time there was a hall suitable for the purpose, essentially the same programme has been carried out every morning. I am, indeed, credibly informed that Mr. Tan Jiak Kim many months ago instructed his sons and brothers not to attend the religious exercises, and I am bound to point out the significant fact that one of your own number, having left the school only about two years ago has often listened to these exercises morning after morning.

As to your alleged compact with Mr. Oldham that no religious instruction whatsoever was to be carried out in the school, I have known nothing about it and must say it does not seem credible in view of the contract that the school was established as a Mission School, and the well-known fact that the Boarding School, of which alone you were trustees was started as a Christian home, with the distinct understanding that the boys in the home were expected to be present during family devotions.

In face of the fact that I have asked for a public investigation as to whether compulsion has been used to compel boys who objected to attend religious services, it hardly seems competent for you to say that on enquiry you are convinced that there has been compulsion.

In conclusion, you will permit me to express my conviction that instead of doing a public duty, you have done the public and the school a great injustice by hastily accepting as true false rumours, and drawing wrong conclusions from reports as basis for your action without giving me a reasonable opportunity to explain matters.

Yours faithfully,
C.C. Kelso

Source:
Straits Times Archives,
Lee Kong Chian Reference Library, National Library Board

Appendix F-7

The Straits Times, 30 Jul 1896

Proselytising in Mission Schools

The Rev. C. C. Kelso informs us that Messrs Tan Jiak Kim, Tan Hup Seng and Tan Boo Liat are not trustees for the Anglo-Chinese School, but only trustees to hold certain real estate to the benefit of the boarding school under the management of the Methodist Mission. We are further informed by Mr. Kelso that the absence from the school during the last few days is not so great as, by reason of the dispute, we expected and had implied. On Friday last (before the discussion began in our columns), there were, we were told, 624 boys at school. On Monday, there were only 545, and on Tuesday only 515. On Wednesday, however, there were 534 and on Thursday (to-day) 537. The school management surmise that, of the 85 still absent, it may be that some, as is the nature of boys, are taking advantage of the circumstances to play truant.

Mr. Tan Jiak Kim's reply to Mr. Kelso's letter

To the Editor of the "Straits Times":

Sir, in the interests of education, since Mr. Kelso continues to deny that "pressure" had been used to induce boys to attend the religious meetings, we feel it our bounden duty to lay before the public all the facts that are within our knowledge. Will Mr. Kelso deny that, up to 1890, Mr. Oldham's School was purely a secular school like the Raffles Institution and the Eastern School? In 1891, the religious exercises were introduced, and we heard of them through the boys. Mr. Jiak Kim, depending on what Mr. Oldham had promised, simply told his sons and brothers not to have anything to do with them. Mr. Kelso, in his reply to our letter, went completely outside the facts to express his astonishment at our ignorance of what went on. We said in our letter that we had to choose between the statements of own boys and the firm denial of Mr. Kelso. We had little or no reason to suspect Mr. Kelso of misleading us, and we, therefore, continued our enquiries without taking any steps which might mean injury to the Anglo-Chinese School. When we said we were satisfied after enquiry that compulsion had been used, we referred to enquiries and investigations that had been undertaken days before Mr. Kelso published his letter asking for investigation. We have discovered that a large number of the Chinese boys have already imbibed the doctrines of the Christian religion, leading them to disobedience to their parents. It is, therefore, untrue that religion has not been systematically taught. When *The Gospel in All Lands* reached our hands, we saw for the first time that what we had been hearing was quite true. How could boys ask their parents for baptism unless their innocent hearts had been filled with the Christian doctrines? Which must mean months of steady teaching. By having the service just when school begins, Mr. Kelso thinks he may have a subterfuge should he be attacked. Many boys who refuse to attend service are punished. Pupil teachers, with cane in hand, hunt up the boys who remained outside. If Mr. Kelso says this is not compulsion, we do not know what it is. Let Mr. Kelso answer our questions. Are the boys punished by being made to stand up while those attending the service sit down—and by being kept in a small room? If boys are late they ought to be punished, but not compelled to attend service. Those who are not late had no choice but either to go to the services or to get shut up. The public ought to know how my own boys are treated. The teachers, it seems, treat them *differently* from most other boys, so that my own boys won't complain. My boys now inform me that they could do as they liked, and, when they were threatened with punishment of any kind, they asked the teachers concerned to refer to me. Other boys, whose fathers have little influence, had to suffer. When I found this out I made up my mind that a school capable of making such distinction in order to enforce attendance at religious services in unworthy of support. Mr. Boo Liat, when at school, was treated like the other boys of "influential" families. He was not punished, but had to choose between half an hour's idleness and attending the singing, as the service is known to boys. We have discovered that in the last week even greater efforts were made to force the boys to attend religious services.

It is absolutely incorrect that we Chinese, when we were asked for money to build the boarding school, were informed that it was to be a Christina home where our children were to be brought under the "inevitable Christian influences." Those who are interested in this matter may have a look at the trust deed for this boarding house at present in the hands of Messrs Rodyk and Davidson. In this deed no mention whatever is made of religion or "Christian home." We gave money to build the boarding house on the distinct understanding that, as embodied in the trust deed, that nothing but pure education was to be given to children. It is absurd to imagine that we, who are not Christians, would desire to spend money in order to give our children Christian training. This is so self-evident that it is incredible that Mr. Kelso should have laboured in the public press to prove otherwise.

The matter concerned is a public one, and we cannot help saying that we are sorry we cannot any longer put any trust in Mr. Kelso's promises or words. Whatever may be the public opinion, I personally feel I have been misled by means not altogether worthy of missionaries.

I am &c
Tan Jiak Kim

Source:
Straits Times Archives,
Lee Kong Chian Reference Library, National Library Board

Appendix F-8

The Straits Times, 31 Jul 1896

Proselytising in Mission Schools

Mr. Kelso's reply to Mr. Tan Jiak Kim: An absolute denial of having punished boys for not attending religious services; about pupils from Mr. Tan Jiak Kim's family; the precise scope of the school's Bible teaching; Dr. Lim Boon Keng's part in the controversy.

To the Editor of the "Straits Times,"

Sir, I am grateful for the important admissions made in Mr. Tan Jiak Kim's letter to the *Straits Times* of yesterday. He says that the boys did report to him in 1890 that religious exercises had been introduced. That was, I believe, when religious exercises were introduced, but, so far as I can learn, there was always more or less religious instruction and Bible teaching in the classes.

Boys have not been punished by being made to stand up for not attending service, but those who come into the Chapel late stand instead of creating confusion by passing through the room to seats. Boys who had any real objection to attending the religious exercises, were really encouraged to come late, as nothing whatever was done to them in any occasion when they came immediately after the exercises were over and entered their classes on time. The pupil teachers, whose duty it was to keep order at the entrance during the Chapel exercises, were instructed to require no boy to go upstairs who had any objection to attending the exercises. There were, however, truant boys to look after who had no real objection to the exercises but who tried to take advantage of the opportunity to run away and play. My order on Friday morning had reference only to such boys; for I, having arrived late that morning, had seen a lot of little boys running away from the school after the gong had sounded, and I had them kept in the office until after the other boys were in their classes, and instructed the teachers to keep them in a short time after school with the boys who were detained for not knowing their lessons. For the same reason such boys have, on three or four occasions, been kept in a rooms for a few minutes after the exercises. I repeat emphatically and distinctly that no boy by my order or to my knowledge, has been punished in any way for not attending religious exercises, if he said he had any objection to doing so. So far as I know all boys have been treated alike in this matter. I am not aware of any favouritism to any rich boys or to Christian boys. Personally I have always endeavoured to practise and enforce the strictest impartiality. My own impression is that Christian teachers are likely to lean in the opposite direction in their endeavours to be just, and to show non-Christian boys and poor boys that they have the same regard for their welfare as for others.

I shall be pleased to have any one who likes examine the trust deed as suggested by Mr. Tan Jiak Kim. He will find it as stated by you yesterday. No condition whatever is put upon the mission in regard to the management of the Boarding School. I am prepared to prove that, when Mr. Tan Jiak Kim brought two of his brothers to the Boarding School, Mrs. Oldham had said that she had told him plainly that, if the boys came, they must come with the understanding that it is a Christian Home, and they would be expected to be present at family prayers.

As this is intended to be my last letter on the subjects that have been raised in this unfortunate controversy, I wish to be very explicit and definite on all important points. No catechism or creed is taught to which sectarian teaching alone we understood Mr. Bonser to refer in his remarks on dogmatic teaching. The Bible, especially its historical parts, are read and explained. We have read some Old Testament history, the Gospels of St Luke and St John, and the Acts of the Apostles in regular course to the boys during the past three years. Many of our Chinese friends have said to us that they do not object to our teaching the Bible, but that it will do the boys good. It teaches boys to honour and love their parents. Our Chinese friends have often assured us of their satisfaction in the fact that their boys were receiving a good moral education in our school. We have made no denials of what we are doing. It seems almost absurd to make any statements of this kind in reply to the stout and definite charges that were made in the first part of this controversy, in view of the admissions that have now been made, but I should like to say that the boys have bought and carried home with them at least five hundred copies of "Gospel Songs." Everything has been done in the most open way without any attempt or desire to conceal anything.

It has been said that the hours required by the Code have been infringed upon by religious exercises and teaching. The Code requires three hours of instruction. The school is in session for four and a half hours on four days and three and a half hours on Friday. The religious exercises never occupy more than thirty minutes, usually only twenty minutes. Why, then, it is asked is all this hubbub? It seems to me now that it is due to the public as well as to the school that the facts as now understood should be made known. I have asked for a public investigation, but as our Chinese friends do not seem to want that, I must with your indulgence take it upon myself to make statements that might more properly, perhaps, came before an investigating committee. My first impression was that the animus in the matter was confined to a European correspondent, but, when I found that a certain side of our Chinese patrons was stirred up to such unreasonable excitement, it was inconceivable to me that such a state of affairs could exist without the active agency of at least two or three influential Chinamen. I sought to allay excitement by trying to remove wrong impressions, and went to those patrons whose influence had always been replied upon, but found that the case had apparently been prejudged against the school, and I could say seemed to have little effect, and no time was taken, as I urged, to investigate the facts. I went to Dr. Lim Boon Keng, knowing that he had spoken very kindly of the school, and had recently strongly defended the Bible teaching of the school at a dinner in the home of one of our prominent patrons, when other influential Chinamen and two of our masters were present. He seemed to want to know the facts in the matter, and I left him with the hope that some good would come from the interview. That was on Monday last. That afternoon, a letter signed "Isaiah" was published in the *Straits Times*, and, as it contained certain internal indications that Dr. Boon Keng himself had written the article, and as it was commonly reported among the boys that he was advising their parents to take them out of the school, and send them to another school, we concluded to interview the Doctor again. Accordingly, Mr. Shellabear and I went to his house early on Tuesday morning. I said to Dr. Boon Keng that, when I had seen him on Monday, it had not occurred to me that he was using his influence against us,, but I had become convinced that he was. We told him that the article in the *Straits Times* of Monday signed "Isaiah" contained internal evidence that he himself had written it, and that the boys of the school were execrating him for the part he was playing, in trying to influence their parents to take them out of the school, in spite of his recent praise of the school which some of them had heard. He seemed to hesitate, but, finally, said frankly that he had written the articles signed "Isaiah" and acknowledged that he had spoken to some parents in professional visits. He claimed that he was influenced by the reports, which he said he had gotten from certain boys that compulsion was used. We discussed every point raised fully, and he said he accepted my explanations and denials, and volunteered to write the *Straits Times* a letter that day over his own signature, stating that he had an interview with me and was satisfied with my statements. I expressed appreciation, and Mr. Shellabear and I retired. After announcing to the boys in Chapel that morning that those who do not think it right to attend the religious exercises, and those whose parents objected could go into another room during the exercises, I wrote Dr. Boon Keng a note telling him of what I had done, and giving him the liberty to use the note in his communication to the *Straits Times*. I take the liberty of quoting his reply:

> *To the Rev. C. C. Kelso,*
>
> *Dear Sir, In reply to your note, I beg to state that I am not sending any correspondence to-day. I have seen the trustees and told them what you have said, and I will inform them of what you have written; and I do not wish to act on one side, as I am not concerned in the school in any way.*
>
> *Yours truly,*
>
> *Lim Boon Keng*

We at once went to him for an explanation. He said he had no time that day to write, and was not satisfied as to writing the next day. He said he felt a delicacy about having his name appear in the papers, so that we had to come away with small satisfaction. I believe that the opposition to the School is confined to a small coterie of men who have done what they can to influence their friends against us. There is, I believe, no strong objection to the Bible among intelligent Chinamen. Nor is there any good reason why there should be. The Bible properly interpreted is not antagonistic to such a religion as Confucianism. It supplements the national religion with clearer light about God. It does not teach that those who do not have the Bible are lost, but those who have never had the Bible shall be judged according to what light they had. We do not, therefore, teach the boys that their parents and friends are not saved because they have not had the Bible, but that those who have never heard the Bible will be judged according to the light which God had given to them. You suggest, Sir, that I should define what it meant by "Christian influence." You have given me an inspiring thesis, but too large a subject for discussion in this place. It is a subject in divine dynamics. "Christian influence" includes the influence of the Christ. Who said as he was ascending into heaven:

"All power is given unto me in heaven and on earth. So I am with you always even unto the end of the world."

I am, &c
C.C. Kelso

With reference to Mr. Kelso's statements published in this journal yesterday, a correspondent says that the reason some of the boys returned was owing to a report zealously spread by the teachers and some of the "professed Christian" boys, that a compromise had been arrived at. The Chinese local papers are giving wide publicity to the utter impossibility of reconciling the sentiments of the Chinese with those of the missionaries on the educational policy pursued in the Anglo-Chinese School. Some of the leading Chinese have approached the managers of the Raffle Institution and the Anglo-Chinese Free School on the subject of providing teaching staff and accommodation for a large number of boys, and, as soon as this is settled, the great bulk of the boys will be withdrawn from the Anglo-Chinese School.

Source:
Straits Times Archives,
Lee Kong Chian Reference Library, National Library Board

Appendix F-9

The Straits Times, 1 Aug 1896

Proselytising in Mission Schools

From a Correspondent:

The Chinese now fully perceive that the letters written to the public papers during the past few days, on this subject, by Mr. Kelso, contain an absolute repudiation of the charges that have been brought against the present religious system of education in the Anglo-Chinese School. He has also endeavoured to make the people of Singapore believe that his school was conducted on a mission basis, unfettered by any condition of the Chinese, and that the present agitation was raised by a small coterie of men only, and that the majority of parents were favourable.

Now it is necessary to show the public that the effort of Mr. Kelso, in alluding to the coterie of men, was to mislead the people by concealing what he is well aware was the fact, that these men were his leading supporters, without whose influence and pecuniary help neither the mission nor the school would have its existence in Singapore. It may now be made clear that the Methodist Mission has always endeavoured to throw dust in the eyes of the public, and especially the Chinese. In 1893, when the Government, with a view to retrenchment, proposed to hand over the public education of the Colony to the Methodists, the trustees of the Raffles Institution made the following remarks in a report, reproduced in the *Straits Times* of 26th May 1893:

> "The Mission Schools, as already pointed out, are branches of foreign societies, whose sympathies and ultimate loyalty is due to

foreign Powers. This alone would make it impossible to hand over to them public education in a British Colony. They are, moreover, sectarian schools; and in a Colony where only a small proportion of the population are Christians, and where the greater part of the revenue comes from the non-Christian element, &c."

This roused the ire of the *Malaysia Message*, the local Methodist organ, with the result that the following appeared in it, as quoted in the *Straits Times* of the 2nd June 1893:

> "The best testimony to the Mission of the Straits Settlements is the confidence the leading Chinese gentlemen put in them. Chinamen possess as much intelligence as Europeans, and may be trusted to know when their interests are being served. If there were any reason for doing so, The Chinese community would withdraw their patronage. The fact that this is not done is a sufficient reply to this stricture upon both the 'sectarianism' and 'ultimate loyalty' of our missionary institutions."

Hitherto, the Chinese community have relied on the assurances of the Methodist missionaries, although, from time to time, warned by European friends that the object of the school was not as described to them. But, when the Chinese obtained documentary evidence, signed by Mr. Kelso, showing that the missionaries had been doing quite the opposite of that which they had openly professed to those influential men who were, on certain definite conditions, led to support them, the Chinese patrons felt it their duty to make themselves thoroughly acquainted with the facts, and communicate the result of their enquiries to the public.

It will be seen, then, that the prediction of the writer in the *Malaysia Message* has been realised. The eyes of the Chinese have been opened, and, true to the prophecy alluded to, they have withdrawn their patronage.

To the Editor of the "Straits Times":

Sir, it is difficult to say who comes worse out of this discreditable squabble between the heads of the American Mission School, their Chinese supporters, or those still more ungracious persons who put sparks to powder and showed the tolerant Towkays that the religion of their fellow citizens, of their Rulers, and of the enlightened world is a faith to fly from—an influence for evil. That these Chinese gentlemen were really blinded by the padres' professions of neutrality speaks overwhelmingly for their ingenuousness. But it is hard to believe. Probably custom, comfort, family influence, and the conservative spirit of clan and race were trusted to as a counterpoise to the school teaching. Also, a certain approval of the moral doctrines of Christ is possible to the intelligent Chinese, who can see that the effect of a liberal education on their sons tends to a modified scepticism not accentuated enough to interfere with those duties which a Chinaman is brought up to consider sacred.

No doubt most Chinese of the better classes would share the dislike of other persons of deep religious convictions to the alienation of their sons form the ancestral faith. We may even allow that the consequences of a sincere conversion may seem to them infinitely more objectionable than we can understand, since a total uprooting of preconceived ideas on the religious customs, so intimately involved with Chinese social and family, is at least *implied* by a version from the doctrines of Confucian to those of the American missionaries. Imagine Confucian etiquette in Wall Street.

Without prejudice—I am afraid that missionary methods, and, above all, mission literature loses missionaries many friends. Let it be so. But the odium cast on the agents of the American by one or two of us, presumably Europeans and professing Christians, is very especially calculated to injure not alone Mr. Kelso and others who make the same blunders, but also the abstract cause of a religion which has been the most powerful reforming and civilising agent of historical time, and which our Chinese fellow subjects might to be taught to respect, because it is ours—if for no other reason. The spiritual side of the question is one which I am not skilled enough to discuss.

The ultra-Protestant branch of the Catholic Church reprobates diplomacy as a weapon. From the layman's point of view, that is wise and right, but a line must be drawn somewhere. These concessions of the spiritual and instinctive to the moral and material, this moulding of inspiration and the individual conscience to the taste of a practical and self-indulgent world, this general laxity of belief and demand for a *"rabattement de prix"* in matters of salvation is a big mischief which has found a little, half-conscious voice in this affair of the American schools and the betrayed Chinamen. It is not a thing to be proud of; nor is this affectation of fair play a sentiment which will win us credit or respect from our Chinese neighbours whose own present attitude is one of righteous horror at having been numbered for a moment, even by implication, amongst the Laodiceans.

Appendix F-9

I am, &c
One of the Latter

Source:
Straits Times Archives,
Lee Kong Chian Reference Library, National Library Board

Appendix F-10

The Straits Times, 4 Aug 1896

Proselytising in Mission Schools

To the Editor of the "Straits Times"

Sir, one statement has been made in the controversy now going on regarding the alleged attempts of the American Missionaries to proselytise which, if not contradicted, would be a great injustice to a gentleman with whom many of us in this Colony were intimate, and whose integrity and uprightness can never be seriously questioned. I refer to the Rev. Mr. Oldham.

Mr. Tan Jiak Kim, in his last letter, asserts that the money subscribed for the boarding school was given on the distinct agreement that secular education only was to be given. As a subscriber at the time, I took a certain interest in the Mission, and I am certain that the pupils, Mr. Tan Jiak Kim's brothers included, were compelled to attend Bible reading, prayers and singing every morning from the very first day the boarding was opened up to the day Mr. Oldham left for American. Does, then, Mr. Tan Jiak Kim seriously allege that Mr. Oldham broke his compact the very first day, and that it is only now, after nearly ten years, that he has found out this alleged act of perfidy?

There are other evidences that not only is this not the case, but that Mr. Tan Jiak Kim and his friends have known this all along, and acquiesced in it by not offering the slightest objection to the practices, probably, as Mr. Kelso has pointed out, because he was distinctly informed from the beginning that his boys would be accepted only on the understanding that they were to be considered as members of a Christian family.

I enclose my card and remain,
I am &c,
"Tanglin"

The Anglo-Chinese Free School

It will be interesting to the public, says a correspondent, to learn that this school, which was founded by Mr. Gan Eng Seng, is in a fair way of being in time well endowed. Periodical subscriptions are being collected. Already the endowment fund reaches over twenty thousand dollars, and, in a matter of ten years, it is expected to show something like a hundred thousand dollars or more. The object of this is to place in the hands of the Chinese a school which shall be on a free and independent basis. It will be seen from this that the Chinese are subscribing munificently to the cause of secular education. It is in contemplation to increase the accommodation of the school, and thus afford it greater scope for usefulness. Until the Chinese have a commodious institution of this kind, they feel they are rather at the mercy of the managers of the other schools.

Mission Schools (From a Correspondent)

The excerpt from the *Monthly*, a Presbyterian Mission paper, in Wednesday's issue of the *Straits Times*, will have the effect of drawing attention to other Mission schools in our midst besides the Anglo-Chinese School. This is as it should be; for it would be an invidious thing to single out for attack the schools of one denomination if there are others of the same nature in the place.

It does not appear to be well understood by many of the Chinese that the "Eastern School," at present under the direction of the Rev. J.A.B. Cook, a very zealous missionary of the Presbyterian Church, is a *Mission* school. True, it has not so far developed its evangelistic side as the Anglo-Chinese School, though it is fairly on the way to do so. But the fact is that the Principal, the Rev. Mr. Lamont, is following the deliberate lead of Mr. Oldham in this respect, and hopes, as Mr. Oldham did, and as the Presbyterian *Monthly* suggests, *silent* and *slowly* to sap the foundations of Confucianism. Mr. Lamont is at present in Europe collecting money from the promoters of foreign missions for the purpose of developing the Presbyterian Eastern Mission School, and Mr. Lamont is a missionary supported by by the friends of foreign missions.

The Roman Catholic School of St Joseph is a pronounced mission school, professedly working on the "voluntary system." The Mission schools of this city are: the Anglo-Chinese School, the Eastern School, and the St Joseph's. This takes no account of the S.P.G. School conducted by Mr. Gomez.

Source:
Straits Times Archives,
Lee Kong Chian Reference Library, National Library Board

Appendix F–11

The Straits Times, 5 Aug 1896

Proselytising in Mission Schools

Mr. Tan Jiak Kim's family and Christianity (From a Correspondent)

In an important decision of the Chief Justice, published in the *Straits Times*, yesterday, in which Mr. Tan Jiak Kim was one of the plaintiffs, a provision is noticed, by the terms of which it is made clear that any of the male descendants of the late Mr. Kim Seng, who should, at any time, forsake the Chinese religion, would have to forfeit his share in the estate. It is well known that this family, of which Mr. Tan Jiak Kim is the present head, is the richest in the Colony. It is scarcely conceivable, therefore, that this gentleman should himself act in a way, or encourage any member of his family so to do, as would imperil his position in connection with the will alluded to. Mr. Tan Jiak Kim has certainly been a most generous patron and benefactor to the Anglo-Chinese School, but it is obvious from the foregoing that he never, in the last degree, contemplated the version of any of his family to Christianity. This should be a sufficient reply to those who imply he rather encouraged than otherwise Christianity teaching in the school.

An Appeal to the Chinese

Sir, as a consequence of the excitement over the charge of proselytism, a certain number of boys have left, and are leaving, the Anglo-Chinese School for other educational institutions. Might I, as one who has followed the discussion with interest, and believing that there have been some faults on both sides, appeal first to the Chinese gentlemen concerned on a point of common honesty? It is well known that the monthly fee charged each pupil is quite inadequate to pay the cost of the instruction given, and that without the Government grant the work could not go on. Now the annual examination is in October, and I ask that the pupils should not be taken away and should attend the school until after the examination, so that the results obtained for secular education should come into the possession of those who have done the work. I, also, appeal to Mr. Kelso to agree that, in the day school between the hours of ten and three, no religious education shall be given of any nature whatever, and that no points connected with this unfortunate estrangement shall be spoken of. I trust, Sir, you will use your influence on this behalf, and I am sure the independent public will appreciate the honesty of the Chinese should they follow this course.

I am &c,
Fair Play

Investigation Solicited

A Correspondent writes:

A full investigation has been offered by Mr. Kelso, but refused by Mr. Tan Jiak Kim and his friends. I fear that these Chinese gentlemen are allowing themselves to be merely the catpaws in the monkey's hands. Why refuse a full, frank, and thorough sifting? Perhaps, the motive of this sudden attack may come to light, and astonish those who are not behind the scenes. It may be awkward for some who have been pulling the wires to have the facts of the case bought to the light of day. At any rate, the Methodists ought to court an investigation, or even go further and invite a number of disinterested gentlemen of the Colony to go into this question. Let the Court of Enquiry be impartial—there must be no minister, schoolmaster or such on the board; and reporters should be present to take down the case as it evolves itself for the public. The laymen should be, say, six Europeans, men of known integrity and disinterestedness, and six Chinese, also, men of uprightness, and who have shown no *animus* in the controversy; this would, of course, exclude the Hon. Dr. Lim Boon Keng, *alias* "Isaiah," &c, &c, &c. It seems ridiculously absurd to say that this has all come to a head on the charge that boys were punished for not attending to the religious instruction. However, "speak the truth and shame the devil." Let us have the truth. Those who are true to themselves "cannot be false to any man." There is, I feel sure, no need of Jesuitic evasions. For the moment, popular feeling may be against the Methodists, but, if the attacking party have not been speaking the truth, they will find they have over-reached themselves, and the tide of opinion, both Chinese and European, will turn, and some may even awake to find they have been befooled to serve some personal purpose. The present writer has not been consulted by, nor has he spoken to the Methodists on this subject, but he feels sure they are one with him in wishing for the largest publicity of the real facts of the case.

Source:
Straits Times Archives,
Lee Kong Chian Reference Library, National Library Board

Appendix F–12

The Straits Times, 27 Sep 1899

Chinese Schoolboys and American Wives

In another column we publish a letter entitled "Straits Chinese and School Influences." The letter is, in substance, an assertion that at the Anglo-Chinese School the children of Straits Chinese are subjected to continuous influence in the direction of adopting the Christian faith. That is a controversy that was discussed very fully in the *Straits Times* some years ago, and about which it is difficult to arrive at any definite conclusion. The Anglo-Chinese School of Singapore is a school conducted by American missionaries, and financed in its earlier stages on the faith that funds could be collected through missionary agency. It is in the nature of things that such a school must have a tendency to influence its scholars towards the adoption of Christian religion or ritual. There is, it is true, an understanding that such influences, if exerted at all, shall be exerted by life and behaviour, rather than by teaching or by prospect of reward. From that arrangement we arrive at the point of our correspondent's letter which is the allegation that, to a Chinese boy of seventeen years of age or thereabouts, there was offered the prospect of his obtaining an American wife. That inducement, as our correspondent framed it, reads somewhat grossly; but the story is not admitted by the lad. The boy's father appears to have satisfied himself, apparently from the boy's elder brother that an American wife was talked of; but the boy now says it was not so.

A charitable view of the question might be that if a lad of seventeen were talking of going to American and were talking of joining the mission, a school teacher might quite naturally, and without meaning any harm, suggest that perhaps the lad would marry some American young lady who might assist him in continuing in the higher walks of life. But if such suggestion were made to a lad of seventeen years of age in a tropical climate, the suggestion must be held to be indiscreet. But then, again, it may be that the teacher was not accurately understood. However, it is a fact that the Straits Chinese are much exercised over the matter. The father of the boy finds that he has lost touch with his child and he is exceedingly indignant and is full of a desire for a remedy, except that remedy he can find none. It thus appears that whatever the precise influences or words that may have been used, the influence of the Anglo-Chinese School in the case under discussion has achieved the evil result of causing great unhappiness to a father, and of disassociating a lad, at a most critical age, form the wholesome influences of parental confidence and the important safeguards of his traditional beliefs and customs.

There, of course, remains the broad fact that a mission school, in the ultimate motive of its founders and conductors, must be intended to Christianise. The Straits Chinese probably face that risk at the Anglo-Chinese School in the knowledge that Christian teaching has a tendency to leave a Chinaman's mind very easily. But a vision of prospects of a pretty American wife may possibly be more lasting and more alluring than the doctrines of abstract theology. It might, therefore, be well that we should hear from the Anglo-Chinese School that the teachers are cautioned to be very discreet in any conversation they may hold with the pupils concerning American wives.

Source:
Straits Times Archives,
Lee Kong Chian Reference Library, National Library Board

Appendix F-13

The Straits Times, 27 Sep 1899

Straits Chinese and School Influences

<u>An Accusation of Proselytising</u>

To the Editor of the "Straits Times"

Sir, Some three years ago, an exciting correspondence was passing through the columns of your journal on the subject of proselytising that was then alleged to be developed among Chinese pupils in the Anglo-Chinese School. I and others with me thought it was then understood between Chinese parents and the American Methodist teachers that a *modus vivendi* had been arrived at, and that there would be no more complaints on the score of proselytising. It is to be regretted that this does not prove to be the case. For some little time after the period referred to, only those boys who wished it attended prayers and the religious exercises held on Friday afternoons. This, of course, is very well in theory, but every boy who has been to school fully appreciates the influence of the wishes of his teacher. Rewards in a small way were always held out to those boys who showed aptitude in committing to memory texts of scripture, but it has been left to the present time to suggest to a Chinese boy of seventeen years or thereabouts the prospects of prizes of a more alluring nature. A lad of this age, who has now been withdrawn from the school and its influences, alleges that a prospect held out to him for becoming a Christian was the possession of an American wife! This, of course, presupposed that the boys would join the mission and go to America. The prize held out to this lad may have been held out to others. But whether so or not so, it certainly does not inspire respect for the methods used to bring about the version of Chinese Babas. I have been permitted to read a copy of a protest sent by the elder of a Chinese family to one of the American teachers, complaining of the measures adopted to proselytise, and withdrawing his boy. The main ground of complaint is that the proceedings are covert, the parents being purposely left in ignorance of what is being done with their boys. It was the same before. Now, while I feel disapproval of the ways pursued in the endeavour to proselytise Chinese boys, I feel but little sympathy for the Chinese elders who suffer through their own indifference. The Chinese possess a tolerably large non-sectarian school, the one founded by the late Mr. Gan Eng Seng, to which they might send their younger boys with safety; and their elder lads could find accommodation at the Raffles Institution. It is in this as in everything else. If the Chinese would not look after their own domestic and family affairs, they must expect that others will meddle with them in a disagreeable way.

I am &c,
Anti-Proselytiser

Source:
Straits Times Archives,
Lee Kong Chian Reference Library, National Library Board

Appendix F-14

The Straits Times, 28 Sep 1899

Straits Chinese and School Influences

To the Editor of the "Straits Times"

Sir, in reference to the editorial and letter regarding the Anglo-Chinese School published in yesterday's *Straits Times*, all the American masters of the emphatically deny having ever, in the least, spoken of, or hinted at, the possibility of any Chinese boy here marrying an American woman. They would regard such a marriage as exceedingly unwise from both the American and Chinese standpoints. No Chinese man, the Mission considers, with a foreign wife would be likely to prove a useful member of the Mission, working among his own people, nor is it likely that he would be received as a member of the Mission Conference. No boys of the Day School have, since I succeeded to the Principalship, at least, have been asked to learn Bible verses, nor of course have any prizes been offered for such learning. The master would considerate especially unwise to make any discrimination between pupils from the standpoint of their religious tendencies; the growth of Christian spirit in the school would, it should be easily understood, be hindered rather than helped by such discrimination.

It is only just to the Chinese parents of our school lads to relate the history of the boys of seventeen in his religious relation to the school. We desire, and endeavour to act accordingly, that all pupils of the school shall in chapel learn the elements of Christian history and Christian faith; this is for their moral as well as intellectual welfare. If a boy by coming to the voluntary Friday afternoon Bible classes and to the Sunday meeting of the Methodist Church has manifested more than usual interest in religious things, we have found by inquiry form parents if this was known by them, and approved by them. If so, well and good; if not, the lad was not encouraged to continue his attendances. In no case has a boy baptised without the free and full consent of his parents. This lad referred to, it was known, came to Bible classes with the consent of his father. To ascertain this, the father was visited by myself and two other members of the Mission. He expressed his full approbation of what was being done, and hoped that the lad, if the other parent consented, would be baptised. Through outside influences, I am told, the father changed his opinion; so the present estrangement between father and son, if such there be, came about—not through any covert act of any of the American masters, but through the fluctuations of the parent's own mind. Such happenings are always possible in Mission work, and as our religious teaching is clearly advertised we cannot justly be blamed.

I am surprised that any doubt should be expressed as to what the religious course of the school is. Just what the school is doing and proposes to do is clearly set forth in my last year's report published in our catalogue and widely distributed, and also copied from there into the daily papers. As given in the historical statement of the catalogue the original subscription list, now in possession of the school, had this statement in the heading:

> *The ultimate aim is to help in the evangelisation and elevation of the non-Christian peoples of this island.*

Dr. Oldham positively denies his having ever promised any course contrary to this, nor had any following principal any right to take any other stand. I certainly have not done so, as my school reports bear witness to. The Anglo-Chinese School was, then, expressly founded to elevate the people and to spread the knowledge of Christianity, and naturally to do it in the way or ways that seemed best to its successive controllers. Any other than a free, open, non-coercive way to accomplish this would be contrary to the spirit of Christ and to the workings of the Methodist Church.

For the year 1898, I allowed any parent who desired it to sign a statement desiring that his children be not compelled to attend chapel. No Chinese parent signed it. For the year 1899, and probably hereafter, attendance at chapel is required of all. The instruction, as far as possible, is desired to be unsectarian, and we consider, as before stated, such attendance strictly necessary for the moral and intellectual growth of the pupils. No pupil is required to attend Bible classes. In closing, allow me to state that I have, since holding this position, endeavoured to explain clearly what we desired to do; and then to live up to such statement. The masters have been specially requested to follow the plans of the school, and I believe have faithfully done so. All true missionaries of Christ are directly or indirectly concerned in proselytising which has to do with the winning of the people to the Christian faith and practice. All we claim is that we endeavour to do this openly and fairly.

I am, &c
J.E. Banks
Principal

Source:
Straits Times Archives,
Lee Kong Chian Reference Library, National Library Board

Appendix F-15

The Straits Times, 29 Sep 1899

Straits Chinese and School Influences

To the Editor of the "Straits Times"

    Sir, I have read with much interest Mr. Banks's letter published in yesterday's issue of the *Straits Times*. It must be admitted that he has stated a good case for the school, and well defended its policy. His argument is strong against the idea of a Chinese missionary marrying an American woman. He means it to be clearly inferred that the utterance of the Chinese lad on this point, if such utterance there were, and his family are responsible for the statement that there was such an utterance, was untrue. The boy now says he never said anything about an American woman, and one of his brothers, who was talked to yesterday, modifies the word American into Foochow. Mr. Banks's denial does not exclude the idea that marriage may have been spoken of, but only that the lady should not be an American. While I am willing to accept Mr. Banks's statement—for I believe him to be a sincerely upright man—so far as it relates to himself and to his personal knowledge of matters appertaining to the working of the school, I must ask to be permitted to point out that there is no sect, Christian or other, has ever yet acknowledged itself in error as to its methods of evangelising and elevating peoples not of its way of thinking. "The end justifies the means" was in practice before religions were. I regret that Mr. Banks has mentioned Dr. Oldham, but, since he has, it may be as well to say that this gentleman was too wise to commit himself to any statement about evangelisation, for the simple reason that,s had he done so, the American Mission would never have gained a footing here at all. Cultivation of the mind was his idea; he left evangelisation to the remote future. Mr. Banks has now made himself clear as to the future religious policy of the school; all children now are required to attend chapel, and, in future, Chinese parents can have no possible right to complain of the outcome of such attendance. After such a declaration it would be wrong to say that there is anything covert about the matter. The policy is, however, a decided advance of Mr. Kelso's arrangement, three years ago, which left such attendance voluntary.

I am &c,
Anti-Proselytiser

The following is taken from this year's report of the Anglo-Chinese School. We publish it at the request of Mr. Banks, the Principal of the school:

The religious instruction of the Day School is as follows:

1. Chapel exercises in the lecture hall from 10 to 10.30 am, consisting of hymn reading and explanation of Bible by master or visitor, prayer, closing with the Lord's Prayer, Doxology and Benediction.
2. Explanation by teachers of Bible references in ordinary English reading books.
3. Cambridge Local Examination Bible portions to those of the Special Class whose parents do not object.
4. Voluntary Friday afternoon Bible classes for one hour, attended by about one-third.
5. Personal talks of teachers with scholars.

About fifty lads are members of the International Bible Reading Association, and read a few verses of the Bible each day at home.

No boy under any circumstances is advised or urged to attend Bible classes or any church, or perform any Christian ceremony without his parent's consent. The teaching is meant to be unsectarian.

Source:
Straits Times Archives,
Lee Kong Chian Reference Library, National Library Board

Appendix G

Bishop Oldham's *Memorandum of Dissent*

Source: Lee Kong Chian Reference Library, National Library Board

STRAITS SETTLEMENTS AND FEDERATED MALAY STATES
OPIUM COMMISSION.

MEMORANDUM OF DISSENT BY THE REVD. BISHOP W. F. OLDHAM, D.D.,
FROM THE MAJORITY REPORT.

In writing this note of dissent from the finds of the other Commissioners, I do not cite paragraphs or enter into details, but would briefly sum up my findings on the three questions asked:—

(1) Much evidence shows that the course of the opium user is from "playing with the pipe" occasionally, to the steady use, in which the tendency is to an increase of the daily dose. There is, from this time, pressure upon the individual's money and time to minister to the appetite already fixed. At stated times every day the drug must be used, or the person be utterly unfit for work. Whether the dose be large or small unfitness for the daily task is the penalty of omitting it. This, with the fact that, circumstances permitting, the dose tends to increase until it reaches large proportions, leads one to conclude that "moderation" in opium smoking does not exist.

(2) The implications of (1)—being noted—no dissent.

(3) I agree with all but the last paragraph, for which I would substitute :—

"We are of opinion that the price of chandu in the Federated Malay "States should be gradually raised to the price obtaining in the Colony, "and that as public opinion grows, and all classes demand further restriction, "the Government department having the matter in charge should be "empowered to increase the price of chandu, or adopt such other measures "as may lead to the increased restriction and ultimate extinction of the "opium traffic. Both in restriction and ultimate prohibition, Government "action should not be permitted to lag behind Chinese public opinion."

W. F. OLDHAM.

NEW YORK, U.S.A.
27th July, 1908.

Appendix H

Bishop Oldham's *Personal Note*

Source: Lee Kong Chian Reference Library, National Library Board

STRAITS SETTLEMENTS AND FEDERATED MALAY STATES
OPIUM COMMISSION.

PERSONAL NOTE BY THE REVD. BISHOP W. F. OLDHAM, D.D.

When asked to accept the appointment to the Commission on Opium, I was told the conclusions would be reached in six months. The end of this period left the Commission far from concluding this work. I was therefore unable to meet with the other Commissioners when making their findings.

I am obliged now, with regret and some hesitation, to express dissent from some conclusions reached, though I agree in the main with the practical measures outlined.

And while wholly in sympathy with what is called the "Anti-opium" view, I would earnestly advise against any sudden measures of repression which would outrun public opinion, disorganize the finances of the Colony, and work harm rather than good to a considerable body of users of opium who have acquired the habit and who steadfastly believe that their health would be sacrificed in any attempt to suddenly cease the use of the drug without ample provision for medical help.

All the parties to the traffic which is now perceived, more or less clearly, not to be conducive to the public good, must patiently and intelligently find their way to better methods of restriction until by successive steps prohibition is reached. Haste and suddenness now are to be deprecated quite as much as lethargy and inaction.

W. F. OLDHAM.

NEW YORK, U.S.A.,
27th July, 1908.

Bibliography

BOOKS

Abdullah Abdul Kadir, Munsyi. *The Hikayat Abdullah*. Kuala Lumpur: Oxford University Press, 1970.

Abdullah, Ali. *Raffles and Singapore*. Singapore: Academic Exercise, Raffles College, 1949.

Abdullah, Noorman. *Exploring Constructions of the "Drug Problem" in Historical and Contemporary Singapore*. Department of Sociology Occasional Paper. Singapore: National University of Singapore, 2005.

Abeel, David. *Journal of a Residence in China and the Neighbouring Countries, from 1829–1833*. New York: Leavitt, Lord, 1834.

Alatas, Hussein Syed. *Thomas Stamford Raffles, 1781–1826: Schemer or Reformer?* Sydney, Australia: Angus and Robertson, 1971.

Aljunied, Syed Muhd Khairudin. *Raffles and Religion: A Study of Sir Thomas Stamford Raffles' Discourse on Religions amongst Malays*. Kuala Lumpur, Malaysia: Other Press, 2004.

Ang, Dennis, et al. *Hearts, Hopes and Aims: The Spirit of the Anglo-Chinese School*. Singapore: Times Books International, 1986.

Badley, Benton T. *Oldham: Beloved of Three Continents*. Lucknow: Lucknow Publishing, 1937.

Barber, Noel. *The Singapore Story: From Raffles to Lee Kuan Yew*. London: Fontana, 1978.

Barclay, Wade C. *History of Methodist Missions*. Vols. 1–3. New York: Board of Missions and Church Extension of the Methodist Church, 1949.

Basri, Ghazali. *Christian Mission and Islamic Da'wah in Malaysia*. Kuala Lumpur: Nurin Enterprise, 1992.

Bebbington, D. W. *Evangelicalism in Modern Britain: A History from the 1730s to the 1980s*. London: Unwin Hyman, 1989.

Bevans, S., and Schroeder R., eds. *Mission for the Twenty-First Century*. Chicago: CCGM, 2001.

Blythe, W. L. *The Impact of Chinese Secret Societies in Malaya: A Historical Study*. London: Oxford University Press, 1969.

Bosch, David J. *Transforming Mission: Paradigm Shifts in Theology of Mission*. Maryknoll, NY: Orbis, 1992.

Boulger, Demetrius Charles. *The Life of Sir Stamford Raffles*. London: Charles Knight, 1973. Reprint. Originally published, 1897.

Braga-Blake, Myrna, ed. *Singapore Eurasians: Memories and Hopes*. Singapore: Times Editions, 1992.

Brown, Theodore L., H. Eugene LeMay Jr., and Bruce E. Bursten, eds. *Chemistry the Central Science*. 7th ed, Upper Saddle River, NJ: Prentice Hall, 1997.

Brown, William. *The History of the Propagation of Christianity Among the Heathen Since the Reformation*. Vol. 1. Edinburgh, UK: A Fullarton & Co, 1823.

Browne, Laurence E. *Christianity and the Malays*. London: SPCK, 1936.

Buckley, C. B. *An Anecdotal History of Old Times in Singapore: From the Foundation of the Settlement under the Honourable East India Company, on Feb. 6th 1819, to the Transfer to the Colonial Office as part of the Colonial Possessions of the Crown on April 1st 1867*. Singapore: Oxford University Press, 1984. Reprint. Originally published, 1902.

Butcher, John G. *The British in Malaya 1880-1941: The Social History of a European Community in Colonial South-East Asia*. Kuala Lumpur, Malaysia: Oxford University Press, 1979.

Cameron, John. *Our Tropical Possessions in Malayan India*. Kuala Lumpur, Malaysia: Oxford University Press. 1965. Reprint. Originally published in London, 1865.

Cannadine, David. *Ornamentalism: How the British Saw Their Empire*. London: Penguin, 2001.

Canton, William. *A History of the British and Foreign Bible Society*. Vol. 5. London: John Murray, 1910.

Carberry, J. J. *Chemical and Catalytic Reaction Engineering*. New York: McGraw-Hill, 1976.

Carnoy, Martin. *Education as Cultural Imperialism*. London: Longman, 1974.

Carpenter, Joel A., and Wilbert R. Shenk, eds. *Earthen Vessels, American Evangelicals and Foreign Missions, 1880-1980*. Grand Rapids, MI: William B. Eerdmans, 1990.

Carver, William Owen. *Missions and Modern Thought*. New York: Macmillan, 1910.

Chang, Cynthia Yee Ping. "Church and Community: Roman Catholicism in Singapore." (M. Soc. Sc.) Thesis, Dept of Sociology, National University of Singapore, 1997.

Chelliah, D. D. *A History of the Educational Policy of the Straits Settlements with Recommendations for a New System based on Vernaculars*. Kuala Lumpur, Malaysia: Government Press, 1947.

———. *A Short History of Educational Policy in the Straits Settlements, 1800-1925*. Singapore: G. H. Kiat & Co, 1960.

Chew, Ernest C. T., and Edwin Lee, eds. *A History of Singapore*. Singapore: Oxford University Press, 1991.

Chew, Maureen. *The Journey of the Catholic Church in Malaysia 1511-1996*. Kuala Lumpur: Catholic Research Centre, 2000.

Chiang Hai Ding. *A History of Straits Settlements Foreign Trade, 1870-1915*. Singapore: National Museum, 1978.

———. "Sino-British Mercantile Relations in Singapore's Entrepot Trade, 1870-1915." In *Studies in the Social History of China and Southeast Asia: Essays in Memory of Victor Purcell*, edited by J. Chen and N. Tarling, 247-67. Cambridge: Cambridge University Press, 1970.

Chiew Seen Kong. "The Chinese in Singapore: From Colonial Times to the Present." In *Southeast Asian Chinese: The Socio-Cultural Dimension*, edited by Leo Suryadinata, 42–66. Singapore: Times Academic Press, 1995.

Christensen, Torben, and William R. Hutchison, eds. *Missionary Ideologies in the Imperialist Era: 1880–1920*. UK: Aros, 1982.

Clammer, R. John. *Singapore: Ideology, Society, Culture*. Singapore: Chopman Publishers, 1985.

Cole, R. Alan. *Emerging Pattern in the Diocese of Singapore and Malaya*. London: China Inland Mission, 1961.

Collis, Maurice. *Raffles*. London: Faber and Faber, 1966.

Comaroff, Jean, and John Comaroff. *Of Revelation and Revolution: Christianity, Colonialism and Consciousness in South Africa*. Vol. 1. Chicago: University of Chicago Press, 1991.

———. *Of Revelation and Revolution: The Dialectics of Modernity on a South African Frontier*. Vol. 2. Chicago: University of Chicago Press, 1997.

Cook, J. A. Bethune. *Sir Thomas Stamford Raffles, Founder of Singapore, 1819, and some of his friends and contemporaries*. London: Arthur H. Stockwell, 1918.

———. *Sunny Singapore: an Account of the Place and its People, with a Sketch of the Results of Missionary Work*. London: Elliott Stock, 1907.

Coppleston, J. I. *Twentieth Century Perspectives, 1896–1939*. History of Methodist Missions 4. New York: Board of Global Ministries of the United Methodist Church, 1973.

Coupland, Reginald. *Raffles of Singapore*. 3rd ed. London: Collins, 1946.

Cowan, C. D., ed. *Early Penang and the Rise of Singapore, 1805–1832: Documents from the Manuscript Records of the East India Company*. Singapore: Malaya Publishing, 1950.

———. *Nineteenth Century Malaya: The Origins of British Control*. London: Oxford University Press, 1961.

Crawfurd, J. *Journal of an Embassy from the Governor General of India to the Courts of Siam and Cochin China*. 2 vols. Kuala Lumpur, Malaysia: Oxford University Press, 1967. Reprint. Originally published in London, 1828.

Cribb, Robert. "Imperialism in Asia: A Comparative Perspective." In *Eastern Asia: An Introductory History*, edited by Colin Mackerras, 131–41. 3rd ed. Kuala Lumpur, Malaysia: Longman, 2000.

David, M. D., ed. *Western Colonialism in Asia and Christianity*. Bombay, India: Himalaya Publishing, 1988.

Davies, John D. "The Growth and Development of Local Government in Singapore, 1848–1887." Academic Exercise, Dept. of History, University of Malaya, Singapore, 1954.

DeBernardi, Jean. "Lim Boon Keng and the Invention of Cosmopolitanism in the Straits Settlements." In *Managing Change in Southeast Asia: Local Identities, Global Connections*, edited by J. DeBernardi, G. Forth, and S. Niessen, 173–87. Montreal, Canada: Canadian Council for Southeast Asian Studies, 1995.

Dena, Lal. *Christian Missions and Colonialism: A Study of Missionary Movement in Northeast India with Particular Reference to Manipur and Lushai Hills 1894–1947*. Shillong, India: Vendrame Institute, 1988.

Dennys, N. B. *A Descriptive Dictionary of British Malaya*. London: Ganesha Publishing, 2002. Reprint. Originally published, 1894.

Dharmaraj, Jacob S. *Colonialism and Christian Mission: Postcolonial Reflections.* Delhi, India: SPCK, 1993.

Diocese of Singapore. *Visions Unfold: Story of the Growth of the Anglican Church in Singapore from 1909-1999.* Singapore: Kairos Design, 1999.

Doraisamy, Theodore. R., ed. *150 Years of Education in Singapore.* Singapore: Teachers' Training College, 1969.

———, ed. *Forever Beginning I: One Hundred Years of Methodism in Singapore.* Singapore: The Methodist Church in Singapore, 1985.

———, ed. *Forever Beginning II: One Hundred Years of Methodism in Singapore.* Singapore: Methodist Book Room, 1986.

———, ed. *Heralds of the Lord: Personalities in Methodism in Singapore and Malaysia.* Singapore: Methodist Book Room, 1988.

———. *The March of Methodism in Singapore and Malaysia 1885-1980.* Singapore: Methodist Book Room, 1982.

———. *Oldham, Called of God: Profile of a Pioneer.* Singapore: Methodist Book Room, 1979.

———. *Sophia Blackmore in Singapore.* Singapore: General Conference, Women's Society of Christian Service, 1987.

———. *What Hath God Wrought: Motives of Mission in Methodism from Wesley to Thoburn.* Singapore: Methodist Book Room, 1983.

Egerton, Hugh Edward. *A Short History of British Colonial Policy 1606-1909.* London: Methuen & Co Ltd, 1945.

———. *Sir Stamford Raffles: England in the Far East.* London: T. Fisher Unwin, 1900.

Eldridge, C. C., ed. *British Imperialism in the Nineteenth Century.* New York: St. Martin's Press, 1984.

Elson, Robert E. "International Commerce, the State and Society: Economic and Social Change." In *The Cambridge History of Southeast Asia.* Vol. 3, *From c.1800 to the 1930s,* edited by Nicholas Tarling. Cambridge: Cambridge University Press, 1999.

Emerson, Rupert. *Malaysia: A Study in Direct and Indirect Rule.* Kuala Lumpur: University of Malaya Press, 1964.

Ferguson, Niall. *Empire: The Rise and Demise of the British World Order and the Lessons for Global Power.* New York: Basic Books, 2002.

Findlay, George G., and W. W. Holdsworth. *The History of the Wesleyan Methodist Missionary Society.* 5 vols. London: Epworth, 1921-24.

Fletcher, Irene M. *London Missionary Society in the Malay Archipelago.* London, 1952.

Goh, Robbie B. H. *Sparks of Grace: The Story of Methodism in Asia.* Singapore: The Methodist Church in Singapore, 2003.

Greer, Robert McLeish. *A History of the Presbyterian Church in Singapore.* Singapore: Malaya Publishing, 1956.

Guiness, Os, and John Seel. *No God but God: Breaking with the Idols of our Age.* Chicago: Moody, 1992.

Gullick, J. M. *Rulers and Residents: Influence and Power in the Malay States 1870-1920.* Singapore: Oxford University Press, 1992.

Hackler, Rhoda E. A. "Americans in Singapore, 1819-1850." Singapore: unpublished paper, Dept. of History, University of Malaya, 1960.

Hahn, Emily. *Raffles of Singapore: A Biography.* Garden City, NY: Doubleday, 1946.

Haines, Joseph Harry. "A History of Protestant Missions in Malaya During the Nineteenth Century, 1815–1881." DTh Thesis, Princeton Theological Seminary, 1962.
Hancock, T. H. H. *Coleman's Singapore*. Kuala Lumpur, Malaysia: The Malaysian Branch of the Royal Asiatic Society in association with Pelanduk Publications, 1986.
Harcus, A. Drummond. *History of the Presbyterian Church in Malaya*. London: Presbyterian Historical Society of England, 1955.
Hardy, P. *The Muslims of British India*. Cambridge: Cambridge University Press, 1973.
Harrison, Brian. *Holding the Fort: Melaka under Two Flags, 1795–1845*. Kuala Lumpur, Malaysia: Malaysian Branch of the Royal Asiatic Society, 1985.
———. *Waiting for China: The Anglo-Chinese College at Malacca, 1818–1843 and Early Nineteenth-Century Missions*. Hong Kong: Hong Kong University Press, 1979.
Hempton, David. *Methodism and Politics in British Society: 1750–1850*. Stanford: Stanford University Press, 1984.
———. *Religion and Popular Culture in Britain and Ireland: From the Glorious Revolution to the Decline of Empire*. Cambridge: Cambridge University Press, 1996.
Heussler, Robert. *British Rule in Malaya*. Oxford: Clio Press, 1981.
Ho Seng Ong. *Methodist Schools in Malaysia: Their Record and History*. Petaling Jeya: Malaysia: The Board of Education of the Malaya Annual Conference, 1964.
Holmes, B., ed. *Educational Policy and Mission Schools: Case Studies for the British Empire*. London: Routledge & Kegan Paul, 1967.
Howell, Julia, and David Schak. "Religious Traditions in Asia." In *Eastern Asia: An Introductory History*, edited by Colin Mackerras, 51–64. 3rd ed. Kuala Lumpur, Malaysia: Longman, 2000.
Hunt, Robert. *Islam in Southeast Asia*. New York: The General Board of Global Ministries, The United Methodist Church, 1997.
———. *William Shellabear: A Biography*. Kuala Lumpur, Malaysia: University of Malaya Press, 1996.
Hunt, Robert A., John Roxborogh, and Lee Kam Hing, eds. *Christianity in Malaysia, A Denominational History*. Kuala Lumpur: Pelanduk, 1992.
Institute of Asian Cultural Studies. *Comparative Chronology of Protestantism in Asia 1792–1945*. Tokyo: Institute of Asian Cultural Studies of the International Christian University, 1984.
Jackson, R. N. *Pickering: Protector of Chinese*. Kuala Lumpur, Malaysia: Oxford University Press, 1965.
Johnson, Anne. *The Burning Bush: A History of the Presbyterian Church in Singapore*. Singapore: Dawn Publications, 1988.
Jung, Karl. *CW 18*. Translated by R. F. G. Hull. 2nd ed. Princeton: Princeton University Press, 1965.
Kaplan, Steven, ed. *Indigenous Responses to Western Christianity*. New York: New York University Press, 1995.
Keay, John. *Empire's End: A History of the Far East from High Colonialism to Hong Kong*. New York: Scribner, 1997.
———. *The Honourable Company: A History of the English East India Company*. London: Harper Collins, 1993.
Kesselring, Ralph Adolph. "Christian Missions in Malaya." BD dissertation, Chicago Theological Seminary, Chicago, 1943.

Khoo Chit Seng. "Administration in the Straits Settlements 1826–1832." Academic Exercise, Dept. of History, University of Malaya, Singapore, 1959.

Khoo Kay Kim. "The Municipal Government of Singapore, 1887–1940." Academic Exercise, Dept. of History, University of Malaya, Singapore, 1960.

———. *The Western Malay States, 1850–1873: The Effects of Commercial Development on Malay Politics.* Kuala Lumpur: Oxford University Press, 1972.

Khor Eng Hee. *The Public Life of Dr. Lim Boon Keng.* Singapore: University of Malaya, 1958.

Kiong Beng Huat. "Educational Progress in Singapore, 1870–1902." Singapore: Academic Exercise, Dept. of History, University of Malaya, Singapore, 1953.

Kratoska, Paul H., ed. *Honourable Intentions: Talks on the British Empire in South-East Asia Delivered at the Royal Colonial Institute, 1874–1928.* Singapore: Oxford University Press, 1983.

———, ed. *South East Asia: Colonial History—Empire Building During the Nineteenth Century.* Vol. 2. London: Routledge, 2001.

Kwa Kiem Kiok. "Towards a Model of Engagement in the Public Realm for the Methodist Church." PhD Dissertation, Asbury Theological Seminary, 2004.

Latourette, Kenneth Scott. *A History of Christian Missions in China.* New York: Russell & Russell, 1929.

———. *A History of Christianity.* Vol 2. New York: Harper and Row, 1975.

———. *A History of the Expansion of Christianity.* Vol. 6, *The Great Century, AD 1800–AD 1914, North Africa and Asia.* London: Eyre and Spottiswoode, 1914.

Lau, Earnest. *From Mission to Church: The Evolution of the Methodist Church in Singapore and Malaysia: 1885–1976.* Singapore: Genesis Books, 2008

Lau, Earnest, and Peter Teo, eds. *The ACS Story.* Singapore: ACS Board of Governors, C.O.S. Printers, 2007

Lau, Maria. "Mission Schools and Changing Values in Singapore." Academic Exercise, Dept. of Sociology, University of Singapore, Singapore, 1977.

Lee, Edwin. *The British as Rulers: Governing Multiracial Singapore.* Singapore: Singapore University Press, 1991.

Lee Kuan Yew. *From Third World to First: The Singapore Story.* New York: HarperCollins, 2000.

Lee Poh Ping. *Chinese Society in Nineteenth Century Singapore.* Kuala Lumpur: Oxford University Press, 1978.

Leong P. "Methodism and Education in Singapore 1886–1914." BA Academic Exercise, Nanyang Technological University, Singapore, 1997.

Liew, Clement. "The Roman Catholic Church of Singapore, 1819–1910: From Mission to Church." Academic Exercise, Dept. of History, National University of Singapore, Singapore, 1994.

Lloyd, Trevor Owen. *Empire: The History of the British Empire.* London: Hambledon and London, 2001.

Lo Wai Fun. "The Transfer of the Straits Settlements from the Indian Office to the Colonial Office in 1867." Academic Exercise, Dept. of History, University of Malaya, Singapore, 1957.

Loh Keng Aun. *Fifty Years of the Anglican Church in Singapore Island, 1909–1959.* Singapore: University of Singapore, 1963.

Loo Choo Kheam. The Methodist Impact of Malaya 1885–1953." Academic Exercise, Dept. of History, University of Singapore, Singapore, 1955.

Low Aik Lim. "Anglo-Chinese School, 1886–1941: Case Study of a Mission School." Academic Exercise, Dept. of History, National University of Singapore, Singapore, 1991/1992.
Makepeace, Walter E., Roland St. John Braddell, and G. S. Brooke, eds. *One Hundred Years of Singapore*. 2 vols. Singapore: Oxford University Press, 1991. Reprint. Originally published in London, 1921.
Means, Nathalie Toms. *Malaysia Mosaic: A Story of Fifty Years of Methodism*. Singapore: Methodist Book Room, 1935.
Mills, Lennox A. *British Malaya 1824–1867*. Kuala Lumpur: Oxford University Press, 1979.
Moore, Donald and Joanna Moore. *The First 150 Years of Singapore*, Singapore: Donald Moore Press Ltd, 1969.
Neill, Stephen. *Colonialism and Christian Mission*. New York: McGraw Hill, 1966.
Nkrumah, Kwame. *Neo-Colonialism: The Last Stage of Imperialism*. Fifth Printing. New York: International Publishers, 1965.
Norwood, Fredrick A. *A Sourcebook of American Methodism*. Nashville: Abingdon, 1982.
———. *The Story of American Methodism*. Nashville: Abingdon, 1974.
Nyce, Ray. *The Kingdom and the Country: A Study of Church and Society in Singapore*. Singapore: Institute for the Study of Religions and Society, 1972.
Oldham, William F. *India, Malaysia and the Philippines: A Practical Study in Missions*. New York: Eaton and Mains, 1914.
———. *Thoburn: Called of God*. New York: The Methodist Book Concern, 1918.
Ong Tiong Whatt. "Farquhar's Administration of Singapore, 1819–1823." Academic Exercise, Dept. of History, University of Malaya, Singapore, 1959.
Ooi Swee Lee. "The First Colonial Governor: Sir Harry Ord, 1867–1873." Academic Exercise, Dept. of History, University of Malaya, Singapore, 1959.
Parkinson, C. Northcote. *British Intervention in Malaya, 1867–1877*. Singapore: University of Malaya Press, 1960.
Peterson, A. D. C. *The Far East: A Social Geography*. London: Gerald Duckworth, 1949.
Philips, C. H., ed. *The Evolution of India and Pakistan 1858–1947: Select Documents*. London: Oxford University Press, 1962.
Porter, Andrew, ed. *The Imperial Horizons of British Protestant Missions, 1880–1914*. Grand Rapids, MI: Eerdmans, 2003.
———. *Religion versus Empire? British Protestant Missionaries and Overseas Expansion, 1700–1914*. Manchester: Manchester University Press, 2004.
Purcell, Victor. *The Chinese in Southeast Asia*. 2nd ed. London: Oxford University Press, 1965.
Raffles, Sophia, Lady. *Memoir of the Life and Public Services of Sir Thomas Stamford Raffles*. Singapore: Oxford University Press, 1991. Reprint. Originally published, 1830.
Raffles, Thomas Stamford. *Statement of the Services of Sir Stamford Raffles*. Kuala Lumpur: Oxford University Press, 1978.
Rajah, Thavamani Devi. "Crawfurd, Resident of Singapore, 1823–1826." Academic Exercise, Dept. of History, University of Malaya, Singapore, 1959.
Reid, Anthony. "Merchant Imperialist: W. H. Read and the Dutch Consulate in the Straits Settlements." In *Empires, Imperialism and Southeast Asia: Essays in Honour*

of Nicholas Tarling, edited by Brooke Barrington, 34–59. Clayton, Australia: Monash Asia Institute, 1997.

Retnam, Eric Selvaretnam. "The Trade of Singapore, 1869–1896." Academic Exercise, Dept. of History, University of Malaya, Singapore, 1961.

Russell, Frederick S., ed. *Advances in Marine Biology*. Vol 5. London: Academic Press, 1967.

Sadka, E. *The Protected Malay States, 1874–1895*. Kuala Lumpur, Malaysia: University of Malaya Press, 1968.

SarDesai, D. R. *British Trade and Expansion in Southeast Asia 1830–1914*. New Delhi, India: Allied Publishers, 1977.

Saw Swee Hock. *The Population of Singapore*. Singapore: Institute of Southeast Asian Studies, 1999.

Sine, Tom. *Mustard Seed Versus McWorld: Reinventing Life and Faith for the Future*. Grand Rapids, MI: Baker, 1999.

Sng, Bobby. *In His Good Time: The Story of the Church in Singapore 1819–2002*. Singapore: Bible Society of Singapore, 2003.

Song Ong Siang. *One Hundred Years' History of the Chinese in Singapore*. Singapore: Oxford University Press, 1984. Reprint. Originally published in London, 1902.

Spence, Jonathan. *God's Chinese Son: The Taiping Heavenly Kingdom of Hong Xiuquan*. New York: W. W. Norton, 1996.

Stanley, Brian. *The Bible and the Flag: Protestant Missions and British Imperialism in the Nineteenth and Twentieth Centuries*. Leicester: Apollos, 1990.

———, ed. *Christian Missions and the Enlightenment*. Grand Rapids, MI: Eerdmans, 2003.

———, ed. *Missions, Nationalism and the End of Empire*. Grand Rapids, MI: Eerdmans, 2001.

Stanley, Brian, Kevin Ward, and Diana Witts, eds. *The Church Mission Society and World Christianity, 1799–1999*. Grand Rapids, MI: Eerdmans, 1999.

Stenson, Michael. *Class, Race and Colonialism in West Malaysia: The Indian Case*. Vancouver: University of British Columbia Press, 1980.

Stevenson, Rex. *Cultivators and Administrators: British Educational Policy towards the Malays, 1875–1906*. Oxford: Oxford University Press, 1975.

Sunquist, Scott, et al. eds. *A Dictionary of Asian Christianity*. Grand Rapids, MI; Eerdmans, 2001.

Swettenham, Frank Athelstane. *British Malaya: An Account of the Origin and Progress of British Influence in Malaya*. London: George Allen and Unwin Ltd., 1906.

Tarling, Nicholas. *British Policy in the Malay Peninsula and Archipelago, 1824 to 1871*. London: Oxford University Press, 1969.

———, ed. *The Cambridge History of Southeast Asia*. Vol. 2, *The Nineteenth and Twentieth Centuries*. Cambridge: Cambridge University Press, 1999.

———, ed. *The Cambridge History of Southeast Asia*. Vol. 3, *From c. 1800 to the 1930s*. Cambridge: Cambridge University Press, 1999.

———. *Imperial Britain in Southeast Asia*. Kuala Lumpur: Oxford University Press, 1975.

———. *Imperialism in Southeast Asia: "A Fleeting, Passing Phase."* London: Routledge, 2001.

———. "Mercantilists and Missionaries: Impact and Accomodation." In *Eastern Asia: An Introductory History*, edited by Colin Mackerras, 132–66. 3rd ed. Kuala Lumpur, Malaysia: Longman, 2000.

———. *Nations and States in Southeast Asia*. Cambridge: Cambridge University Press, 1998.

Teo, Peter, Earnest Lau, and George Martzen, eds. *The People Called Methodists: The Heritage, Life and Mission of the Methodist Church in Singapore*. Singapore: The Methodist Church in Singapore, 2003.

Thio, Eunice. *British Policy in the Malay Peninsula, 1880–1910*. Vol. 1, *The Southern and Central States*. Singapore: University of Malaya Press, 1969.

Thoburn, James. *India and Malaysia*. New York: Hunt and Eaton, 1892.

Tong Teck Ing. "Opium in the Straits Settlements, 1867–1909." Singapore: Academic Exercise, Dept of History, University of Malaya, 1955.

Townsend, W. J., H. B. Workman, and George Eayrs, eds. *A New History of Methodism*, Vols. 1 and 2. London: Hodder and Stoughton, 1909.

Tregonning, K. C. *The British in Malaya: The First Forty Years, 1786–1826*. Tucson: The University of Arizona Press, 1965.

Trocki, Carl A. *Opium and Empire: Chinese Society in Colonial Singapore, 1800–1910*. New York: Cornell University Press, 1990.

Turnbull, C. M. *A History of Singapore 1819-1975*. Kuala Lumpur: Oxford University Press, 1982.

Vaggioli, Dom Felice. *History of New Zealand and Its Inhabitants*, Dunedin, New Zealand: University of Otago Press, 2001.

Vaughan, J. D. *The Manners and Customs of the Chinese of the Straits Settlements*. Kuala Lumpur, Malaysia: Oxford University Press, 1974. Reprint. Originally published, 1879.

Wang, Gungwu. *China and the Chinese Overseas*. Singapore: Times Academic Press, 1991.

Warren, Max Alexander Cunngingham. *The Missionary Movement from Britain in Modern History*. London: SCM, 1965.

Webster, Anthony. *Gentlemen Capitalists: British Imperialism in South East Asia, 1770–1890*. London: Tauris Academic Studies, 1998.

Wild, Antony. *The East India Company: Trade and Conquest from 1600*. New York: Lyons Press, 1999.

Wilkinson, R. J. *A History of the Peninsular Malays*. Singapore: Kelly & Walsh, 1923.

Winter, Ralph, and Steven C. Hawthorne, eds. *Perspectives on the World Christian Movement*. Pasadena, CA: William Carey, 1999.

Wong Chan Kok, and Chuck Lowe, eds. *Ministry in Modern Singapore: The Effects of Modernity on the Church*. Singapore: Singapore Bible College, 1987.

Wong, Francis H. K., and Gwee Yee Hean, eds. *Official Reports on Education: Straits Settlements and the Federated Malay States: 1870–1939*. Singapore: Pan Pacific Books Distributors, 1980.

Wong, H. K., and Ee Tiang Hong. *Education in Malaysia*. London: Heinemann, 1975

Wong, James Y. K. "The Church in Singapore." In *Church in Asia Today: Challenges and Opportunities*, edited by Saphir Athyal. Singapore: Asia Lausanne Committee for World Evangelization, 1996.

———. *Singapore: The Church in the Midst of Social Change*. Singapore: Church Growth Study Centre, 1973.

World's Student Christian Federation. *History's Lessons for Tomorrow's Mission: Milestones in the History of Missionary Thinking*. Geneva, Switzerland: World's Student Christian Federation, 1960.

Wright, Arnold, and H. A. Cartwright, eds. *Twentieth Century Impressions of British Malaya: Its History, People, Commerce, Industries, and Resources*. Abridged ed. Singapore: Graham Brash, 1989. Reprint. Originally published in London, 1908.

Wright, Arnold, and Thomas H. Reid. *The Malay Peninsula: A Record of British Progress in the Middle East*. London: T. F. Unwin, 1912.

Wurtzburg, C. E. *Raffles of the Eastern Isles*. Singapore: Oxford University Press, 1984. Reprint. Originally published in London, 1954.

Yen Ching Hwang. *Community and Politics: The Chinese in Colonial Singapore and Malaysia*. Singapore: Times Academic Press, 1995.

———. *A Social History of the Chinese in Singapore and Malaya 1800–1911*. Singapore: Oxford University Press, 1986.

JOURNAL ARTICLES

Bartley, W. "The Population of Singapore in 1819." *Journal of the Malaysian Branch of the Royal Asiatic Society* 42.1 (1969) 112–13.

Bastin, John, ed. "Sir Stamford Raffles' Letters to Nathaniel Wallich." *Journal of the Malaysian Branch of the Royal Asiatic Society* 54.2 (1981).

Blackburn, Kevin, and Pauline Fong Lai Leong. "Methodist Education and the Social Status of the Straits Chinese in Colonial Singapore (1886–1914)." *Paedagogica Historica* 35.2 (1999) 333–57.

Bogaars, George. "The Effect of the Opening of the Suez Canal on the Trade and Development of Singapore." *Journal of the Malayan Branch of the Royal Asiatic Society* 38.1 (1955) 99–143.

Braddell, T. "Notices of Singapore." *Journal of the Indian Archipelago and Eastern Asia* 8 (1853) 97–111, 329–48, 403–19.

———. "Notices of Singapore." *Journal of the Indian Archipelago and Eastern Asia* 9 (1854) 53–65, 442–82.

———. "Notices of Singapore." *Journal of the Indian Archipelago and Eastern Asia* 7 (1855) 325–57.

Bunnag, S. C. "The Founding of Singapore, 1819." *Asian Studies* 4.3 (1966) 532–48.

Cangi, Ellen C. "Civilizing the People of Southeast Asia: Sir Stamford Raffles' Town Plan for Singapore, 1819–23." *Planning Perspectives* 8.2 (1993) 166–87.

Cavani, Fabrizio, Gabriele Centi, Carlo Perego, and Angelo Vaccari. "Selectivity in Catalytic Oxidation." *Catalysis Today* 99 (2004) 1–3.

Cheng Siok Hwa. "Government Legislation for Chinese Secret Societies in the Late 19th Century." *Asian Studies* 10.2 (1972) 262–71.

———. "Sir Cecil Clementi Smith as Colonial Secretary and Governor of the Straits Settlements, 1878–1885, 1887–1893." *Journal of the South Seas Society* 28.1/2 (Dec. 1973) 34–71.

Cheng U Wen, Lena. "Opium in the Straits Settlements, 1867–1910." *Journal of South East Asian History* 1 (March 1961) 57–75.

Crawfurd, John. "Notes on the Population of Java." In *Journal of the Indian Archipelago and Eastern Asia* III (1849) 32–55.

Doraisamy, Theodore R. "Women Pioneers of Methodism in Singapore and Malaysia: Messengers of Love." *Asia Journal of Theology* 4.2 (1990) 344–55.
Ee, Joyce. "Chinese Migration to Singapore, 1896–1941." *Journal of Southeast Asian History* 2.1 (1961) 33–51.
Freedman, Maurice. "Immigrants and Associations in 19th Century Singapore." *Comparative Studies in Society and History* 3 (1960) 25–48.
Freedman, Maurice, and Marjorie Topley. "Religion and Social Alignment among the Chinese in Singapore." *Journal of Asian Studies* 21.1 (1961) 3–23.
Galbraith, J. S. "The 'Turbulent Frontier' as a Factor in British Expansion." *Comparative Studies in Society and History* 2 (1960) 150–68.
Gallagher, John, and Ronald Robinson. "The Imperialism of Free Trade." *The Economic History Review* 6.1 (1953) 1–15.
Gamba, Charles. "Chinese Associations in Singapore." *Journal of the Malaysian Branch of the Royal Asiatic Society* 39.2 (1966) 123–68.
Gibson-Hill, C. A. "The Singapore Chronicle 1824–37." *Journal of the Malaysian Branch of the Royal Asiatic Society* 42.1 (1969) 166–91.
Grasselli, Robert. "Selectivity Issues in (Amm)Oxidation Catalysis." *Catalysis Today* 99 (2004) 23–31.
Hunt, Robert A. "William Shellabear." *International Bulletin of Missionary Research* 26.1 (Jan. 2002).
———. "William Shellabear and His Bible." *Methodist History* 29.1 (1990).
Jackson, R. N. "Grasping the Nettle: First Successes in the Struggle to Govern the Chinese in Singapore." *Journal of the Malaysian Branch of the Royal Asiatic Society* 40.1 (1967) 130–39.
Kathirithamby-Wells, J. "Early Singapore and the Inception of a British Administrative Tradition." *Journal of the Malaysian Branch of the Royal Asiatic Society* 42.2 (Dec. 1969) 48–73.
Khoo Kay Kim. "Malay Society, 1874–1920s." *Journal of Southeast Asian Studies* 5.2 (1974) 179–98.
Legge, John. "The Colonial Office and Governor Ord." *Journal of Southeast Asian Studies* 29.1 (1998) 1–7.
Lim, L. U. "British Opium Policy in the Straits Settlements, 1867–1910." *Journal of Southeast Asian Studies* 2.1 (1961) 52–75.
Loh Fook Seng, P. "The British Approach to Slavery in the Straits Settlements and the Malay States 1819–1910." *Journal of the Historical Society* 5 (1964) 23–55.
Pearson, H. F. "Lt. Jackson's Pan of Singapore." *Journal of the Malayan Branch of the Royal Asiatic Society* 26.1 (1953) 200–204.
Pickering, W. A. "Chinese Secret Societies and Their Origin, Part 1." *Journal of the Straits Branch of the Royal Asiatic Society* 1 (1878) 63–84.
———. "Chinese Secret Societies and Their Origin, Part 2." *Journal of the Straits Branch of the Royal Asiatic Society* 3 (1879) 1–18.
Png Poh Seng. "The Straits Chinese in Singapore: a Case of Local Identity and Sociocultural Accommodation." *Journal of Southeast Asian History*, 1969, 10(1):95–114.
Ponniah, Moses. "The Situation in Malaysia." *Transformation* 17.1 (January/March 2000) 31–34.
Roff, William R. "The Malayo-Muslim Community of Singapore in the late 19th Century." *Journal of Asian Studies* 24 (1964) 75–89.

Roxborogh, John. "Early Nineteenth-Century Foundations of Christianity in Malaya: Churches and Missions in Penang, Melaka and Singapore from 1786–1842." *Asia Journal of Theology* 6.1 (1992) 54–72.

Saw Swee Hock. "The Changing Population Structure in Singapore during 1824–1962." *Malayan Economic Review* 9.1 (1964) 90–101.

Sharom, Ahmat. "American Trade with Singapore, 1819–1865." *Journal of the Malaysian Branch of the Royal Asiatic Society* 38.2 (1965) 241–57.

———. "The Singapore Malay Community." *Journal of the History Society* (1970–71) 39–46.

Stewart, R. J. M. "Raffles of Singapore: The Man and the Legacy." *Asian Affairs* 13.1 (1982) 16–27.

Tarling, Nicholas. "The Prince of Merchants and the Lion City." *Journal of the Malaysian Branch of the Royal Asiatic Society* 36.1 (1964) 20–40.

Tay, J. S. "The Attempts of Raffles to Establish a British Base in South-East Asia, 1818–1819." *Journal of Southeast Asian History* 1.2 (1960) 30–46.

Turnbull, Mary. "The European Mercantile Community in Singapore, 1819–1867." *Journal of Southeast Asian History* 10.1 (1969) 12–35.

Wilson, Harold E. "An Abortive Plan for an Anglo-Chinese College in Singapore." *Journal of the Malaysian Branch of the Royal Asiatic Society* 40.2 (1972) 97–109.

Wong Lin Ken. "The Trade of Singapore, 1819–1869." *Journal of the Malayan Branch of the Royal Asiatic Society* 30.4 (1960) 1–315.

Yen Ching Hwang. "Early Chinese Clan Organization in Singapore and Malaya 1819–1911." *Journal of Southeast Asian Studies* 13.1 (1981) 62–87.

ANONYMOUS ARCHIVAL RECORDS

Anglo-Chinese School Magazine, 1927. Singapore: Methodist Archives.

Annual Report, Methodist Episcopal Mission, 1894 to 1905. Singapore: Methodist Archives.

CO273/22 203 of 8 Oct. 1868 Ord to Kimberly. Singapore: National Archives.

CO273/57 29 dated 2 May 1872, Ord to Kimberley. Singapore: National Archives.

CO273/65 24 of 20 Jan. 1873, Ord to Kimberley enclosing Report of Commission of Enquiry on the Oct. 1872 riots. Singapore: National Archives.

CO273/148 435 of 15 Oct. 1887 Weld to Holland enclosing Weld's address to the Legislative Council 13 Oct. 1887. Singapore: National Archives.

CO 273/328, G.D. No 308, 24 July 1907. Singapore: Singapore National Archives.

Code of Regulations and Government and Grants-in-Aid English and Vernacular Schools in the Federated Malaysian States, 1902. Singapore: National Archives.

Malaysia Message, Vol I No 4 Jan. 1892. Singapore: The Methodist Archives.

Malaysia Message, June 1893. Singapore: The Methodist Archives.

Malaysia Message, January, 1895. Singapore: The Methodist Archives.

Malaysia Message, June 1896. Singapore: The Methodist Archives.

Malaysia Message, Vol IX No. 6 March 1900, Singapore: The Methodist Archives.

Malaysia Message, Vol X No 7 Apr 1901. Singapore: The Methodist Archives.

Malaysia Message, February 1905. Singapore: The Methodist Archives.

Malaysia Message, 1907. Singapore: The Methodist Archives.

Malaysia Message, Vol XVIII No 4, January 1909. Singapore: The Methodist Archives.

Malaysia Message, Nov. 1911. Singapore: The Methodist Archives.

Malaysia Message, Jan.–Feb. 1935. Singapore: The Methodist Archives.
Methodist Episcopal Church Missionary Society Book of Annual Reports, 1889. Madison, NJ: United Methodist Archives.
Methodist Message, May 1929. Singapore: The Methodist Archives.
Minutes of the Malaysia Mission Annual Meeting, 1892. Madison, NJ: United Methodist Archives.
Oldham to Dr. Peck, 7 August 1890, No 1261-1-2: 30, Madison, NJ: United Methodist Archives.
Oldham's Letter to the Board of Missions, 1889. Lake Junaluska, NC: Commission on Archives and History, United Methodist Church.
Oral transcripts of Dr. Low Cheng Gin (Singapore Archives, Access No. 287, Reel 18), and Teong Ah Chin (Singapore Archives, Access No. 47, Reel 3) Singapore: National Archives.
Quarterly Review of the Minneapolis Branch of the WFMS Vol 20 No 1 Jan. 1913, Singapore, Methodist Archives.
Report of the Education Committee, Minutes of the Malaysia Annual Conference, 1897 Singapore: Methodist Archives.
Report of Inspector General of Police, S.S. for the year 1875 PLCSS 1876 ccxxiii. Singapore: National Archives.
Report of Inspector General of Police, S.S. for the year 1876 PLCSS 1876 ccxlviii. Singapore: National Archives.
SSAR 1892, 174. Singapore: National Archives.
SSAR 1894, 173. Singapore: National Archives.
SSAR 1898–1906, Report on Education. Singapore: National Archives.
SSLCP, 1885, B150. Singapore: National Archives.
SSLCP, 1902 Report. Singapore: National Archives.
SSLCP, 1907 Report. Singapore: National Archives.
Straits Settlements Education Commission Report, 1902. Singapore: National Archives, 1902.
The Gospel in All Lands, May 1896. Singapore: The Methodist Archives.
The Report of the Wesleyan Methodist Missionary Society for the Year ending April 1857. Wesleyan Missionary Society, London, 1857.
The Singapore Free Press, 25 July 1896. Singapore: The National Library Archives.
The Singapore Free Press, 29 July 1896. Singapore: The National Library Archives.
The Singapore Free Press, 30 July 1896. Singapore: The National Library Archives.
The Straits Times, 25 July 1896. Singapore: The National Library Archives.
The Straits Times, 27 July 1896. Singapore: The National Library Archives.
The Straits Times, 29 July 1896. Singapore: The National Library Archives.
The Straits Times, 30 July 1896. Singapore: The National Library Archives.
The Straits Times, 31 July 1896. Singapore: The National Library Archives.
The Straits Times, 1 August 1896. Singapore: The National Library Archives.
The Straits Times, 27 September 1896. Singapore: The National Library Archives.
The Straits Times, 28 September 1896. Singapore: The National Library Archives.
The Straits Times, 29 September 1896. Singapore: The National Library Archives.
The Straits Times, 17 August 1907. Singapore: The National Library Archives.

ARCHIVAL RECORDS

Amery, A. J., J. E. Banks, and W. T. Kensett. "Report of Committee on Public Morals." In *Minutes of the Malaysian Mission Conference of the Methodist Episcopal Church, 1898*. Singapore: American Mission Press, 1898. Singapore: The Methodist Archives.

Anderson, John. *Report of the Commission Appointed to Inquire into Matters Relating to the Use of Opium in the Straits Settlements and the Federated Malay States*. Singapore: Government Printing Office, 1908. Singapore: National Archives.

Anson, A. E. H. *Sketch of a Scheme for Public Education Straits Settlements*. Archival Reels—Education in Strait Settlements. Singapore: National Archives of Singapore.

Blackmore, Sophia. *A Record of Forty Years of Women's Work in Malaya, 1887–1927*. Unpublished records. Singapore: The Methodist Archives.

———. "Report of Deaconess Home." In *Minutes of the Malaysian Mission Conference of the Methodist Episcopal Church, 1911*. Singapore: American Mission Press, 1911. Singapore: The Methodist Archives.

Blackmore, Sophia, et al. "Annual Report, Women's Foreign Missionary Society." In *Minutes of the Malaysian Mission Conference of the Methodist Episcopal Church, 1899*. Singapore: American Mission Press, 1899. Singapore: The Methodist Archives.

Chen So Lan. *Opium Problem in British Malaya* (pamphlet). Singapore Anti-Opium Society, 1 January 1935, 22. Singapore: Singapore Archives (reel).

Cook, J. A. B. "The Opium Traffic." In *The Malaysia Message*, Vol I No 8 May 1892. Singapore: The Methodist Archives.

Hebinger, Josephine. "Annual Report, Women's Foreign Missionary Society." In *Minutes of the Malaysian Mission Conference of the Methodist Episcopal Church, 1895*. Singapore: American Mission Press, 1895. Singapore: The Methodist Archives.

———. "Annual Report, Women's Foreign Missionary Society." In *Minutes of the Malaysian Mission Conference of the Methodist Episcopal Church, 1896*. Singapore: American Mission Press, 1896. Singapore: The Methodist Archives.

Ho Zhiwen, Peter, "'Not in Your Image'—Conflict and Synthesis in the Education of Colonial Singapore. A Case Study of the Anglo-Chinese School 1886–1914." Oxford University Undergraduate Thesis, 2006. Singapore: Methodist Archives.

Horley, W. E. "The Anti-Opium Movement on the Malay Peninsular." In *The Malaysia Message*, Vol XVI No 3, Dec. 1906. Singapore: The Methodist Archives.

———. "Report of Committee on Public Morals." In *Minutes of the Malaysian Mission Conference of the Methodist Episcopal Church, 1910*. Singapore: American Mission Press, 1910. Singapore: The Methodist Archives.

"An Interview with Bishop Oldham on the Opium Question." In *The Malaysia Message*, Vol IV No 4, Feb. 1895. Singapore: The Methodist Archives.

Jarman, Robert L., ed. *Annual Reports of the Straits Settlements 1855–1941*, Vols. 3, 4, 5, and 6. London: Public Records Office, 1998. Singapore: National Archives.

Lim Boon Keng. "Opium Versus Alcohol." In *The Malaysia Message*, Vol XVIII No 1 Oct. 1908. Singapore: The Methodist Archives.

Luering, H. L. E., Emma Ferris, and W. T. Stagg. "Report of the Committee on Education." *Minutes of the Malaysia Mission Conference of the Methodist Episcopal Church, 1894*. Singapore: American Mission Press, 1984. Singapore: The Methodist Archives.

Luering, Violet M. "Report of Chinese Work." In *Minutes of the Malaysian Mission Conference of the Methodist Episcopal Church, 1894*. Singapore: American Mission Press, 1894. Singapore: The Methodist Archives.

McCallum, H. E. "Memorandum on the Opium Traffic, Straits Settlements, by the Colonial Engineer." In *Correspondence on the Subject of the Consumption of Opium in Hong Kong and the Straits Settlements*. London: Great Britain Colonial Office, May 30, 1892. Singapore: National Archives.

Morgan, F. H. "Report of Committee on Public Morals." In *Minutes of the Malaysian Mission Conference of the Methodist Episcopal Church, 1897*. Singapore: American Mission Press, 1897. Singapore: The Methodist Archives.

Munson, R. W. "Presiding Elder's Report." In *Minutes of the Malaysian Mission Conference of the Methodist Episcopal Church, 1895*. Singapore: The Methodist Archives.

Murray, W. "In Memoriam: Mr. C. Philips." *The Malaysia Message*, July 1904.

Oldham, William. "Malaysia." Archives Manuscript, CAHUMC.

———. *The Malaysia Message*. November 1894. Singapore: The Methodist Archives.

Pykett, G. F. "Report of Committee on Rescue Work." In *Minutes of the Malaysian Mission Conference of the Methodist Episcopal Church, 1906*. Singapore: American Mission Press, 1906. Singapore: The Methodist Archives.

Pykett, G. F., J. E. Banks, and W. T. Kensett. "Report of Committee on Public Morals." In *Minutes of the Malaysian Mission Conference of the Methodist Episcopal Church, 1898*. Singapore: American Mission Press, 1898. Singapore: The Methodist Archives.

Raffles, Stamford. *Singapore Local laws and Institutions, 1823*. London: Cox and Baylis, 1824. Singapore: National Library Archives (microfilm: NL NL7979).

Rutledge, W. P. "Report of Committee on Public Morals." In *Minutes of the Malaysian Mission Conference of the Methodist Episcopal Church, 1902*. Singapore: American Mission Press, 1902. Singapore: The Methodist Archives.

———. "Report of Committee on Public Morals." In *Minutes of the Malaysian Mission Conference of the Methodist Episcopal Church, 1903*. Singapore: American Mission Press, 1903. Singapore: The Methodist Archives.

Shaw, Edward W. *Replies to Questions on Education*. Archival Reels—Education in Strait Settlements. Singapore: National Archives of Singapore.

Shellabear, William. "Annual Report of the Methodist Episcopal Mission, Singapore District." In *The Malaysia Message, Vol IX No. 6*, March 1900. Singapore: The Methodist Archives.

———, ed. "The Education of Chinese Women." In *The Malaysia Message Vol 1 No 9*, June 1892. Singapore: The Methodist Archives.

———. "Opium from the Missionary Standpoint." In *The Malaysia Message*, Vol I No 8 May 1892. Singapore: The Methodist Archives.

———. "Repeal of Our Anti-Gambling Laws." In *The Malaysia Message*, Vol X No 10 July 1901. Singapore: The Methodist Archives.

Shellabear, W. G., W. E. Horley, A. F. Amery, G. F. Pykett, and Ling Thi Kong. "Report of Committee on Public Morals." In *Minutes of the Malaysian Mission Conference of the Methodist Episcopal Church, 1906*. Singapore: American Mission Press, 1906. Singapore: The Methodist Archives.

Urch, W. H. B., C. C. Kelso, and W. G. Shellabear. "Report of Committee on Public Morals." In *Minutes of the Malaysian Mission Conference of the Methodist Episcopal*

Church, April 1–5, 1893. Singapore: American Mission Press, 1893. Singapore: The Methodist Archives.

———. "Report of Committee on Public Morals." In *Minutes of the Malaysian Mission Conference of the Methodist Episcopal Church, 1894*. Singapore: American Mission Press, 1894. Singapore: The Methodist Archives.

West, Benjamin F. "The Opium Question Again." In *The Malaysia Message*, Vol II No 2 Dec. 1892. Singapore: The Methodist Archives.

———. "The Physical Effects of Opium." In *The Malaysia Message*, Vol I No 8 May 1892. Singapore: The Methodist Archives.

———. "Presiding Elder's Report—Singapore District." *Minutes of the 12th Session of the Malaysia Conference of the Methodist Episcopal Church, 1904*. Singapore: American Mission Press, 1904.

Woolley, R. *Report of the Select Committee of the Legislative Council to enquire into the state of Education in the Colony (the Woolley Report), 1870*. Singapore: National Archives of Singapore.

INTERNET RESOURCES

Chew, Earnest. http://www.scholars.nus.edu.sg/post/singapore/history/chew/chew10.html.

Chew, Emrys. *A Merlion at the Edge of an Afrasian Sea: Singapore's Strategic Involvement in the Indian Ocean*. Singapore: RSIS, 2008. http://www.rsis.edu.sg/publications/WorkingPapers/WP164.pdf.

Heng Kian Wai, Andy. "Pangkor Treaty 1874 Revisted." ThM paper (unpublished). http://www.scottsunquist.net/download/files/Sample%20Papers/Sample%20Paper%20-%20Pangkor%20Treaty%201874.pdf

Hwa Yung and Robert Hunt. *The Methodist Church in Malaya*. http://smu.edu/theology/global/Forms%20and%20Documents/Readings%20for%20Courses/Malaysia%20Denominations%20in%20PDF.pdf.

Kampong Kapur Methodist Church. "Our History." http://www.kkmc.org.sg/kkmc_history.html.

Kana, Maria Perpetua. "Christian Mission in Malaysia: Past Emphasis, Present Engagement and Future Possibilities." MPhil Dissertation. Australia: Australia Catholic University, 2004. http://dlibrary.acu.edu.au/digitaltheses/public/adt-acuvp68.25092005/02whole.pdf.

Khondker, Habibul Haque. "Cricket, Colonialism, Culture and Cosmopolitanism." Paper presented at a seminar at School of Social Sciences, Singapore Management University, 2009. http://www.socsc.smu.edu.sg/events/Paper/habib.pdf.

Lau, Earnest. "Teaching Moral Education by Example." *Methodist Message*, March 2009. http://www.methodistmessage.com/mar2009/elaupg.html.

Lopez, Carolina C. *The British Presence in the Malay World: A Meeting of Civilizational Traditions*. http://www.penerbit.ukm.my/jsari19-01.pdf.

O'Brien, Patrick K. *The Pax Britannica, American Hegemony and the International Economic Order, 1846–1914 and 1941–2001*. http://eh.net/XIIICongress/cd/papers/7O%27Brien11.pdf.

Palgrave, Francis T., ed. *The Golden Treasury of the Best Songs and Lyrical Poems in the English Language*. London: Macmillan, 1875. http://www.bartleby.com/106/122.html.

Stevens, Abel. "The History of the Methodist Episcopal Church in the United States of America." http://wesley.nnu.edu/wesleyctr/books/0201-0300/stevens/0244-4613.htm.

Teo Chee Hean. Speech at the Opening Ceremony of the 1997 Pre-University Seminar. "Singapore as Best Home: From Scenarios to Strategies" on 3 June 1997 at NUS. http://www.moe.gov.sg/media/speeches/1997/030697.htm.

Thulaja, Naidu Ratnala. "Sago Lane." In *Infopedia for National Library Board, Singapore.* http://infopedia.nl.sg/articles/SIP_299_2005-01-11.html.

Trinity Annual Conference, MCS. "Publications—Goh Hood Keng." http://www.trac-mcs.org.sg/Download.cfm?DObjID=245&Mode=1&FN=/Goh%20Hood%20Keng.pdf

Wesley Methodist Church. "History." http://www.wesleymc.org/!main/content/view/22/31/.